# MARY ASTELL:
# REASON, GENDER, FAITH

# Mary Astell

Reason, Gender, Faith

*Edited by*
WILLIAM KOLBRENER and MICHAL MICHELSON

**ASHGATE**

Published by
Ashgate Publishing Limited
Gower House
Croft Road
Aldershot
Hants GU11 3HR
England

Ashgate Publishing Company
Suite 420
101 Cherry Street
Burlington, VT 05401-4405
USA

Ashgate website: http://www.ashgate.com

British Library Cataloguing in Publication Data

Mary Astell: reason, gender, faith
1. Astell, Mary, 1668–1731 – Criticism and interpretation
2. Astell, Mary, 1668–1731 – Political and social views
3. Astell, Mary, 1668–1731 – Knowledge and learning
I. Kolbrener, William II. Michelson, Michal
828.4′09

Library of Congress Cataloging-in-Publication Data

Mary Astell: Reason, Gender, Faith / edited by William Kolbrener and Michal
Michelson.
    p. cm.
    Includes bibliographical references.
    ISBN 978-0-7546-5264-5 (alk. paper)
1. Astell, Mary, 1668-1731 – Criticism and interpretation. 2. Astell, Mary,
1668–1731 – Political and social views. 3. Astell, Mary, 1668–1731 – Religion. 4.
Feminism – Great Britain – History. I. Kolbrener, William. II. Michelson, Michal,
1954–
HQ1595.A78M36 2006
305.42092–dc22                                                            2006005233

ISBN: 978-0-7546-5264-5

Printed on acid-free paper

Typeset in Times New Roman by Jonathan Hoare, Pinner, Middx
Printed and bound in Great Britain by MPG Books Ltd, Bodmin, Cornwall

# Contents

# Acknowledgments

In seeing this book into print, we have benefited from the suggestions and advice of many colleagues and friends. A special session on Mary Astell at the MLA annual convention in 2002 began the process which resulted in the current collection.

E. Derek Taylor, Sharon Achinstein, and Ruth Perry made that session possible. Nigel Smith, Helen Thompson, Peter Herman, and Marshall Grossman encouraged the project from the outset; the latter along with Jeffrey Perl, Ellen Spolsky and Peter Herman are gratefully acknowledged for their guidance (and patience) along the way. We would like to convey our thanks to Mark Goldie and Jacqueline Broad for their helpful comments on an earlier draft of the volume introduction. John Shawcross and Elizabeth Fox Genovese offered timely advice; Aden Bar Tura provided expert editorial assistance. We are grateful to our editor at Ashgate, Erika Gaffney. Finally, we express our thanks to the Lechter Institute of Literary Research at Bar-Ilan University for its generous support.

The cover image, the engraved frontispiece from Richard Allestree's *The Ladies Calling* (Oxford, 1693), is reproduced with permission from the William Andrews Clark Memorial Library, University of California, Los Angeles.

# Notes on Contributors

SHARON ACHINSTEIN is Reader in English at Oxford and Tutor at St Edmund Hall. Her work has focused on the intersections of politics, the public sphere, and the histories of radicalism. Her previous books are *Literature and Dissent in Milton's England* (Cambridge, 2003) and *Milton and the Revolutionary Reader* (Princeton, 1994). She has edited *Gender, Literature and the English Revolution* (Routledge, 1995), and is currently working on a new edition of Milton's Divorce Tracts which reconsiders the relations between domestic, religious, and civil liberty.

JACQUELINE BROAD is a Postdoctoral Fellow in the School of Philosophy and Bioethics at Monash University, Melbourne. She is the author of *Women Philosophers of the Seventeenth Century* (Cambridge, 2002), and she has published papers on Mary Astell in *Eighteenth-Century Thought* and the *Dictionary of Literary Biography*. Together with Karen Green, she is currently working on a history of women's political thought, from 1400–1800, funded by the Australian Research Council.

MARK GOLDIE is Senior Lecturer in History at the University of Cambridge and a Fellow of Churchill College. He was formerly co-editor of *The Historical Journal* and Vice-Master of Churchill College. He has published extensively on British political, religious, and intellectual history, 1650–1750. His editions of Locke's writings include *The Selected Correspondence of John Locke* (Oxford, 2002).

CORRINNE HAROL is an Assistant Professor in the University of Alberta's Department of English and Film Studies, specializing in Restoration and eighteenth-century literature. She has recently completed a book called *Enlightened Virginity in Eighteenth-Century Literature* (Palgrave, 2006). Her chapter in this volume is the first step in a new project, which will consider the allegorical relationships between sex and politics in representations of late-seventeenth-century political upheaval.

WILLIAM KOLBRENER is an Associate Professor in the English Department at Bar-Ilan University. He has written extensively on the literature and history of early modern England. His current work on Astell is part of a larger project on the counter-Enlightenment languages employed by Jacobites and the High Church after 1689.

MICHAL MICHELSON completed her doctorate in the Department of English at Bar-Ilan University. Her research focuses on theology, identity, and authority in the works of early modern women writers.

EILEEN O'NEILL is Professor of Philosophy at the University of Massachusetts-Amherst. She published the first modern edition of Margaret Cavendish's *Observations upon Experimental Philosophy* (Cambridge, 2001), and has written on Descartes,

Leibniz, and numerous early modern women philosophers, as well as on the relation of feminism to the historiography of philosophy. Together with Christia Mercer, she co-edited *Early Modern Philosophy: Mind, Matter and Metaphysics* (Oxford, 2005), a collection of new essays in the history of philosophy by top scholars in the field. She is currently completing a book on women philosophers' contributions to seventeenth-century metaphysics.

CLAIRE PICKARD is currently completing a doctorate on Jacobite women writers at St Hilda's College, Oxford.

HANNAH SMITH is a Tutorial Fellow and University Lecturer in History at St Hilda's College, Oxford. She is author of *Georgian Monarchy: Politics and Culture in Britain, 1714–60* (Cambridge, 2006).

HILDA L. SMITH is Professor of History at the University of Cincinnati and is a specialist in early modern England and the history of European women. She has published *Reason's Disciples: Seventeenth-Century English Feminists* (Illinois, 1982), *All Men and Both Sexes: Gender, Politics and the False Universal in England, 1640–1831* (Penn State, 2002), edited *Women Writers and the early modern British Political Tradition* (Cambridge, 1990), and co-edited *Women and the Literature of the Seventeenth-Century: An Annotated Bibliography* (Greenwood, 1990) and *Women's Political and Social Thought: An Anthology* (Indiana, 2000). In addition, she has published a range of articles on the history of political thought, early modern feminism, and broad assessments of the field of women's history.

E. DEREK TAYLOR is an Associate Professor of English at Longwood University (Farmville, VA). His essays related to Mary Astell have appeared in *Eighteenth-Century Fiction* and *Journal of the History of Ideas*. His and Melvyn New's edition of *Letters Concerning the Love of God* (Ashgate) appeared in 2005.

ANN JESSIE VAN SANT is Associate Professor of English at the University of California, Irvine. She is the author of *Eighteenth-Century Sensibility and the Novel* (Cambridge, 1993) and of articles on women and satire, and women in the novel. She is currently working on a project called *Women's Stories*, which explores women's relation to law and equity principally in the novel but in other genres as well. Her courses include Restoration and eighteenth-century literature and culture as well as satire and women and fiction.

MELINDA S. ZOOK is Associate Professor of History at Purdue University. She is the author of *Radical Whigs and Conspiratorial Politics in Late Stuart England* (Penn State, 1999), and the co-editor of *Revolutionary Currents: Nation Building in the Transatlantic World* (Rowman and Littlefield, 2004). She has written articles on women, Whig politics, and Protestant nonconformity in the seventeenth century, and is currently working on a book–manuscript on women, religion, and politics in Restoration England.

# Chapter I

# "Dreading to Engage Her": The Critical Reception of Mary Astell

## William Kolbrener and Michal Michelson

Let me obscured be, & never known
Or pointed at about the Town,
Short winded Fame shall not transmit
My name, that the next Age may censure it:
If I write sense no matter what they say,
Whither they call it dull, or pay
A rev'rence such as Virgil claims,
Their breath's infectious, I have higher aims.
                         "Ambition"

When Mary Astell presented a copy of her poems to Archbishop Sancroft, she wrote, in an accompanying dedicatory letter, that it "was not without pain and reluctancy" that she broke off from what she called her "beloved obscurity."[1] In writing of Astell in his *Memoirs of Several Ladies of Great Britain* of 1752, George Ballard would transform Astell's fondness for "obscurity" into a recurring theme in his account of her life. Astell, according to Ballard, expressed "modesty" in the publication of all of her works, being, as he writes, "extremely fond" of that "obscurity" which "she courted and doted on beyond all earthly blessings." Her only ambition was, Ballard writes (citing from Astell's own preface to *Letters Concerning the Love of God*), "to slide gently through the world without so much as being seen or taken notice of." As Ballard would have it, without the "restless curiosity" of others, Astell would have maintained the obscurity that she desperately cultivated and always desired.[2] Ballard, as Margaret Ezell has written, may have been more "didactic" than "objective," but it was Astell herself who asserted the wish to "most industriously shun a *great* Reputation," declaring herself unwilling to receive praise "from any but an infallible Judge."[3]

---

1  Reprinted in Ruth Perry, *The Celebrated Mary Astell* (Chicago, 1986), 405, 400.

2  George Ballard, *Memoirs of Several Ladies of Great Britain*, ed. Ruth Perry (Detroit, 1985), 383. Astell, according to Ballard, displayed the same reluctance for publicity in the publication of her *Moderation Truly Stated*: "In spite of all the arts she used to conceal herself, the learned soon discovered her to be the author, and accordingly gave her the applause due to her merit," 386.

3  Margaret J.M. Ezell, *Writing Women's Literary History* (Baltimore, 1996), 79; Mary Astell and John Norris, *Letters Concerning the Love of God* (London, 1695), 4.

1

In the *Memoirs*, the emphasis upon Astell's efforts for self-concealment emerges most clearly in Ballard's rendering of the illness of the final years of her life. Astell, Ballard writes, "concealed" her breast cancer "in such a way that the few of even her most intimate acquaintances knew anything of the matter."[4] In her last days, "her thoughts ... fixed upon God and eternity," Astell left instructions that "no company might be permitted to come to her." She would not, Ballard remarks in a tone perhaps more appropriate to the genre of hagiography, "be disturbed in the last moments of her divine contemplations."[5] As one contemporary put it, Astell's desire for concealment was so great that in her final years, ending in her death in 1731, she simply "withdrew into herself."[6]

Ballard's description of Astell's propensities for obscurity emerges as a biographical trope, and also, from about the time when the *Memoirs* were published, a historiographical principle that governed the reception of her work.[7] That, as Ruth Perry writes, no woman "picked up where Astell left off," and that she was "forgotten so quickly," was not simply a function of the proclivities for withdrawal and obscurity emphasized in Ballard's account.[8] Astell herself observes in *Some Reflections upon Marriage* that it is the "Subtilty" of men which both "advances them to the Post of Honour," and also "gets them a Name," conveying it "down to Posterity." It is men, Astell continues, who "dispute for Truth as well as Men who argue against it; histories are writ by them, they recount each others great Exploits, and have always done so."[9] From this perspective, Astell's propensity for self-concealment, or what Elisa New calls (in a different context) "feminist invisibility," would lend itself to the reception that would await her work in a tradition of male historians who were interested, in Astell's own words, only in "each others great Exploits."[10]

As Florence Smith relates in her 1916 monograph on Astell, Ballard's "difficulty in gathering material" for the biography in 1752 would imply that Astell's reputation, by then, already "had died."[11] Astell was, of course, not unknown during her lifetime—especially for her advocacy in *A Serious Proposal to the Ladies* of a philosophical and theological retreat for women. Swift's *Tatler* essay of 1709 points to the irony that though "Madonella," his sardonic figure for Astell, had argued for

---

4   In Ballard's account, the Reverend Mr Johnson, "a gentleman very eminent for his skill in surgery," performed the required operation, but, at Astell's behest, only "in the most private manner possible" (391). For the full account in Ballard of Astell's mastectomy, see *Memoirs of Several Ladies*, 391–92.

5   Ballard, *Memoirs of Several Ladies*, 392.

6   Cited in Florence M. Smith, *Mary Astell* (New York, 1916), 162.

7   Ballard, *Memoirs of Several Ladies*, 391.

8   Perry, *The Celebrated Mary Astell*, 330.

9   Mary Astell, *Reflections upon Marriage* (London, 1706), 88. Astell would echo this sentiment in *The Christian Religion as Profess'd by a Daughter of the Church of England* (London, 1705) where she writes that since men are "the historians, they seldom condescend to record the great and good actions of women," 202.

10   See Elisa New, "Feminist Invisibility: The Examples of Anne Bradstreet and Anne Hutchinson," *Common Knowledge* 2.1 (1993): 99. For a discussion of early modern women and the writing of history, see D.R. Woolf, "A Feminine Past? Gender, Genre, and Historical Knowledge in England," *American Historical Review* 102 (1997): 645–79, as well as Devoney Looser, *British Women Writers and the Writing of History: 1670–1820* (Baltimore, 2000).

11   Smith, *Mary Astell*, 34.

feminine "Solitude," her proposal "had made more Noise in the world" than she intended.[12] Notwithstanding Astell's influence upon her immediate contemporaries, Elizabeth Elstob, in a letter to Ballard after the publication of the *Memoirs*, could offer only her consolation on the fate of the volume commemorating the writings and skill of "learned Ladies":

> I am extremely sorry to hear of the disappointments you have met with … This is not an Age to hope for any encouragement to Learning of any kind. For your part I am sorry to tell you the choice you have made for the Honour of the Females was the wrongest subject you could pitch upon.[13]

The subject of "learned ladies," not least of all Astell, was not, and would not be, a popular one for generations. Astell's expressed desire for obscurity was in the end fulfilled, not out of deference to her own Christian inclinations, but by a historiographical tradition that often overlooked her presence. It was not Ballard's sympathetic treatment of Astell that set the tone for her early reception; rather, it was Bishop Francis Atterbury's remark to George Smalridge, written after the bishop had dined—unsatisfactorily—with Astell. Objecting to Astell having been, in their sole meeting, "a little offensive and shocking in her expressions," Atterbury concluded: "I dread to engage her."[14] Astell's manner was shocking to the Bishop; the refusal to engage with her work, though not the norm during her life, characterized Astell's reception, or rather her relative obscurity, for the next 150 years.[15]

The impetus for Astell's twentieth-century revival began with Smith's monograph on Astell.[16] The revival was informed (and continued to be, in various ways, through much of the twentieth century) by the principles of what Devoney Looser has called "herstorical method." Herstorical method focuses upon constructing "female-centered accounts of the past," and emphasizes, in the context of work on Astell, the ways in which she anticipated more contemporary feminist educational and social agendas.[17] Smith provides a characteristic version of this approach in her affirmation that "the modern viewpoint" reveals the "basic falsity" of Astell's positions; thus her political and theological pamphlets—evidencing her allegiance to Tory politics and High Church theology—passed into justifiable "oblivion." The educational pamphlets, however, held out more "interest" for Smith, because of the way in which

---

12  *The Tatler*, ed. Donald F. Bond, 3 vols. (Oxford, 1987), 1:240.

13  Cited by Smith, *Mary Astell*, 169–70.

14  On Ballard's attempt to protect Astell from Atterbury's insinuations, see Perry, *The Celebrated Mary Astell*, 218–19.

15  For the details of Astell's reputation and reception during her lifetime, see Smith, *Mary Astell*, 25–34.

16  See also Karl D. Bulbring, "Mary Astell: An Advocate of Women's Right Two Hundred Years Ago," *The Journal of Education* (London, 1891): 199–203; Katherine S. Pattinson, "Mary Astell," *Pall Mall Magazine* (June 1893): 133–40; and Harriet McIlquham, "Mary Astell: A Seventeenth Century Women's Advocate," *Westminster Review* 149.4 (1898): 440–49. Bulbring writes that those celebrating Mary Wollstonecraft for promoting women's rights should rightfully mention her predecessor Astell; similarly, McIlquham cites Astell as a forerunner of Wollstonecraft and "a pioneer of the modern 'Women's Rights' Movement" (445).

17  Looser, *British Women Writers*, 1.

they anticipated contemporary models of education for women.[18] Some contemporary scholars, also reading Astell from within the context of a liberal tradition of rights, elaborate more sophisticated versions of Smith's perspective in which, for example, Astell's "conservative values" are seen as "delimitations" of an otherwise "proto-feminist agenda."[19] The implicit attribution of contradiction to Astell's thinking (between progressive educational ideals and conservative political values) may, however, simply register Astell's failure to fit neatly within the expectations produced by contemporary interpretive accounts.[20]

Recent innovations in Astell scholarship can be attributed to several factors— not all of them local to discussions about Astell herself. Indeed, general changes in feminist methodology and historiography have had dramatic implications for studies of early modern women writers in general, and Astell in particular. Looser, for example, departing from those earlier avatars of what she calls "herstory," appeals to contemporary feminists to "define 'history' more broadly," and to acknowledge that women writers "used historical material with widely diverging interests and results." Such an emphasis helps to reveal, Looser argues, the significance of women's contributions to the developments of the "long-eighteenth century," though rarely, she adds, "in the uncomplicated fore-motherly, and proto-feminist ways" that many had hoped.[21] Citing Elaine Hobby's assertion that "we find in the past what we look for" and "only come up with answers to questions we think to ask," Margaret Ezell has called, accordingly, for "a consideration of our historiography"— often based on Whig and evolutionary assumptions—and a reconsideration of those "patterns of inquiry which will determine the future direction of women's literary history."[22] Barbara Lewalski similarly writes that early modern women's writing has been "too narrowly contextualized—studied chiefly in relation to other women's texts, or to modern feminist theory."[23] Traditional feminist concerns may have, as Looser writes, engaged primarily with the works of ostensible "trailblazers," ignoring those texts anomalous to contemporary paradigms.[24] The changes over the past decades, however, have moved contemporary scholars away from

---

18   Smith, *Mary Astell*, 158, 35.

19   See Catherine Sharrock, "De-ciphering Women and De-scribing Authority," in *Women, Writing, History: 1640–1740*, eds. Isobel Grundy and Susan Wiseman (Athens, GA,1992), 122.

20   Herbert Butterfield long ago identified this historiographical tendency (exemplified in Smith's work), describing what he calls the "whig interpretation of history" which comes to organize "the whole course of centuries upon what is really a directing principle of progress." Through "reference to the present day," historians classed historical figures into those "who furthered progress ... and those who tried to hinder it" (*The Whig Interpretation of History* [London, 1931], 101).

21   Looser, *British Women Writers*, 2–3.

22   Ezell, *Writing Women's Literary History*, 9, 12. Explaining the problem with precedent methodologies, Ezell writes: "By unconsciously permitting our perceptions to be shaped by unexamined ideologies, perhaps unwittingly carried over from certain privileged texts or theories, we may have infused the values and standards of those texts and theories in our constructions of the past" (7). Significantly, in Ezell's account, the figure of Astell functions as a means to question feminist literary histories presupposed upon the principle of continuity with present concerns (27). See Elaine Hobby, *Virtue of Necessity: English Women's Writing 1649–88* (Ann Arbor, 1989), 204.

23   Barbara Lewalski, *Writing Women in Jacobean England* (Cambridge, MA, 1994), 1.

24   Looser, *British Women Writers*, 6; Ezell, *Writing Women's Literary History*, 23.

the narrowly contextualizing practices which characterized earlier generations of scholarship.[25]

Within Astell studies, the first critical advances were biographical and editorial, and only after that methodological. Ballard had already noted the diversity of Astell's commitments in his *Memoirs*, emphasizing that she "made herself a complete mistress of everything she attempted to learn with the greatest ease imaginable."[26] But it was not until Ruth Perry's *The Celebrated Mary Astell* (1986) that the full range and details of Astell's learning and commitments became available to Astell scholars. That Astell would write in many genres, to many audiences, was a symptom of her engagement with all aspects of the intellectual world she inhabited. Astell displayed, Perry writes, a "comfortable affection for other women and their gossip about court fashion," while at the same time pursuing "relentless arguments about the Occasional Conformity Bill." "She passed along recipes for medicinal potions one day," Perry continues, "and carefully interpreted results of parliamentary elections the next." In the diversity of her interests and commitments, Perry argues, Astell was "unlike any other intellectual of her time."[27] The inclusive portrait of Astell that Perry revealed through biography, Bridget Hill achieved, the same year, with the publication of a broad selection of her writings in her *The First English Feminist*.[28] Patricia Springborg's scholarly editions of the two parts of *A Serious Proposal to the Ladies*, and later, in a separate volume, *Some Reflections upon Marriage* (along with Astell's other political writings), foreground the extent to which Astell's works were both part of an emergent proto-feminist canon, and also central to the development of early modern discourses of theology, philosophy, and history.[29] Astell's appearance in the

---

25 Hobby's *Virtue of Necessity* was groundbreaking in this regard in providing more thorough historical contextualization of women's engagement with contemporary political and educational issues. For more recent work on women's writing and politics in context, see *Women's Writers and the Early Modern British Political Tradition*, ed. Hilda L. Smith (Cambridge, 1998), especially the introduction, 1–21.

26 Ballard, *Memoirs of Several Ladies*, 382.

27 Perry, *The Celebrated Mary Astell*, 327; Bridget Hill, *The First English Feminist* (London, 1986), in a biographical introduction to *Some Reflections*, also notes Astell's diverse set of commitments. "She has been variously described," Hill writes, "as Platonist, a Cartesian rationalist, a Lockean feminist, an English Femme Savante, and the 'first major English feminist.' If some of these labels are more relevant to her than others," Hill asserts, "there is not one that, by itself, adequately describes her" (49). For a brief introduction to Astell's life and works, see Jacqueline Broad's entry on Mary Astell in *British Philosophers 1500–1799*, vol. 252 of *Dictionary of Literary Biography*, eds. Philip B. Dematteis and Peter Fosl (Detroit, 2002), 3–10. See also Jennie Batchelor's essay on Astell in the *Literary Encyclopedia*, http://www.litencyc.com/php/speople.php?rec=true&UID=168.

28 Hill excerpts from a wide range of Astell's theological, political, and philosophical tracts, as well as some of her poetry. Hill's work was anticipated, though on a more modest scale, by Moira Ferguson's *First Feminists: British Women Writers 1578–1799* (Bloomington, 1985), which includes a selection of Astell's works.

29 *Astell: Political Writings*, ed. Patricia Springborg (Cambridge, 1996); Mary Astell, *A Serious Proposal to the Ladies, Parts I & II*, ed. Patricia Springborg (London, 1997). Hilda L. Smith's *Reason's Disciples: Seventeenth Century English Feminists* (Urbana, 1982) remains an early milestone in the consideration of seventeenth-century women. The publication of scholarly editions of Astell's major works has continued with the publication of the Astell–Norris correspondence, *Letters Concerning the Love of God*, eds. E. Derek Taylor and Melvyn New (Aldershot, 2005).

*Norton Anthology of Literature by Women* (edited by Sandra M. Gilbert and Susan Gubar in 1985) and the fifth edition of the *Norton Anthology of English Literature* (1986) would insure that Astell would not only be a name to be cited (as she may have been in previous generations), but an author of texts to be read by scholar and student alike.[30]

The current volume, indebted both to the recent methodological advances in women's studies, as well as to the biographical and textual work achieved by Perry, Hill, and Springborg follows the implicit imperative of Lewalski's volume by attending to Astell's works in the contexts in which they were articulated. The renewed significance of contexts in the works of feminist scholars like Hobby, Looser, and Ezell dovetails with the methodology of the Cambridge School of history—that is, the works of Quentin Skinner and J. G. A. Pocock. "Cambridge History" has attempted to correct what Pocock calls those "extra-historical" impulses which have lead, especially within early modern historiography, to the twin errors of "anachronism," the "attribution to a past author of concepts which could not have been available to him," and "prolepsis," treating the author "as anticipating the formation of arguments in whose subsequent formation, the role of his text, if any, had yet to be fully demonstrated."[31] As Skinner explains, the "mythology" of both "anachronism" and "prolepsis" emerges when historians are more "interested in the retrospective significance of a given episode than in its meaning for the agent at the time."[32] For both Pocock and Skinner, the antidote for proleptic and anachronistic histories (sometimes manifesting themselves in the versions of "herstory" to which Looser calls attention) is an emphasis on the recovery of the linguistic or discursive contexts for particular utterances. As "texts are concerned with their own questions, and not with ours," the readings of the Cambridge School are governed not by contemporary historiographical traditions, but by the questions—and contexts—to which individual authors respond.[33] With what might be called the second phase of Astell scholarship completed—that is, with the elaboration of Astell's life, and the publication of scholarly editions of her texts—the current volume participates in the task of elaborating Astell's works in their various contexts.

Virginia Woolf famously remarked upon the "deplorable" fact that "nothing is known about women before the eighteenth century." Despairing, Woolf confesses,

---

30 On the politics of anthologies and their role in canon formation, see Ezell, *Writing Women's Literary History*, 39–65.

31 J.G.A. Pocock, "Quentin Skinner: The History of Politics and the Politics of History," *Common Knowledge* 10.3 (2004): 537. For Ezell's discussion of evolutionary models in feminist historiography, see *Writing Women's Literary History*, 21–30.

32 Quentin Skinner, *Visions of Politics* (Cambridge, 2002), 1:73. "For example," Skinner writes, "it has often been suggested that, with Petrarch's ascent of Mount Ventoux, the age of the Renaissance dawned." "Now this might," Skinner continues, "in a romantic sort of way, be said to give us a true account of the significance of Petrarch's action and its interest for us. But no account under this description could ever be true of any action Petrarch intended, or hence of the meaning of his act" (73).

33 Skinner, *Visions of Politics*, 88. For Skinner's extensive response to critics who attack the very possibility of the recovery of authorial intention, see "A Reply to My Critics" in *Meaning and Context: Quentin Skinner and his Critics*, ed. James Tully (Princeton, 1988), 231–88. Similarly, Ezell, observing that early modern women's texts are "part of a dialogue," recommends "approaches that would invite fresh questions about the past rather than silencing its answers" (*Writing Women's Literary History*, 65).

"I have no model in my mind to turn about this way and that."[34] Following Pocock's call to attend to "the patterns of polyvalence" sometimes present in an author's work (what Peter Burke labels "contexts in the plural"), one might argue that there is not merely a need for a single "model," as Woolf calls it, but for various *models* for the consideration of the writings of early modern women—especially the works of Astell.[35]

Astell wrote in a variety of distinctive genres: a chronological account of her writings and their genres provides a schematic sense of her various intellectual engagements. Such a narrative would begin in 1689 with the twenty-three-year-old Astell, the orphaned daughter of a Newcastle coal merchant, presenting the collection of her spiritual poetry to Sancroft (she had traveled alone to London in 1688). Residing in Chelsea, Astell cultivated friendships with the likes of Sancroft and Bishop (later Dean) Atterbury, as well as with the women who became her lifelong friends and patrons—including Lady Catherine Jones, Lady Elizabeth Hastings, Lady Ann Coventry, and Elizabeth Hutcheson. In 1693, she extended these connections by initiating a correspondence with the Malebranchian philosopher, John Norris. *Letters Concerning the Love of God*, the full Astell–Norris correspondence published in 1695, shows Astell delving into the controversy over Nicolas Malebranche's occasionalist metaphysics as well as refining the distinction between divine and human love. For her occasionalist affinities—the belief in the exclusive efficacy of God as sole cause of all events in this world through direct intervention—and the ostensible religious "enthusiasm" it entailed, she was attacked by, among others, Lady Damaris Masham in her *Discourse Concerning the Love of God* in 1696.[36]

While in correspondence with Norris, Astell began to compose her *A Serious Proposal to the Ladies* which, with its sequel *Part II* in 1697, articulated her program for women's educational reform, bolstered (especially in *Part II*) with philosophical arguments from sources ranging from Descartes and Malebranche to the Port Royal school. Astell's proposal for a "Religious Retirement" for women never materialized (though Ballard claims that Astell had collected £10,000 for the project); Astell did, however, go on to help found a charity school in Chelsea in 1709.[37] Although published anonymously, the tract would solidify her contemporary reputation, earning praise from the likes of John Evelyn in his *Numismata* (1697), and emulation from Daniel Defoe in his *Essay upon Projects* (1697), as well as inspiring a generation of young women writers, including Elstob, Lady Mary Wortley Montagu, and Lady Mary Chudleigh.[38] From the success of her considerations of educational reform, in

---

34  Virginia Woolf, *A Room of One's Own* (London, 1967), 69.

35  "When a diversity of such languages is to be found in a given text," Pocock writes (*Virtue, Commerce and History* [Cambridge, 1986]), "it may follow that a given utterance is capable of being intended and read, and so of performing, in more than one of them at the same time." The author, Pocock, continues, "may move among these patterns of polyvalence, employing and recombining them according to the measure of his capacity" (9); Peter Burke, "Context in Context," *Common Knowledge* 8.1 (2002): 174.

36  *Letters* was also attacked by Daniel Whitby, *A Discourse of the Love of God* (London, 1697).

37  Ballard, *Memoirs of Several Ladies*, 383; Perry, *The Celebrated Mary Astell*, 231.

38  See Broad, *British Philosophers 1500–1799*, 7. Astell is considered to be the prototype for Samuel Richardson's *Clarissa* (1747–48), as well as Valeria in Suzannah Centlivre's *The Basset Table* (1705); her *Proposal* the model for Sarah Scott's *Millenium Hall* (1750).

1700, Astell authored her *Some Reflections upon Marriage*, a defense of the Duchess of Mazarine (against the libelous attacks upon her character for alleged marital infidelities), and a formidable analysis of the asymmetries of contemporary courtship and marriage practices. Astell's advice in the tract that "it is not good for a woman to marry" reflects her own commitment to a life of devotion and service to God, as well as her hesitation to enter into a bond that would place her subject to what she calls a "Monarch for Life."[39]

In 1704, Astell turned to politics and history: her three works, *A Fair Way with the Dissenters*, *An Impartial Enquiry into the Causes of Rebellion and Civil War in the Kingdom*, and *Moderation Truly Stated* (responses to the works of Daniel Defoe, White Kennett, and James Owen respectively), elaborated her attack on Whigs and Dissenters, and in particular the practice of occasional conformity. In these texts, Astell outlines her Tory political perspective and her allegiance to a worldview that had its origin and authority in the figure of the "Royal Martyr," Charles I. From politics, the narrative would conclude, Astell turned back to her more youthful concerns of the *Letters*—that is, theology. Her penultimate work, *The Christian Religion, As Profess'd by a Daughter of the Church of England* (which, published first in 1705, was followed by her *Bart'lemy Fair* of 1709, an attack on the third Earl of Shaftesbury's *Letter Concerning Enthusiasm*) provides a systematic distillation of her mature theological views.

Such an account certainly serves a heuristic function, but the unequivocal categorization of Astell's works within different genres obscures the way in which her individual works themselves employ varied sets of vocabularies. In this collection, Springborg's observation that *Some Reflections* is as much about politics as it is about domestic relations becomes emblematic of Astell's work as a whole, in which varieties of vocabularies are invoked within individual texts.[40] The contributors to this volume demonstrate how Astell's different works each transcend the limitations of genre—requiring more than one Woolfian "model" to be adequately understood. For Astell, political, theological, and educational discourses (among others) continuously overlap and help to inform and re-define one another.

Given the emphasis on the plurality of contexts, the current volume includes the work of scholars from a variety of disciplines—literature, philosophy, and history. The turn towards the elaboration of different discourses does not, however, entail an abandonment of the concerns of early generations of Astell critics. To assert with Pocock the importance of discourses, or with Skinner the importance of "linguistic contexts," may, however, mean to turn away from a certain version of "herstory." Such a move entails looking at Astell as one of many (mostly masculine) agents, employing, and inflecting the languages of, for example, Cartesian philosophy, Anglican theology, or Tory politics. Yet to follow the imperative of Melinda Zook to integrate men's and women's studies, and to see the way in which Astell shared the concerns and reference-points of her male contemporaries, does not mean to ignore Astell's feminine (or feminist) voice.[41] Astell, when seen within the various

---

39  Astell, *Reflections*, 88–89, 31.
40  Springborg, introduction to *Astell: Political Writings*, xxviii.
41  Melinda Zook, "Integrating Men's History into Women's History: A Proposition," *The History*

frameworks within which she wrote, will not be left to appear a mere man "in Petticoats" (a phrase Astell herself employs in objecting to the representation of women by contemporary historians).[42] Astell consistently foregrounds her concerns on gender, but those concerns, as the essays in this volume demonstrate, are always *mediated* through a manifold set of convictions.[43] The sub-title of this volume places "gender" as the middle term to emphasize that though Astell's articulation of her conceptions of gender were central, they were always elaborated through the vocabularies which emerge from the dual and sometimes competing registers of "reason" and "faith."


In the essays that open this volume, Sharon Achinstein and Hannah Smith focus on Astell's conception of "faith," demonstrating the ways in which Astell's feminist commitments were in fact mediated by her developing theological commitments. In her "Mary Astell, Religion, and Feminism," Achinstein writes that Astell's theology provides a rich ground for feminist analysis. Achinstein shows that early modern scholars, writing within a liberal historiographical tradition, have often neglected the theological aspects of Astell's works. While, as Achinstein argues, the separation of private and public achieved through liberal political theory and practice was to consign religion to the private realm, the triumph of the "feminist Astell" is that she disrupts the consignment of women to the domestic sphere. Placing Astell in dialogue with Hobbes, Locke, and Charles Davenant (among others), Achinstein demonstrates that Astell denies the fictional positing of the autonomous individual in the state of nature—upon which the relegation of women to the private sphere depended. Through an analysis of Astell's *Some Reflections*, *Christian Religion* and the two parts of *A Serious Proposal*, Achinstein shows how Astell's conceptions of feminist agency, passions, and virtue were presupposed upon a radical form of theological dependence which challenged the emerging perception of emancipation based on voluntarist notions. Through looking at Astell's conceptions of materiality, personhood, and rationality, Achinstein argues that Astell's works elaborate a feminist challenge to her contemporaries—though not one which provides an unequivocal precedent for contemporary feminists.

In her "Mary Astell and the Anglican Reformation of Manners in Late-Seventeenth-Century England," Hannah Smith turns to the context of Anglican morality as a means of providing a re-reading of Astell's *A Serious Proposal* of 1694. *A Serious*

---

*Teacher* 34.1 (2002): 373–87.

42 Astell, *Christian Religion*, 202.

43 Catherine Gallagher's "Embracing the Absolute: The Politics of the Female Subject in Seventeenth-Century England," *Genders* 1.1 (1988): 24–39, stands as an early turning-point in Astell studies in affirming the inter-relation between what had been considered incommensurable commitments in Astell's work. By coining the phrase "Tory Feminism" (in relation to a group of early modern women including Astell and Margaret Cavendish), Gallagher anticipates the work of some of the contributions to this volume by affirming that Astell's work entails a hybrid of radical gender insights and right-wing Tory politics. Gallagher was herself, in some sense, anticipated by Joan K. Kinnaird in "Mary Astell and the Conservative Contribution to English Feminism," *Journal of British Studies* 19.1 (1979): 53–75, which elaborates Astell's feminist languages in the context of traditions of conservative thought.

*Proposal* may have been conventionally viewed as an early argument for "female intellectualism" in an interpretive tradition which views the tract as part of the "first wave" of feminism. Smith, however, argues that for the tract to be fully understood it must be placed in the context of the primarily religious preoccupation with morality of the decades in which it was written. Smith thus places Astell not in the milieu of women writers on education such as Anna Maria van Schurman, Bathsua Makin, and Judith Drake, but in the company of Anglican predecessors such as Edward Chamberlayne, Clement Barksdale, George Hickes, and Richard Allestree. By detailing the late-century preoccupation with moral reform and the various Societies for the Reformation of Manners which then flourished, Smith shows *A Serious Proposal* to be a product of the contemporary concern with the vice and irreligion of Restoration society—part of the Anglican campaign for the reformation of manners. Astell, though complying with orthodox Anglican thought, would be subject to the ridicule and suspicion of the likes of Gilbert Burnet, Smith concludes, because of her emerging profile as a High Church zealot and Tory polemicist.

William Kolbrener, in his "Astell's 'Design of Friendship,'" shows the confluence between Astell's early theological and political arguments. He argues that the metaphysical assumptions which underlie Astell's anatomy of friendship in her contributions to the *Letters* would develop, in *A Serious Proposal, Part I* and later in *Some Reflections upon Marriage*, into categories that would help her to describe the social and political realities of latitudinarian England. Kolbrener demonstrates how the degraded realms of materiality, artifice, and prejudice associated in the *Letters* with desire for the creature would, in both *A Serious Proposal* and *Some Reflections*, come to characterize first the culture of masculine courtship and then latitudinarian orthodoxy in general. By contrast, authentic and substantial love, associated exclusively by Astell in the *Letters* with love for the Creator, manifests itself in the friendships enjoyed in the feminine retreat advocated in *A Serious Proposal*. In Kolbrener's reading of the 1694 tract, Astell salvages friendship as both meaningful and theologically defensible through a rejection of the occasionalist metaphysics of the *Letters* and a return to the metaphysical assumptions of the Cambridge Platonists. In showing the parallel between the metaphysics articulated in Astell's 'Appendix' to the *Letters* and those underlying her conception of feminine friendship in *A Serious Proposal*, Kolbrener gives weight to the speculations of Ruth Perry and Derek Taylor that, though published earlier, *A Serious Proposal* was actually composed after the bulk of the correspondence between Norris and Astell had taken place.

Kolbrener argues that the theological categories of *Letters* would come to inform Astell's later work on courtship, friendship, and marriage in her criticism of latitudinarian culture. In his "Mary Astell and John Locke," Mark Goldie emphasizes the importance of theology in Astell's encounter with the works of John Locke. Against a dominant view in Astell studies, argued most forcefully by Patricia Springborg, that Astell's work was motivated by an animus against Locke's political thought, Goldie argues that Astell's attack upon Locke was primarily philosophical and theological. By detailing the character and chronology of Locke's early reputation (and demonstrating the centrality of Locke's *Essay* and not the *Two Treatises* to his contemporary reception), Goldie contends that Astell's arguments entail an assault on Whigs and Dissenters—and do not anticipate modern feminist critiques of liberal democracy. Astell, in elaborating a politics described by Goldie as "Machiavellian Toryism," may have been thinking about the works of Plato, Machiavelli, and More, but certainly not the Locke of the *Two Treatises*. When Astell does turn to Locke in her *Christian Religion*, the principal terms of the engagement with him are theological and moral, not political. Though not engaging extensively with Locke's political tract, in the 1706 Preface to *Some Reflections upon Marriage*, Astell launches an (heretofore unacknowledged) attack on a different work of Locke's, his posthumously published *Paraphrase and Notes on the First Epistle of St Paul to the Corinthians*. Through re-assessing Locke's early reputation, and refining our conception of Astell's engagement with his works, Goldie argues that Astell's idiosyncratic and complex Tory ideology was guided by theological concerns; when assailing Locke, Astell's target was primarily his materialism and Socinianism rather than his politics.

In Goldie's reading, Astell decidedly did not provide "feminism's first retort to liberal modernity." In her "Mary Astell's Law of the Heart," Corrinne Harol also turns to Astell's engagement with Locke, attempting to recuperate aspects of "the modern or at least radical Astell." By foregrounding the centrality of desire in the two parts of *A Serious Proposal*, Harol argues that Astell articulates a version of the subject in consonance with a different liberal tradition—one that would eventually manifest itself in the moral "perfectionism" of a later tradition of "positive liberalism." In showing how Astell's conception of desire emerges out of the tensions between the Anglican concepts of "laws written into the heart" and Locke's notions of subjectivity from the *Essay*, Harol argues that desire is the key to spirituality for Astell. In contrast to Locke, where the progressive revisions of the *Essay* evoke an increasingly depraved conception of desire, Astell imagines desire as the only guarantor of moral goodness. Where Locke depicts desire as working in opposition to the moral faculty of understanding and therefore requiring suppression, Astell advocates the development of an "autonomous mind" where rationality and passion are not at odds, but rather united in the service of God. For Harol, it is surprisingly Locke who is figured as the "proponent of repression, and even the pseudo-idealist." Astell, by contrast, "enmeshed in the realities of life in society," holds out the promise, through the alignment of reason and desire, of the possibility of spiritual perfection.

While both Goldie and Harol outline the theological underpinnings of Astell's political conceptions, in her "Religious Nonconformity and the Problem of Dissent in the Works of Aphra Behn and Mary Astell," Melinda Zook focuses upon Astell's tracts of the first decade of the eighteenth century to elaborate the parallels between Astell's political conceptions and her perceptions of both gender and sexuality. In the process, Zook identifies an unexpected (and apparently unlikely) context for the political tracts of 1704. Aphra Behn, one of the Restoration theatre's most prolific authors, who wrote before the Glorious Revolution and Act of Toleration in 1689, might seem to endorse views of marriage and sexuality diametrically opposed to those of Astell. Zook argues, however, that as an earlier "Tory feminist," Behn—specifically her views on Dissenters—provides an important precedent for Astell's thought. Behn and Astell not only both equate Dissenters with rebellion and chaos (as did many Restoration royalists); they likewise represent dissent as a direct threat to both social and sexual orders. Astell's representations of Dissenters (including occasional conformists, latitudinarians, and Socinians) parallel Behn's earlier representations of the Puritan-Dissenter in plays such as *The City Heiress* and *The Roundheads*. By focusing on the "image of the hypocritical, ambitious, dissembling, canting, and often lustful Dissenter," Zook outlines the Tory ideology articulated by both Astell and Behn. In this reading, Astell, like Behn before her, linked the religious and political "enthusiasm" of Dissenters with a predatory sexuality. For Zook, Astell's conceptions of gender emerge as a *political* concern—a function of her distrust of dissenting politics which reveals its duplicity through its licentious sexuality.

Claire Pickard also shows the relationship between political concerns and gender in Astell's work, through focusing on the conception of agency in Astell's rarely discussed poetic *oeuvre*. In "'Great in Humilitie': Mary Astell's Poetry," Pickard delineates the relationship between literary, spiritual and political registers in the collection of manuscript poems presented to Sancroft in 1689. For Pickard, Astell's literary ambitions for glory are fulfilled through service, passivity, and even martyrdom. By constructing her own sense of personal ambition through the discourses associated with the Royal Martyr Charles I, Astell's poetry demonstrates that exclusion from the machinations of earthly power—and the possibility of what she calls in *Some Reflections* "Heroic Action"—serves as the necessary pre-requisite for the realization of spiritual ambition. Astell intimates, Pickard argues, that a specifically feminine martyrdom may in fact assure a heavenly reward even greater than that to be achieved by "famous Masculine Heroes." In Pickard's reading of the poems, gender, though an impediment to earthly power, becomes a means in Astell's quest to achieve "a Crown of Glory." The implicit argument of the poems, Pickard claims, anticipates the passivity and martyrdom advocated in the prose—as in *Some Reflections*, where Astell most vigorously argues for a non-material solution to the problems of gender inequality.

In "'Tis better that I endure': Mary Astell's Exclusion of Equity," Ann Van Sant explores another—hitherto unelaborated—context for Astell's major works: early modern property rights. Van Sant traces the emergence of equity from out of the framework of common law (in which the concept of equity remained undeveloped), and elaborates the legal, political, and theological vocabularies of equity contemporary with Astell's tracts. During the early modern period, the separate jurisdiction of equity served as a means of accommodating married women's property rights (before their legal recognition in the Married Women's Property Act of 1882). But Astell herself consistently aligns her thinking with the prescriptive power of law as ancient custom and against the exceptionality implied in equitable thinking. Van Sant thus explores the paradox that though Astell's tracts—in particular *Some Reflections*—elaborate injustices towards women in terms of "inequity," Astell resolutely ignores the ameliorative remedies offered by the rule of equity, deliberately locating both justice and equity solely in the divine. Astell's refusal to bring equity down to earth—into the practical context of marriage and domestic relations—can be attributed, according to Van Sant, to her political and theological principles. The ironic dismissal of Defoe in her *A Fair Way with the Dissenters* and the appeal to obedience in *A Christian Religion* stand as Astell's affirmation of obedience and authority against the lawlessness implied in the exceptionalism of equity—which was increasingly associated with dissent, non-conformity, and religious toleration.

The triptych of essays by Eileen O'Neill, Jacqueline Broad, and Derek Taylor, focusing more specifically on languages of "reason," articulate the philosophical contexts for Astell's work. In "Mary Astell on the Causation of Sensation," O'Neill examines Astell's arguments with Norris in *Letters Concerning the Love of God* in the framework of longstanding debates between Aristotelian naturalist philosophers, on the one hand, and theologians advocating occasionalism, on the other. O'Neill demonstrates how Astell's philosophical arguments are dependent upon the philosophical discourses developed by contemporaries, as well as the older philosophical traditions that informed them. Thus O'Neill considers Astell's debate with her contemporary Nicolas Malebranche on occasionalism in relation to Thomas Aquinas's attack upon the occasionalism advocated by the Islamic theologian al-Ghazali. In elaborating Astell's own position on occasionalism, and its ramifications for mind-body interaction, O'Neill identifies Astell's stance with that of Descartes—whose concurrentist position about bodies as partial efficient causes of sensation she would come to emulate. From out of the earlier medieval debate, Astell appears as a figure opposing both Malebranche's and Norris's occasionalist rationalism and Locke's materialistic empiricism—advocating instead something close to the "orthodox Cartesian position."

O'Neill emphasizes the congruities between what she sees as Astell's anti-occasionalist philosophical perspective and that of Descartes. In her "Astell, Cartesian Ethics, and the Critique of Custom" Jacqueline Broad focuses on the so-called tension between Astell's conservative political commitments and her Cartesian philosophy. In Broad's reading, these tensions disappear if we interpret Astell's "Cartesian challenge to custom" according to an ethical rather than epistemological model of Cartesianism. In the second part of *A Serious Proposal*, Broad points out, Astell appeals to Descartes's conception of ethics, and not solely to the Cartesian epistemology that figures so broadly in thinkers advocating what Jonathan Israel has called "radical enlightenment." Broad shows how Astell's appropriations of Cartesian philosophy are modeled upon those of Cambridge Platonists (such as Henry More) who also try to accommodate Cartesian rationalism within the context of Anglican practice and ethics. Acknowledging Astell's primarily prudential aims—"her design to effect a moral reformation in women"—reveals the proper context for Astell's engagement with Descartes. For Broad, a closer examination of Astell's pursuit of Cartesian ethical ideals enables a more nuanced understanding of her feminist views in consonance with her conservative political ideals.

Continuing the focus upon Astell's philosophical discourses, in "Are You Experienced?: Astell, Locke, and Education," E. Derek Taylor also acknowledges Astell's debt to Descartes, but in the service of a discussion of Astell's attitudes towards pedagogy and education. Notwithstanding Astell's concession to Descartes's conception of the immateriality of reason, Astell's own accommodations to pedagogy and sensationalist psychology would seem to reveal a surprising affinity to her philosophical nemesis, John Locke. While Patricia Springborg has remarked that Astell makes "a surprising concession to the principles of a Lockean sensationalist psychology," Taylor asks whether Astell was "implicitly a true empiricist, and of Locke's party without knowing it?" Focusing on Astell's arguments about education in works that span four decades—from *Letters* to *A Serious Proposal* to *Some Reflections* to *Christian Religion*—Taylor shows how Astell's commitment to education gained its energies primarily from the educational theories of Descartes, Malebranche, and Norris, and not from an engagement with Locke's work. Astell, Taylor argues, may concede that in the acquisition of truth "bodies matter." Yet while Locke asserts that sensory perception is central to the acquisition of all human knowledge, Astell emphasizes an educational practice which at once acknowledges, but simultaneously helps to undo, the "prejudices of senses." Taylor concludes that Locke's sensationalist psychology was not, for Astell, ineluctable; Astell's own program for educational reform for women, rescued from the senses, is based on an essentially rationalist account of learning ultimately deriving from Cartesian philosophy.

With the concluding essay, Hilda L. Smith's "'Cry up Liberty': The Political Context for Mary Astell's Feminism," the volume returns to an analysis of the political vocabularies in Astell's work to explicitly address the connection between Astell's royalist politics and her feminist arguments. Writing against those who point to the ostensible contradiction of Astell's positions, Smith shows that it was, in fact, Astell's Tory politics that enabled her arguments on behalf of women. Situating Astell's thought in relationship to the Protestant sectaries of the 1640s and 1650s, Smith shows how the contradiction of Puritan opposition to the King and their assertion of strong patriarchal authority within the family (a contradiction inherited by Astell's dissenting contemporaries), provided an opening for Astell's Tory defense of women. It is Astell's royalism, Smith argues, that allows her to raise questions about women's standing in society which, in fact, eluded the likes of Locke (who cited the Fifth Commandment in arguing equal respect for fathers and mothers, but asserted the authority of men in the domain of property rights). In Smith's readings of *A Serious Proposal* and *Some Reflections*, Astell elaborates arguments in defense of women that go even further than those of Margaret Fell, whose *Women's Speaking Justified* is often cited as a less ambiguous, and therefore more appropriate, antecedent for contemporary versions of feminism. Smith points out that Fell's focus was on "future life," while Astell, by unmasking the "partial universalism" of Civil War sectarian discourses (and their later Whig embodiment), provides a *practical* analysis and critique of the dynamics of the early modern family. Paradoxically, it is Astell more than sectaries, Quakers, or Locke who provides concrete arguments in defense of women in the context of early modern Britain.

Was Mary Astell, then, a proto-feminist? A feminist? For Smith, as for some of the other contributors to this volume, the answer is, unequivocally, yes. But the Mary Astell who emerges from Smith's analysis is a feminist who perplexes the categories of contemporary feminism, and whose own arguments in defense of women were always complicated and—as Smith shows—in some sense energized, by her Tory political commitments. When discussing the early modern period, "women," as Rachel Weil has noted, "is not always a useful term for political and social categorization."[44] The category, when unqualified, fails in relation to Astell because her defense of women emerges out of the totality of her complex and sometimes enigmatic set of commitments and convictions—whether theological, political, legal, or philosophical—which the contributors to this volume endeavor to elaborate.

While the first phase of the recovery of early modern women's writings was in the mode of an archeological dig for "first feminists," and the second a presentation of their texts to a modern audience, by the 2000s we are ready to re-embed Astell in the thicker contexts of the history and philosophy of her time. The feminists of the 1980s have succeeded triumphantly within a quarter century in persuading historians, philosophers, and literary scholars (who do not necessarily identify themselves with feminist studies) that they too cannot leave Astell out of their reckoning. The essays presented in this collection, following on the achievements of earlier scholars, show Astell to be not only a figure in the proto-feminist canon, but a major innovator in the long eighteenth century.

---

44 Rachel Weil, *Political Passions: Gender, the Family and Political Argument in England: 1680–1714* (Manchester, 1990), 4.

# Chapter II

# Mary Astell, Religion, and Feminism: Texts in Motion

Sharon Achinstein

In this chapter I intend to raise questions about the relations between feminism and the Enlightenment, and open up the issue of explaining the historical transition from one form to another. It has long been a claim in women's history that during the early modern period, women's activities, whether economic, political, legal, or religious, became consigned to a sphere of the domestic. Social, political, and legal historians are debating this hypothesis, but this story of "the long ebb" remains vested in a genealogical narrative about the rise of liberal political ideologies.[1] For instance, Patricia Springborg, who has done the most to retrieve Mary Astell for mainstream political theory, claims that the early feminist deserves preeminence as the first opponent of the separation of "the public and private worlds into which social life was divided and which it was the intention of the theoreticians of the early modern state to entrench," a separation which was founded, as Springborg continues, "on homologous contracts: the social contract, which constituted the political world of men, and the marriage contract, which governed the private world of women."[2] Sara Mendelson and Patricia Crawford, along these lines, in the conclusion to their rich and beautifully synthesizing account of women's history in early modern England, lay a measure of the blame for the consignment of women to the domestic on liberal political theories, and in doing so follow the powerful political analysis of Carole Pateman. "What seems to have undermined women's formal participation [in politics] by the end of the seventeenth century," they write, "was the changing paradigm of political theory." They continue, and I quote in full because their account is as succinct as it is typical:

> From the Civil War onwards, when seventeenth-century political writers and theorists considered questions of political rights, they conceptualized the citizen more clearly than before as male. Democratic paradigms of the rights of men and brothers excluded women more decisively than did patriarchal discourses, in which lineage and inheritance provided grounds for the formal political privileges of élite property-holders of both sexes.[3]

---

[1] Though Amy Erikson provides some evidence to the contrary in *Women and Property in Early Modern England* (London, 1993), 159.

[2] Patricia Springborg, "Mary Astell (1666–1731): Critic of Locke," *American Political Science Review* 89.3 (1995): 621.

[3] Sara Mendelson and Patricia Crawford, *Women in Early Modern England, 1550–1720* (Oxford, 1998), 429–30; and Ruth Perry, "Mary Astell and the Feminist Critique of Possessive Individualism,"

For this narrative, the triumph of the feminist Astell is that she disrupts a history of the consignment of women to the domestic and the separation of public from private. This story of a separation of private and public has been a topic of recent interest to literary historians, although no longer as simple a binary as it once seemed. [4]

There is also a clear modernist bias of seeing religion as a central concern only in the period before the Enlightenment. The great scholar of the Enlightenment, Peter Gay, epitomized that period as the era of the "rise of modern paganism." Keith Thomas has similarly argued for the eighteenth century as a time of "disenchantment of the world." [5] These theorists convey a powerful assumption that secularization and modernity march in step.[6] When historians have recognized the significance of religion, even radical religion, in Enlightenment society, it is often seen as a foil: J. G. A. Pocock, for example, titles an essay: "Religion: the Antiself of Enlightenment."[7] When historians of English intellectual life have treated religion, they have focused on its political—and therefore "public"—aspects, seeing religion as "priestcraft," emphasizing the political functions of religion in party politics, or considering worship as a social practice.[8] Only recently, in studies of contemporary epistemology, have intellectual historians been coming to see the surprising correlation between

---

*Eighteenth-Century Studies* 23.4 (1990): 444–57, 445; Carole Pateman, *The Sexual Contract* (Stanford, 1988), 90–91; Patricia Springborg, "Astell, Masham, and Locke: Religion and Politics," in *Women Writers and the Early Modern British Political Tradition*, ed. Hilda Smith (Cambridge, 1998), 105–25. For contrast, see Melissa A. Butler, "Early Liberal Roots of Feminism: John Locke and the Attack on Patriarchy," in *Feminist Interpretations and Political Theory*, eds. Mary Lyndon Shanley and Carole Pateman (University Park, PA, 1991), 74–94; and Kathryn J. Ready, "Damaris Cudworth Masham, Catharine Trotter Cockburn, and the Feminist Legacy of Locke's Theory of Personal Identity," *Eighteenth-Century Studies* 35.4 (2002): 563–76.

4  On the liberal consignment of women to a "separate sphere" of the domestic, see Susan Okin, "Women and the Making of the Sentimental Family," *Philosophy and Public Affairs* 11.1 (1982): 65–88; and for the "long ebb" argument by social historians, see Alice Clark, *Working Life of Women in the Seventeenth Century* (London, 1919), 290–308; Chris Middleton, "Women's Labour and the Transition to Pre-Industrial Capitalism," in *Women and Work in Pre-Industrial England*, eds. Lindsey Charles and Lorna Duffin (London, 1985), 181–206. Questioning the private/public sphere dichotomy with particular relevance to feminist concerns are Amanda Vickery, "Golden Age to Separate Spheres? A Review of the Categories and Chronology of English Women's History," *Historical Journal* 36.2 (1993): 383–414; and Lawrence E. Klein, "Gender and the Public/Private Distinction in the Eighteenth-Century: Some Questions about Evidence and Analytic Procedure," *Eighteenth-Century Studies* 29.1 (1995): 97–109.

5  Keith Thomas, *Religion and the Decline of Magic* (London, 1983), 640.

6  Peter Gay, *The Enlightenment: An Interpretation* (New York, 1996); "secularization theory" enters into cultural history via indirect means, as for example in the work of Jurgen Habermas; for a contemporary critique, see Peter L. Berger, "The Desecularization of the World: A Global Overview," in *The Desecularization of the World: Resurgent Religion and World Politics*, ed. Peter L. Berger (Washington, DC, 1994), 1–18.

7  Lawrence E. Klein and Anthony J. La Vopa, eds., *Enthusiasm and Enlightenment in Europe, 1650–1850* (San Marino, CA, 1998), 3. See also Dominique Colas, *Civil Society and Fanaticism*, trans. Amy Jacobs (Stanford, 1997); Jonathan Israel, *Radical Enlightenment: Philosophy and the Making of Modernity, 1650–1750* (Oxford, 2001), 4, which sets out the modernization/rationalization/secularism thesis.

8  Important exceptions are the classic essays by Hugh Trevor-Roper, "The Religious Origins of the Enlightenment," in *Religion, the Reformation and Social Change* (London, 1984), 193–236; J.G.A. Pocock, "Post-Puritan England and the Problem of the Enlightenment," in *Culture and Politics*, ed. P. Zagorin (Los Angeles, 1980), 91–109.

theology and the rise of modern political ideologies.[9] The link has yet to bear fruit in the study of early modern women's ideas.

The writings of Mary Astell form a corpus of accounts peculiarly suited to unravel these analytical strands. Astell's brave polemics about marriage, women's education, and the like have been severed from her serious interest in theology; and a recovery of her religious writing is long overdue. It is simply not enough to say her attacks on Dissenters were a mere polemical reflex. In them, she engages seriously with theological concerns, connecting the specific controversies to the main philosophical debates in her own day. Recently, Astell's writings, along with those of other early "feminists" have been placed in the context of party polemic.[10] In the present study, I suspend judgment on whether Astell belongs to "modernity" or to "feminism" in order to inquire into the internal structure of argument. I should like to begin my analysis by reminding us that the separation of private and public achieved through liberal political theory and practice was to consign religion to the private sphere.

Our ignoring of Astell's religious writings is not simply oversight. For the Restoration and post-1688 period—that in which we find that fabled separation between private and public; the origins of liberalism; and the emergence of our Tory Feminism—the study of religion has generally been reduced to political analyses of polemics about the shape of the church, ecclesiological controversies that took place in and around the public sphere, specifically over dissent, atheism, and the fears about Roman Catholicization and priestcraft.[11] However, to reduce religion to politics (or economics) is a mistake; theology, I suggest, is a wrongfully neglected arena that could prove very rich for feminist analysis, especially because a thinker as engaged with theological questions as Astell wrote extensively about the topic, addressing some of her most searching questions about the nature of human agency, personal relationships, the passions, and virtue—all questions central to feminism—through the discourse of religion. In the early modern period, it is hard to ignore the way that theological discourse was a means to express existential purpose, to construct subjectivity and community, indeed to mediate public and private. Further, to occlude theology from a feminist account is to ignore means and to privilege ends.

"If *all Men are born free*, how is it that all Women are born slaves?"[12] In the history of feminism, this statement seems a remarkable step forward for women's rights. Yet

---

9 See John Marshall, *John Locke: Resistance, Religion and Responsibility* (Cambridge, 1994), esp. 329–83.

10 Rachel Weil, *Political Passions: Gender, The Family and Political Argument in England, 1680–1714* (Manchester, 1999), puts *Reflections* in relation to the allegiance controversies of the 1690s; Hannah Smith, "English 'Feminist' Writings and Judith Drake's *An Essay in Defense of the Female Sex* (1696)," *Historical Journal* 44.3 (2001): 727–47, in relation to party politics and to the rise of sociability.

11 Justin Champion, *Pillars of Priestcraft Shaken: The Church of England and its Enemies, 1660–1730* (Cambridge, 1992); Mark Goldie, Paul Seaward and Tim Harris, eds., *The Politics of Religion in Restoration England* (Oxford, 1990); Roger Lund, ed., *Margins of Orthodoxy: Heterodox Writing and Cultural Response, 1660–1750* (Cambridge, 1995).

12 Mary Astell, *Some Reflections upon Marriage*, in *Astell: Political Writings*, ed. Patricia Springborg (Cambridge, 1996), 18. This edition, hereafter cited parenthetically as *SRM*.

Astell wrote not simply concerning women; Astell's theological program is to defeat the *premise* of this theorem: humans are not, in her mind, "born free." Astell has two targets in writing this pithy statement in her *Some Reflections upon Marriage*, first published in 1700: Robert Filmer, the patriarchalist political theorist, as well as those sponsors of contract theory such as John Locke, who were developing arguments about social order from abstract principles. Against Filmer, Astell argues that the inequalities between men and women perceptible in the world are not a matter of divine command to Adam, but merely a historical fact, a matter of custom and prejudice. "'Tis true that GOD told *Eve* after the Fall that *her Husband shou'd Rule over her*," admits Astell, but she continues by pointing out another Biblical example of hierarchy that ought not be made a precedent, one specifically evoking the class warfare of her own day:

> And so it is that he told *Esau* by the mouth of *Isaac* his Father, that he shou'd serve his *younger Brother*, and shou'd in time, and when he was strong enough to do it, *break the Yoke from off his Neck*. Now why one Text shou'd be a Command any more than the other, and not both of them be Predictions only. (*SRM* 19–20)

Thus Astell asks, tweaking Filmer for the contradiction in his argument, and appealing to the same class interests.[13] Astell lays blame for gender inequality not on God's injunction to Adam and Eve, therefore, but on historical eventualities; evoking the specter of the elder brother serving the younger one was also a not-so thinly disguised scare tactic in the Civil War period, rousing the threat of popular insurrection.

After she dismisses the Biblical precedent for male superiority, as Filmer postulates it, Astell turns to thinkers on the left and to arguments for a *natural* male superiority. She asks "why the former [God's injunction to Eve after the Fall] shou'd prove *Adam's* natural Right to Rule" [underlining added]. As feminists have long argued, Adam's having been created *before* Eve ought not justify male dominance over women: "For the Earthly *Adam's* being *Form'd* before *Eve*, seems as little to prove her Natural Subjection to him, as the Living Creatures, Fishes, Birds and Beasts being Form'd before them both, proves that Mankind must be subject to these Animals" (*SRM* 21). In her drive to demolish arguments from *natural* law, Astell retrieves instead the authority from *scripture*, citing Paul: "the Scripture commands *Wives to submit themselves to their own Husbands*. True; for which St. *Paul* gives a Mystical Reason (Eph 5.22 etc) and St. *Peter* a Prudential and Charitable one (1 St. Pet. 3.) but *neither of them derive that Subjection from the Law of Nature*" (*SRM* 20, italics added). Astell sees hierarchy in Christian marriage not as a natural, but as a divine institution, citing Paul's command in Ephesians 5.22 for "*Wives to submit themselves to their own Husbands*," and backing this up with Peter's call in 1 Pet. 3:1 for "*ye wives*" to "*be in subjection to your own husbands*." The hierarchy visible in the world is, then, not because of Adamic example, women's natures, their deficiency in reason, or from their weakened physical capacity (*SRM* 20–21). It is from the gospel that women's subjection is enjoined, a gospel that is the testament of the Lord.

---

13   Sir Robert Filmer, *The Anarchy of a Limited or Mixed Monarchy* (1648), in *Patriarcha and Other Writings*, ed. Johann Sommerville (Cambridge, 1991), 138.

Recent scholars have seen Astell's attack on natural subjection as a feminist move, a critique of liberal ideology, because it underscores the ways that male superiority is often predicated on a little-admitted notion of natural differences between men and women. A closer look at Astell's work tells another story. For Astell, divine edict justifies male superiority as an indisputable rule. For this reason, Astell supports the idea of women's refusing to marry at all. "She then who Marrys," she declares,

> ought to lay it down for an indisputable Maxim, that her husband must govern absolutely and intirely, and that she has nothing else to do but to Please and Obey. She must not attempt to divide his Authority, or so much as dispute it, to struggle with her Yoke will only make it gall the more. (*SRM* 62, 49)[14]

The solution to women's "slavery" then, is that women should never agree to enter into marriage in the first place, because to marry is to submit to an authority that is by institution unassailable.

In her attacks on arguments from nature, Astell does not, however, anticipate current feminist thought by pointing out the ways that male superiority is often predicated on the seldom-avowed concepts of natural *differences* between men and women. Her reasoning derives from other premises, and her goal is utterly different from current feminist agendas of recognizing and valuing difference. Her line of thinking instead parallels that of Filmer, whose goal is to deny any arguments from nature. Astell's point of departure is God, and with that divine authority she shores up an antidemocratic program. "Where there is an equality by nature, there can be no superior power," Filmer writes in *The Anarchy*. To prove this, Filmer brings up what is meant to be seen as a ridiculous possibility—women's natural equality—which is why Astell takes a swipe at him. The notion of a basic female equality, he writes, "cannot but be mischievous always at the least to all infants and others under age of discretion—not to speak of women, especially virgins, who by birth have as much natural freedom as any other and therefore ought not to lose their liberty without their own consent."[15] From these words, it could appear that Filmer is arguing for women's "freedom." Astell, however, exposes Filmer as no proto-feminist; he rather used the instance of women's natural liberty to point out the absurdity of the contractarian argument which bases its claims on the equal rationality of all people, a claim Filmer most fervently rejects.

In rejecting Filmer's sexism, however, Astell does not produce arguments for an essential equality of men and women *prior* to society, in a state of nature. By urging women to stay single, she is not suggesting they hold on to their own freedoms and remain in that equal state of nature. On the contrary; that freedom was never theirs to begin with, for there is no state of nature, not even in theory. Astell, in refuting Davenant's argument that people may reassume fundamental rights if their safety is threatened by their sovereign, writes:

---

14  Ruth Perry also reads this ironically in *The Celebrated Mary Astell: An Early English Feminist* (Chicago, 1986), 166.

15  Filmer, *Anarchy*, 142. See, for another reading, Margaret R. Sommerville, *Sex and Subjection: Attitudes to Women in Early-Modern Society* (London, 1995), 217–19.

*I have hitherto thought, a State of Nature was a meer figment of* Hobb's *Brain, or borrow'd at least from the Fable of* Cadmus, *or* Aeacus *his* Myrmidons, *till you were pleas'd to inform me* 'of that Equality wherein the Race of men were plac'd in the free State of Nature.' *How I lament my Stars it was not my good Fortune to Live in those Happy Days when Men spring up like so many Mushrooms or* Terrae Filii, *without Father or Mother or any sort of dependency!*[16]

Astell's language of dependency may seem to echo our contemporary feminist critiques of the abstract individual, Hobbes' self-generated "mushroom," a premise that denies important ties of kinship, family, and society.[17] Astell indeed criticizes the fictional positing of the autonomous individual in the state of nature, removed from ties of generation. However, Astell, unlike current feminists, takes the argument for dependency back a step. She points to a fundamental dependency that state-of-nature arguments deny: the dependence of humans upon God.

Natural liberty was a philosophical postulate Astell would not entertain because she held that humans were bound by a prior and inalienable relation, obedience to God. To Astell, discussions of natural liberty and the like smacked of mere morality, of materialism, in short, of atheism; and the language in which she registered her assault on the natural liberty of all people, against their potential as rational subjects and citizens, took place in religious categories that today seem arcane. The ferocious theological debates in the early modern period, as historians of science and epistemology have long understood, did not solely pertain to the long-afternoon sermonizing of hairsplitting divines; there were matters of enormous political and ethical consequence in these controversies. As early modern politics became an autonomous sphere, carved out from the sphere of religion, morality, and the eternal (the "modernity-secularizing" story), it was precisely over the nature of human knowledge, autonomy, and freedom, that theology came to be a mediating discourse, preparing the world for the removal of spiritual dependence and triggering real change. Theology, as I see it, is both the effect and the cause that sparks historical restructuration. In the life of women, then, theology may be seen as a means to understand and to practice agency, an agency that might properly be called "feminist." For Astell, and for many of her time, the means now were becoming *more* rather than less religious even as the ends were growing ever more secularized. That is to say, the public presence of women making intellectual arguments made their identity newly visible, and constituted a coming into the public that belied any particular advocacy to the contrary. Women's arguments worked to make them visible in the public, secular sphere even as they advocated something to the contrary.

To miss Astell's theological mode of expression and the spiritual contours of her political writings is to misunderstand her account of liberty, equality, and sociability.

---

16  [Mary Astell,] *Moderation Truly Stated* (London, 1704), xxxv. The mushroom analogy may derive from Hobbes' *De Cive*, in which he asks us to "consider men as if but even now sprung out of the earth, and suddenly, like mushrooms, come to full maturity, without all kind of engagement with each other" (Thomas Hobbes, *The Citizen*, in *Man and Citizen: Thomas Hobbes's De Homine and De Cive*, ed. Bernard Gert, [Garden City, 1972], 205).

17  See Christine Di Stefano, "Masculinity as Ideology in Political Theory: Hobbesian Man Considered," *Women's Studies International Forum* 6.6 (1983): 633–44.

This essay seeks to restore theology to its function as the dispensable mediator of the transition from early modern to modern. Astell, by theological discourses, directed her writings to a very modern problem: the liberal premise of self-sufficiency or human autonomy. Astell denied this starting point: with or without the presence of human governments in Church and state, she argued, people were under God's government, their self-worth defined by the condition, and direction, of their souls. Further, there was a need for the divinely ordained institution of the Church to solicit obedience, because of the condition of humans as fallen and dependent upon the workings of Grace through the Holy Spirit.[18] Social bonds, Astell believed, must be enforced by convention and institution and not simply by "contract." A new model of sociability, it has been argued, was coming into place in the early Enlightenment, one in which Astell may be seen as an important contributor.[19] Although Astell works to negate the assumptions of liberal epistemology and political theory, her work is in dialectical response: she is, along with Masham and Locke, an early diagnostician of secularization.

From her theology, Astell starts with a principle of the inadequacy of human reason, which explains the need for revelation's authority and assistance. "Reason," Astell writes,

> can judge of things which she can comprehend, she can determine where she has a compleat, or at least a clear and distinct Idea, and can judge of *a contradiction in terms*, for this is within her compass; but she must nor affirm in opposition to Revelation, that there is any *contradiction in the nature of things that are Infinitely above her*; nor deny a Truth because it is out of her reach. An *Indian*, or a *Ploughman*, may as peremptorily as he pleases, deny all the Propositions in *Euclid*, but they don't cease to be True, because the poor Ignorant does not understand them.[20]

Writing against the democratic capacity of humans for reason, as found in Locke's *Essay Concerning Human Understanding*, Astell makes three counter-claims: reason is distributed unequally; reason has need of Revelation; and Revelation is embodied in the English Church.[21]

In her major theological treatise of 1705 from which this pronouncement upon reason is drawn, *The Christian Religion as Profess'd by a Daughter of the Church of England*, Astell contests with Locke and others over key theological points about agency, personhood, and rationality. She disputes the grounds upon which Locke builds an edifice for a political theory based upon contract, and challenges his views

---

18 On reason's impairment with the Fall, see Astell, *SRM*, 15; and Astell, *A Serious Proposal to the Ladies*, ed. Patricia Springborg (London, 1997), 105, 156. This edition will be cited parenthetically as *SP I* and *SP II* in this essay, although the author has also consulted Springborg, ed., *A Serious Proposal to the Ladies* (Toronto, 2002). On reason's lack of self-sufficiency, see [Astell,] *The Christian Religion* (London, 1705), 17, 50, 53.

19 Laura Runge notes Astell's stress on the social function for gallantry and civility, in "Beauty and Gallantry: A Model of Polite Conversation," *Eighteenth-Century Life* 25.1 (2001): 54.

20 Astell, *Christian Religion*, 18.

21 On Locke's "democratic intellect," see Jeremy Waldron, *God, Locke, and Equality: Christian Foundations in Locke's Political Thought* (Cambridge, 2002), 83–107.

of the sufficiency of people to make choices in politics.[22] In relation to Lockean principles, Astell's theology *can* support a kind of egalitarianism, but one that one would be hard pressed to call *feminism*. Its understanding of liberty is limited to positive liberty, its mode essentially dependent. The aim of human existence is, finally, anti-social and otherworldly; this *telos* undercuts the possibility of the expression of human agency. Indeed, Astell posits an essential mode of radical dependence for all humans, resolving her concept of person in a master/slave model of relation between God and humankind. Her view of liberty, then, is a moral, epistemological, and political challenge to the notion of emancipation based on agency of persons in the material world.

It is hard to overestimate the otherwordly focus of Astell's concern. Current philosophers and historians of political thought who have analyzed Astell's engagements over epistemology that reflect her contest with Locke and Masham point to vital elements in Astell's theories of agency, linking will, cognition, and reason. Yet an emphasis on cognition and reason has slighted attention to her notion of personhood, a concept essential to any theory of consent.[23] On the aim of human life, Astell asserts,

> 'tis certainly no Arrogance in a Woman to conclude, that she was made for the Service of GOD, and that this is her End. Because GOD made all Things for Himself, and a Rational Mind is too noble a Being to be Made for the Sake and Service of any Creature. The Service she at any time becomes oblig'd to pay to a Man, is only a Business by the Bye. (*SRM* 11)

And further:

> The Relation between the two Sexes is mutual, and the Dependence Reciprocal, both of them Depending intirely upon GOD, and upon Him only; which one wou'd think is no great Argument of the natural Inferiority of either Sex. (*SRM* 13)

These arguments may be seen as tactical or opportunistic ways of challenging arguments about female natural subordination, but when we turn away from Astell's explicitly "feminist" discourse to her religious ideas, the picture that emerges is even more complex. Thus when Perry claims that Astell opposes marriage because she "recognized that women lost their political rights when they married—along with their property rights," it's hard to figure out how *anyone* in Astell's system could have "political rights" at all.[24] Nor is Astell in this respect close to Hobbes, because,

---

[22] See E. Derek Taylor, "Mary Astell's Ironic Assault on John Locke's Theory of Thinking Matter," *Journal of the History of Ideas* 62.3 (2001): 505–22.

[23] Kathryn J. Ready, in "Damaris Cudworth Masham," has explored Locke's definitions of person as they bear on conceptions of reason, asking why his conceptions were taken up by feminist philosophers Masham and Trotter. Ready suggests that Locke offers feminists a solution to the mind/body problem that had held women subordinate on account of their impaired physical capacities; see also Kathleen M. Squadrito, "Mary Astell's Critique of Locke's View of Thinking Matter," *Journal of the History of Philosophy* 25.3 (July 1987): 433–39.

[24] Perry, "Mary Astell and the Feminist Critique," 448.

unlike in Hobbes, for Astell the individual can never offer consent.[25] Basing her argument upon a religious conception of identity as dependent, Astell begins at a fundamentally different starting point for an analysis of political agency than that supplied by the voluntarist politics of contract or liberty of conscience.

For instance, in her critique of natural law arguments, Astell focuses on the central (populist) principle of a natural right of self-preservation. But this principle shares little with contemporary feminist interest in ownership of one's own body, in issues such as prostitution, abortion, female genital mutilation, and marital rape. Instead, Astell posits ownership of the body in God. In her *A Serious Proposal to the Ladies, for the Advancement of their true and greatest Interest* (1694), the premise of the women's educational institution is that

> we were not made for our selves ... Religion is the adequate business of our lives, and largely consider'd, takes in all we have to do; nothing being a fit employment for a rational Creature, which has not either a *direct* or *remote* tendency to this great and *only* end. (*SP I* 21)

The affairs of the world, the sensations of the body, can give delight, but they can also divert humans from their true interest, which is in God (*SP I* 160). In her fascinating series of letters with the Anglican Divine John Norris, Astell poses questions about human relations in the context of this principle.

This revision of Malebranche, whom Astell had only understood through Norris's mediation, offers a ripe area for examining one early modern woman's account of human desire and the passions.[26] Astell asks if love of human creatures is compatible with a love for God; and her conclusion over the course of this dialogue is no. The Soul, she stresses, cannot have "a twofold Desire" both for God and for fellow humans; as she puts it, "we may as reasonably expect that a Stone should go up Hill and down Hill at the same time."[27] This was a point about which Damaris Masham took special notice; in her reply to the Norris–Astell correspondence, Masham asserts that cultural effects can help direct our earthly love properly towards benevolence.[28]

Astell takes a firmer line. Despite her emphasis on female education, she is doubtful about cultural reform, and expresses concern about the dangers of this misplaced allegiance. "Thus we are insensibly betrayed," she worries," into a wrong Motion, and blindly follow on in it, till at length we become so glew'd to the Creature, that 'tis almost as difficult to wean us from it, as it is to change the Leopard's Spots, or whiten

---

25 Thus I disagree with Penny Weiss, "Mary Astell: Including Women's Voices in Political Theory," *Hypatia* 19.3 (2004): 63–94, who finds many points of contact between Astell and Hobbes; in contrast, Sarah Ellenzweig's elegant essay, "The Love of God and the Radical Enlightenment: Mary Astell's Brush with Spinoza," *Journal of the History of Ideas* 64.3 (2003): 379–97, offers a splendid account linking Astell's feminism and her theology.

26 On the debate over the passions in seventeenth-century thought, see Anthony Levi, *French Moralists: The Theory of the Passions, 1585–1649* (Oxford, 1964); and on Malebranche, see Susan James, *Passion and Action: The Emotions in Seventeenth-Century Philosophy* (Oxford, 1999), 108–23.

27 [Mary Astell and] John Norris, *Letters Concerning the Love of God* (1695), 201–2.

28 [Damaris Masham,] *Discourse Concerning the Love of God* (1696), 10–11.

the Negro's Skin."[29] The images here are striking; affection and attachment for fellow humans may lead us to shift our very natures, a shift with irrevocable consequences, here figured as the physically fixed markers of color (with images recalling a long-standing tradition of sin as spotted and of blackness as denoting sinfulness). The metaphor of "weaning," however, is seen positively; humans must be "weaned" from their affections and attachments—here the most basic of all nurturing and bodily attachments, the breast—in order to live up to their obligations to love God. Near the end of her series of letters, Astell approves, "Sure I am that a Man may be much happier by withdrawing his Heart from the Creature than he can be in cleaving to it."[30] This language is a daring revision of the biblical injunction that the male shall "cleave" to the female (Gen 2:24, Mat 19:5, Mark 10:7). Liberation from earthly marriage—and its depressing subordination of women—is emancipating for women, but Astell's conception of withdrawal from earthly ties denotes a much broader ideal than mere corporeal liberation from temporary human subjugation.

Her approach was surely ascetic, and as such a brace against the controlling structures of marriage and patriarchal authority. It was, nonetheless, a revolutionary assault on matter *tout court*. Damaris Masham worried about the political and social consequences of this line of thinking, responding to what she saw as "raptures," and arguing that "the duty to love with Desire, nothing but God only, Every Decree of Desire of any Creature whatsoever, being Sin" was a dangerous "Enthusiasm, or even Irreligion."[31] Masham's response to Astell's asceticism was an extended defense of "a lawful love of the *Creatures*," including children, friends, and relations.[32] Instead of removal of earthly affection, Masham encourages the proper regulation of passion.

Was Astell recommending the evacuation of human affection? Astell's views on the body are remarkable. The experiences of the body are not "to be Contemn'd," Astell asserts in the second part of her *Serious Proposal* (1697), "since they set forth the Wisdom, Power and Goodness of their Maker. But if we compare them with the Human Soul," she continues, "they appear of little value, and of none at all in comparison of Him who made them; and since their Nature is beneath, and their Worth much less than ours, we cannot find our Happiness in 'em." Astell then talks of being "buried alive in a crowd of Material Beings" (*SP II* 160). With her essentially otherworldly conception of personhood, Astell is thus liberated from the confines of a body rendered in early modern culture as weak, infirm, and prone to sin; it is through the language of dependence however, that she expresses that liberation, as she erupts in an incantation that is something like a prayer:

> For whether we consider the Infinite Perfection of his Nature, or the Interest we have in, and our intire dependance on him. Whether we consider him as Maker and Governor of all things, as filling all places, intimately acquainted with all Events, as Righteous in all his ways, and holy in all his works. Whether we contemplate his Almighty power; or what seems more suitable to our Faculties and Condition, the Spotless Purity of his Nature,

---

29   Astell and Norris, *Letters*, 212.

30   Astell and Norris, *Letters*, 254.

31   Masham, *Discourse Concerning the Love of God*, 27, 6.

32   Masham, *Discourse Concerning the Love of God*, 10.

which guided by Infallable Wisdom always Chuses what is Best. And more particularly his infinite Goodness, his Beneficence to the Children of Men; that he is not only Good in himself, but that he is also *Our* Good, the only Amiable Being, who is altogether Lovely and worthy of All our Love, the Object of our Hope, the Sum of our Desire, the Crown of our Joy. (*SP II* 160)

This is a far cry from Catharine Gallagher's conception of the Tory Feminist's "absolutist self"; the absolutism Astell longs for is that of complete union with God (*SP II* 180).[33] Mary Astell, in fact, is at pains to obliterate the ideology of self-possession: for the religious woman, she opines, "her Self-Esteem"—these are Astell's words—"does not terminate in her *self* but in GOD, and she values her self only for GOD's sake" (*SP II* 179). Indeed, this conception of the self as it registers in the early modern religious sensibility has the potential for extraordinary political consequence: either it could fire up radical protestant identity, as it did during the English civil war to motivate many women to take action, to become prophets and leaders; or it could support a logic of obedience, grounding an argument for submission to the state and its Church, as it does here. It was precisely against this logic of dependence that Locke's religious philosophy and his epistemology were directed.

For Astell, education would lead to "improvement" of "intelligent Souls," but the aim was to "fit us to propagate Religion when we return to the World. An habitual Practice of Piety for some years will so root and establish us in it, that Religion will become a second nature," to replace fallen, human nature (*SP I* 37). The "interest" to which her education is directed is not the "present interest," but that of heaven, "so [that humans might become] absolutely Conform'd to the Divine Will" (*SP II* 135, 171). Because of the condition of dependence and impairment with the Fall, Astell dismisses both popular sovereignty based upon natural freedom and claims to liberty of conscience:

In a word, order is a Sacred thing, 'tis that Law which GOD prescribes Himself, and inviolably observes. Subordination is a necessary consequence of Order, for in a State of Ignorance and Pravity such as ours is, there is not any thing that tends more to Confusion than Equality. It do[e]s not therefore become the gross of Mankind to set up for that which is best in their own conceit; but humbly to observe where GOD has Delegated his Power, and submit to it, *as unto the Lord and not to Man.*[34]

The "State of Ignorance and Pravity such as ours is," is that state after the Fall, in which human reason and will are impaired. In the late seventeenth and early eighteenth centuries, it was precisely over the consequences of the Fall, specifically for human reason and volition, that theological dispute took place.

Astell's engagement with John Locke and Damaris Masham focused precisely on this question. In the proto-liberal schemes, the Fall of mankind had left no indelible scar upon human rationality. From this difference, many consequences for human

---

33    Catharine Gallagher, "Embracing the Absolute: The Politics of the Female Subject in Seventeenth-Century England," *Genders* 1.1 (1988): 24–39.

34    Astell, *Moderation Truly Stated*, 59.

autonomy in the political and religious sphere were to follow: if humans were free from the stain of original sin, they could develop concepts of social justice and fairness weaned from their dependence upon the otherworldly. According to the Levellers, for instance, the meanest capacity is fully capable of rightly understanding the essential tenets of Christianity. Locke's views in *The Reasonableness of Christianity* and *Essay Concerning Human Understanding* are potentially democratic: the fundamental truths of Christianity are duties capable of being understood by all. "GOD has furnished Men with Faculties sufficient to direct them in the Way they should take."[35] Locke's search for the epistemic and ontological contours that make such a proposition possible led him to his heresies.[36] Mary Astell's critique of liberal contract theory resisted this direction; it was shored up by an assertively otherworldly approach.

To return, then, to the question of the public and the private, we must reassess from the standpoint of theology that dichotomy upon which modern feminists have grounded their accounts of women's exclusion from political life. The theological account to find full explication in Astell's *Christian Religion* is that of an interpenetration of spiritual and civic life. "To speak as a mere Natural Person," Astell remarks, "our Duty to our Selves consists in making the best use of our Talents, and hereby aspiring to the highest degree of happiness and perfection of which we are capable." But that is not enough, she continues: "But considering it as a Christian, I place it in doing nothing that misbecomes the Relation we bear to Christ as Members of His Body, and in Living suitably to so high a Dignity."[37] The distinction drawn, then, is not between public and private so much as between atheist and Christian.

To miss the spiritual orientation here is not only to miss something necessary about the pre-enlightenment organization of religion and the state, but also to miss something about early feminism. Specifically, this otherworldliness enabled Astell's contribution to the historical modes of the organization of gender as a strategic intervention regarding hierarchy, identity, and subjectivity. Astell may have been opportunistically motivated by a High Church–Tory rejection of constitutional theory in the wake of the Glorious Revolution; her attacks on dissent, indeed her indictment of the Civil War rebellion, are mounted as a defense of class privilege against the incursions upon authority by the lower orders. But it is my argument here that her thought be understood through the lens of theology, as a *recherche* effort not only to brace against Lockean contractual theory, but to shore up a concept of agency that renders the person as ultimately dependent upon authority. Perry has argued that Mary Astell "distrusted the rhetoric about individual freedom and the rights of the governed that justified the Glorious Revolution. It was empty cant, she believed, in

---

35  John Locke, *An Essay concerning Human Understanding*, ed. Peter H. Nidditch (Oxford, 1975), 4:20.3, 708.

36  Richard Ashcraft, "Faith and Knowledge in Locke's philosophy," in *John Locke: Problems and Perspectives*, ed. John W. Yolton (Cambridge, 1969), 194–223; see John Marshall, *John Locke*.

37  Astell, *Christian Religion*, 245.

the service of party politics."[38] This is certainly true; and yet we must look ever deeper into the serious way she attended to theological problems raised by the political positions adopted by those who would become Whig theorists; her public exercise of female reason, what Carla Hesse has called, in context of the French women, the "other" Enlightenment, was in some sense to contradict her own theological positions.[39] Nonetheless, a justification of conservative monarchy derives from her ontology of the person, with premises quite different from Masham and Locke, but which may be aligned to mainstream religious doctrines of scholastic thought, and against which Locke's account of liberty, and with it, the separation of the religious from the political, should be seen as genuinely radical, if still problematic.

Astell's is an intricate argument from divine authority, and an argument that considers the flourishing of human beings as normatively of less importance than the flourishing of the state and Church insofar as they serve God. So, along with her withdrawal from notions of sociability and community, Astell is only peripherally interested in questions of human justice as fairness. Although in her work there is a commitment to the equal reasoning capacity of women and men, she believes all humans were alike impaired at the Fall, so that reason alone is never fully capable of grounding good actions.[40] In her refusal to take the individual as the basic unit for political thought, Astell refused to submit to the sexist discourse of her own day; but she also refused the priority of lived, embodied experience: to be human for her is to be a means to an end which is otherwordly. As we think about the history of liberalism, and its relation to feminism, this orientation deserves further investigation.

---

38 Ruth Perry, "Mary Astell and the Feminist Critique," 447.

39 Carla Hesse, *The Other Enlightenment: How French Women Became Modern* (Princeton, 2001), 55.

40 Thus Astell's "Cartesian" defense of women's rational capacity can offer equality with men's rational capacity, as argues Margaret Atherton, "Cartesian Reason and Gendered Reason," in *A Mind of One's Own: Feminist Essays on Reason and Objectivity*, eds. Louise M. Antony and Charlotte Witt (Boulder, CO, 1993), 19–34. This argument however misses the essential point: human reason is insufficient to acquire knowledge. We need to be careful about asserting Astell's "Cartesianism," given the importance of Malebranche to Norris and Astell's defense of Love of God (and to take into account her qualifications regarding Malebranche in the Appendix to the *Letters*); Astell's commitment to the Augustinian notion of impairment of human reason at the Fall is the heart of debates with Locke's *Reasonableness of Christianity*, and her assault of his alleged Socinianism which would deny that original impairment; see Melvyn New and E. Derek Taylor, introduction to *Letters Concerning the Love of God*, by Mary Astell and John Norris (Aldershot, 2005).

Chapter III

# Mary Astell, *A Serious Proposal to the Ladies* (1694), and the Anglican Reformation of Manners in Late-Seventeenth-Century England

Hannah Smith

The first part of Astell's *Serious Proposal* has frequently been read as an indictment of contemporary female education and an early argument for female intellectual activity. In this relatively short, but lively and vigorous pamphlet, framed as an epistle to the female sex, Astell urged her readers to abandon their frivolous pursuits and, instead, to devote their time to improving their minds—a scheme which would assist them in furthering their religious understanding and which would heighten their sense of spiritual self-worth. Women were not born ignorant and immoral any more than men, Astell resolutely argued. This was a state which was "acquired not natural," for women as well as men had been endowed with the "faculty of Thinking."[1] The crux of the problem lay with the prevailing trends in female education, rather than with the female sex, and Astell proposed a remedy in the form of a "*Religious Retirement*" (*SP* 165), an institution where girls might receive an intellectually serious education, and where unmarried women might be able to withdraw from the world.

Astell's trenchant criticism of contemporary standards of female education has ensured her place in the pantheon of female writers on women's education, such as Anna Maria van Schurman, Bathsua Makin, and Judith Drake.[2] Yet, while a reading of the *Serious Proposal* as a proto-feminist educationist tract holds true in general terms, the more specific purposes of *Part I* of *A Serious Proposal* require reappraisal and further exploration. For it has become increasingly clear over the last few years that the texts of Schurman, Makin, Astell, and Drake need to be read, not only alongside earlier "pro-women" writings and in tandem with the philosophic movements of the era, but also placed in the context of the political and religious preoccupations of the decades in which they were written.[3] This is especially true for

I wish to thank Mark Goldie for reading an earlier version of this chapter.

1  [Mary Astell], *A Serious Proposal to the Ladies for the Advancement of their True and Greatest Interest: By a Lover of Her Sex* (London, 1694), 23, 79. Hereafter cited parenthetically as *SP*.

2  Bridget Hill, "A Refuge from Men: The Idea of a Protestant Nunnery," *Past and Present* 117 (1987): 107–9; Ruth Perry, *The Celebrated Mary Astell: An Early English Feminist* (Chicago, 1986), 99–100.

3  For works that place Astell in an historical context see Perry, *Celebrated Mary Astell*; Patricia Springborg, "Astell, Masham, and Locke: Religion and Politics," in *Women Writers and the Early Modern*

Astell.[4] She was famed as a devoted member of the Church of England, who went on to write several explicit defenses of the Church's position during the period of transition when it no longer came to have a monopoly on English spiritual life. The *Serious Proposal* can be read as both reflecting Astell's anxieties over the future of the Church and as a product of the mounting Anglican concern with the vice and irreligion of society. Thus, in the *Serious Proposal*, Astell appears more as the High Church moralist, reacting against contemporary mores, than as a "first feminist." For, as will be argued, she aimed to enable women to live as devout Anglicans rather than intellectually liberated individuals, and her prime ambition—which she shared with a host of Anglican clerics—was the reformation of female manners.

A key preoccupation of the 1690s was the idea of moral reform.[5] Propounded by some of the highest and lowest in the land, interest in moral reform transcended party boundaries and sectarian differences, encompassing Jacobites and Williamites, Anglicans and Dissenters alike. The movement took a variety of forms, both political and social. It had a parliamentary political dimension, with "Country" MPs campaigning against instances of parliamentary corruption.[6] It also received royal endorsement from William III and Mary II, who were keen to make the royal court a fount of morality and piety. Their supporters depicted the king and queen as actively bringing about a new era in which vice and irreligion would be swept away.[7] Moral reform also had a strongly voluntarist social dimension, and no more so than in the shape of the Societies for the Reformation of Manners. These were interdenominational associations, formed by a number of the clergy and laity, and were independent of the state. Their aim was to promote morality and enforce the moral legislation that was already on the statute books; they did this by disseminating moral tracts and sponsoring keynote sermons, while their members policed the conduct of neighbors and associates, informing on drunkards, blasphemers, sabbath-breakers, and fornicators to the civil authorities for prosecution.[8]

This extraordinarily widespread and fervent concern about the moral state of the nation, and the explosion of activity in attempting to reform it, can be seen as a direct response to the three decades which preceded 1688, a period which, from

---

*British Political Tradition*, ed. Hilda L. Smith (Cambridge, 1998), 105–25; Van C. Hartmann, "Tory Feminism in Mary Astell's *Bart'lemy Fair*," *Journal of Narrative Technique* 28.3 (1998): 243–65; Isobel Grundy, *Lady Mary Wortley Montagu: Comet of the Enlightenment* (Oxford, 1999), 193–94, 240–42; Hannah Smith, "English 'Feminist' Writings and Judith Drake's *An Essay in Defence of the Female Sex* (1696)," *The Historical Journal* 44.3 (2001): 727–47.

    [4] For possible "proto-feminist" influences on the *Serious Proposal*, see Perry, *Celebrated Mary Astell*, 72–73.

    [5] See Craig Rose, *England in the 1690s: Revolution, Religion and War* (Oxford, 1999), 195–209. See also D.W.R. Bahlman, *The Moral Revolution of 1688* (New Haven, 1957); Tina Isaacs, "The Anglican Hierarchy and the Reformation of Manners, 1688–1738," *Journal of Ecclesiastical History* 33 (1982): 391–411; David Hayton, "Moral Reform and Country Politics in the Late Seventeenth-Century House of Commons," *Past and Present* 128 (1990): 48–91; Shelley Burtt, *Virtue Transformed: Political Argument in England, 1688–1740* (Cambridge, 1992); Tony Claydon, *William III and the Godly Revolution* (Cambridge, 1996).

    [6] Hayton, "Moral Reform," 48–91.

    [7] See Claydon, *William III and the Godly Revolution*.

    [8] Isaacs, "The Anglican Hierarchy," 391–94.

the standpoint of the 1690s, had allowed decadence, debauchery, and irreligion to flourish almost unchecked. To allow such behavior to continue would bring down upon England the unmitigated wrath of an angry God. Such a characterization of the Restoration period was, of course, a particularly helpful take on the reigns of Charles II and James VII and II for those who had supported the Revolution and wished to validate it. But anxiety over morality and religion had predated the Revolution; in the words of John Spurr, it was "one of the fundamental components of Restoration Anglicanism."[9]

Such an obsession was, in part, fired by the loose-living, irreligious behavior of Charles II and his courtiers, which became a major theme of the opposition critiques of the 1670s and early 1680s.[10] But it was fuelled by the Restoration regime's attitude towards religion. The king favored religious toleration and—in 1662 and 1672—tried to bring about the toleration for Protestant dissent that he had promised in 1660, thus undercutting the status of the Church of England. Not only was Charles lukewarm in his support for the Church, but, by the mid 1670s, he appeared to be favoring Catholics as well as Protestant Dissenters. His court had a distinctly Catholic tone, and his brother and heir, James, Duke of York was a Catholic convert (openly acknowledged from 1673). The succession of James proved disastrous for the Church, for the new king also tried to push through plans for toleration for both Protestant Dissenters and Catholics.

While the Church of England was saved from James II by the arrival of William of Orange in 1688, its status as *the* Church of England began to disintegrate with the passing of the Toleration Act in 1689, which permitted Protestant Dissenters to separate themselves from the established Church and worship elsewhere, and with the subsequent decline of legal mechanisms which had previously compelled attendance at Anglican services. Lacking the official support they had previously enjoyed, devout Anglicans now had to shift for themselves in the battle against schism and vice, and they increasingly went on the offensive with characteristic vigor and enterprise.[11] Probably the most successful and far-reaching of their efforts was the Society for Promoting Christian Knowledge (SPCK), founded in 1699. Its aim was to promote not so much Christian knowledge as Anglican knowledge; as Craig Rose has demonstrated, the Society placed great emphasis on holy living and good works as well as on helping others to obtain salvation.[12] The SPCK set about this task in several ways, but its chief weapon in the fight against impiety and Protestant Dissent was education. Although the Society was mindful of the need to

---

9   John Spurr, *The Restoration Church of England, 1646–1689* (New Haven, 1991), 234.

10   See, for examples, Paul Hammond, "The King's Two Bodies: Representations of Charles II" in *Culture, Politics, and Society in Britain, 1660–1800*, eds. Jeremy Black and Jeremy Gregory (Manchester, 1991), 13–48.

11   Spurr, *Church of England*, 234, 238.

12   For accounts of the Society see Craig Rose, "Politics, Religion, and Charity in Augustan London, c. 1680–c. 1720" (PhD diss., University of Cambridge, 1988), 64 ; Craig Rose, "'Seminarys of Faction and Rebellion': Jacobites, Whigs, and the London Charity Schools, 1716–1724," *The Historical Journal* 34.4 (1991): 831–55; Craig Rose, "The Origins and Ideals of the SPCK, 1699–1716," in *The Church of England, c. 1689–c. 1833: From Toleration to Tractarianism*, eds. John Walsh, Colin Haydon, and Stephen Taylor (Cambridge, 1993), 172–90.

ensure that the children of the elite received some training in Anglican devotion, it was especially prominent in establishing charity schools to ensure that the poor, and particularly the female poor, received a sound Anglican upbringing.[13] This was not because the SPCK was especially interested in expanding the intellectual horizons of girls, or even equipping them with some fragments of functional literacy. The SPCK's interest was entirely sectarian. The practices and beliefs of the Dissenting churches were seen as having a strong appeal to the female sex, and women were widely believed to make up a large part of Dissenting congregations—an opinion which appears to be supported by some evidence.[14] Moreover, while it was important that young women were trained in Anglican doctrines for the sake of their own souls, it was also important because girls were the mothers of the future, who, if taught the tenets of Anglicanism, would raise their children according to such principles. Schism and immorality would be stamped out at the source.[15] Indeed, such a project was so close to the heart of the benefactor of one London charity school that he left money to fund the dowries of former pupils who continued to be devout Anglicans and whose proposed husbands were also staunchly Anglican.[16]

Despite the vast scholarly literature on moral reform, Astell's contribution to the reformation of manners movement has been rarely acknowledged, except in the context of the charity school initiative. Ruth Perry has shown how Astell became actively involved in this enterprise in 1709, with the foundation of a charity school for girls at Chelsea, the London suburb where she had long lived. Like its sister institutions, there was a strong religious element to the Chelsea school's curriculum. Although the pupils were taught reading, writing, accounting, and sewing, they were also taught Anglican precepts, were catechized twice a week, and went to church twice on Sundays. They were confirmed when they became old enough.[17] Yet the charity school at Chelsea should not be seen as Astell's only contribution to moral reform. So, too, can the first part of the *Serious Proposal*, if it is set against the backdrop of the prevailing Anglican obsession with education as a means of creating—and stabilizing—an Anglican society, where neither debauchery nor dissent could exist. Situating Astell within this context reveals her as a key participant in the moral reform movement and illuminates the ideas which she would develop with a sharper polemical edge in the 1700s.

# I

Astell's piety infuses the *Serious Proposal* at every turn, from her assessment of what was wrong with contemporary female educational practices to her plan for remedying it. Indeed, she openly declared that the "*main*, I may say ... *only* design" of her institution—which she termed a *Religious Retirement*—was religious, and

13  Rose, "Politics, Religion and Charity," 75–76.
14  John Spurr, *English Puritanism, 1603–1689* (Basingstoke, 1998), 195–97.
15  See Rose, "Politics, Religion and Charity," 108.
16  Rose, "Politics, Religion and Charity," 119.
17  Perry, *Celebrated Mary Astell*, 238–39.

she couched its importance in terms of a mission, appealing to her readers to come forward and support it, thereby "saving their own and their neighbours Souls" (*SP* 74, 164–65).

Astell was of the opinion that it was ignorance and the "narrow Education" which many women received that laid "the Foundation of Vice" (*SP* 44). Women were not taught to distinguish between what was important and what was trivial. Indeed, they were tutored by the received wisdom of society and by customary practice to accept false values, to set store on false merit, and to be more concerned with externals rather than the inward matters of the soul. Consequently, they were susceptible to the allurements of sin, while remaining immune to the beauties of religion. What was to be done? According to Astell, the answer was a sound education which inculcated a good understanding, uprooted ignorance, and created the right conditions for religion—by which Astell meant the doctrines of the Church of England—to germinate and grow.

Astell's Anglican intentions were evident both in the daily life and in the curriculum that she proposed for her institution. It would be ordered along strictly Anglican lines, with its inmates "pay[ing] a strict conformity to all the Precepts of their holy Mother the *Church*," whose "sacred Injunctions" Astell believed were "too much neglected." There would be "daily performance of the Publick Offices after the Cathedral manner, in the most affecting and elevating way," a weekly Communion, and "solid instructive" preaching and catechizing (*SP* 90). Such an emphasis on Anglican liturgical and devotional practices was mirrored by the school syllabus. Although she praised the scholarly and literary achievements of Anne Dacier and Katherine Philips, and urged her readers to emulate them, nevertheless, the course of study Astell set down was highly focused and didactic (*SP* 10). The greatest ambition she appears to have desired for her students was that they were "at least so far learned, as to be able to form ... a true Idea of Christianity" (*SP* 84).

For this reason, Astell damned the reading of "Plays and Romances," since she considered that they provided a type of learning that was "worse than the greatest Ignorance," instructing women in "the greatest Follies" and promoting the false values which she was condemning (*SP* 83). "Love and Honour," Astell remarked, "are what every one of us naturally esteem," yet "... these venerable Names" were "wretchedly abus'd, and affixt to their direct contraries." "How," Astell asked, "can she possibly detect the fallacy, who has no better Notion of either, but what she derives from Plays and Romances?" (*SP* 36–37). "Plays and Romances" were not the only works that were barred from Astell's curriculum. Astell's students were not to "waste their time, and trouble their heads" about what "the vogue of the world has turn'd up for Learning." They need not worry themselves with learning foreign languages, unless for reading "useful Authors." Nor were they required to read extensively. Rather, they were to furnish their minds with "a stock of solid and useful Knowledge" and to "take care to understand and digest a few well-chosen and good [books]" (*SP* 75–77).

Moreover, although Astell wished for women to "inquire into the grounds and Motives of Religion" and to be a Christian "out of Choice, not in conformity," she did not intend that her students should launch themselves upon some spiritual quest and explore the various forms of Christianity (*SP* 53). Indeed, Astell was confident that "thoroughly to understand Christianity as profess'd by the *Church of England*" would be "sufficient to confirm [them] in the truth" (*SP* 77–78). It appears to have been beyond her comprehension that a woman might rationally choose a Christian denomination other than Anglicanism, and it is noticeable that when she attacked those who were religious by their "Affections" rather than their "Judgment," she did so in a rhetoric generally used by High Churchmen to characterize Dissenters. It was conventional in such circles to condemn religious "enthusiasm" in the strongest possible terms, for it was seen as proceeding hand in hand with dissent, schism, and— glancing back to the Civil Wars—political and religious rebellion. Astell complained about those affected by "indecent Raptures" and "unnecessary Scruples," who were "very furious" and "violent," and had "more *Heat* than *Light*" to their religious zeal (*SP* 55–56). And she was careful to underline that her proposal that women should undertake directed religious study was in no way an attempt to push for a more formalized role for women in Church life. With a glance at the Quaker practice of female preachers, Astell maintained that she did not pretend "that Women shou'd teach in the Church, or usurp Authority where it is not allow'd them." "Permit us only to understand our *own* duty, and not be forc'd to take it upon trust from others," she modestly requested (*SP* 84).[18]

In her proposals, Astell had predecessors, for there existed considerable concern amongst the Anglican clergy and laity about the piety and morality of the female elite, and the lightness of what passed "in the Language of this loose age" as "*a Lady's Religion*."[19] Edward Chamberlayne in 1671, Clement Barksdale in 1675, and Astell's acquaintance George Hickes in 1684 had all argued for the creation of educational establishments for women where the doctrines of Anglicanism might be imbibed.[20] Chamberlayne and Hickes had been particularly insistent about the denominational bias of their proposed "colleges," and had envisaged them as vital weapons in the war against dissent. According to Hickes, such institutions would prevent women straying into "Enthusiasm" and "Schism," and he believed that women were "so silly and deceivable for want of Ingenious and Orthodox Education, and not for want of Parts." Like Astell, he had called upon the female laity to sponsor and promote these Anglican "Colleges."[21]

It is difficult to determine what influence, if any, the proposals of Chamberlayne, Barksdale, and Hickes had upon Astell when she came to write the *Serious Proposal*. There was, however, at least one other Anglican writer, who, if he did not formulate

---

18  It might be noted that the SPCK was vehemently opposed to the Quakers. See Rose, "Politics, Religion, and Charity," 85.

19  The phrase belongs to Astell's acquaintance, Francis Atterbury. See Francis Atterbury, *A Discourse Occasion'd by the Death of the Right Honourable the Lady Cutts* (London, 1698), 13.

20  [Edward Chamberlayne], *An Academy or Colledge: Wherein Young Ladies and Gentlewomen May at a Very Moderate Expense be Duly Instructed in the True Protestant Religion* (Savoy, 1671); [Clement Barksdale], *A Letter Touching a Colledge of Maids or, a Virgin-Society* (London, 1675); George Hickes, "A Sermon Preached at the Church of St. Bridget on Easter-Tuesday Being the 1st of April 1684" in *A Collection of Sermons Formerly Preached by the Reverend George Hickes D.D.*, 2 vols. (London, 1713), 397–98. See Smith, "English Feminist Writings," 731–34.

21  Hickes, "A Sermon Preached at the Church of St. Bridget," 398.

plans for a female "college," anticipated Astell on a range of points—Richard Allestree, author of the devotional treatise, *The Ladies Calling* (1673), whose influence can be ascribed with a fair degree of certainty. Astell cited *The Ladies Calling* in *Part II* of the *Serious Proposal*, where she lauded Allestree as an "excellent Author," and remarked that she wished that his "Ingenuous and Kind Advice" to women was "not only to be seen in their Closets, but transcrib'd in their Hearts and Legible in their Lives and Actions."[22] Given Astell's keen endorsement of Allestree, it is fruitful to explore in greater depth the similarities between their writings.[23]

It is now generally accepted that Allestree, the Regius Professor of Divinity at Oxford from 1663 to his death in 1681, and a prominent Restoration Anglican cleric, was the author of the bestselling and almost ubiquitous Anglican devotional handbook *The Whole Duty of Man* (1658), as well as a number of other very popular works, including *The Gentleman's Calling* (1660), of which *The Ladies Calling* was the companion volume.[24] Like Astell, Allestree's commitment to the Church cause was unswerving, although his loyalty was put to much severer trials than hers. During the 1650s he had kept the flame of Anglicanism alight in the winter of Interregnum Puritan England, holding Anglican services even though they had been proscribed. After the Restoration, when his services to the Church were rewarded, he continued to fight to preserve the influence of his Church through inculcating Anglican attitudes in the laity via his devotional writings.

Like the *Serious Proposal*, the *Ladies Calling* was the work of an Anglican missionary. Allestree wrote to reform, to "awaken some Ladies from their stupid Dreams, convince them that they were sent into the World for nobler purposes, then only to make a little Glittering in it."[25] Allestree was convinced that women were capable of great virtue and he decried the practice of deducing "Generals from Particulars," and tarring all women with the same brush. He argued that this was especially dangerous because it corroded female self-worth and the inclination to reform:

> If it can once pass into a Maxim, that women are such silly or vicious creatures ... Themselves may imbibe the common opinion, charge all their personal faults on their Sex, think that they do but their kind, when indeed they most contradict it.

Like Astell, Allestree wanted to "acquaint them with their own valu" and to inspire them to form "higher thoughts of themselves" (*LC* Preface). Although Allestree was altogether more conservative in his opinions about the intellectual capabilities of women (following the received opinion that they were below those of men), he did

---

22 [Mary Astell], *A Serious Proposal to the Ladies for the Advancement of their True and Greatest Interest: In Two Parts. By a Lover of Her Sex* (London, 1697), 259–60.

23 For a discussion of Astell and Allestree, see Mary Astell, *A Serious Proposal to the Ladies Parts I and II* (London, 1997), ed. Patricia Springborg, xix, xxxiv, n. 9, xxxix, n. 56, 168, 188 n. 91, 194–95, n. 169.

24 For Allestree, see Mark Purcell, "Useful Weapons for the Defence of That Cause: Richard Allestree, John Fell, and the Foundation of the Allestree Library," *The Library* 21.2 (1999): 124–28; Spurr, *Restoration Church*, 281–84.

25 [Richard Allestree], *The Ladies Calling. In Two Parts* (Oxford, 1673), 235. Hereafter cited parenthetically as *LC*.

not hesitate to concede that men benefited from a better education. If women had the same advantages, he acknowledged, they might equally profit from them for "what ever vicious impotence Women are under, it is acquired, not natural," a phrase which Astell later echoed in the *Serious Proposal* (*LC* Preface).

Astell and Allestree shared other concerns. According to Allestree, one reason why female behavior was so faulty was because women had a cloudy idea of what religion actually meant (*LC* 33). This needed to be remedied, and he recommended his female readers to "look into the inside of the Religion they profess" (*LC* 35). Although Allestree did not make much mention of formal education *per se* (he seems not to have placed a great deal of store on it as a way to change mores, either male or female), he encouraged women to educate themselves in their faith.[26] Like Astell, he was not contemplating that they should concern themselves in what he termed "a maze of controversies." Rather, they should read "only to discern those plain grounds of Truth on which our Church builds; which if well digested, will prove a better amulet against delusion then the reading whole Tomes of Disputations, more apt to distract then fortify." Indeed, he believed that

> had our she-zealots first consulted som sober guides, and from them understood upon what grounds the Practice as well as Doctrin of our Church was founded, they could not so easily have bin carried away by *every wind of doctrine*, as the Apostle phrases it." (*LC* 34–35)[27]

Reading, thus, was crucial to Allestree's project—but it had to be the right type of reading and he was as forthright as Astell about the ill effects that "Romances" had on young female minds. Such matter placed flirtation, gallantry, and deceit in a favorable light. Allestree feared that "those amorous passions, which tis their design to paint to the utmost life, are apt to insinuate themselves into their unwary readers, and by an unhappy inversion, a copy shall produce an original." Like Astell he believed that they created "false notions" of "Love and Honor" (*LC* 151–52).

While it can be speculated that Astell drew several of her points from Allestree, nevertheless, it is important to note that such ideas were also held by a number of Astell's Anglican contemporaries. Here it is instructive to turn to the tributes paid to a woman who departed the world in December of the same year in which the *Serious Proposal* came into it—Queen Mary II. It is highly debatable as to whether Astell would have acknowledged Mary II's title, but possibly she may have been prepared to acknowledge her piety, and it could be conjectured that it was modesty rather than politics which prevented Astell from dedicating *Part I* of the *Serious Proposal* to her—the fact that *Part I* had not been "ill receiv'd" led Astell to dedicate *Part II* to Mary's sister, Princess Anne of Denmark, later to reign as Queen Anne.[28] Certainly, it would have been very difficult for Astell to deny the queen's religious fervor entirely.

---

26  For Allestree's criticisms of male education see [Richard Allestree], *The Gentleman's Calling* (London, 1673), 37–39.

27  The phrase is from Ephesians 4:14. Astell was more radical than Allestree in her attitudes towards female ability and it is noteworthy that while Allestree and, later, George Hickes, portrayed women as being swayed by "every wind of doctrine," Astell applied the phrase to men when making the point that even men might be swayed into error if they were insufficiently knowledgeable (*SP* 75).

28  [Astell], *Serious Proposal, Part II*, Dedication.

During her brief reign, Mary had been zealous in propounding the idea that 1689 had been a "godly Revolution," and she was keenly and anxiously interested in the moral reform movement. She was well known for her genuine religious devotion and her interest in the Church of England—a devotion which was reflected in the private writings and religious reflections she left behind.[29]

Mary's godliness was the main theme of the sermons preached and published after her generally widely lamented death from smallpox at the age of thirty-two.[30] The queen's piety was lauded as worthy of "General Imitation" by Thomas Manningham, and her example justly upbraided "many other Ladies, even of the First Rank" according to John Finglas. Her decease was used as a platform for yet another call for a national reformation of manners in what the Archbishop of Canterbury described as "an *Atheistical* and *Profane* Age, the Seeds of which Impiety have been sowing for some years."[31] In their concern with moral reform, such works shared the sentiments of the *Serious Proposal*; moreover, they also corresponded closely with its drift when they came to describe the foundations of Mary's religious conviction.

The queen was depicted as possessing a piety which was grounded upon reason and self-education. William Wake presented her as endowed with an intelligence that "with a very moderate Exercise, [would] have carried Her into a Perfect Knowledge of Her Religion." Wake was quick to point out, however, that Mary had not relied solely upon her natural abilities and, like Astell's students, had taken care to diligently "Improve Her Understanding." She was a careful and judicious reader: "Piety and Instruction were indeed the Ends She aim'd at ... She read for Profit, not Curiosity; and sought for Use, not Diversion, in it."[32] Moreover, Mary was careful to draw limits to her religious enquiries. Thomas Tenison, the Archbishop of Canterbury, who preached the official sermon at Mary's funeral, assured his listeners that the queen did not trouble herself with "curious Questions which the Prudent neither ask, nor think themselves concern'd to answer." If she did encounter difficulties with the texts she was studying, he continued, she consulted "some Person of especial Ability" about it.[33] Mary also was diligent in her devotional exercises but, here again, the queen followed a *via media* between "*Transport*" and "*coldness*." This was crucial, for, as Thomas Manningham remarked in keeping with prevailing Anglican opinion,

29   Rose, *England in the 1690s*, 203–5.

30   For some of these sermons and elegies on her death, see Lois G. Schwoerer, "Images of Queen Mary II, 1689–1694," *Renaissance Quarterly* 42.4 (1989): 717–48; Rachel Weil, *Political Passions: Gender, the Family, and Political Argument in England, 1680–1714* (Manchester, 1999), 105–17.

31   Thomas Manningham, *A Sermon Preach'd at the Parish-Church of St. Andrew's Holborn, the 30th of December 1694 on the Most Lamented Death of our Most Gracious Sovereign Queen Mary* (London 1695), preface; John Finglas, *A Sermon Preached at the Chappel Royal in the Tower upon Sunday the Sixth Day of January 1694/5 Being the Feast of the Epiphany: as also the Day Whereon the Greatest Part of that Audience Appeared in Deep Mourning upon the Death of her Sacred Majesty our Late Gracious Queen Mary* (London, 1695), 28; Thomas Tenison, *A Sermon Preached at the Funeral of her Late Majesty Queen Mary of Ever Blessed Memory in the Abbey-Church in Westminster upon March 5 1694/5* (London 1695), 17.

32   William Wake, *Of Our Obligation to put our Trust in God rather than in Men and of the Advantages of it. In a Sermon Preached before the Honourable Society of Grayes-Inn: upon the Occasion of the Death of our Late Royal Sovereign Queen Mary* (London, 1695), 31–33.

33   Tenison, *A Sermon Preached*, 4–5.

it was a short step from "earnest *Devotion*, to Heats of *Enthusiasm*, or to weaknesses of *Superstition*."[34] Thus, Astell's thinking on female education and piety can be seen as part of a shared Anglican discourse which laid great stress on the importance of prayer and private study in strengthening religious faith.

## II

Astell designed her "*Religious Retirement*" as a "Retreat from the World for those who desire that advantage" (*SP* 61). However, Astell did not see the rejection of the wicked world as the only possibility, or indeed the most laudable course of action, for the genuinely pious. Her institution was not an enclosed confraternity, grilled away from the world, but a sisterhood which sent out its members to preach to the unconverted. Not that Astell was, in any way, enamored with fashionable society. It was a "constant Scene of Temptations" and a locus of "ill company," "foolish Amours," and "idle Amusements," a sphere of life in which "many persons who had *begun* well [and] might have gone to the Grave in peace and innocence" fell from virtue (*SP* 106, 116, 150). It was in part for such women that Astell's institution was designed, in order that the frail might be "supported by the prop of Vertuous Friendship, and confirm'd in Goodness by holy Examples, which alas! they will not often meet with in the world" (*SP* 151). Astell, however, recognized that not all of womankind could shelter from the raging impieties of the world behind the walls of a cloister. Thus, her institution was designed to equip ladies with the necessary knowledge to live outside its walls as good Anglicans. Furthermore, it equipped them to live there as agents of change.

There were several ways in which the "pious and prudent" students of Astell's "Seminary" might go about changing the world (*SP* 73). One way was to set a good example which would influence other women, Astell suggested. But she also had in mind a more active course of action. Astell puzzled over the "unaccountable backwardness" she had noticed which "too many good persons" displayed when it came to advocating "the Piety they profess" (*SP* 48–49). Astell's institution would ameliorate this situation. At the same time that her students acquired "substantial Piety and solid Knowledge" they would also acquire that wisdom which, according to Astell, was enough to ensure that they were not slow in standing up for their faith. The wise woman was "not content to be wise and good her self alone"; she would, rather, endeavor to "propagate Wisdom and Piety to all about her." Having "calmly and sedately observ'd and rectify'd what is amiss in our selves, we shall be fitter to promote a Reformation in others," Astell believed (*SP* 141, 152–53).

Astell rhapsodized about this "Reformation" and outlined her dream of a new society, which possessed new rules of social conduct, a society where, through genteel sociability, a corps of lady evangelists would bring the Bible out of the church and into the drawing room. She fantasized that "instead of that froth and impertinence, that Censure and Pragmaticalness, with which Feminine Conversations so much abound,

---

34  Manningham, *A Sermon Preach'd*, 11–13.

we should hear their tongues employ'd in making Proselytes to heaven." It would not be the "Follies of the Town" but "the Beauties and the Love of Jesus" which would be "the most polite and delicious Entertainment," and it would be thought "rude and barbarous to send our Visitors away uninstructed." In such a society there would exist a new measure of gentility—virtue and piety—and it was by these qualities that "Ladies of Quality," who had the necessary time and leisure to act as evangelists, would be able to "distinguish themselves from their Inferiors, by the blessings they communicated, and the good they did" (*SP* 144–45).

It was a dream which others shared and—in at least one case—tried to translate into a reality. Thomas Manningham believed that Mary II had made works of practical divinity "part of her Entertainment when *She* sate at work with her *Maids of Honour*," and he trumpeted her as a "Pattern for all our *Ladies* to imitate."[35] Three decades earlier, Allestree, too, had set great weight on the idea of "social evangelism," although he focused on the role that gentlemen could play in advocating the gospel. Gentlemen had both time and status to do this, and Allestree believed that they would prove more successful than clerics, for "what comes only out of the Pulpit, passes for ... the discourses of those whose Trade it is to inveigh against sin." Gentlemen, however, might be seen as disinterested parties.[36]

Gentlewomen, perhaps even more than gentlemen, could play an instrumental role in promulgating religion in society, for the pious lady's influence extended beyond the drawing room. The important role that mothers played in shaping the minds of their children was almost universally acknowledged in late seventeenth-century England. As we have seen, it was a fundamental premise behind the charity school movement, and it also preoccupied Anglican writers. It was the linchpin of Edward Chamberlayne's argument for Anglican "colleges" for women, and Allestree endorsed it as well, encouraging mothers to cultivate piety in their children themselves and not to leave the task to servants.[37] It was also significant for Astell. Astell enjoys a reputation as a staunch defender of spinsterhood and a celibate life, but although she was no great enthusiast for marriage and her institution was, in part, designed as a refuge for those who did not want to marry, or had, for whatever reason, failed to do so, nonetheless, she set considerable importance on motherhood. "Great is the influence we have over them in their Childhood," she remarked, in which time, "if a Mother be discreet and knowing as well as devout, she has many opportunities of giving such a *Form* and *Season* to the tender Mind of the Child, as will shew its good effects thro' all the stages of his Life" (*SP* 154–55). This, of course, relied upon the mother being educated and religious-minded, and Astell was sensitive to the charge that an ill-educated woman could be an influence for the worse. Perhaps with this in mind, Astell came up with an alternative, one which bypassed the other possibility of paying an individual to teach a child. Like Mary II, who was reported to have insisted on catechizing her god-daughter herself, Astell was averse to the practice of employing a person to instill essential truths, believing that "mercenary people"

---

35  Manningham, *A Sermon Preach'd*, 9.

36  Allestree, *Gentleman's Calling*, 124. For interest in the idea of a reformation of gentlemanly manners at the time of the Restoration, see Spurr, *Church of England*, 30.

37  Chamberlayne, *Academy or Colledge*, 1–2; Allestree, *Ladies Calling*, Preface, 194.

held "short views of things," and since they had "sordid and low Spirits," they were not likely to "form a generous temper in the minds of the Educated." The answer, therefore, was to enlist volunteers. Thus, while Astell's students—"the Children of Persons of Quality"—were instructed in lesser matters by "meaner persons," Astell intended that the gentlewomen resident in her institution would play an influential role in forming their minds (*SP* 147–49).[38]

Astell was keenly concerned with reforming female manners, but while this was her prime aim, she was almost as concerned with the manners of men. For women might not only influence the behavior of their own sex; they could also bring their influence to bear on the manners of the other. As mothers they wielded influence over their sons, and indeed Astell believed that maternal piety could "go a great way towards reclaiming the men" (*SP* 154). But women also wielded another type of influence—as objects of male admiration.

Astell held a scathing view of men, but there was a particular species of the sex whom she detested as an embodiment of immorality—the "Wit." Here, she was, once again, not alone, for it was commonplace among Anglican clerics and writers to attack the mores of fashionable, dissolute, and satirically-minded men, and the irreligious views that they were believed to proclaim.[39] But Astell saw them as her particular enemies, and she would go on to attack their "Whiggish" philosophy in *Bart'lemy Fair or an Enquiry after Wit* in 1709. It was they, she maintained, who played a prominent role in undermining the tenets of religion by disseminating atheistic creeds and living out a debauched existence. In Astell's eyes, this was not only morally despicable, it was also dangerous; what made it especially so, for others as well as Astell, was the rhetorically beguiling way the "Wit" went about justifying this mode of life, using wit to make religion appear absurd and trivial.[40] Astell was convinced that the Wits would ridicule her proposal, but she was confident that she would have the last laugh (*SP* 162). Her "*Religious Retirement*" might be the subject of their scoffing, but under its auspices, women would be trained to detect the false values of such men, and would "have more discernment than to esteem a Man for such Follies as shou'd rather incline them to scorn and despise him." Having obtained a due appreciation of religion, women

> wou'd never be so sottish as to imagine, that he who regards nothing but his own brutish Appetite, shou'd have any real affection for them, nor ever expect Fidelity from one who is unfaithful to God and his own Soul. (*SP* 163)

The "Wit," finding no female admirers in Astell's ideal world, would effectively be stopped in his tracks.

---

38  For Mary II's refusal to allow a servant to undertake the task, see Edward Fowler, *A Discourse of the Great Disingenuity and Unreasonableness of Repining at Afflicting Providences: and of the Influence which they Ought to Have upon us on Job 2.10. Publish'd upon Occasion of the Death of Our Gracious Sovereign Queen Mary of Most Blessed Memory* (London, 1695), "The Preface Relating to the Queen," 23.

39  Spurr, *Church of England*, 250.

40  Finglas complained of how "a religious and devout Temper, is expos'd to Ridicule." Mary II also was believed to dislike (and probably did dislike) "the Ignorance, and Impudence, of those (tho esteem'd Wits) who pretend to deny the being of a Deity." Finglas, *A Sermon Preached*, 28, 30.

Husbands, too, might be reformed by the influence of their pious wives. Astell was of the opinion that a sound moral education might enable a woman, through her subsequent virtuous conduct, to retain the affection of her spouse when "the Passion of a Lover is evaporated into the cool temper of a Husband" (*SP* 170). Moreover, her good example might win him back to the ways of righteousness if, perchance, he had strayed. It was something of a trope in this period to suggest that the pervasive influence of a beautiful and good woman would be "enough to convert a Libertine."[41] Astell employed a variant form when she argued, optimistically perhaps, that "a good and prudent Wife wou'd wonderfully work on an ill man; he must be a Brute indeed, who cou'd hold out against all those innocent Arts, those gentle persuasives and obliging methods she wou'd use to reclaim him." "Piety is often offensive, when it is accompanied with indiscretion," Astell added, "but she who is as Wise as Good, possesses such Charms as can hardly fail of prevailing." And because a husband was "well entertain'd" at home, he would not seek his pleasures outside it (*SP* 155–56).

Astell's "*Religious Retirement*" was her response to one social trend, the lack of more intellectually rigorous forms of female education; it was also a response to what Astell saw as another—the declining marital prospects of daughters from impoverished gentry backgrounds (a background from which, incidentally, Astell herself sprung) when faced with competition from mercantile heiresses.[42] While this was, in late-seventeenth-century terms, a social problem, Astell also saw it as a moral problem produced by the faulty values of a corrupt society which "set a much higher value on Money than it deserves" (*SP* 157). And this love of lucre had unfortunate consequences. Gentlewomen were valued on their financial worth rather than on their qualities of mind and character. They were thus often priced out of the marriage market by the practice of aristocratic and gentry families "chusing rather to fill their Coffers than to preserve the purity of their Blood" and preferring "a wealthy Upstart before the best Descended and best Qualified Lady" (*SP* 158–59). In turn, this brought about the socially and morally undesirable result—which Allestree, and later George Wheler also commented on—of desperate gentlewomen, flying from the reproach of spinsterhood, to some "dishonourable Match" and to their "own irreparable Ruin" (*SP* 160–61).[43] In the reformed world which Astell envisaged, the daughters of decayed gentry families would be educated in her institution, thus preserving them from "great Dishonours." "Prudent men" would eschew the corrupting dictates of cash, reckoning up such an education as "a sufficient *Dowry*," and considering that "a discreet and virtuous Gentlewoman will make a better Wife than she whose mind is empty, tho' her Purse be full" (*SP* 149–50).

41  See Wake, *Of Our Obligation*, 17.

42  Perry, *Celebrated Mary Astell*, 42. For the background to this and concerns of contemporaries see R.B. Outhwaite, "Marriage as Business: Opinions on the Rise in Aristocratic Bridal Portions in Early Modern England," in *Business Life and Public Policy: Essays in Honour of D.C. Coleman*, eds. Neil McKendrick and R.B. Outhwaite (Cambridge, 1986), 34–35; Sara Heller Mendelson, "Debate: The Weightiest Business: Marriage in an Upper-Gentry Family in Seventeenth-Century England," *Past and Present* 85: 127.

43  See also Allestree, *Ladies Calling*, 146–47; George Wheler, *The Protestant Monastery or, Christian Oeconomicks* (London, 1698), 17; Perry, *Celebrated Mary Astell*, 133.

We have seen how Astell's themes had precedents in the writings of a number of Anglican clerics. However, it can be further argued that she drew on the work of yet another Anglican clergyman for her thinking on the moral consequences of the prevailing trend in matrimony, as well as much else that related to female education. He was Adam Littleton, schoolmaster, lexicographer, royal chaplain, and the rector of Chelsea from 1669 until his death in the year that the *Serious Proposal* was published. He was the author of countless sermons, a number of which attacked the Dissenters, but one work is of particular note—his sermon preached on the death of Lady Jane Cheyne in 1669.[44] Lady Jane Cheyne had been born Lady Jane Cavendish, the daughter of the Earl (later Duke) of Newcastle and thus was the step-daughter of the famed writer and literary "personality" Margaret Cavendish, Duchess of Newcastle.[45] It is not beyond the bounds of probability that Astell knew of Lady Jane Cheyne, and of Littleton's funeral sermon. Lady Jane may have attracted Astell's interest as the royalist writer of a number of verse works. She had lived in Chelsea, had been an active patron of its church, and her widower was buried there in 1698.[46] Littleton's sermon was addressed to his Chelsea parishioners and it is possible that a Chelsea acquaintance lent a copy of the sermon to Astell. Indeed the bibliophile Littleton (who was recorded as being "easy of access" and "wonderfully communicative of his rare learning") may have done so, for Astell, as a Chelsea resident, was among his flock.[47]

If Astell did read Littleton's sermon, it is almost certain that she would have found much of interest in it. She may have appreciated his depiction of Lady Jane, who undertook extensive reading of "good Discourses" and who so jealously prized her opportunities for devotion that she "lookt upon all Occasions, that Interrupted That, as Impertinent and Uneasie" and who, for this reason, disliked "the Multitude of Formal Visits which she could not avoid receiving ... and returning that took off her time from these Spiritual Exercises" (Astell, with her condemnation of "impertinent Visits" would have empathized [*SP* 106]).[48] Perhaps of greater interest was Littleton's sympathetic stance regarding the issue of female equality. He attacked the notion that women were designed by God solely to serve men, and he argued that since woman was formed from man that this "doth plainly evince the Equality of the *Woman's* Merits and Rights with *Man*." He also addressed the issue of women's education, in the process noting the work of "a Learned Woman of *Utrecht*," Anna Maria van Schurman, and her spirited defense of the female sex. Women, he remarked, were as intellectually capable as men

---

44  Adam Littleton, *A Sermon at the Funeral of the Right Honourable the Lady Jane, Eldest Daughter to His Grace William, Duke of Newcastle, and Wife to the Honourable Charles Cheyne Esq at Chelsey*, (London, 1669).

45  *Kissing the Rod: An Anthology of Seventeenth-Century Women's Verse*, ed. Germaine Greer, Jeslyn Medoff, Melinda Sansone, and Susan Hastings (London, 1988), 106–18; Oxford DNB, "Lady Jane Cheyne."

46  Basil Duke Henning, ed., *The House of Commons 1660–1690: The History of Parliament*, 3 vols. (London, 1983), 2:51–2.

47  DNB and Oxford DNB, "Adam Littleton"; Perry, *Celebrated Mary Astell*, 63–64, 287, 289.

48  Littleton, *A Sermon*, 45–46.

of those *Improvements* which by the Efforts of Reason and the Methods of Education and the Instincts of the Blessed Spirit are to be made upon it, and no less fitted in her natural Ingeny for all kind of *Studies* and *Imployments*.[49]

Littleton's comments are striking in the context of the *Serious Proposal*, but so, too, are his comments on marriage, which bear close resemblance to Astell's lamentations over the corrosive power of mammon. Littleton looked back to an age when "Piety, alone, was accounted a sufficient Portion," and he railed against the state of affairs when "*Vertue* and good Education are undervalued, and *Wealth* is become the Lovely Thing, and all the Shafts of Mens Desires are Tipt with Gold and Silver" or by physical beauty. Indeed, with regard to the latter point, Littleton castigated his own sex. It was the fault of men if women frittered away their time in dressing or pursuing frivolous and immoral aims, for women were only trying to comply with male expectations.[50] Thus, even Astell's critique of contemporary trends in matrimony need to be set in the context of earlier Anglican thinking on the matter.

## III

Astell's *Serious Proposal* had much in common with the Anglican writings of the three decades preceding its publication. Indeed, aside from the fact that its author was female, there was little in the *Serious Proposal* that was strikingly out of keeping with its era. Astell's ideas were not held only by an obscure, impoverished young woman. They were also shared, in some form or other, by those of both "high" and "low" Church sentiment at the top of the Church of England's hierarchy, such as Allestree, Regius Professor of Divinity at Oxford; Littleton, a royal chaplain; Tenison, Archbishop of Canterbury; Wake, who would become Archbishop of Canterbury after Tenison's death in 1715; Manningham, who would become Bishop of Chichester in 1709; and, of course, Hickes, who would have undoubtedly obtained high clerical office, had he not become a nonjuror after the Revolution.

Why, then, did Astell and her proposal receive the suspicion and ridicule that it did, given that it was, in a sense, highly respectable and in keeping with orthodox Anglican thinking? Arguably, it was because it became irrevocably enmeshed in the party political strife of the 1700s. According to Astell's biographer, George Ballard, publishing in the early 1750s but on information received in the late 1730s, a "great lady"—either Princess Anne of Denmark or Lady Elizabeth Hastings—had been willing to donate ten thousand pounds to build Astell's institution but had been persuaded to desist by Gilbert Burnet, Bishop of Salisbury, since it looked too popish a plan.[51] Astell's "Religious Retirement" was indeed rather monastic—in tenor if not in practice—and her determined emphasis upon the merits of celibacy and her rejection of physical sensuality, may have sounded just a little too popish for

---

49  Littleton, *A Sermon*, 19–20.
50  Littleton, *A Sermon*, 24–25.
51  Perry, *Celebrated Mary Astell*, 134, 502, n. 35.

Burnet's Protestant liking.[52] After all, Astell hailed it as a "Happy Retreat!" which would introduce women "into such a *Paradise* as your Mother *Eve* forfeited" (*SP* 67). Indeed, at one stage, she portrayed the ideal inhabitant of her institution as a type of bride of Christ, "dead to the World" and devoting herself "entirely to the contemplation and fruition of her Beloved" (*SP* 70). It is telling that Astell felt obliged to state in the second part of the *Serious Proposal* that her institution was designed to be "*Academical*" rather than "*Monastic*."[53]

But monasticism was not alien to Burnet's thinking—indeed, he also thought that "something like monasteries without vows" would be "a glorious design" for promoting a more serious and religious-minded form of education for women.[54] And it was certainly not alien to other Anglican thinkers.[55] That pillar of the Restoration Church, Richard Allestree, regretted that female monastic houses had been abolished at the Reformation rather than being reformed (*LC* 145). So, too, did John Evelyn, who praised Astell for her proposal, and similarly wished that after the Reformation some "Religious Foundations" might have been spared "both for Men and Women." In such a place, he writes,

> single Persons devoutly inclined, might have retired and lived without Reproach or insnaring Vows; tho' under such Restraint and Religious Rules, as could not but have been approved by the most averse to *Popery* or Superstition.

It was in keeping with this Anglican tradition that, for Evelyn, Astell's proposal called to mind the Anglican community established by the Ferrar family at Little Gidding in the 1620s and 1630s.[56] And George Wheler, whose *The Protestant Monastery* (1698) also acknowledged Astell's proposal, suggested establishing a type of monastery for women.[57]

It is not known when Burnet dissuaded the "great lady" from sponsoring Astell's institution—if indeed he did—but it may not necessarily have been in the years immediately after the publication of the first part of the *Serious Proposal*, when the work appears to have been generally well received by Whigs and Tories alike. It may rather have occurred in the 1700s when Astell again made a name for herself, this time as a resolute scourge of dissent.[58] Astell attacked the practice of occasional conformity to the Church of England by Dissenters in her three pamphlets of 1704 at the time of the debate in parliament of the Occasional Conformity Bill, a bill which Burnet, who favored toleration for Protestant Dissenters, opposed. And it is

---

52  For Astell's distaste for physical sensuality, see Perry, *Celebrated Mary Astell*, 144.

53  [Astell], *Serious Proposal Part II*, 286.

54  Gilbert Burnet, *The History of My Own Times*, 6 vols. (Edinburgh, 1753), 6:205; Hill, "A Refuge from Men," 118.

55  See Burnet *The History of My Own Times*, 110–12 for the sixteenth- and seventeenth-century nostalgia for monastic life.

56  John Evelyn, *Numismata: A Discourse of Medals, Antient and Modern* (London, 1697), 265. For the possible influence of the Little Gidding project upon Astell, see Perry, *Celebrated Mary Astell*, 135.

57  Wheler, *The Protestant Monastery*, 14–18.

58  For the early reception of *Serious Proposal*, see Perry, *Celebrated Mary Astell*, 99–100, 103, 111–12.

also noteworthy that attacks upon Astell's educational plans by Whigs, in particular Richard Steele, who satirized Astell twice, in numbers thirty-two and sixty-three of *The Tatler* in 1709, occurred at the height of Astell's fame as High Church pamphleteer.[59] Indeed, as Ruth Perry notes, Astell believed, in 1722, that the attack upon her, and her proposal, was in response to her pamphlet of 1709, *Bart'lemy Fair* which assailed the philosophy of toleration.[60] Furthermore, in *The Tatler*'s second attack on Astell, she appears alongside two other Tory literary women, Delariviere Manley and Elizabeth Elstob.[61] It is equally telling that on the other side of the party divide, during the same period, in 1707, George Hickes praised Astell's works and recommended that they should be included as part of a young lady's education.[62] Owing to Astell's political activities, the *Serious Proposal* had become a heavily politicized text. What made Astell's institution so unappealing to the likes of Burnet and Steele was not that it was too Catholic in sentiment but rather that it was too uniformly Anglican. The establishment of an institution to instruct ladies in the ways of piety was perfectly acceptable; the establishment of a seminary to rear High Church zealots, run by a Tory pugilist, could neither be taken too seriously—or too lightly—by Whigs, who were coming to look askance at the charity school movement itself for the same reasons.[63]

Mary Astell's intellectual career has long appeared something of an ideological contradiction to those seeking the foundations of modern feminism. How do we reconcile the author of a tract on female education, who so forthrightly assailed customary thinking about women's intellectual abilities, with the intolerant High Church pamphleteer howling that the Church was in danger? One approach has been to analyze how Astell employed the language of contemporary political debate and applied it to dissect the politics of gender. All her work was, in some way, political. But, there is another way in which we can trace a link between Astell's dual careers as a proto-feminist and a Tory High Church political commentator. By reading the first part of the *Serious Proposal* as an Anglican tract that was deeply indebted to the writings of earlier Anglican writers, and which was as much concerned with preserving the spiritual monopoly of the Church as with training female minds, we can discern the uninterrupted intellectual trajectory followed by Astell from the 1690s through into the 1700s when she explicitly began to defend her Church of England.

---

59   *The Tatler*, ed. Donald F. Bond, 3 vols. (Oxford), 1:238–41, 439–40; Springborg ed., *Serious Proposal*, xxxv, n. 25, xxxvi, n. 26. It has been argued that Swift rather than Steele wrote these numbers—but Astell believed it was Steele.

60   [Mary Astell], *An Enquiry after Wit: Wherein the Trifling Arguing and Impious Raillery of the Late Earl of Shaftesbury in his Letter Concerning Enthusiasm and other Profane Writers are Fully Answer'd and Justly Exposed*, 2nd edition (London, 1722), "Advertisement"; Perry, *Celebrated Mary Astell*, 223–31; *Astell: Political Writings*, ed. Patricia Springborg (Cambridge, 1996), xv; Hartmann, "Tory Feminism," 244–49.

61   *The Tatler*, 1:439–40.

62   Perry, *Celebrated Mary Astell*, 498, n. 60.

63   See Rose, "Seminarys of Faction and Rebellion."

# Chapter IV

# Astell's "Design of Friendship" in *Letters* and *A Serious Proposal, Part I*

## William Kolbrener

"A true Lover of God," Astell writes in "Letter XI" of *Letters Concerning the Love of God*, "is always consistent with himself." "One Part of his Life," she continues, does not clash and disagree with the other"; indeed, "that Life only is truly religious which is all of a piece."[1] Though Astell's works fall within different genres—political, philosophical, and theological—her contributions to the *Letters Philosophical and Divine* not only blur the distinction between philosophy and theology, but also have implicit within them the categories which Astell would use in her writings on politics and gender. Astell's reflections on love and friendship in her letters to Norris may have been, at least in their early reception, most generally noted for their theological sublimity.[2] Her arguments in the *Letters*, however, as much they are written in the languages of metaphysics and philosophy, already contain within them the sociological and political categories which would dominate her later discussions of both gender and politics in England—specifically as they would be developed in her *A Serious Proposal to the Ladies, Part I*.

Ruth Perry has suggested that though *Letters* was published in 1695, and the first part of *A Serious Proposal* in 1694, the latter may have actually been written at the same time or after her correspondence with Norris.[3] Indeed, the tropes of humility that characterize her introduction to the letters, and her persistent use of the categories from *Letters* in *A Serious Proposal* (not to mention the explicit reference to Malebranche), suggest the correspondence with Norris may have, as Derek Taylor and Melvyn New suggest, "emboldened her to speak her mind for the first time … to a public audience."[4] In my argument, in *A Serious Proposal* (and later in *Some Reflections upon Marriage*), the typologies of love and friendship developed in *Letters* would be employed in the service of an analysis of domestic relations, as well as latitudinarian politics. Astell's writings, in this reading, are not simply unrelated endeavors in different genres, but are consistent with one another—"all of a piece."

I am grateful to Michal Michelson and Derek Taylor for their guidance in helping to formulate the argument of the current essay.

1  [Mary Astell and] John Norris, *Letters Concerning the Love of* God (London, 1695), 273–74. Hereafter cited parenthetically as *L*.

2  Mary Astell and John Norris, *Letters Concerning the Love of God*, eds. E. Derek Taylor and Melvyn New (Aldershot, 2005), 4.

3  Ruth Perry, *The Celebrated Mary Astell: An Early English Feminist* (Chicago, 1986), 82.

4  Astell and Norris, *Letters*, eds. Taylor and New, 11.

Despite the continuities between the two tracts, there are also significant differences, registered primarily, I will argue, in *A Serious Proposal*'s departure from the occasionalist metaphysics which characterized what I conceive to be, following Perry, her *earlier* exchange with Norris. By foregrounding such a disparity, I hope to make Perry's speculations about the actual dating of the composition of *Letters* and *A Serious Proposal* more compelling by showing that the metaphysics implicit within *A Serious Proposal* dovetail with those articulated in Astell's "Appendix" to *Letters*.[5] That is, although the theological categories of the *Letters* allow for the articulation of Astell's critique of domestic relations in *A Serious Proposal*, what I call the latter tract (despite its earlier publication date), through its abandonment of the extremes of Malebranchian metaphysics, provides an idealized conception of feminine friendship not present—or even possible—in the *Letters*.

# I

Diagnosing what T. S. Eliot would centuries later call, in a very different context, a "dissociation of sensibility" where "thought" was separated from "feeling," Norris, in his introduction to the *Letters*, lamented that in the age of Enlightenment "heads should be so full of Life and Spirits," and "yet that the Pulse of our Hearts should beat so low." Though "Knowledge," Norris writes, "is now in its Meridian," in "this cold frozen Age of ours," the "Love of God is declining and ready to set" (*L* a6r).[6] Neither Norris, however, nor Astell, despite the arguments of their critics (like Masham who would attribute "wild" Enthusiasm to their position), argued for love as a merely mystical principal: indeed, for Norris and Astell, the emphasis on love emerged as a philosophical necessity, consistent with the rigors of reason and Enlightenment.[7] While Locke of the *Essay* would argue "that it is the *Understanding* that sets Man above the rest of sensible Beings," for Norris, consciously overturning the Lockean philosophical hierarchy, understanding plays a merely secondary role, and has importance only "as it influences and determines our Love."[8] Love, as conceived by Norris, was a principle of philosophical import; indeed, so central was love in not only the metaphysics but in the philosophy of Norris that he accorded it a role parallel to the role of gravity in Newtonian physics. What Norris calls "the Moral Gravity of the Soul" is acted upon, he writes, by the "*great Magnet*, Good in general or God, and … with as much Necessity as a Stone falls downwards."[9] As Norris would write in *Letters*, emphasizing the centrality of love for both metaphysics and ethics, "no sooner does a Creature begin to be, but he begins to love" (*L* 122). Astell

---

5   Astell's first letter was written on Saint Matthew's Day, September 21, 1693; her last to Norris June 21, 1694. *A Serious Proposal* received its licensing imprimatur on July 16, 1694. Astell's "Appendix" is dated later, August 14, 1694.

6   T.S. Eliot, "Metaphysical Poets," in *Selected Essays* (New York, 1950), 247.

7   [Damaris Masham,] *Discourse Concerning the Love of God* (London, 1696), 120.

8   John Locke, *Essay Concerning Human Understanding*, ed. Peter H. Nidditch (Oxford, 1975), 43; John Norris, *The Theory and Regulation of Love* (London, 1694), 61.

9   Norris, *Regulation*, 17

would similarly affirm this centrality of love, borrowing the conceptual vocabularies refined by Norris in his earlier tracts: "the Soul," she writes, "may as well cease to *be* as cease to love" (*L* 95).

The Hobbesian Samuel Parker had associated "amorous romance" with fancy and enthusiasm, outside of the realm of philosophical rationality.[10] Against the emerging discourses of Enlightenment which had emphasized the philosophical irrelevance of love (associating its excesses with what Pocock calls "Giant Enthusiasm," and the inferior epistemological realms of emotion and imagination), for Norris, and Astell of the *Letters*, love would be at the very center of their philosophical systems.[11] In the *Letters*, love and friendship are not merely categories adjunct to the understanding, but rather understanding is subordinate to a love which, properly refined, leads to the proper *philosophical* service of God. Love, for both Norris and Astell, was not to be resurrected as a mystical alternative to philosophical discourse, but as the central philosophical category within that discourse. Thus Astell's "Divine Amorist" of the *Letters* is also a philosopher (*L* 268). For both Astell and Norris, the cure elaborated in the *Letters* for the "slow pulse of the heart" is to re-invigorate philosophy through love of the divine.

For Astell, of course, such a love would be defined in relation to its opposite— desire for the creature. Norris had already distinguished in his *Theory and Regulation of Love* between love as mere *desire*, properly directed only to the Creator, and love as *benevolence*, the selfless desire of good to others, which was the proper relation of man to his fellow. Norris's vaunted occasionalism provides the metaphysical foundations for the conception of friendship as benevolence. Not only because occasionalism directs the creature to the understanding that God is the cause of all things, but because occasionalist metaphysics bequeaths a world which is emptied of any remnant of spirituality. As matter is merely an efficient cause or occasion, sense experience has no independent efficacy or function. As Norris wrote in *Practical Discourses*, "the whole matter of the Creation" is "an idle, dead, unactive thing."[12] When Astell emphasizes the importance of disabusing her mind of that "early Prejudice that sensible Objects do act upon our Spirits," she extrapolates to the realm of human relations, re-affirming her own conviction that creatures must be "sought for our good, but not loved as our Good" (*L* 76). Astell elaborates, in the *Letters*, the "Design of Friendship" entailed by an occasionalist metaphysics (*L* 144).

Within the context of occasionalist metaphysics, the relationship that friendship entails only serves as a means to a higher goal: love of the divine. Astell does concede that "the Soul of our Neighbor has the most plausible Pretence to our Love, as being the most Godlike of all the Creatures"; nonetheless, she affirms that it cannot supply "our Wants" or "be the proper Object of Desires" (*L* 133). The very "Boundlessness of Desire" of human love is for Astell "a plain indication" that such desire "was never made for the Creature," for there is nothing "in the whole Compass of Nature that can satisfie Desire" (*L* 131). Man may be the most Godlike of creatures, but in

---

10    Samuel Parker, *A Free and Impartial Account of the Platonick Philosophy* (Oxford, 1666), 76.

11    J.G.A. Pocock, "Within the Margins: The Definitions of Orthodoxy" in *The Margins of Orthodoxy*, ed. Roger D. Lund (Cambridge, 1995), 43.

12    John Norris, *Practical Discourses upon several Divine Subjects*, vol. 3 (London, 1693), 55.

the metaphysics inherited from Norris, there is no resemblance between the divine and human to countenance the love of the creature. Astell, probably troubled by the Biblical conception of man created in the image of God (a seeming proof text against Malebranchian occasionalism), returns to that scriptural notion, and nonetheless affirms that those "that bear the nearest Resemblance to our Maker" are simply "dearest Idols" (*L* 213). The occasionalism of the *Letters* thus undermines what Erica Harth describes as an earlier cultural sensibility informed by the "mediation of resemblance" characterized by "metaphorical and analogical thinking," and licensed by the conviction of the link between spiritual and material realms.[13] In the occasionalist metaphysics of the *Letters*, the principle of resemblance, so characteristic of the earlier Renaissance sensibility which asserted correspondence between divine and physical realms has been completely erased. As such, the creature—always revealing its insufficiency as a proper object of love—comes only to emphasize the need for the understanding of the philosophical priority of the exclusive love of God. The "Tyes" that had "glewed" us to the world, Astell writes, are broken—revealing, in her stark metaphysics of friendship, the creaturely friend as a mere idol of the divine (*L* 265).

Indeed, Astell's own friendships (or rather their failure) become for her, the experiential context in which she comes to recognize the centrality of the love of God. Admitting that "none ever love more generously then I have done," she nonetheless attributes what she calls "ungrateful Returns" to "the Kindness" of God whom she refers to as her "best Friend." Seeing "how apt my Desires were to stray from him," Astell continues, God orchestrated the "frequent Disappointments" of friendship to have her "learn more Wisdom" rather than let loose her "Heart to that which cannot satisfie" (*L* 49–50). The very persistence of desire in Astell (which so many critics have noted) leads her to understand friendship not as the proper realm for the fulfillment of that desire, but rather as the means for its re-direction to the divine. Thus, she attributes the failures of her friendships to the ostensible "kindness" and "wisdom" of God who disciplines his creatures in the requisites of divine love. How often, Astell asks, "do we force the Almighty to deprive us of these dear Idols that have usurped our Hearts?" For Astell, the idol of friendship is tolerated by God, only "so he may convince us how improper it is to permit our Souls to cleave to any Creature, which [though] allowing it to be able to entertain us at present, can give no Security for the future." The "Crosses and Disappointments," as Astell adopts the language of martyrdom to the realm of friendship,

> show us experimentally since we will not sufficiently attend to what Reason suggests, the Emptiness and Unsatisfactoriness of all created good, that so we may more directly pursue, and inseparably cleave to the uncreated. (*L* 182–83)

Love of the divine emerges, in Astell's merging of the discourses of empiricism and martyrdom, out of the always failed experiment entailed through connection to the creature. Unmoved by the precepts of reason alone, only the failure of human love

---

13   Erica Harth, *Cartesian Women: Versions and Subversions of Rational Discourse in the Old Regime* (Ithaca, 1992), 7–8.

leads, painfully, but necessarily, to the divine. This ideal of friendship is realized, paradoxically, through its absence: "Our Kindness," Astell writes, when "he [sic] no longer returns it is the more excellent and generous, because more free." Though Astell concedes that "it can't be called Friendship when the Bond is broke on one side," she affirms that there may be a "most refined and exalted Benevolence on the other" (*L* 146). Friendship in the context of occasionalist metaphysics, then, does not provide fulfillment, but only a consciousness of that *lack* which human friendship always entails—the requisite precursor for a true love of God.

The rehabilitation of love for the divine as a philosophical principle only comes, however, through Astell's more elaborate articulation of the differences between love of the creature and love of God. In *Letters*, Astell associates the desire for the creature and created world with the degraded realm of fancy and imagination, and the love of God with rationality and philosophical rigor. That is, Astell, like many of her Tory and High Church compatriots, would borrow the distinction between truth and imagination so prominent among avatars of Enlightenment, to associate the former with a philosophical love of God, and the latter with the degraded love of the creature.[14] Within this framework, human friendship functions properly only in its failure—a source of censure and correction, presupposed not on a mutuality of shared feeling, but on a distance—even a withdrawal tending towards martyrdom. Already in her 1689 collection of verses, Astell had referred to "Enemies" as her true friends, since they act as "Monitors," telling her of her "faults," thus serving as "Benefactors" whose "spurs" come to "correct and mend."[15] To be sure, the emphasis on the importance of censure in feminine relationships was not unique to Astell. Halifax's *Advice to a Daughter*, the tract which Perry calls "the seventeenth-century *locus classicus* of patriarchy," contains a section entitled "Censure." But where Halifax elaborates the importance of censure only as a pragmatic means of self-protection for the purposes of social advancement, Astell's conception of corrective censure is in the service of philosophical, and ultimately theological, refinement.[16]

For Halifax, the idealized reader of his tract should beware of being either "first in fixing a *hard Censure*," or "too hasty" to join "the other side to defend" a friend, lest she "draw an *ill* appearance" upon her self.[17] Halifax offers no idealized sense of reciprocal friendship. Rather, his advice upon friendship, more particularly on the proper form of a censure of a friend, revolves around the pragmatic principle that his feminine readers might themselves be "well thought of by the world."[18] For Astell, however, "the great Design of Friendship" is corrective in a philosophical sense: "to discover and correct the most minute Irregularity, and to purifie and perfect the Mind with the greatest Accuracy" (*L* 144). Not only does friendship refine—experimentally, as she puts it—what Astell calls the prejudices of senses, as attention is moved from

---

14    See my "The Charge of Socinianism: Charles Leslie's High Church Defense of 'True Religion,'" *Journal of the Historical Society* 3.1 (2003): 1–25.

15    Reprinted in Perry, *Celebrated Mary Astell*, 404.

16    Perry, *Celebrated Mary Astell*, 160.

17    George Savile Halifax, Marquis of (1688), *The Lady's New-years Gift, or, Advice to a Daughter*, 121–2.

18    Halifax, *New-years Gift*, 132.

created beings to the divine, but her conception of friendship dovetails with the agendas of philosophical Enlightenment.

Arnauld in the *Art of Thinking* had argued that "accuracy of mind is infinitely more important than any speculative knowledge acquired from the truest and most established science."[19] In Astell's work, it is the proper friendship of benevolence which serves the ends of philosophy—the purification of the mind with the "greatest Accuracy"—and leads ultimately to divine service. While desire "hoodwinks our Souls, and makes us blind to our Friend's Imperfection," the true friend overcomes the love which "finds or fancies Excellency and Perfection" and finds the defect which "embitters its Delight," encouraging "a pure and disinterested Benevolence" (*L* 144, 176). For Astell, a friendship modeled on martyrdom and inevitably asymmetrical in structure ("delighting in *doing* good, and having no Regard to *receiving it*"), serves the interest not of an enthusiastic and blind fancy, but of a disinterested "philosophy" (*L* 145). Censure, for Astell, is not a matter of pragmatic self-protection, but the essence of the relationship between friends—which can lead to both metaphysical and philosophical perfection.

While Astell celebrates withdrawal from the creature as a primary means of philosophical refinement, her republican contemporary Robert Molesworth seeks such refinement in "Society," attacking the kinds of withdrawal which both Norris and Astell go on to celebrate. In his 1692 *Account of Denmark*, he attacks the "Prejudices" of the "Old Philosophy" and the "Narrow Spiritedness" of the "Monastick Life," proclaiming instead the benefits of a cosmopolitan and rational philosophy.[20] Molesworth employs an argument which anticipates Masham's critique of the *Letters* in which she accuses the authors of advocating a withdrawal into "Monasteries" and "Hermitages"—associated for her with "Sottish and Wicked Superstitions."[21] For the Astell of the *Letters*, by contrast, the martyrdom of friendship (and the withdrawal which it entails) is put in the service of rational philosophy and the enlightenment ideals of accuracy and disinterested benevolence. Human nature, writes Astell, tends towards a "Narrowness" which seeks to "monopolize a worthy Person to our selves" (*L* 143). But such narrowness, associated by Molesworth (as well as Masham) with the prejudices of monasticism is in Astell's work connected with an unrepentant love of the creature. Molesworth celebrates a cosmopolitanism which combats a prejudice which he associates with Tory and Jacobite politics and theology. For Astell, "narrowness" is a function of association with the creature, to be overcome only by a friendship which expands "in Acts of Kindness and Beneficence." Such Beneficence, however, is utterly devoid of desire, to be pursued as "uncircumscribedly and universally as the Capacity" of one's "Nature will permit," marking both a distance from the creature, and a readiness for a philosophical closeness to God (*L* 141).

In *Letters*, friendship never results in the positive embodiment of relationship, but functions rather as a check on human desire leading towards a true love—of

---

19  As cited by Perry, *Celebrated Mary Astell*, 85. On Arnauld's role in Astell's thought, see Springborg's "Introduction," in Mary Astell, *A Serious Proposal to the Ladies Parts I & II*, ed. Patricia Springborg (London, 1997), xxv.

20  Sir Robert Molesworth, *An Account of Denmark, As It was in the Year 1692* (London, 1692), c1r.

21  Masham, *Discourse*, 120.

God—which will only serve to "greaten and inlarge the mind" (*L* 140). Molesworth councils travel to the northern countries in Europe as a cure to single minded "bigotry," associated in his work with the very principles which Astell would extol; for Astell, paradoxically, an openness of mind, which "cuts off all narrow and illiberal Thoughts," comes about through total withdrawal from the creature (*L* 267).[22] Disinterestedness, benevolence, liberality, and accuracy—all staples of an emerging latitudinarian philosophy—were to be embodied in Astell's conception of Divine Love. Masham's attribution of "enthusiasm" and "pompous rhapsodies" to the *Letters* was an attempt to relegate Astell's perspective (with that of Norris) to the epistemologically inferior realm of emotions and imagination; Astell's defense of love for the divine, however, is framed not in terms of appeals to the emotion, but rather a turn to the disinterested languages of philosophical argument.

The typology of love elaborated in *Letters*, as suggested, would be adapted, in her later works, for the purposes of social and political critique; indeed, the distinctions in *Letters* already contain an implicit political argument. To be sure, Norris had already alluded to the centrality of love not only as an intellectual principle, but as a political one. In *The Theory and Regulation of Love* he wrote that the "Irregularity of Love" not only undermines "the Pillars of Happiness," putting the "Foundations of the Intellectual World out of Course," but also has consequences for "Political Happiness," leading "either to *Generation* or *Corruption*."[23] Astell of the *Letters* further elaborates the political principles which emerge from the distinction between love and desire. In the seventh letter, she amplifies the contours of an almost Hobbesian state of nature, founded on the principle of desire: "How is it possible," she asks,

> but that Multitude of Lovers who all desire the same thing, which is very far from being able to satisfy one, much less all of them, should cross each other in these Desires and Pursuits, and consequently destroy that Peace and mutual Benevolence which ought to be cherished among rational Beings? (*L* 138–39)

Such a world, reminiscent of the state of war described by Hobbes in *Leviathan*, is presupposed on a world of desire—a world which Astell associates with imagination, idolatry, and passion. Desire—"loving amiss," as Astell terms it—leads to lashing out in "a thousand Extravagancies," falling prey to "pleasant Dream[s]," and thus becoming "our evil" by deluding "our Expectations" and causing "us to fall into Air and Emptiness" (*L* 131, 180).

For Astell, this desire, associated with delusion and imagination, comes into being as a function of the misrepresentation which plays on the weakness of the senses. "Herein," Astell writes:

> appears the Devil's greatest Masterpiece, that he can give such a false Representation of things, and so much to our Disadvantage as to put us upon the violent Pursuit of good where we can never find it, and to blind us so that we may not discern it where it is, and our own most notorious Folly in being so wretchedly imposed on by him. (*L* 258)

---

22  Molesworth, *Account of Denmark*, clv.
23  Norris, *Regulation*, 58.

It is not any natural aversion "that sets us in Opposition to God," but it is rather the machinations of the Devil—and "false Representation" which give precedence to a desire of sense, "the true source of all our Disorder, the corrupt Root of all our Faults" (*L* 213, 194). Desire for the creature, for Astell of the *Letters*, is associated with the artifice of the devil, and a misrepresentation which removes desire from its true object, God. Pursuit of the desires engendered by satanic misrepresentation will "open a Bank to all the Mischief, Malice and Uncharitableness that is in the World"; for the pleasures of this world can never "satisfie Desire" (*L* 138, 132). Here, desire for the creature undermines political stability. Contemplation of "divine Perfections," however, leads the Mind, writes Astell, to move with "Alacrity" and "unwearied Vigor"; while the "force of Temptations" and the machinations of the "Devil" lead man "to doat on the Creature" such that "all is unhinged and falls into disorder" (*L* 192). While Astell continues to associate love of the divine with the rigors of philosophical "alacrity" and "vigor," love for the creature is affiliated with a desire instigated through satanic misrepresentation that has both spiritual and political consequences.

In Astell's argument of the *Letters*, the "disorder" instigated by desire is overcome through the redemptive powers of divine love. Where for Hobbes, the world is circumscribed by passion and only redeemed through the arbitrary covenant of Leviathan, Astell finds the supposition that "*all Human Love is a Love of Desire* … a great Reproach to Human Nature." For "as bad as it is," she continues, human nature "is not incapable of a pure and disinterested benevolence" (*L* 177). Astell's philosophical love—emerging through the martyrdom of friendship—provides a salvific alternative to the endless strife and disorder imposed by Hobbesian desire. Hobbes finds such desire in the State of Nature; Astell, by contrast, argues that desire for the creature is not intrinsic to the human condition, but a product of "voluntary Error, superinduced Habits, and evil Customs" (*L* 213). The "Design of Religion" thus parallels the "Design of Friendship" which is "to retrieve the original Rectitude and Perfection of Human Nature" (*L* 184). Divine love, in this sense, comes into being not only as a metaphysical or intellectual principle, but a political one as well—the "only effectual Means of securing Obedience." "In vain," Astell writes, "do we search for Rules to regulate our Manners, and prescribe Remedies to cure our Infirmities." Such "Prescriptions," she writes, "will do us but little Service till we have reformed our Love" (*L* 193–94). Not Hobbesian covenant, nor Lockean contract, nor latitudinarian manners will secure "mutual Benevolence" but only— and more simply—the proper regulation of desire (*L* 139). In Astell's reading, the Hobbesian state of nature is an historical deviation from a more original connection with the divine that can be rectified in an obedience born out of love.

While desire breeds "Hearts Lusts" and the pursuit of "Imaginations," Astell advocates the use "of such Methods as will infallibly secure us from Delusion and Disappointment"—the philosophical rectification of the chaos of Hobbesian politics (*L* 200). In the anatomy of love elaborated by Astell in *Letters*, love of God provides a philosophical method for the overcoming of imagination, passion, and a delusion associated with idolatry. "Let us once banish our Idols from our Hearts whatever they are," she intones, "and we shall quickly find that all will be well again" (*L* 193).

Divine love thus provides not only a theological, but political and philosophical antidote to the excesses of desire, sense, and the artifices of the imagination.

It is important to note, however, that for Astell of the *Letters*, even while accounting creaturely love and satanic misrepresentation the cause of political instability, the pleasures of the imagination are not banished. They are merely sublimated in the pleasures of the divine. "Thought," Astell writes, "seems to me nothing else but the Determination of the Soul to some certain Object which she desires either to contemplate or enjoy." Such thought, she continues, asserting the ineradicable presence of the imagination, is presupposed upon the "forming in her self the Images and Representations of what she delights in" (*L* 190). Desire, for Astell, following Norris, must be properly regulated, but it is always focused through representations—even in the context of the love for the divine. One must, Astell writes, seek out not the imaginative pleasures associated with the creature, but only those offered by the Creator. That is, divine love also has its pleasures. Indeed, for Astell, the pleasures of this world remain only a "Shadow" of the real "substance" of pleasures offered by the divine (*L* 203). Astell's "divine amorist" feels "the silken Bands of Love, these odiferous Perfumes drawing after him, uniting them to him by the most potent Charms!" (*L* 262). These divine "charms" provide a *substantial* realm in which, "our grateful Passions" may indeed "freely take their Range." In this realm the satanic powers of the unredeemed imagination hold no sway: "There is no Serpent lurks in the Grass, all is calm and placid, secure and entertaining" (*L* 131–32). Divine love not only provides charms, but entertainment, offering its own pleasures to an imagination that can be finally and fully fulfilled. "Blessed is the man," Astell writes, who is "so overcome" by such authentically divine Charms:

> He never lived till now, nor knew what Pleasure meant; some Shews of it might tantalize and abuse him, but now he is delivered from that Enchantment, and has free Access to the Ocean of Delight, he may now take full Draughts of Bliss without fear of want or Danger of Satiety! (*L* 263)

The creature offers mere "Shews and Enchantment," while the creator, in a language no less sensual, offers "full Draughts of Bliss." In Astell's language, verging on the kind of terminology employed in metaphysical conceits, Norris's "cold frozen age" is transformed, not through a mystical abandonment of philosophy, but through the "Charming and Ravishing" pleasures of a divine—and rational—service.


## II


In *A Serious Proposal, Part I*, the theological opposition between desire for the creature and love of the Creator developed in the *Letters* emerge as categories which help to describe sociological and political realities—more specifically the realm of courtship dominated by an unequivocally masculine form of desire and the competing realm of feminine friendship. The desire of the *Letters*, associated with the "false Representations" of satanic artifice is figured, in *A Serious Proposal*, as a principle which governs courtship and domestic relations. By contrast, the principle of authentic love, associated in *Letters* exclusively with love of the divine, manifests itself in *A Serious Proposal* in the "holy Conversation" of Astell's proposed religious community. Here, in a departure from the conception of friendship of the earlier tract, in which Astell disparagingly speaks of those in pursuit of friendship as seeking to cleave "to little dirty Creatures," women enjoy the "charms" not only of God, but of friendship itself (*L* 207). Such a shift in Astell's conception of friendship is made possible through a more fundamental change in metaphysical assumptions, elaborated in Astell's "Appendix" to the *Letters*, and paralleled in *A Serious Proposal*.

Astell's condemnation of love for the creature transforms in *A Serious Proposal* to a condemnation of masculine courtship. Indeed, in *A Serious Proposal*, Astell conceives of that masculine realm of courtship as one governed entirely by the dictates of creaturely love, where the Hobbesian principles of desire and misrepresentation find cultural embodiment in "the rude attempts of designing men."[24] In a world dominated by "Hearts Lusts" and artifice now harnessed for the ends of masculine seduction, women find themselves at the mercy of those lovers who offer a "plausible resemblance" to what women, schooled only in "Plays and Romances," imagine they desire (*SP* 12, 14). Without sufficient education to distinguish between "reality" and the "pretence" of men, women are subject to those "silly Artifices which are us'd to ensare and deceive them" (*SP* 13, 12). Desire for the creature, described in the *Letters* in terms of satanic desire and misrepresentation, now emerges as a cultural principle where the mechanisms of imagination are employed by men within the realm of courtship in pursuit of their feminine objects of desire. In Astell's sociology of courtship, women, not properly educated to distinguish between authentic love and the "few airy Fancies" proffered by men, may "chuse amiss," though the "Crime," Astell affirms, remains "the Deceivers" (*SP* 12). Observing the "vain and the gay" who are "making Parade in the World and attended with Courtship," women's eyes are "dazzled with the Pageantry" of a Hobbesian world of masculine seduction, and condemned, as a result, to a "mechanical way of living" (*SP* 16, 32). Like in the *Letters*, where desire for the creature leads to "narrow and illiberal thoughts," so in *A Serious Proposal*, the rituals of courtship lead women, under the spell of masculine imagination, to a way of life which, Astell writes, "shortens our Views" and "contracts our minds" (*SP* 32). As in *Letters*, the cultivation of love of the creature has both political and philosophical consequences, rendering "improvement impossible" (*SP* 32). For Astell of *A Serious Proposal*, the ostensibly cosmopolitan realm of courtship leads to contraction of the mind and "narrowness."

Without proper education, a woman, Astell writes, "will easily open her Ears to whatever goes about to nourish and delight them," channeling her "desires to the creature" and not the "Love of God." When, Astell continues, "a cunning designing Enemy from without," has drawn her over to "his Party," he "has the Poor unhappy Person at his Mercy" who "credulously hearkens to the most disadvantageous Proposals, because they come attended with a seeming esteem" (*SP* 12). The

---

24   Mary Astell, *A Serious Proposal to the Ladies Parts I & II*, ed. Patricia Springborg. Hereafter cited parenthetically as *SP*.

"cunning designing Enemy," the satanic force of deception, which, in the earlier tract, had diverted the desire fit for the Creator to the creature, now comes in the guise of the courtier. His seductions are based upon artifice—"trifling Arts"—and misrepresentation which come to characterize social relations as dictated by the requisites of masculine courtship and desire. Further, the metaphor of political party elaborated here in *A Serious Proposal*, becomes explicit in *Some Reflections* where Astell shows the parallels between domestic relations and a public sphere also governed by artifice employed in the service of seduction. That is, in *Some Reflections*, the sensibility and strategies of the courtier inform the public sphere—increasingly gendered as masculine—as a whole. "When a Man," Astell writes,

> and for certain much more when a Woman, is fallen into this Toyl, that is, when either have been so unwary and indiscreet as to let another find out by what Artifices he may manage their Self-Love and draw it over to his Party, 'tis too late for anyone who is really their Friend, to break the Snare and disabuse them.[25]

In this passage, Astell freely adopts the languages which she had employed to describe domestic deceit in her description of the political process now also wholly governed by manipulation and the "Artifices" and interests of Party.[26] The avatars of party politics, with their self-serving machinations and interests, represent a political manifestation of the "passions," "lusts," and "artifice" described in the *Letters*. In *Some Reflections*, as in *A Serious Proposal*, it is a particularly masculine "Prejudice" which through its manipulations—"Pretence," "Plot," "Policy," and "Design"—gives rise to and sustains feminine "Passion" (*SRM* 63, 64). The educational program advocated in *A Serious Proposal* detains the masculine economy of passion and interest, so that women will neither be "inveigled and impos'd" upon by the "rude attempts of designing men," nor "bought and sold" in the marketplace of the courtier (*SP* 39).

Desire, beginning in *Letters* as a perversion of divine love, adopted in *A Serious Proposal* as a primary feature of the culture of courtship, appears in *Some Reflections* as a principle which informs the culture of latitudinarian orthodoxy as a whole. In *Letters*, desire had been associated with the "Prejudices of Sense" and in *A Serious Proposal* with a specifically masculine imagination (*L* 221). Later, in *Some Reflections*, Astell offers a sardonic tribute to the "topping Genius of Men," founded on their indulgence in the powers of artifice and manipulation. Their "Subtilty in forming Cabals and laying deep Designs" leads them to break "through all Tyes Sacred and Civil" in pursuit of "Honor" and a "Name." "All famous Arts," she continues, "have their Original from Men, even from the Invention of Guns to the Mystery of Eating" (*SRM* 87–88). *Some Reflections*, by providing its own anthropology of late-seventeenth-century courtship, demonstrates the ways in which the rites of courtship are themselves reflective of a contemporary culture dominated

---

25  [Mary Astell,] *Some Reflections on Marriage* (London, 1700), 73–74. Hereafter cited parenthetically as *SRM*.

26  For a further development of this argument, see my "Gendering the Modern: Mary Astell's Feminist Historiography," *The Eighteenth Century: Theory and Interpretation* 44.1 (2004): 1–24.

by self-interested masculine designs enamored with the physical and the artificial. Indeed, the attribution of artifice and absorption in the physical, emerging first in the typology of desire of the *Letters*, recurs in Astell's works as a means of describing not only latitudinarian culture, but also, in Astell's polemical writings of the early 1700s, the culture of the regicides which Astell shows as its antecedent.[27]

Just as Astell did not abolish images and their attendant physical pleasures in *Letters*, so *A Serious Proposal* rejects the pleasures of courtship, but upholds the possibility of a more authentic—and substantial—delight. In the occasionalist universe of *Letters*, such delight would only be located in the divine; in *A Serious Proposal*, however, such delights can be found in the realm of the creature—that is, the realm of feminine friendship. Like in *Letters*, Astell distinguishes between the "fruitless search after new Delights" now associated specifically with the "pretence" of "feigned lovers," and "the innocent Pleasures" of "a much sweeter and more durable delight" (*SP* 19, 21). If in her contributions to the *Letters* Astell had insisted upon the persistence of the imagination, Astell in *A Serious Proposal* also provides an alternative to the impoverished satisfactions of creaturely desire. Astell thus exhorts her feminine readers to abandon those "Amusements which you now pursue" which simply "toll you on with fair pretences and repay your Labours with defeated hopes." For such amusements, masquerading as authentic pleasures, are merely the product of "false Representations and Impostures" (*SP* 30). "Come hither," she therefore enjoins,

> and take a true view of 'em that you may no longer deceive your selves with that which profits not, but spurning away these empty nothings, secure a portion in such a Bliss as will not fail, as cannot disappoint you. (*SP* 35)

Like the *Letters*, *A Serious Proposal* distinguishes between mere "enchantments," products of "false representation," and authentic "bliss." In *Letters*, such bliss is associated solely with love of the divine, while desire is associated with the degradation and "mean Enjoyments" of the creature (*L* 183). In *A Serious Proposal*, by contrast, "innocent Pleasures" are associated with "a noble and Vertuous and Disinterress'd Friendship" (*SP* 20). By employing the typology of desire as a sociological category, Astell opens up the way for a conception of friendship which is not merely corrective as in *Letters*, but also both satisfying and redemptive. In the sociology of *A Serious Proposal*, it is not the generic world of friendship, but rather a specifically masculine world of courtship which is impoverished. The withdrawal from the "little Toys and Vanities" of that world into "Religious Retirement" results not in the languages of martyred withdrawal, but rather the reciprocity of the fully embodied feminine relationship of true friendship (*SP* 31).

In the *Letters*, the perfection of the mind is enabled through the always failed experiment entailed by desire for the creature. Philosophical disinterestedness and the enlarging of the mind for Astell of the *Letters* result from the acknowledgement of the insufficiency of all aspects of the creation, including the "Soul" of one's

---

27  See my "'Forc'd into an Interest': High Church Politics and Feminine Agency in the Works of Mary Astell," *1650–1850: Ideas, Aesthetics, and Inquiries in the Early Modern Era* 10 (2004): 3–31.

"Neighbor." That is, the "Rectitude and Perfection of Human Nature," in the correspondence with Norris, is achieved not through what Astell calls stooping to the image of the creature, but rather through exclusive attention to the perfection of "that beautiful Image of our Maker" (*L* 184). Withdrawal in *A Serious Proposal*, however, has its justification not in the languages of personal martyrdom achieved through an exclusive love of God, but through a feminine retirement "from the noise and hurry of the world." From this (masculine) world, women can withdraw to a realm where, Astell affirms, "having calmly and sedately observ'd and rectify'd what is amiss in our selves, we shall be fitter to promote a Reformation in others" (*SP* 41). The withdrawal of martyrdom of *Letters* (a necessary part of a "friendship" always figured as asymmetrical) gives way, in *A Serious Proposal*, to a withdrawal from the sensual realm of the masculine into the perfecting realm of feminine friendship. Rectification in *A Serious Proposal*, unlike the *Letters*, emerges as a function not of mere social censure, but rather social interaction.

Further, where in *Letters*, the pleasures of imagination only have their proper theological and philosophical satisfaction in the substantial "charms" of the creator, in *A Serious Proposal*, virtue is embodied in the charms—equally substantial—of the creature. "Adorn'd with a thousand charms," the "charming Creature" nourished through this "blessed Retirement," will provide a "perpetual Display of the beauties of Religion" and thus "attract the eyes and enamour the hearts of all who behold her" (*SP* 28–29). Genuine friendship, Astell writes, will afford "a much more durable delight, than all those pitiful diversions, those revellings and amusements, which now thro your ignorance of better, appear the only grateful and relishing Entertainments" (*SP* 21). In contrast to those "Entertainments" proffered by courtiers, Astell of *A Serious Proposal* celebrates what she calls the "innocent Arts" and "Charms" of women that can overcome and redeem the most brutish and ill-disposed of men. She thus contrasts the "curious Artifices and studied Arts" which characterize the realm of courtship with the "native innocency and unaffectedness" of those "whose Charms, and the unblameable Integrity of their Lives, are abundantly more taking" (*SP* 45). In the occasionalist sensibility of the *Letters*, all charms and arts not associated with divinity are condemned as dreamlike and idolatrous. Through the transformation of the typologies of love and desire developed in *Letters*, Astell is able to extol, in *A Serious Proposal*, the "Beauties of our *Religious*" (*SP* 45). The "never failing charms" of divinity of *Letters* are now embodied in the innocent—and "prevailing"—arts of the feminine (*SP* 42).

The shift from the conception of friendship in which "Martyrdom is the highest Pleasure" to one that affords and *embodies* the "durable" charms of innocent pleasures is made possible, however, not only by the use of desire as a sociological category— condemning the interested love which dominates domestic relations as specifically masculine (*L* 45). That charms can be manifested in this world through feminine friendship entails, as well, a revision in metaphysical world view from that of the earlier correspondence with Norris. Indeed, Astell's contribution to the "Appendix" to the *Letters*, where she shows herself, and not Norris, to be the true inheritor of the Cambridge Platonists, provides a natural transition to the implicit metaphysics of *A Serious Proposal*. By invoking More's conception of "plastic power" at the end of

*Letters*, Astell argues for "*a sensible Congruity*" between the "Powers of the Soul that are employed in Sensation, and those Object which occasion it." By asserting the "congruity" between spirit and matter achieved by the "plastic power," Astell rejects Norris's occasionalist position that God acts immediately, preferring rather the notion that God acts "*mediately* by his Servant Nature" (*L* 281–82). The possibility of a congruity between soul and body, so absent from the occasionalism of Norris and Malebranche, allows, as Taylor writes, for a function for sense organs, but it also affirms the possibility that the created world can embody—however mediately— aspects of the divine.[28] "Plastic power" provides the means of re-asserting, in a post-Cartesian universe, an earlier metaphysical worldview, allowing for the manifestation of spirit in the material world. By "passing through the universe," the "plastic power," as Ralph Cudworth glosses it, brings "all particulars of the Creation," both physical and spiritual, "into one General Harmony in the Whole."[29] Where the bulk of the *Letters*, steeped as they are in the metaphysics of Malebranche, entailed a complete denial of an earlier conception of resemblance or analogy between divine and human spheres (what Harth calls the "mediation of resemblance"), Astell's gesture to More's plastic power re-instates the possibility of resemblance, and, as a consequence, the possibility of the radically different conception of friendship articulated in *A Serious Proposal*.

Astell of the *Letters* had lamented that even man, created in the image of God, was an inappropriate object for human affection. In *A Serious Proposal*, however, the "beauties" of religion are embodied in human—specifically feminine—charms. Such a conception of embodiment would be impossible had Astell remained loyal, in *A Serious Proposal*, to Norris's occasionalism. For in vain will the divine amorist, in the context of occasionalism, search for an earthly object of love. In *A Serious Proposal*, by contrast, God, rather than overseeing a world in which friendship is only the failed experiment that leads to martyrdom, ordains a reciprocal relation whose virtues are both "substantial" and satisfying. Such friends become an "emblem" of what Astell calls "this blessed place"—"a blessed World ... shining with so many stars of worship" (*SP* 37). The very notion of an emblem would be anathema to the occasionalist metaphysics of Norris; for, in the occasionalist context, the pleasures of divine worship are exclusive to God and can never have any material manifestation. Indeed, the emblem, presupposed upon the continuity between divine and human realms (where material part can stand in for spiritual whole) hearkens back to an earlier metaphysics—of Donne, Milton, and the Cambridge Platonists. Synecdoche, a staple of an earlier metaphysical sensibility, underlies the worldview of *A Serious Proposal* where the proposed monastery is both "a Type and Antepast of Heav'n" (*SP* 21).

The emblematic resemblance between Astell's utopian feminine community— itself a "Paradise"—and Heaven similarly sanctions a view of friendship not based merely on correction and censure, but resemblance and relation (*SP* 38). Before "contracting so important a Relation," Astell advises "it were well if we could look

---

28  E. Derek Taylor, "Mary Astell's Ironic Assault on John Locke's Thinking Matter," *Journal of the History of Ideas* 62.3 (2001): 509.

29  Ralph Cudworth, *Treatise Concerning Eternal Morality* (London, 1731), 295.

into the very Soul of the beloved Person, to discover what resemblance it bears to our own." Friends are not merely corrective "Monitors" (though they remain that as well), but their "Souls bear an exact conformity to each other" in both their "*make* and *frame*"—and are, Astell affirms, "purposely design'd by Heaven to unite and mix" (*SP* 37). With their "God-like temper," "*like* him who made them," Astell writes, friends "diffuse their benign Influence" (*SP* 38). In the bulk of *Letters*, following Norris's lead, Astell had assiduously avoided any suggestion of a metaphysics based upon resemblance. In *A Serious Proposal*, the resemblance between friends, authorized—that is, "design'd"—by Heaven comes to sanction a version of friendship which embodies those "charms" that adumbrate the divine.[30]

In this reading, the celebration of feminine society in *A Serious Proposal*, perpetually displaying "the Beauties of Religion," comes into being as a result of both continuities and differences with the exchange with Norris. By adopting the typologies of love and desire from *Letters* for her own social anthropology of domestic relations, Astell could mark off a realm of genuine friendship—removed from the Hobbesian desire which characterized the realm of courtship. By implicitly elaborating a metaphysics more indebted to More and the Cambridge Platonists than to Norris and Malebranche, Astell was able to show how "charms," associated in the *Letters* solely with the divine, might be positively embodied in the emblem of feminine friendship.

*A Serious Proposal*, however, proves to be an anomaly in Astell's corpus. For in her later works, it would only be the socio-political categories of desire which would survive. Indeed, starting with *Some Reflections*, tropes of martyrdom would appear with greater frequency, with friendship functioning less as an embodiment and diffusion of divine virtue, but more, as in the *Letters*, a mere source of censure and correction. To be sure, artifice, design, and imagination, associated in *Letters* with desire, would continue to function in Astell's social, political, and historiographical writings: such languages would be the primary means by which she would come to characterize and reject the various manifestations of the latitudinarian orthodoxy she would oppose throughout her life. But the celebration of friendship, made possible, as I have argued, by the adaptation of the metaphysics of the Cambridge Platonists, would be short-lived. As Taylor has compellingly argued, *Christian Religion* would return finally and firmly to the occasionalist metaphysics articulated by Norris.[31] In such a context, Astell does not celebrate the powers of feminine charm diffusive of heavenly virtue, but rather a friendship which consists primarily in "Advising, Admonishing, and Reproving," and, when all else fails, unleashing "the Truth that

---

30   Astell's Preface to *Letters*, written shortly before the "Appendix" (dated July 2, 1694), describes Lady Catherine Jones (to whom the work was dedicated), in terms very similar to those employed in *A Serious Proposal*. Jones, Astell writes, "so nearly resembles" the "Glorious Author of Perfection." The principle of resemblance is not only manifest in Jones's similarity to God, but in all "those true Lovers of God" who "like excited Needles … cleave not only to him their *Magnet*, but even to one another." Astell concludes her preface, affirming the substantive delights of the feminine, with the hope that "Ladies may be at last convinced that the Beauty of the Mind is the most charming Amiableness," and that no "Ornaments are so becoming to a Lady as the Robe of Righteousness" (*L* a24v, a25v). Astell's praise of Jones, I would argue, emerges from the same sensibility—and metaphysics—that informed the "Appendix" to *Letters*.

31   Taylor, "Ironic Assault," 510.

wounds."[32] Friendship, from this perspective, provides no paradisial ante-type to, or emblem for, a divine world. Rather, *Christian Religion*, again asserting a metaphysics which undermines any resemblance between creature and Creator, re-instates a notion of friendship based upon a martyrdom set in the service of philosophical truth—returning to the notion of friendship asserted by both Norris and Astell in *Letters*, that is, in the correspondence which began in 1693.

---

[32] [Mary Astell,] *The Christian Religion as Profess'd by a Daughter of the Church of England* (1705), 162, 164.

# Chapter V

# Mary Astell and John Locke

## Mark Goldie

## I

The contest between Mary Astell, "the first English feminist," and John Locke, "the father of liberalism," has become a compelling postmodern melodrama. Astell exposed the contradictions of Lockean liberalism by showing that the rights it accorded to men were not to be extended to women, and thereby guaranteed that, at its very birth, liberalism was challenged by feminism. Under the mask of rationalist universalism, liberalism hid its bias toward the masculine. Astell saw this and quarreled with it. Accordingly, she strikes an approving chord among contemporary feminists, who doubt the emancipatory character of the Enlightenment political orthodoxies that came to dominate the modern world.

In this contest, Astell and Locke carry heavy symbolic burdens. They are in danger of becoming ciphers, archetypes of "feminism" and "liberalism." When this occurs, our reading of them tends to lose sight of textual and historical specificity. The two authors become canonized, their writings elevated above the mêlée of contemporary controversy, such that Astell is assumed to have Locke permanently in her sights, and constantly to be antagonistic towards him. It is time to reduce this contest to more modest proportions.

The Astell–Locke quarrel has sharpened in recent decades, principally because of developments in feminist orientations towards Locke and liberalism. While feminism remained modernist, that is to say, saw itself as an extrapolation of liberalism, it was possible to hold that Lockean doctrine was sympathetic towards women.[1] The feminist potential in Locke, however, received a severe blow in Carole Pateman's *The Sexual Contract* (1988). Pateman argued that contractual theory was patriarchal, because the agreement to create the state was made by men and presupposed the prior subjection of women. This cohered with a claim among historians that in the birth of modernity "separate spheres" emerged in which women and the family came to constitute a private sphere distinct from the public sphere of men in civil society.[2]

---

For commenting on a draft of this essay I am grateful to James Buickerood, Hannah Smith, Jane Spencer, Sylvana Tomaselli, and the volume editors.

[1] For example, Melissa Butler, "Early Liberal Roots of Feminism: John Locke and the Attack on Patriarchy," *American Political Science Review* 72.1 (1978): 135–50; Hilda Smith, *Reason's Disciples: Seventeenth-Century English Feminists* (Urbana, IL, 1982).

[2] For a survey and critique, see Amanda Vickery, "Golden Age to Separate Spheres?," *Historical Journal* 36.2 (1993): 383–414.

A corresponding shift occurred in the interpretation of Astell. While feminism remained close to liberalism, her ardent Toryism and pious Anglicanism seemed contradictory bedfellows of her feminism. More recently, however, her Toryism has come to seem less problematic, and less eccentric among feminists of her era.[3] It is now commonplace to argue that Toryism—together with Royalism, its earlier Civil War phase, and Jacobitism, its later post-Revolution phase—had an affinity with feminism. The female poets, playwrights, and philosophers of the seventeenth and early eighteenth centuries were, it is held, overwhelmingly Tory.[4] The alienation of Tory and Jacobite women lent them an angle of vision that enabled them to see through the cant of the Whig Revolution. "Reactionary" though they were, they spoke for a fading familial and aristocratic world in which women had enjoyed a real presence—in the golden age before the separate spheres.

Locke published his *Two Treatises of Government* in 1689. The "Glorious Revolution," which conventionally is held to have inaugurated the Whig-liberal state, occurred in the same year. The Revolution, some claim, damaged rather than enhanced the position of women.[5] And Astell published her critiques in the two decades after 1689. This is a concatenation that ensures Astell's stature as feminism's first retort to liberal modernity. The case is classically stated by Ruth Perry:

> from the beginning, women were suspicious of the modern democratic state and their place within it. ... The Glorious Revolution, to Astell's mind, served the interests of Whigs, of Dissenters, and of men. For what is significant about Mary Astell's reaction to the dispensation of 1689 is that it contains elements of an early feminist critique of liberal political theory. ... Locke's *Second Treatise on Government*, which provided the theoretical justification for the revolutionary settlement, in separating the rights of citizens from the obligations of families, announced a paradigm shift from a political world populated by men and women involved in a web of familial and sexual interconnections to an all-male world based solely on contractual obligation.[6]

It is, however, Patricia Springborg who has most copiously maintained the claim that Astell's work was pervasively driven by an animus against Locke's political thought.[7]

---

3   Joan Kinnaird led the way in "Mary Astell and the Conservative Contribution to English Feminism," *Journal of British Studies* 19.1(1979): 53–75. For a recent survey, see William Kolbrener, "Gendering the Modern: Mary Astell's Feminist Historiography," *The Eighteenth Century* 44.1 (2004): 1–24.

4   Carol Barash, *English Women's Poetry, 1649–1714* (Oxford, 1996); Paula McDowell, *The Women of Grub Street* (Oxford, 1998); Kathryn King, *Jane Barker, Exile* (Oxford, 2000). The Tory women include Margaret Cavendish, Anne Finch, Aphra Behn, Jane Barker, and Mary Manley.

5   Ruth Perry, "Mary Astell and the Feminist Critique of Possessive Individualism," *Eighteenth-Century Studies* 23.4 (1990): 444–57; McDowell, *Women of Grub Street*, chs. 3–5. For a survey see Rachel Weil, *Political Passions: Gender, the Family, and Political Argument in England, 1680–1714* (Manchester, 1999), ch. 1.

6   Perry, "Mary Astell and the Feminist Critique," 445, 447, 449–50.

7   In the introductions and footnotes to her two editions of Astell's writings: *Political Writings* (Cambridge, 1996), hereafter cited as *PW*; and *A Serious Proposal to the Ladies* (London, 1997) hereafter cited as *SP*; and in her "Mary Astell (1666–1731), Critic of Locke," *American Political Science Review* 89.3 (1995), 621–33, hereafter cited as *MA*. See also her "Astell, Masham, and Locke: Religion and Politics," in *Women Writers and the Early Modern British Political Tradition*, ed. Hilda Smith (Cambridge, 1998); and "Mary Astell and John Locke," in *The Cambridge Companion to English*

She asserts that "in each of Astell's works the principal, but largely unacknowledged, target is Locke" and that Astell was "more single-mindedly devoted to the refutation of Locke than any of her contemporaries." Consequently, Astell's exposure of Locke "anticipated, to a surprising degree, modern feminist critiques of a liberal democratic state as yet unborn" (*PW* xix; *MA* 624, 621). More specifically, Springborg argues for Astell's claim to be the earliest critic of Locke's *Two Treatises of Government*. Whereas scholars have hitherto held that the first critique did not appear until 1703, and the first extended treatment not until 1705, Springborg holds that Astell refuted the *Two Treatises* in all her works from 1694 onwards (*MA* 621, 623–24, 628–29; *PW* xxii–xxiii, 4–5, 234; *SP* xix–xxiii). Furthermore, she detects, scattered throughout Astell's works, innuendo against Locke's personal life and career.

At the core of the theoretical case lies what has been called Astell's homology argument: her use of the parallel between the state and the family to expose the double standard whereby principles of equality and justice demanded in the social contract are not accorded in the marriage contract. This is the force of Astell's justly celebrated epigram, "If all men are born free, how is it that all women are born slaves?"[8] Astell's question is undoubtedly arresting, and on this occasion she certainly had Locke's *Two Treatises* in view. What may be doubted is that this epigram is the key to unlock her polemical career.

The aim of this chapter is to examine Astell's confrontation with Locke's politics. Springborg rightly asks, "how can we be sure that he [Locke] was really her target?" (*MA* 622). I shall first point to some general difficulties with Springborg's answer, and then turn to Astell's specific remarks on Locke. I shall argue that Astell's encounter with Locke's *political* theory came late in her authorial career, that her interest in Locke's politics was always subordinate, even incidental, to her interest in his philosophy and theology, that admiration mingled with consternation in her appraisal of Locke, and that, in most of her political tracts, her polemical target was not Locke but the Whigs and Dissenters as a body, just as she said it was. Finally, somewhat paradoxically, I shall demonstrate that Astell's most often quoted work, the 1706 Preface to *Some Reflections upon Marriage*, was more thoroughly directed against Locke than scholars have hitherto recognized: yet not against his *Two Treatises*.

The general difficulties with Springborg's account have to do with the character and chronology of Locke's early reputation. Astell wrote very early in the history of the reception of his works. Some precision is needed before assuming that the *Two Treatises* loomed large in the landscape of contemporary controversy. Locke's *Two Treatises* and *Essay Concerning Human Understanding* appeared in 1689, the *Reasonableness of Christianity* and its *Vindication* in 1695, and the third *Reply to the Bishop of Worcester* in 1699: these are the works to which Astell explicitly refers. Her own publications, ten in number, appeared between 1694 and 1709.[9] In these

---

*Literature, 1650–1740*, ed. Stephen Zwicker (Cambridge, 1998), 276–306.

8   Mary Astell, *Some Reflections upon Marriage*, in *Astell: Political Writings*, ed. Patricia Springborg, 18. Hereafter cited as *SRM*.

9   *A Serious Proposal to the Ladies, Part I* (London, 1694), *Letters Concerning the Love of God* (London, 1695), *A Serious Proposal to the Ladies, Part II* (London, 1697), *Some Reflections upon Marriage* (London, 1700), *Moderation Truly Stated* (London, 1704), *A Fair Way with the Dissenters*

works, which totaled over fifteen hundred pages, she mentioned the *Two Treatises* on four pages, and not before 1705.[10] She silently quoted the *Two Treatises* on one further occasion, in the 1706 Preface (*SRM* 18–19).[11] Prior to her *magnum opus, The Christian Religion* (1705), the only book of Locke's she named, doing so several times, was the *Essay*. In the *Christian Religion* the book she by far most liberally cited was the *Reasonableness*. This pattern of citation is a fair reflection of Locke's public reputation by the mid-point of the first decade of the eighteenth century.

The dates of publication of Locke's works distort our perception of his contemporary reputation. The work he put his name to was the *Essay*, and he took trouble to project this as his defining work, commissioning an engraved portrait of himself for the second edition of 1694. About most of his other works he was obsessively secretive. He did not admit authorship of the *Two Treatises* until he wrote his will in 1704. By the time of his death that year, whereas the *Essay* and the *Reasonableness* had received some two dozen treatises dedicated to refuting them, the *Two Treatises* had received none.[12] It is true that his authorship of the *Two Treatises* was rumored, though we cannot be sure of Springborg's claim that it was "a widely circulated secret in the 1690s" (*MA* 631). Nobody named him in print as the author before 1698.[13] The turning point seems to have been the furor over the Kentish Petition in 1701, when Whig writers, notably John Somers and Daniel Defoe, adopted a dramatic defense of the sovereignty of the people against a Tory parliament, citing or paraphrasing the *Two Treatises*.[14] In the following year the term "Lockian," of a political doctrine, was coined.[15] In 1703 Charles Leslie launched his critique of the *Two Treatises* in his *New Association of those called Moderate Churchmen with the Modern Whigs and Fanatics*; and in 1705 appeared the anonymous *Essay Upon Government: Wherein the Republican Schemes Reviv'd by Mr Lock, Dr Blackhall, &c, are Fairly Consider'd and Refuted*.[16] It is almost certainly Leslie's assault, pursued repeatedly in his tracts and journalism in 1703–5,[17] that drew the *Two Treatises* to Astell's attention, for the

---

(London, 1704), *An Impartial Enquiry into the Causes of Rebellion and Civil War* (London, 1704), *The Christian Religion as Profess'd by a Daughter of the Church of England* (London, 1705), Preface to the 3rd edition of *Reflections* (London, 1706), *Bart'lemy Fair* (London, 1709).

10   Astell, *Christian Religion*, 133–34, 305–6. Hereafter cited as *CR*.

11   In the index to *Political Writings*, Springborg lists some 150 references under "Locke": Astell mentions Locke once, on page 177.

12   Jean Yolton and John Yolton, *John Locke: A Reference Guide* (Boston, 1985). See also John Attig's online Locke bibliography at www.libraries.psu.edu/tas/locke.

13   William Molyneux, *The Case of Ireland* (London, 1698), 38–39, 119. For a checklist of early citations of the *Two Treatises*: *The Reception of Locke's Politics*, ed. Mark Goldie, 6 vols. (London, 1999), 1:lxxiii–lxxiv; also at the website cited above.

14   John Somers (?), *Jura Populi Anglicani* (London, 1701), 30–31; Daniel Defoe, *The Original Power of the Collective Body of the People* (London, 1702); in Goldie, ed., *Reception of Locke's Politics*, 1:336n, 325–53.

15   Humphrey Michel, *Sanguis Carolinus Exclamans* (London, 1702), sig. A3v; in Goldie, ed., *Reception of Locke's Politics*, 1:359.

16   Goldie, ed., *Reception of Locke's Politics*, 1:326; 2:62, 75–106.

17   Charles Leslie, *Cassandra* (London, 1704), 14; *The Rehearsal* (London, Apr.–Oct. 1705), nos. 36–66; in Goldie, ed., *Reception of Locke's Politics*, 2:1–74. For Leslie's role, see Martyn Thompson, "The Reception of Locke's *Two Treatises of Government*, 1690–1705," *Political Studies*, 24.2 (1976): 184–91.

*Two Treatises* made no mark on her trio of political tracts of 1704, and only surfaced in 1705–6.[18]

The scholarship of the past thirty years on the reception of Locke's politics and the political ideologies of the post-Revolution era has demonstrated that Lockean politics was far from ubiquitous.[19] The presumed nexus of Revolution, Whiggism, and Locke is no longer so plausible. Astell scholars are curiously resistant to these findings, anxious to retain Locke as the presiding ideologue of the Revolution and hence as the monolithic target of Astell's critique. Yet the Revolution was as much a Tory as a Whig achievement, and Tory ideologies survived and revived, for which the energy of Astell's pamphleteering is itself evidence. Locke's radical claims about the right of rebellion against tyrants did not suit the moderate consensus that surrounded the Revolution settlement. In the controversy over allegiance, Locke was marginal, and Tories spoke not of deposing kings but of abdication, hereditary right, and divine providence. These circumstances allowed for Astell's own studied ambiguity about the Revolution, her voice always as much that of a Revolution Tory as of a Jacobite recidivist. For Tories, 1689 was not 1649, and those who spoke of deposing tyrants were identified as an anarchic remnant of a superannuated Puritan fanaticism. In so far as Tories troubled to engage with the *Two Treatises*, they construed it not as a novel departure in political theory but as a familiar echo of a long tradition of radical Calvinist resistance theory. Astell was herself preoccupied with exorcizing that tradition, but, as we shall see, she did not think it worthwhile to add Locke's name in her analysis of it.

It is mistaken therefore to assume that Locke acquired a reputation as a *political* philosopher quickly, and mistaken to think of that reputation as canonical in contemporaries' understanding of the Revolution. What Locke did speedily acquire was a reputation as a philosopher.[20] He was pre-eminently the author of the *Essay*. Astell engaged with Locke at an early stage of her writing, but her encounter was with his epistemology. One of her most lasting works was the series of philosophical letters she exchanged with John Norris, published in 1695.[21] Her stance was more favorable than Norris's toward the Lockean theory of knowledge. By the time she assailed the *Essay* and especially the *Reasonableness* in *The Christian Religion* she had formed a harsher view.[22] The changing environment of Locke's reputation made a

---

18 That she was keenly aware of Leslie is clear from the title page of *A Fair Way with the Dissenters and their Patrons*, which states it is "not writ by Mr L----y, or any other furious Jacobite"; she also cites *The New Association* (Astell, *Fair Way*, in Springborg, ed., *Political Writings*, 106).

19 John Dunn, "The Politics of Locke in England and America in the Eighteenth Century," in *John Locke: Problems and Perspectives*, ed. John Yolton (Cambridge, 1969); J.G.A. Pocock, *The Machiavellian Moment* (Princeton, 1975); John Kenyon, *Revolution Principles* (Cambridge, 1977); J.G.A. Pocock, "The Myth of John Locke and the Obsession with Liberalism," in *John Locke*, eds. Pocock and Richard Ashcraft (Los Angeles, 1980), 1–24; J.C.D. Clark, *English Society, 1688–1832* (Cambridge, 1985). For a survey see Goldie, "Introduction," in *Reception of Locke's Politics*, 1.

20 John Yolton, *John Locke and the Way of Ideas* (Oxford, 1968).

21 *Mary Astell and John Norris: Letters Concerning the Love of God*, eds. E. Derek Taylor and Melvyn New (Aldershot, 2005).

22 For the evolution of her attitude see E. Derek Taylor, "Mary Astell's Ironic Assault on John Locke's Theory of Thinking Matter," *Journal of the History of Ideas* 62.3 (2001): 505–22; also, *The First Feminist: Reflections upon Marriage and Other Writings of Mary Astell*, ed. Bridget Hill (Aldershot, 1986), 49.

difference. After 1695, attacks on the *Essay*, notably by Bishop Edward Stillingfleet, came to dwell on its theological heresies. It was Astell's alarm on behalf of Christian orthodoxy that prompted her frontal assault in 1705. Her sense that the discursive field of "Locke studies," as it then existed, was primarily philosophical and theological was enhanced by her belief that Locke had written two other books with which she took issue, *The Ladies Religion* and *A Discourse of the Love of God*.[23] What mattered most to Astell about Locke was his apparent Socinianism and the specter of atheistic materialism that lay in his notorious proposition that "matter might think."[24] Her *Christian Religion*, a treatise on natural and revealed religion, lacks a modern edition, and lacks extensive scholarly appraisal, lacunae which unbalance our sense of her priorities. Certainly the work is remarkable for its integrated account of Locke's works, and for its address to ethical and social themes, yet it remains fundamentally a work of philosophical and moral theology. This made of Astell a more intellectually ambitious critic of Locke than was Charles Leslie, but it also made her indifferent to Locke *on government*.

There is a final general point to make about Locke's early reputation. Springborg holds, as she must, that, taking Astell's writings as a whole, the Lockean target was "largely unacknowledged," for Astell rarely named Locke (*PW* xix). How then to explain the *prima facie* absence of Locke? Springborg argues that Astell felt inhibited from making a frontal assault on Locke while he was alive because he was an influential servant of King William III (*MA* 632; *SP* xvi). This is unpersuasive. In that libelous age, the most senior of politicians were fair game for rancorous public denunciation. There is, moreover, no sign that Locke's philosophy was protected by his public persona, for his *Essay* was subjected to savage indictments from the mid-1690s onwards.[25] Perhaps Astell, as a woman, felt a greater sense of inhibition, yet all her work is marked by vehemence, and she was not generally hesitant about identifying her enemies. Nor was Locke's being still alive relevant. When, late in 1704, she prepared her major assault on Locke for the press, only at proof stage did she discover that Locke had recently died. In her errata list she amended Locke "is ... of another mind" to Locke "was ... ."[26]

Locke was in no special sense an "employee" of William III. Like hundreds of others, he held publicly salaried posts.[27] He was not employed in the royal household. Tory and Jacobite polemicists were not backward in targeting Whig "placemen," usually dwelling on MPs who waxed prosperous on public pensions.[28] It was plausible

---

23  The author of the first (1697) is unknown, of the second (1696) is Damaris Masham. It is possible, however, that Astell feigned her belief that Locke was the author.

24  See Kathleen Squadrito, "Mary Astell's Critique of Locke's View of Thinking Matter," *Journal of the History of Philosophy* 25.3 (1987): 433–40; Taylor, "Ironic Assault"; John Yolton, *Thinking Matter: Materialism in Eighteenth-Century Britain* (Minneapolis, 1983).

25  Besides Stillingfleet, John Edwards was particularly brutal, in four works, 1695–97.

26  Astell, *Christian Religion*, sig. A6v, 406. Locke died in October; Astell's book was in press at Christmas (403).

27  Commissioner of Excise Appeals, 1689–1704; Commissioner of the Board of Trade, 1696–1700.

28  A list of placemen, *c.* 1693, which names Locke's fellow commissioners who were MPs, was drawn up by the Jacobite Samuel Grascome: Bodleian Library, MS Rawlinson D486, fos. 1–5. For other such lists see: G.M. Ditchfield, David Hayton, and Clyve Jones, *British Parliamentary Lists, 1660–1800:*

to include Locke among the Court Whig apparatchiks of the Revolution state, and at least one diatribe did so.[29] But Locke, an elderly scholar living in the Essex countryside, hardly ranked weightily alongside the great City financiers and army contractors. Nor was he alone or prominent in having had a former, pre-Revolution, life as a Whig conspirator in the circle of the Earl of Shaftesbury. Amid the din of Tory assaults on Whig hypocrisy and sleaze in the 1690s and 1700s Locke scarcely figures. His most prominent public role by far was in the great recoinage of 1696, and there was material here for assaults on him for the economic suffering that followed his advice. Astell did not address the topic. She evinced no interest in Locke's public career, and Springborg's detection of supposed allusions to it lacks credibility.


## II


I have assumed that we should be attentive to Astell's *explicit* naming of Locke or his books, and that ordinarily we should read silence as absence. This of course might be thought a naive way of reading her. Her silences may mask allusion and innuendo. Astell was a skilful literary artificer and a supreme ironist. But alertness to the possibility of innuendo ought not to decline into slack reading, in which references to commonplace political vocabulary are assumed to be references to Locke's *Two Treatises*, nor to reductive reading, in which philosophical arguments are assumed to be political jibes. Still less should it collapse into cabalistic reading, in which assaults against a class of persons—Whigs, Dissenters, politicians, men—are taken to be personal vitriol against Locke. I turn now to consider Astell's references to Locke in the order she made them, and to Springborg's allegations of innuendo.

Astell's first reference to Locke occurs in *A Serious Proposal to the Ladies, Part II* (1697), the continuation of her remarkable prospectus for a female academy devoted to learning and piety, and indictment of women for their worldly vanity and slavery to fashion. Here the "ingenious author" of the *Essay Concerning Human Understanding* is cited approvingly for his advice on good grammar.[30] No reservations are expressed, and it is hard to detect in her passing remark an ironic or polemical intent. On the contrary, the element of respect for the *Essay* needs to be noted as evidence for her embrace of recent philosophical developments. She was a keen reader of Descartes and the Port Royal school, as well as of Locke, and her Tory Anglicanism did not entail stubborn defense of Scholastic Aristotelianism, of which there were still redoubts in the universities. At this stage, as Derek Taylor has argued, Astell "refuses to attack [Locke] directly or to break completely with his philosophical methods."[31]

We can find a parallel treatment of the *Essay* in Judith Drake's *Essay in Defence of the Female Sex* (1696), a work sometimes attributed to Astell. Like Astell, Drake

*A Register* (London, 1995).

29  Anon., *An Attempt to Show How Far the Land and Trade of England are Affected by Usury* (London, n.d., c. 1712?); in Goldie, ed., *Reception of Locke's Politics*, 6:159–68.

30  Springborg, ed., *Serious Proposal*, 139, citing the *Essay*, bk. 3, ch. 7, "Of Particles."

31  Taylor, "Ironic Assault," 514.

was a high Tory, a devoted Anglican, and a feminist. Like Astell, she was open to new developments in philosophy. In her tract she recommends a library of books for women to read. Immediately after praising such diehard Tory authors as Sir Roger L'Estrange and Sir George Mackenzie, she offers, on the art of reasoning, "the greatest master of that art Mr Locke."[32] Like Astell, Drake sought in post-Scholastic philosophy arguments for the sexlessness of the mind. Locke's reputation was not yet sullied by association with religious heresy or political fanaticism.

During the 1690s Astell was unquestionably an attentive reader of Locke's *Essay*. But Springborg argues that both parts of the *Serious Proposal* (1694 and 1697) also contain an embryonic critique of Locke's politics (*PW* xv ff). She singles out one passage in which Astell writes that intellectual prejudice and customary ideas are

grand hindrance[s] in our search after truth; these dispose us for the reception of error, and when we have imbibed confirm us in it; contract our souls and shorten our views, hinder the free range of our thoughts and confine them only to that particular track which these have taken, and in a word, erect a tyranny over our free born souls ....

This remark is glossed as "an important anticipation of the argument mounted against the social contract theory," which she and Leslie will later develop, and because the "introduction of the argument here with specific reference to the word contract has not been previously noticed," it follows that "debate over the reception of Locke's ... *Two Treatises* ... has never given Astell her due" (*SP* 89, 184n). Yet Astell is here plainly using the word "contract" merely in the sense of "lessen," and there is no shadow here of "social contract theory." The metaphors of "tyranny" and "free born" are indeed political, but they were utterly commonplace not only in politics but also in discussion of the fettered and unfettered mind.

In another passage, where Astell is discussing how, by habitual and unreflective association of ideas, virtues like "honour" or "greatness" become falsely attached to their opposites, she exclaims, "what do they think of greatness who support their pomp at the expense of the groans and tears of many injured families?" By this, Astell means that people (and no doubt women and children especially) suffer at the hands of those who hold perverted worldly notions of greatness. Yet Springborg holds that "here Astell anticipates her challenge to Locke and the Whigs ... to apply in the private sphere the democracy they advocate in the public," a cry that would be "echoed" in her remark in 1706 that "is it not then partial in men to the last degree, to contend for, and practise that arbitrary dominion in their families, which they abhor and exclaim against in the state?" (*SP* 121, 189n, xxi–xxii; *SRM* 17). It is hard to see the homology argument in Astell's remark, and there is no sign that she was thinking about "democracy." Rather, Astell's instance is given in the course of her—rather Lockean—case for conceptual clarity, the "improvement of our understandings" by the getting of "right ideas" and the "managing all our words" (*SP* 120). Her chosen instance is typical of her habitual homilies against the cruel vanities of worldliness.

---

32  Judith Drake, *Essay in Defence of the Female Sex* (London, 1696), 53–54, 11–12. See Hannah Smith, "English 'Feminist' Writings and Judith Drake's *An Essay in Defence of the Female Sex* (1696)," *Historical Journal* 44.3 (2001): 727–47.

In glossing other passages, Springborg finds it sufficient that Astell uses commonplace terms like "interest" or "empire" to indicate a reflection on the *Two Treatises* (*SP* 8, 30, 49n, 60n). The term "slavery," which Astell, like her contemporaries, uses in respect of "the captivation of our understandings," prompts a gloss about Locke's involvement in the Earl of Shaftesbury's slave-owning colonies, this being a "new twist" in Astell's indictment of Locke's politics (*SP* 136, 192n; cf. 191n).

Furthermore, Springborg takes Astell not only to be quarrelling with Locke's politics but also to be engaging in crude *ad personam* libels about Locke's relationship with Lady Damaris Masham at the Essex manor house of Oates. She holds that when Astell speaks of "the seduction of their unwary neighbours" by men who seek to maintain their own opinions without regard to truth, she "appears to be impugning Locke as the seducer of Masham" (*SP* 118, 189n; cf. xvi).[33] It is true that John Edwards, in 1697, referred to Locke's "seraglio" at Oates,[34] yet it is surely a misjudgment of the character of Astell's treatise to suppose that in the midst of a discussion of Antoine Arnauld's *Art of Thinking*, the classic text of Port Royal logic, she intends her readers to detect such an innuendo.[35]

## III

After 1697 Astell made no further reference to Locke until 1704. There is no mention of him in the first edition of *Reflections upon Marriage*, published in 1700. However, Springborg holds that here Astell again "anticipated" Leslie's "arguments against Locke" (*PW* xxiii, 5, 85, 234; cf. *MA* 626; *SP*, 184n, 189n).[36] Leslie would provide a detailed and overt critique of Locke on government, whereas Astell offers a sustained assault on the oppressiveness of contemporary marriage: her subject matter is different and Locke is nowhere mentioned. There is, however, one point made by Leslie that is made by Astell, and it is a striking one, for it is the homology argument. The clearest instance in *Reflections* is this:

> Patience and submission are the only comforts that are left to a poor people, who groan under tyranny, unless they are strong enough to break the yoke, to depose ... which I doubt would not be allowed of here. For whatever may be said against passive obedience in another case, I suppose there's no man but likes it very well in this; how much soever arbitrary power may be disliked on a throne, not Milton himself would cry up liberty to poor female slaves, or plead for the lawfulness of resisting a private tyranny. (*SRM* 46–47)[37]

---

[33] Locke was not a "neighbour" of Masham's but lived in the Masham household. Springborg further contends that a remark about those "whose lives are a direct contradiction to reason, a very sink of corruption," may refer to Locke's relationship with Masham (14, 52n). See also 195n.

[34] Maurice Cranston, *John Locke: A Biography* (Oxford, 1957), 431. The remark was not published.

[35] For further alleged allusions to Locke, see: Springborg, ed., *Serious Proposal*, 61n, 187n, 188n, 193n.

[36] Springborg specifically cites passages in *Political Writings*, 46–47, 48–49, 51–53, 77–79. See also further alleged allusions to Locke: 59n, 63n.

[37] As Springborg notes, in the fourth edition (1730, 45), Astell inserts after "Milton himself" the phrase "nor B.H. –, nor any of the advocates of resistance," a reference to Benjamin Hoadly.

Here Astell alludes to the Revolution and to Whig denigration of the Tory doctrine of passive obedience. She then draws a parallel between government in the state and government in the family, and challenges Whigs to apply to the latter the principles they insist upon in the former. Leslie would later charge that if Whigs were true to their principles they would "call a council of their wives, children, and servants" and "give up the government of your house entirely into their hands."[38] Undoubtedly Astell made a powerful polemical move in order to expose Whig hypocrisy. The difficulty, however, is that her argument was far from novel, and she did not make it against Locke. As Rachel Weil has shown, the homology argument had been used by Tories much earlier. The author of a pamphlet of 1679 wrote:

> If all power be originally in the people, then it will by consequence follow, that the lawful authority of a father over his children, and a husband over his wife, are derived from the children and wife, and the children and wife in some cases may resume their power ... and their native liberty.

In a sermon of 1682 George Hickes, a savage enemy of Whiggism, argued the case more expansively:

> If men only have an interest in the supreme power, by whose order and authority, or by what Salic law of nature were women excluded from it, who are as useful members of the commonwealth, and as necessary for human societies, as men are? Who gave men authority to deprive them of their birthright, and set them aside as unfit to meddle with government; when histories teach us, that they have wielded sceptres as well as men, and experience shows, that there is no natural difference between their understandings and ours, nor any defects in their knowledge of things, but what education makes?[39]

Likewise, Bridget Hill has shown the presence of the homology on the stage. In Thomas Otway's *The Atheist* (1685) Portia asks, "Do not our fathers, brothers, and kinsmen ... bid fair for rebellion against their sovereign. And why ought not we, by their example, to rebel as plausibly against them?" Lady Brute in John Vanbrugh's *The Provok'd Wife* (1697), discussing marital infidelity, says that since her husband "han't kept his word, why then I'm ... absolved from mine ... The argument's good between the king and the people, why not between the husband and the wife?"[40]

The version of the homology argument that most frequently occurs in seventeenth-century Royalist and Tory treatises is the claim that sovereigns in the state no more derive their authority from the consent of the people than do husbands derive theirs from their wives. This was often coupled with the drawing of a distinction between authorization and designation: subjects may designate who shall rule, but they do not confer authority upon them. A people might elect a ruler, a wife a husband, or

---

38  Charles Leslie, *New Association*, Part II, Supplement, 6–7; in Goldie, ed., *Reception of Locke's Politics*, 2:65; Leslie, *Rehearsal* (London, 9–16 Dec., 1704) , no. 20.

39  Anon., *A Letter to a Friend, Shewing ... how False that State-Maxim is, Royal Authority is ... in the People* (1679), 7; George Hickes, *A Discourse of the Sovereign Power* (1682), 22; quoted in Weil, *Political Passions*, 41, 43.

40  Quoted in Hill, *First Feminist*, 41.

the cardinals a pope, but in every case authority comes from God.[41] In this and other versions of the homology argument, the Tory case was that a single and not a double standard should apply as between the state and the family.[42]

## IV

After 1697, Astell's next mention of Locke occurs in *Moderation Truly Stated* (1704). This tract is an assault on the Dissenters for their misuse of the liberty allowed them by the Toleration Act of 1689, and in particular their practice of "occasional conformity" by which they "hypocritically" took the Anglican sacrament in order to qualify themselves for public office. The Act allowed Dissenters liberty of worship but continued their exclusion from civic life. Astell's tract was a contribution to the furor over the Tories' Occasional Conformity Bills, which would have outlawed the practice, and thereby closed the loophole by which Dissenters got into office. Astell deplored the appeasement of Dissenters by Whigs and Low Church Anglicans. They and the Dissenters talked up religious "moderation" as an antidote to High Church intolerance. Astell's theme is the dishonesty of using the term "moderation" to denote acquiescence in hypocrisy and false religion. At one point she asserts that "lukewarmness and indifferency ... is the only sense in which moderation can be taken in the present contest; if with the great Mr Locke, it be our constant care to annex to the word a determinate idea."[43] This single reference to Locke in a tract of 120 pages glances at what had become a commonplace of Lockean epistemology. Astell's tone is much as it was in the second part of *A Serious Proposal*. Locke urged conceptual hygiene, the avoidance of the abuse of language. Once more, Astell's cites the *Essay* and not the *Two Treatises*, and she recommends its authority. There is, perhaps, an ironic play on "great" Mr Locke. Whigs and Dissenters will surely, she suggests, not wish to do other than follow the precepts of a writer whom they so much admire.

There is, to be sure, a further hint at Lockean epistemology elsewhere in this tract, and this time in closer relation to political theory. In her preface she attacked Charles Davenant. Finding in him an endorsement of contractarian ideas, she jeers at his notion that men originally found themselves in a condition of natural equality in a free state of nature.[44] This was "a mere figment of Hobbes's brain" and was contrary to the Biblical truth that we are all of Adam's race (*MTS* xxxv). Noting that the concept of a condition of natural freedom was ingrained in Whig thinking, Astell slyly calls it their "innate idea." Her implication is that Locke's epistemology,

---

41  For example, William Sherlock, *The Case of Resistance* (London, 1684), 124–25; Sir Philip Warwick, *A Discourse Concerning Government* (London, 1694), 14.

42  See John McCrystal, "Revolting Women: The Use of Revolutionary Discourse in Mary Astell and Mary Wollstonecraft Compared," *History of Political Thought* 14.2 (1993): 189–203, esp. 192.

43  Astell, *Moderation*, 10–11, hereafter cited as *MTS*; Locke, *Essay Concerning Human Understanding* (Oxford, 1975), bk. 3, ch. 10, "Of the Abuse of Words" (hereafter cited as *Essay* by book, chapter). There is no modern edition of *Moderation*.

44  Davenant was an erstwhile Tory, now widely accused of turncoating.

here his critique of innate ideas, is well-known and authoritative. The Whigs, she suggests, are mistaken in their fixed dogma of the state of nature, in a philosophical world in which we now accept that our ideas are not innate but must be demonstrated from "experimental"—experiential—knowledge. The state of ungoverned nature, she insists, had no historical or anthropological basis whatsoever.

In this tract there is still no sign that Astell took any interest in the *Two Treatises* or in Locke's public persona. Notwithstanding, Springborg argues that substantial sections form "a long disquisition on Locke" and "trace the contours of Locke's career," being coded critiques of Locke as a time-serving, scheming political opportunist, and party scribbler (*PW* xxiv, 126n; *MA*, 625, 630). This is fanciful. The tract is manifestly an assault on Dissenters, and their Puritan forebears, and on the whole Whig party and Low Church Anglicans who took the Dissenters' side. It is similar to numerous other Tory attacks on occasional conformity. Locke was not a Dissenter, nor a religious or political leader, and he did not publish any contribution to this controversy. In this crisis he was not consequential. When Astell attacks "new men" who seek "their own advancement" she means Dissenters who want access to office. This and other remarks quoted by Springborg as innuendo on Locke occur in a passage that begins, "Let Dissenters then enjoy their toleration ... but ... let us not give them power and opportunity to destroy the establishment" (*MTS* 92–93). When Springborg asks rhetorically, "Who but Locke made such 'a bustle about liberty and property'?"—the latter phrase is Astell's—the answer must be, a large army of Dissenters and Whigs.[45]

Springborg has a more specific textual case to make. She holds that when Astell refers to a highwayman she has a particular section of Locke's *Two Treatises* in mind. The "highwayman" acquires key importance for her as a "test case of [Astell's] method of refutation," and she repeats her claim in respect of similar passages in two of Astell's other works (*MA* 626–28; *SRM* 16–17n; *SP*, 193n). Astell makes an ironic exclamation: "and if a thief meets me on the highway and goes off with my purse, therefore he has a right to it, and God approves the action!" In *Reflections*, Astell puts it this way: "and if mere power gives a right to rule, there can be no such thing as usurpation; but a highwayman so long as he has strength to force, has also a right to require our obedience" (*MTS* 80). Springborg contends that Astell is referring to Locke's discussion of tacit consent in paragraph 119 of the *Second Treatise*, where Locke refers to the consent presumed to be given to the sovereign by a person "traveling freely on the highway" (*PW* 16). This reading is surely erroneous. In paragraph 119 Locke discusses a person who travels upon the highway, not a "highwayman." Locke means a person who benefits from the security provided by the state and who thereby may be deemed to have given consent and owe obedience. By contrast, a highwayman, of course, is a robber who assaults travelers. Astell uses the highwayman as a metaphor for usurpation: Locke's passage on tacit consent is not about usurpation. Elsewhere, Locke does himself, like Astell, use the image of

---

45  Springborg, "Mary Astell (1666–1731), Critic of Locke," 630. For Astell as a critic of Dissent, see William Kolbrener, "'Forc'd into an Interest': High Church Politics and Feminine Agency in the Works of Mary Astell," *1650–1850: Ideas, Aesthetics, Inquiries in the Early Modern Era*, 10 (2004): 3–31.

the highwayman as a metaphor for usurpation and rogue government.[46] Springborg insists that Astell has all these passages in mind and is deliberately conflating them, in order to embroil Lockean consent theory in the defense of King William III's usurpation. She holds that, for Astell, Locke's use of the highwayman metaphor can be turned against him, casting the Whigs as bandits and the Revolution as banditry. Astell drew a parallel "between rogue government and the state, scarcely veiled by the fiction of tacit consent" (*MA* 628). Yet all that occurs is that Astell and Locke use the same commonplace analogue of highwaymen and usurpation. In none of Astell's remarks upon highwaymen does she go beyond this metaphor, and there is no hint of an allusion to Locke's discussion of consent, tacit or otherwise.

If we return to Astell's highwayman metaphor in *Moderation* we find that it occurs in a discussion of Milton's *Iconoclastes* (1649), a classic defense of the English Republic and of the trial and execution of Charles I. She is attacking the ideologues of the Civil War—naming also the Parliamentarian lawyer William Prynne and the rebel preacher John Goodwin—whom, she charges, discovered God's providential approbation in the success of their cause. For the victorious soldiers of Cromwell's army, for the fanatic preachers and republicans, might was right. It was a doctrine, she continued, by which any exertion of brute force, any successful human exigency, might be deemed God's work. There is no reason to believe that Astell's target is other than who she says it is: the rebels of the Civil War whom she frequently and bitterly assailed. Astell was ever alert to the moral repugnancy of Puritan providentialism (*MTS* 80).

There is, in *Moderation*, another place where the *Two Treatises* might more plausibly have been cited. Astell's preface against Davenant is a remarkable political essay, in many ways her most interesting and neglected, containing as it does a theme that might be called Machiavellian Toryism, in its admiration for Spartan virtue and Roman Stoicism, and its preoccupation not with rights and liberties, but with virtue, frugality, counsel, and faction. It displays her familiarity with a range of major political treatises, for she cites Plato's *Republic*, Machiavelli's *Discourses*, More's *Utopia*, Bacon's *New Atlantis*, and Hobbes's *Leviathan*. She deplores "fine schemes of government, [that] have traced it up to the state of nature, original contract and all that." In speaking of the state of nature as "a figment of Hobbes's brain," she cites the fables of Cadmus's teeth and of mushroom men, both of which supposed the spontaneous generation of human beings, without paternity (*MTS* xx, xxxv). Critics of Hobbes had for decades used exactly these images.[47] In the spirit of Plutarch's analysis of the cycle of political regimes, Astell predicts that Whig populist demagoguery will end in arbitrary rule—as it had in the 1640s. She returns to her contempt for Dissenters, who threaten a "distinct state" (*MTS* xxxvii–xxxviii, xlviii). In none of this does she find it relevant to mention Locke's *Two Treatises*.

---

46 John Locke, *Two Treatises of Government*, ed. Peter Laslett (Cambridge, 1967), *Second Treatise*, paras. 182, 186, 207.

47 For example, Thomas Tenison, *The Creed of Mr Hobbes* (London, 1670), 131–33; Edward Hyde, Earl of Clarendon, *A Brief View and Survey of … Leviathan* (London, 1676), 38–39; John Eachard, *Mr Hobbes's State of Nature* (London, 1672), 76–80.

**V**

Astell's next reference to Locke occurs in *An Impartial Enquiry into the Causes of Rebellion and Civil War* (1704). This tract was an assault on White Kennett's sermon on January 30, which had, she thought, abused the solemn anniversary of Charles I's execution by defending the regicide. Her tract is a threnody on the tragedy of the royal martyr and an analysis of the politics of Charles's reign. She objects to the Whig cant of liberty, estates, and self-preservation. Such vocabulary was commonplace and she cites it from Kennett's sermon. There is no reason to suppose that this is a furtive attack on Locke and that Kennett was Locke's "surrogate" (*PW* xxxv; *MA* 626). Astell's single reference to Locke is a sarcastic aside to the effect that Kennett's knee-jerk association of Stuart monarchy with French slavery is best explained by reading "Locke's chapter of the Association of Ideas."[48] Once again Astell has turned to the *Essay* and not to the *Two Treatises*: to a chapter added in the fourth edition of 1700, for evidently Astell kept up with Locke's successive revisions of the *Essay*.

It is true that Astell adds a remark about Locke's political color. Kennett "need not be afraid to read it, for that ingenious author is on the right side, and by no means in a French interest!" Springborg holds that this is the key to unlock the presence of an attack on Locke. She argues that Astell's next remark clinches the case. Having observed that Locke is "by no means in a French interest," Astell continues: "And indeed, till people will observe the excellent precepts of our holy religion, and that in particular, of calling no man master upon earth, of following no popular speaker and leader of a party, they will easily be persuaded to think, as every cunning and factious man will have them." For Springborg, "the passage must be read as an elaborate satire of Locke's views," since Locke, while professing "holy religion," was a latitudinarian, and, while professing to call "no man master," had been the henchman of the "leader of a party," the Earl of Shaftesbury, who "exactly fitted that description" (*IE* 177 and n; *MA* 625; *SP* 61n). This reading is deeply improbable. Astell is writing about the politics of Charles I's reign and inveighing against Whigs in Queen Anne's reign; she is not thinking of Charles II's reign. More important, Astell is not here deprecating or satirizing Locke. On the contrary, she is recommending the intellectual independence that Locke advocates. She suggests that until people learn to think for themselves, to call nobody their leader in thought, to put aside the tyranny of mental habit and fashionable opinion—"the constant din of their party," as Locke puts it—they will be the victims of devious demagogues. The passage draws not on Locke's career but his epistemology.[49]

Springborg finds another reference to Locke, where Astell puts the argument that since people do not have a right to dispose of their own lives, their consent cannot be the source of sovereign authority: sovereigns *do* have a right over people's lives—the right of capital punishment—hence their authority must derive from God.[50] Yet this

---

48   Astell, *Impartial Enquiry*, 177 hereafter *IE*, cited from Springborg's edition of *Political Writings*; Locke, *Essay*, bk. 2, ch. 33.

49   Locke, *Essay*, 2:33, para. 18; see bk. 4, ch. 20 ("Of Wrong Assent, or Errour"), para. 17 ("leaders of parties"); bk. 4, ch. 19 ("Of Enthusiasm").

50   See Astell, *Impartial Enquiry*, 170, allegedly against the *Second Treatise*, para. 23.

point was a cliché of seventeenth-century Royalist and Tory political thought, and her point is neither novel nor has any special bearing on Locke.[51]

There is a section elsewhere in *An Impartial Enquiry* where Lockean political theory might more naturally have been cited. With considerable erudition, Astell provides a genealogy of Calvinist and Catholic resistance theory, of the ideology of "mutual compact between king and people" that issued in a defense of the right to depose or assassinate tyrants. Her charge was that radical Protestants redeployed the "king-killing doctrine" developed by the Papists. She cites authors from the early sixteenth century onwards: Major, Bellarmine, Suarez, Molina, Parsons, Buchanan, Milton, and other "mercenary scribblers whom all sober men condemn." She had offered a similar litany in *Moderation*, there naming Mornay, Hotman, Knox, Buchanan, Parker, Milton, Rutherford, and Baxter (*IE* 163, 153–63; *MTS* 70–77).[52] This was the history of political thought as Royalists and Tories regularly explained it.[53] Locke's critics would soon add him to this litany.[54] But in 1704 it did not seem relevant to Astell to do so.

## VI

We come now to *The Christian Religion*, which contains Astell's sustained consideration of Locke, in which for the first and only time she explicitly cites the *Two Treatises*. In this book she definitely associates Locke's political with his other writings. She refers to "our modern authors, who not only refine upon philosophy, by which they do service to the world; and upon politics, by which they mean to serve their party; but even upon Christianity itself, pretending to give us a more reasonable account of it" (*CR* 135). This is Locke the author in turn of the *Essay*, the *Two Treatises*, and the *Reasonableness of Christianity*.[55]

Her treatise is, *inter alia*, a theological, moral, and political meditation on the cardinal Tory doctrine of "passive obedience," a doctrine which entailed a categorical denial that it was ever right to take up arms against the sovereign. What is striking about Astell's account is that she returned this doctrine to its theological roots. For "passive obedience" took its origin as a term to denote Christ's resignation in the face of his crucifixion. The Christ-like response to human oppression is patient endurance and stoic acceptance. "Love is the only retaliation our religion allows us" (*CR* 236). Christ upon the cross contains, she argues, a complete refutation of Whig political theory.

---

51 For example, John Maxwell, *Sacro-Sancta Regum Maiestas* (London, 1644), 49–52; William Falkner, *Christian Loyalty* (London, 1679), 420.

52 She adds one contemporary author, Defoe: Astell, *Moderation*, 68, 72.

53 She gives the sources of her erudition: Henry Foulis's *History of the Romish Treasons* (London, 1671), and Richard Bancroft's *Dangerous Positions* (London, 1593).

54 For example, Luke Milbourne, *The Measures of Resistance* (London, 1710), 3: "Mariana, Suarez, Bellarmine, Hotman, Buchanan, Bradshaw, Milton, Baxter, Owen, Goodwin, Sidney, Locke."

55 Locke is still an author "for whom I have a due esteem" (252) because of "his excellent *Essay*" (252); he is "deservedly celebrated" (403), "that great master of good sense" (256). Much depends on whether we judge Astell to be sustaining an unrelenting ironic tone.

The Gospel, she continues, teaches us not to value our temporal welfare above eternal life. Self-preservation, so much vaunted by the Whigs, is not our cardinal aspiration. Or, rather, not as ordinarily considered, for it is the preservation of our spiritual rather than our bodily self that we ought to seek.

> What then is self-preservation, that fundamental law of nature, as some call it? ... it does not consist in the preservation of the person or composite [mind and body], but in preserving the mind from evil, the mind which is truly the self ... It is this self-preservation and no other, that is a fundamental sacred and unalterable law.

The last phrase is Locke's, and she adds, with deliberate irony, that in *this* sense the *Two Treatises* is right—right that self-preservation is cardinal—although its author applied it "in another case where it will not hold" (*CR* 305–6).[56]

Astell adverts once more to the *Two Treatises* in discussion of the same theme. She holds Whig doctrine to be materialistic and hedonic, for it privileges earthly and sensual felicity over spiritual and eternal. For the Epicurean, love is constituted by a "bare sentiment of pleasure" or a "disposition of mind towards that which pleases" (*CR* 132). Yet we are commanded by the Gospel to love our persecutors, and it cannot be supposed that our persecution is something which pleases, and it is impossible to think of the invasion of our estates, employments, and lives as pleasurable. When Christ commands us to love those who cause us pain, he commands contrary to sense, to sensuousness. Astell now elaborates this point in a series of quotations of Lockean phrases.

> To submit to and bear with a persecutor, *the common enemy and pest of mankind*, much more to delight, to rejoice, and take complaisance in him, is contrary to all sense and reason, to *our just and natural rights*, and can go down with none but *such servile flatterers*, who would have all *men born to what their mean souls has fitted them, slavery*.

The italicized passages occur in the Second Treatise, which she cites in the margin (*CR* 133–34).[57]

Astell's position involves a complete repudiation of the political language of self-preservation. The only triumph over earthly tyranny lies in martyrdom. Freedom consists in the soul's transcendence of temporal slavery and not in the body's rebellion. The pacifism of the Gospel is incompatible with Locke's advocacy of political violence. This categorical alienation from the mental world of Whig political theory exempted Astell from offering anything like a sustained textual critique of the *Two Treatises*. Her encounter with Lockean politics remains on the plane of moral theology rather than political casuistry, and her two brief references to the *Two Treatises* are minor episodes in a long and complex work.

---

56 Here she cites *Second Treatise*, para. 149.

57 Astell here cites *Second Treatise*, paras. 230, 239; ("just and natural rights" is not an exact quotation). She also cites again para. 149 ("fundamental, sacred, and unalterable") and para. 23 ("nobody can give more power than he has himself").

## VII

The fifth work in which Astell refers to Locke—though not by name—is in the Preface she added to the third edition of *Reflections upon Marriage* in 1706.[58] In her most memorable and often cited passage, it is clear that she is quoting the *Two Treatises*, and the phrases she italicizes are Locke's:

> If *all men are born free*, how is it that all women are born slaves? as they must be if the being subjected to the *inconstant, uncertain, unknown, arbitrary will* of men, be *the perfect condition of slavery*? and if the essence of freedom consists, as our masters say it does, in having a *standing rule to live by*? And why is slavery so much condemned and strove against in one case, and so highly applauded and held so necessary and so sacred in another? (*SRM* 18–19)[59]

Here of course is the homology argument, classically stated, and now addressed to Locke. She restates the point in a scarcely less telling phrase: "if absolute sovereignty be not necessary in a state, how comes it to be so in a family? or if in a family why not in a state; since no reason can be alleged for the one that will not hold more strongly for the other?" (*SRM* 17).

Taken as a whole, however, Astell's 1706 Preface dwells only briefly on the homology argument and the *Two Treatises*. Its chief burden is scriptural, and the bulk of it is devoted to investigating the position of women in the Old and New Testaments, against the claims of critics who say that her feminist principles "were not agreeable to scripture" (*SRM* 14). She especially takes issue with conventional readings of St Paul's proscription of women's "praying and prophesying" in public worship. What has never before been noticed is that Astell here launches an attack on a different work of Locke's, his posthumously published *Paraphrase and Notes on the First Epistle of St Paul to the Corinthians*.[60] Hers is in fact the first critique of that work, for Locke's book was fresh off the press.[61]

Locke had, in extensive explanatory notes on 1 Corinthians 11:2–16, provided a remarkable discussion of women's religious role.[62] His conclusion was ambiguous. On the one hand, where most commentators had read Paul as absolutely prohibiting a role for women, Locke argued that in special circumstances, where a woman was directly inspired by God, she might speak and "prophesy," provided she remained veiled. "That the spirit of God and the gift of prophecy should be poured out upon women as well as men in the time of the Gospel is plain."[63] So striking was this claim

---

58 There was, later, a final work in which Locke was cited: *Bart'lemy Fair*, where Astell quotes "the great Mr Locke" for his definition of wit (77); Locke, *Essay*, 2:11.

59 The italicized phrases occur in the *Second Treatise*, paras 61, 22, 24, and 22, respectively. Cf. Springborg, "Mary Astell (1666–1731), Critic of Locke," 629; Springborg, ed., *Political Writings*, 19n.

60 Including by me in my edition of the Preface: Goldie, ed., *Reception of Locke's Politics*, 2:107–32.

61 Locke's book was advertised in the *Term Catalogue* in Hilary (February) 1706 and Astell's in Trinity (July).

62 John Locke, *A Paraphrase and Notes on the Epistles of St Paul*, ed. Arthur Wainright, 2 vols. (Oxford, 1987), 1:219–23; and see Wainright's commentary, 44, 59–62, 68–69, 442–43.

63 Locke, *Paraphrase*, 1:221, reiterated 222, 245; citing Acts 2:17 and Joel 2:28.

that Quaker authors invoked Locke's authority in defense of the Quaker tradition of female preaching. The topic was a pressing one, in light of the eruption of female preaching among the Civil War sects and the attempt by conservative Quakers to suppress this legacy of mid-century radicalism.[64] The topic retained polemical force: a hostile cartoon of 1710 shows a woman preaching at a Quaker meeting.[65]

On the other hand, Locke also argued that in ordinary circumstances women should remain silent as well as veiled, the veil being a "token of her subjection." He underscored this religious subordination by insisting that Paul did not disrupt the natural condition of things. Locke's remarks at this point constitute the starkest endorsement in any of his writings of women's natural inferiority. The passage is remarkable for its absence in modern scholarship on Locke and gender.

> The Christian religion was not to give offence by any appearance or suspicion that it took away the subordination of the sexes and set the women at liberty from their natural subjection to the men. And therefore we see that, in both these cases, the aim was to maintain and secure the confessed superiority and dominion of the man and not permit it to be invaded so much as in appearance. Hence the arguments in the one case for covering and in the other for silence are all drawn from the natural superiority of the man and the subjection of the woman.[66]

It was this passage which provoked Astell's fury. She names neither Locke nor his book, but it is certain that he is the "learned paraphrast" to whom she refers (*SRM* 12, 20).[67] The certainty lies not only in her use of that term, but also in her noting the two contrasting claims that Locke makes: that Paul offered a limited allowance for female prophesying—the paraphrast "endeavours to prove that inspired women as well as men used to speak in the church, and that St Paul does not forbid it"—and that Paul's general teaching coincides with the natural subordination of women (*SRM* 20; cf. 11). No less than six times Astell refers to the terms "natural superiority," "natural inferiority," or "natural subjection," because the "paraphrast ... lays so much stress" on it (*SRM* 9, 12, 13, 14, 20, 24). That Locke's *Paraphrase* is her target is clinched by an even more precise reference, which allows her to suggest that Locke has arrogantly overreached himself in pronouncing an interpretation of Paul. Locke

---

64    Josiah Martin, *A Letter ... on the Paraphrase and Notes of the Judicious John Locke, Relating to Women's Exercising their Spiritual Gifts in the Church* (London, 1716): in Goldie, ed., *Reception of Locke's Politics*, 5:129–42; William Rawes, *The Gospel Ministry of Women ... Defended from Scripture and from the Writings of John Locke* (London, 1801). See Peter Huff, "John Locke and the Prophecy of Quaker Women," *Quaker History* 86.2 (1997): 26–40; Wainright, ed., *Paraphrase and Notes*, Introduction, 68–69. For background, see Keith Thomas, "Women and the Civil War Sects," *Past and Present* 13 (1958): 42–62; Phyllis Mack, "Women as Prophets during the English Civil War," in *The Origins of Anglo-American Radicalism*, eds. Margaret Jacob and James Jacob (London, 1984), 214–30.

65    F.G. Stephens, Edward Hawkins, and M.D. George, *Catalogue of Political and Personal Satires Preserved in the Department of Prints and Drawings in the British Museum*, 11 vols. (London, 1870–1954), 2:1556: "Green-aproned sisters whine."

66    Locke, *Paraphrase*, 1:222.

67    The paraphrast is not, therefore, William Nicholls in his *Duty of Inferiours* (London, 1701), as suggested by Goldie (*Reception of Locke's Politics*, 2:111n, 113n), following Springborg (*Political Writings*, 5, 12n, 14n, 20n), following Hill (71n, 73n, 77n).

declares himself foxed by Paul's remark that women should be veiled "because of the angels," saying "what the meaning of these words is I confess I do not understand." Astell retorts that the verse "because of the angels" is "so very obscure a text, that that ingenious paraphrast who pleads so much for the natural subjection of women ingenuously confesses, that he does not understand it." Paul, she says, probably referred to "some custom among the Corinthians ... which we are ignorant of, and therefore [we are] apt to mistake him" (*SRM* 12–13).[68]

Astell's fundamental objection is that Locke had falsely used Paul to support an argument from natural law. She indignantly balks at the idea of "natural inferiority" which "our masters lay down as a self-evident and fundamental truth." Paul "argues only for decency and order, according to the present custom and state of things ... he says not a word of inequality, or natural inferiority." Paul's case is based on "prudential reasons ... not ... any law of nature." Paul in fact says that "man is not without the woman, nor the woman without the man, but all things of God," so that "the relation between the two sexes is mutual, and the dependence reciprocal, both of them depending entirely upon God ... which one would think is no great argument of the natural inferiority of either sex." Scripture should not be used to settle issues which "ought to be decided by natural reason only." Scripture can no more settle the question of the relations between the sexes than it can settle the argument between Copernican and Ptolemaic astronomy (*SRM* 9, 11–13, 20).[69]

It is striking that Astell here adopts the characteristic position of the Enlightenment rationalist speaking against scriptural fundamentalism, and she does so against Locke. She turns the screw by invoking Locke's own principles in the *Reasonableness*. The purpose of scripture, she writes, is to make us "excellent moralists and perfect Christians, not great philosophers ... [scripture] being writ for the vulgar as well as for the learned." In other words, it is not the function of the Bible to solve our philosophical and scientific problems, but to teach us to lead virtuous lives. She exclaims against her "adversary" who, when

> reason declares against him, he flies to authority, especially to divine, which is infallible ... But scripture is not always on their side who make a parade of it, and through their skill in languages and the tricks of the schools, wrest it from its genuine sense to their own inventions. (*SRM* 14)[70]

She rounds off with a protest at women's deprivation of the opportunity to learn the ancient languages necessary for scriptural scholarship—Locke of course constantly referred to the Greek originals of the New Testament texts (*SRM* 14).[71]

---

68  See Locke, *Paraphrase*, 1:223; 1 Corinthians 11:10.

69  See 1 Corinthians 11:11–12.

70  Cf. Locke, *The Reasonableness of Christianity*, ed. John Higgins-Biddle (Oxford, 1999), ch. 15, esp. 169–70: "This is a religion suited to vulgar capacities ... The writers and wranglers in religion fill it with niceties ... as if there were no way into the church, but through the academy ... The greatest part of mankind have not leisure for ... distinctions of the schools"; also ch. 14.

71  Judging by remarks in this passage it is just conceivable that Astell regarded Locke's *Paraphrase* as a critique of her *Reflections*. Locke possessed a copy of the first edition: John Harrison and Peter Laslett, *The Library of John Locke* (2nd edition, Oxford, 1971), 185.

This tirade notwithstanding, Astell's general argument on women and scripture is characteristically paradoxical and not in fact much different from Locke's: there were once prophetic women, but in the post-prophetic church women do not have a public role. She launches into a disquisition on female prophetesses, holy women, and rulers, such as Ruth, Esther, Rebecca, Miriam, Deborah, and Abigail in the Old Testament and Mary, Elizabeth, Martha, Tabitha, Anna, and Priscilla in the New. This partly proves a religious point, but also a political, for Deborah's government shows that "the sovereignty of a woman is not contrary to the law of nature," a theme which culminates in Astell's celebration of Queen Anne's imperial prowess (*SRM* 24, 30).[72]

At the same time, Astell, while categorically denying the natural inequality of women, insists that she has no intention of disrupting the modern church's tradition of masculine ministry. Under post-prophetic conditions, women's religious role is not in public ministry. "As for [Paul's] not suffering women to speak in the church, no sober person that I know of pretends to it" (*SRM* 20).[73] As a hater of the Civil War sects—the "enthusiasts" as opposed to the "sober"—she could hardly hold otherwise. In fact she offers her own novel reading of Paul: the Apostle's purpose was to condemn sects of Dissenters who promoted "indecent behaviour" among their female followers. In the Epistle to Timothy Paul had attacked wicked men, who "having a form of godliness ... lead captive silly women." Astell suggests that at Corinth "the same cunning seducer employed ... women," and "therefore St Paul thought it necessary to reprove them so severely in order to humble them" (*SRM* 13).[74] In other words, Paul condemned female "prophesying" at Corinth because of the antics of pseudo-godly nonconformists.

That Astell has contemporary Dissenters in mind is reinforced by her remarks in *Moderation Truly Stated* about the prominence of women among the Dissenters. It was a common complaint among Anglicans that the Dissenters indecently flattered female religiosity.[75] For Astell, the female Dissenter was a type of the flighty, vain, unthinking, fashion-conscious woman whom she so constantly condemned. Women Dissenters are "noisy women ... the witty and the gay, the intriguing and politic ladies ... on the factious side," as against "the old and the ugly, the praying and the women of thought ... on the other" (*MTS* li, xlix–li). As ever, Astell insists upon the modesty of women while upholding their natural equality.

## VIII

In preparing *The Christian Religion* Astell had decided to mount a general critique of Locke. This had not been the purpose of any of her earlier works. And in her *magnum*

---

72 See Barash, *English Women's Poetry*, 237.

73 Cf. Springborg, ed., *Serious Proposal*, 23–24: "We pretend not that women should teach in the church, or usurp authority where it is not allowed them."

74 See 2 Timothy 3:5–6. Cf. Springborg, ed., *Serious Proposal*, 24.

75 See, for example, *The Conventicle Courant* (London, 1682), nos. 3, 6, 16, 17. On dissenting women see John Spurr, *English Puritanism, 1603–1689* (Basingstoke, 1998), 195–97.

*opus* her target was primarily Locke's materialism and Socinianism, not his politics. By 1706 Astell had the Lockean bit between her teeth. She eagerly seized upon Locke's posthumous work coming off the presses. What provoked her to compose her famous Preface was indeed Locke, but not his *Two Treatises*, rather a work which modern readers of Locke are scarcely aware of, the *Paraphrase*. Astell found in the *Paraphrase* Locke's categorical statement of women's natural inferiority. Her Preface defends natural equality and modest piety. Her topic is the interpretation of scripture. It is true that she deployed the homology argument with devastating effect, and with the *Two Treatises* in mind. Yet this is a slim foundation for the anachronistic hyperbole that Astell "anticipated ... modern feminist critiques of a liberal democratic state as yet unborn," not least because it allows the brightness of a single epigram to darken the complex mental landscape of Astell's Tory ideology.

## Chapter VI

# Mary Astell's Law of the Heart

Corrinne Harol

If you *approve*, Why do you not follow?
And if you *Wish* why shou'd you not *Endeavor*?
*A Serious Proposal to the Ladies Part II*, 120

Much has been made of Mary Astell's rationalist critique of John Locke's epistemology, but Astell is generally not considered a theorist worth contemplating with regard to the emerging arena of human subjectivity to which Locke's postulation of a rights-bearing subject, conflicted between desire and will, is seen as an important early contribution.[1] While Astell's feminism is generally considered to have had historical legs, in all other respects she has, for most of her legacy, been seen as on the losing side of both historical causality and political correctness. Locke's empiricism, his Whig interpretation of history, and his emergent view of subjectivity are all markers of his greater importance for modernity. Astell's quaint rationalism, her flirtations with occasionalism and her Tory and theological commitments all consign her, feminism aside, to the dustbin of historical might-have beens, and they compel her defenders to offer historical or instrumental reasons for what appear to be her illogical combinations of politics, theology, philosophy, and feminism. The emergent interest in Mary Astell, to which this collection both testifies and contributes, attempts to transcend this rather limited defense of Astell and to imagine ways that Astell might matter to modernity. Patricia Springborg has been spearheading this effort with such claims as her recent one that Astell conceives a critique of liberalism on the level of rhetoric that her successors will later literalize.[2] Sarah Ellenzweig has discovered ways that Astell's philosophical conservatism paradoxically aligned her with the radical Enlightenment figure Spinoza.[3] And Ruth Perry has shown how Astell presciently predicted the "asocial and androcentric" implications of liberalism even at its inception.[4]

I would like to thank William Kolbrener, Michal Michelson, Brenda Lyshaug, and the participants of the 2005 WESECS meeting, especially David Mazella and Laura Stevenson, for helpful comments on this essay.

1 For example, Charles Taylor credits Locke with a strong version of "disengaged reason," which Taylor calls the "punctual self," that is a marker of modern subjectivity. *Sources of the Self: The Making of Modern Identity*, (Cambridge, MA, 1986), 159–76.

2 Patricia Springborg, "Republicanism, Freedom from Domination, and the Cambridge Contextual Historians," *Political Studies* 49.5 (2001): 851–76.

3 Sarah Ellenzweig, "The Love of God and the Radical Enlightenment: Mary Astell's Brush with Spinoza," *Journal of the History of Ideas* 64.3 (2003): 379–97.

4 Ruth Perry, "Mary Astell and the Feminist Critique of Possessive Individualism," *Eighteenth-*

This essay is also an attempt to show how Astell's conservative critique of the emergent Whig compromise, and in particular of Locke's arguments of the *Essay*, can lead us to see aspects of the radical, or at least the modern Mary Astell. It reads the second part of Astell's *A Serious Proposal to the Ladies* as a response to the revived interest, among mainstream Anglican thinkers, in the theory of "law written in the heart" and as a response to Locke's emerging ideas about subjectivity. Via her mediation of these theories, Astell imagines a different kind of relationship between desire and morality, and she imagines a subject who is neither repressed nor limited to the kinds of negative freedoms that are often considered the legacy of Locke's subject of rights. As such, she prefigures certain critiques of what we now call negative liberalism. The line of descent from Astell to a positive version of liberalism cannot of course be made directly. The effort to do so, however speculatively, must be seen as a product of my own desire and not Astell's, for she would of course be appalled to be associated with secular liberalism. But the argument hinges, nonetheless, on the unexpected centrality of desire to Astell's *Serious Proposal*.

In the first installation of *A Serious Proposal to the Ladies*, Astell grounds her argument for a Protestant nunnery on reason: in particular, on the importance of reason to society and to spirituality, and on woman's reasonableness. She argues for the commonly held conception that Protestantism is the reasonable choice over mystical Catholicism and against the likewise commonly held notion that women are less reasonable than men. This allows her to be simultaneously both feminist and staunchly Anglican. Astell figures reason's chief opponent to be the desires of the body. Her philosophical view is rationalist, depending upon a mind–body separation and upon a veneration of reason and the mind over the body. As such, her argument for a Protestant cloister rests on transcending the material world as much as possible. A Christian life, according to Astell, "requires a clear understanding as well as regular affections, that both together may move the will to a direct choice of God."[5] Her monastery will allow women to withdraw themselves "as much as may be from Corporeal things, that pure Reason may be heard the better" (*SP II* 164). Astell famously and vehemently disagrees with Locke's empiricism, and argues that true reason transcends the body rather than depends upon it. Despite her explicit theological commitment Astell proposes an overtly secular institution. Although she denigrates material satisfactions in favor of philosophical and theological pursuits, Astell's arguments for a female community are secular and worldly, based on the "real interest" of the potential members but also on larger sociological grounds. Her convent will, she claims, "amend the present and improve the future age" (*SP I* 67–68, 73). Astell's *Proposal*, like most seventeenth- and eighteenth-century schemes for Protestant convents, promises the earthly benefit of female education.[6] Astell, as Protestants from all ends of the spectrum, imagines that humans have to live in this world and that secluding oneself from the world for religious purposes procures

---

*Century Studies* 23.4 (1990): 444–57, 457.

    5  Mary Astell, *A Serious Proposal to the Ladies, Parts I and II*, ed. Patricia Springborg (Toronto, 2002), 70. Hereafter cited parenthetically as *SP I* or *SP II*.

    6  For more on this point, see Bridget Hill, "A Refuge from Men: The Idea of the Protestant Nunnery," *Past and Present* 117 (1987): 107–30.

neither spiritual nor social benefits. Ironically, Astell's High Church Anglicanism seems inflected here with latitudinarianism, in that it emphasizes reason and implies that sacred goals are indistinguishable from secular ones, namely personal happiness and social stability.

While the first *Proposal* stresses reason and social benefits, in order to argue for female education, its sequel, published two years later in response to critics of the original treatise, makes its case more enigmatically, philosophically, and originally. In Ruth Perry's words, the sequel proposes a "formal set of rules for thinking," based on the philosophies of Descartes and Arnould.[7] In adapting these French models to her English female Protestant audience, Astell articulates a theory of desire that intervenes in the seventeenth-century debate over free will, which developed from the central theological problems of the day: How does one reconcile belief in God's omnipotence with the absence of sure evidence of God's will? And how does one conform to God's will in the absence of knowledge of it, or in the face of selfish desires for something different? These questions link problems of epistemology with dilemmas of theology, psychology, and ethics. Early Protestant reformers challenged the Catholic emphasis on free will and good works as well as the humanist theory of the unbounded human will. Luther, for example, argues that the human will, by itself, is in bondage to sin. In arguing for justification by faith alone, Luther claims that "without the grace of God, the will produces an act that is perverse and evil."[8] In its most radical forms, such as Antinomianism, Protestant theology's rejection of human free will leads to a rejection, at least in the eyes of its detractors, of any ethical code. The relative importance of—and the relationships among—reason, grace, faith, and morality form the foundation of most of the theological theory of the seventeenth century, with latitudinarians stressing the harmony of reason and morality, while the non-conformists continue to insist, to varying degrees, on the priority of grace over both reason and morality.[9]

The task of political theorists of the seventeenth century was to link philosophy of the mind with a political theory that could guarantee social stability. Theories of the will and desire were central to sorting out the contours of a new political system because these problems were central to debates about human morality and thus to theories of governance. Earlier in the century, the Cambridge Platonists along with other moderate Protestants argued that human beings, endowed with innate ideas and reason, have a natural tendency to desire the good, an argument that, at least superficially, circumvents the problems of tension between human will and God's will, and between morality and spirituality. This revival of the Pauline and Thomist concept of "laws written into the heart" at once challenges a number of contemporary doctrines: Hobbes's argument for the necessity of arbitrary and absolute power; radical Protestant claims that spirituality is virtually irrelevant to secular ethics; as well as the Catholic emphasis on the importance of freely chosen moral actions

---

7  Ruth Perry, *The Celebrated Mary Astell: An Early English Feminist* (Chicago, 1986), 83.

8  Cited in Dolora Wojciehowski, *Old Masters, New Subjects* (Stanford, 1995), 91.

9  See Isabel Rivers, *Reason Grace and Sentiment* (Cambridge, 1991) for a thorough treatment of the history of these debates.

as the route to salvation.[10] Although this view is, like Locke's political theories, a justification for natural law, it becomes a chief instigator for (and a central antagonist of) Locke's critique of innate ideas and his sensationalist epistemology.

In its original latitudinarian sense, the seventeenth-century version of "law written into the heart" emphasizes reason and is based on a "heart" synonymous with the mind. But as this doctrine develops, and as the heart comes to take on its modern connotation as the site of both moral and romantic feeling, a philosophical theory of love becomes crucial to resolving these debates over free will and epistemology.[11] That is, while latitudinarians emphasize reason, their descendants, who include both freethinkers as well as a number of High Church Anglicans, become more divided over the relative importance of the affections to morality. This is the debate into which Astell, following John Norris, enters. In *The Theory and Regulation of Love: a Moral Essay* (1688), Norris, an Anglican divine, links love of God with secular ethics. Norris asserts the "obvious" though neglected truth that "all Virtue and Vice" can be reduced to "the various Modifications of Love."[12] He explicitly links love of God with secular or "corporeal" love. Though the former is "simple desire" and the latter "wishing well to," nonetheless, for Norris, love of God and love of humans are both aspects of the "motion of the soul towards Good."[13] Norris declares that secular love is linked to spiritual love and that it is this connection that provides the moral foundation of society. Although this newly revised notion of "laws written in the heart" would lose out to empiricism as a mode of knowing, the idea that virtue inheres in secular, especially romantic love, would be the foundation for companionate marriage and the sentimental novel, and thus would be an important precursor to the secular ethics that emerge in the eighteenth century.[14]

Intrigued by Norris's arguments, Astell undertakes a correspondence with him on the question of God's love. In *Letters Concerning the Love of God*, Astell pushes Norris to consider that God may be equally the author of human pain and human pleasure, challenging him to integrate a response to Locke's sensationalist epistemology (and

---

10   Paul writes that people not tutored in Christianity might still be moral, since "the requirements of the Law are written on their hearts, their consciences also bearing witness, and their thoughts now accusing, now even defending them." Romans 2:15. For Thomas Aquinas's ideas on this issue, see J. Budziszewski, *Written on the Heart: The Case for Natural Law* (Downer's Grove, 1997), 51–94.

11   For interesting analyses of the historical relationship between the physical heart, whose circulatory functions were just being accepted, and the emotional heart, an important locus for the cult of sensibility, see Robert Erickson, *The Language of the Heart, 1650–1750* (Philadelphia, 1997) and Scott Manning Stevens, "Sacred Heart and Secular Brain," in *The Body in Parts: Fantasies of Corporeality in Early Modern Europe*, eds. David Hillman and Carla Mazzio (New York, 1997), 263–82.

12   John Norris, *The Theory and Regulation of Love: A Moral Essay* (London, 1688), from the preface "To the Reader."

13   Norris, *Theory and Regulation*, 9.

14   The classic scholarly accounts of these trends—for example, J.G.A. Pocock, *Virtue, Commerce and History: Essays on Political Thought and History, Chiefly in the Eighteenth Century* (Cambridge, 1985); Jürgen Habermas, *The Structural Transformation of the Public Sphere: An Inquiry into a Category of Bourgois Society*, trans. Thomas Burger (Boston, 1991); Lawrence Stone, *The Family, Sex and Marriage in England, 1500–1800* (London, 1977)—have all been subject to rigorous (and legitimate) critique based on rethinking the public/private distinction from historical, feminist, and Marxist (as well as other) viewpoints. For the purposes of this essay, however, I am accepting their general applicability.

the realities of a life of pain) within his Anglican theology. But it is in the second part of her *Serious Proposal* (along with *Some Reflections upon Marriage*) that Astell's most significant deviance from Norris occurs. Whereas Norris, as part of his ethical and political program, diminishes the distinction between secular and sacred objects of desire, Astell, for the rest of her career, insists upon the vast dissimilarity between them, especially for women. Portraying the human condition as torn between the desires of the body and the truths of the understanding, Astell makes a case for learning as a key to morality. While Norris's secularized "law of the heart" claims that people will naturally follow God's law, Astell, especially in the second part of the *Proposal*, demonstrates the difficulty that inheres in directing one's will, and one's love, toward God. The realms of sexual desire and procreation present the largest obstacles to these ethical and spiritual goals. In this critique of Norris, Astell participates in what Deborah Shuger has identified as a late-seventeenth-century trend in which eros and agape, or romantic and divine love, became irrevocably separated.[15] Astell effects this split, not as others (mainly poets working in secular modes) do—that is, by elevating romantic love to a spiritual good that is impeded by religious institutions—but rather by arguing that men are unworthy objects of desire and inadequate substitutions for God. Astell points to a conflict in the social order: the needs of society and the contemporary standards for female virtue inhibit the development of real social virtue in women by perverting their desires away from God and towards men. Astell is interested in a world in which all objects of desire presented to women are unsatisfying substitutes for God, and she argues that social ethics, as well as female happiness, will bear the burden of this social transformation. In other words, social ethics and female happiness both suffer from the worldly convention that women seek fulfillment of their desires through men, and will thus benefit equally from a transfer of that desire to the divine.

This argument of Astell's depends upon a theory of human nature that is neither deterministic nor quietist, two theories heretical to a state-sanctioned religion like the Church of England. For Astell, the keys to happiness and to spiritual fulfillment are a correct understanding of God's nature as benevolent and of human nature as reasonable but necessarily much more limited than God's. This is why "understanding" leads to a desire to do God's will and why doing God's will makes us happy. If we misunderstand either our nature or God's, our "inclinations take a wrong bias" (*SP II* 210). These deviations from God's will happen, according to Astell, for two reasons: the social customs that prevent people (especially women) from thinking for themselves, and the structure of human nature and development, in which the will asserts itself before the understanding has a chance to develop. "We Will," according to Astell, "e're we are capable of examining the Reasons of our Choice" (*SP II* 206).

In Astell's philosophy, if the "understanding" is not developed through education (as it is not in seventeenth-century women), then both spiritual destiny and happiness are thwarted. Because women are encouraged to make themselves materially

---

15 Deborah Kuller Shuger, *The Renaissance Bible: Scholarship, Sacrifice and Subjectivity* (Berkeley, 1994), 179–82.

attractive to men, and because society encourages them to keep their desires focused on men and material objects and their energies focused on reproduction, women in particular, Astell argues, are spiritually imperiled by the priorities of the emergent secular society's priorities. Although Astell adamantly maintains the equality and fundamental similarity of men and women, in thinking about the lack of parity in their social experiences—the marriage contract in particular—Astell theorizes the relationship between desire and spirituality in a way that predicts problems for a society organized to thwart the development of true female happiness. Such happiness is obviated both by directing female desire to mortal objects and by discouraging the development of women's "understanding" that would correct that desire. Astell's feminist perspective—that is, her interest in theorizing the problem of desire from a vantage point that accounts for the material conditions of women—allows her to elaborate a philosophy of mind that neither naively believes in the essential harmony between individual desire, God's will, and political stability nor that cynically insists upon their inherent antagonism.

In her challenges in the second part of the *Proposal* to the ideas that morality is innate and that sacred and domestic happiness are linked, Astell moves away from emergent Church of England orthodoxy. In this, she shares something with Locke, who is otherwise one of the principal antagonists of her ideas. Locke's theories about personality and morality change over the course of his revisions of the *Essay Concerning Human Understanding*. In the first edition (1690), Locke accepts the notion that humans have a general tendency to desire the good. Given freedom of action (as opposed to freedom of will), humans will make choices towards future good. For Locke, this future good is figured as both spiritual and political. God, he argues, made an "inseparable connection" between "*Virtue* and Public Happiness" and made "the Practice thereof, necessary to the preservation of Society, and visibly *beneficial* to all."[16] In the first edition of the *Essay*, the will tends naturally (though not innately) towards moral, spiritual, and social good. The second edition of the *Essay* (1695) shifts emphasis from the "ethical" will, in Jonathan Kramnick's words, to the "morally neutral concept of desire."[17] In this revision, Locke relocates morality from the will to the understanding: instead of an essentially good individual who sometimes errs, the subject's unavoidable defects of desire need to be compensated by reason. Locke argues that an agent has the "Power to suspend his determination"; that is, humans can abstain from immediate pleasures in order to regulate their conduct to God's law.[18] The moral sense is thus mainly a negative force: the power to suspend and repress desires. As such, Locke's nascent theory of human psychology challenges the innate morality of the "law written into the heart" (as espoused by the Cambridge Platonists), as well as the radical depravity of the reformed will and the pessimistic Hobbesian view that people are doomed to be ruled by an amoral and mortal power. The revised *Essay* depicts a conflict between human desires and

16  John Locke, *An Essay Concerning Human Understanding*, ed. Peter Nidditch (Oxford, 1975), 69.

17  Jonathan Brody Kramnick, "Locke's Desire," *YJC* 12.2 (1999): 189–208, 197. For similar readings of Locke's revisions, see Ian Harris, *The Mind of John Locke* (Cambridge, 1994) and John Sitter, *Arguments of Augustan Wit* (Cambridge, 1991).

18  Locke, *Essay*, 271.

human will that will become the key to modern notions of subjectivity. The final version of the *Essay* does not, however, retreat from the position that "*Virtue* and Publick Happiness" are insuperably linked; rather, it posits the central conflict on the level of the individual, between will and desire, and not between individual agents and social or political organizations.

The second part of Astell's *Serious Proposal* responds directly to Locke's theories of the will and desire. Astell's philosophy of the will follows Locke's developing theory—and contrasts with Norris's—by making the understanding, and especially the understanding of the self, a key to morality. Astell, like Locke, imagines a psychological subject who must "procure sufficient Acquaintance" with itself, indeed even to "suspect" itself sometimes, in order to make moral decisions (*SP II* 216, 186). "Nothing less than a continual Watch" will do, according to Astell, and the subject must be willing to "Restrain" passions as needed (*SP II* 216). One difference between Locke's and Astell's thought is that Astell believes that reason needs nurturing from within the mind itself: for her, seclusion rather than the Lockean reliance on experience will promote reasoned morality. But the most significant difference between Astell and Locke is that the former, especially in the second part of the *Proposal*, retains a sense of the significance of both desire and individual (as opposed to "publick") happiness to moral goodness. For Locke, desire must be checked in order for the moral faculty of understanding to take over, but for Astell, desire is a critical component, in fact the end point of reason; indeed desire is the key to spirituality.

In asking her female audience "Can you be in love with servitude and folly?," Astell begins the second part of her *Proposal* with a decided emphasis on desire (*SP II* 120). In admonishing her audience, "if you *Wish*, Why shou'd you not *Endeavor*?," Astell encourages women to yolk their will to their desire, which she imagines will lead them to follow her plan (*SP II* 120). In language that would provide later critics ammunition to charge her with enthusiasm, Astell diminishes the role of reason by suggesting that it is, though crucial, merely a tool for passionate devotion to God. Reason allows us to "draw aside the clouds" that "hide the most adorable face of GOD from us" so we can "lose our selves with Wonder, Love and Pleasure!" Such pleasures are "too ineffable to be named, too Charming, too Delightful not to be eternally desir'd" (*SP II* 212). Astell explicitly contrasts this love of the divine with the demands of corporeal objects of desire, which keep us "sunk into sense, and buried alive in a crowd of Material beings"—preventing, rather than facilitating, spiritual development (*SP II* 212). According to Astell, human desire and "adoration" should turn towards God, not things of this world. We do not have "narrow groveling hearts" capable of only base objects of desire but rather are "all on Fire"; thus, we do not need to enervate our desire but rather to direct it to the correct object (*SP II* 133). Consequently, despite Astell's commitments to reason (especially in the first part of the *Proposal*) and to the importance of the understanding to morality, she insists that it is not our "sentiments" that must be censured, but rather our understandings, which "willfully and unreasonably" allow us to adhere to material objects of desire (*SP II* 137). For Astell, the function of reason is to direct passion (towards God) rather than to suppress it. The second part of her proposal, dedicated to the happiness of its adherents, instructs women to replace the "Pleasures" of their "Animal Nature" with the superior and "unspeakably delightful" pleasure of aligning their desires with God's will (*SP II* 144).[19]

Thus, while the revisions of Locke's essay evoke an increasingly depraved desire, Astell's *Proposal* develops in the opposite direction. In positing depravity of desire as a problem of understanding that can be rectified—if we understand our divine possibility, we will desire it—Astell imagines desire as something to be cultivated, rather than repressed. Whereas Locke's *Essay* invites its readers to study their own minds, Astell's *Proposal* encourages them to peruse the "springs and windings" of their "Hearts" (*SP II* 216). Further, where Locke asks us to use our will to suspend our desires so that we may act as reasonable moral agents, Astell implores us to suspend our "assent" and to train the understanding so that love of God, and of truth, can take over (*SP I* 110–17). While the first part of her proposal claims social benefits, in her response to her critics (and to Locke) in the second part, Astell focuses instead on the problem of female *pleasure*. In the latter tract, she makes her case to women by arguing that in aligning their wills and their desires, they may be happy, virtuous, and spiritually purified. Moreover, Astell argues for the radical autonomy of the mind from material and social concerns, advocating the imperative to perfect reason through education so that individual happiness—and its corollary in God's law—may prevail. This may be a rhetorical strategy, aimed at convincing her original audience rather than her critics, but in the process Astell significantly revises Anglican, and Lockean, philosophy.

Astell's rhetorical strategy reinforces her critique of Locke's theories. For example, between Locke's first and second version of the *Essay*, the word "uneasiness" creeps in to assume a crucial role in articulating his nascent theory of subjectivity. Locke aligns uneasiness with the very fabric of desire, arguing that "uneasiness alone determines the will" because "it alone is present." Locke also argues that uneasiness— the experience of absence—rather than delight, is inevitably the strongest human motivation.[20] Astell suggests something much different, by arguing that the full presence of happiness can be experienced and is indeed much more powerful than "unease." She also worries (perhaps rhetorically), that her proposal will give the ladies "unease." This suggests, as Astell admits, that her proposal is designed to act as much on the desirous part of the subject as on the reasoning faculties she so glorifies. But she also insists that it is a moral good to remove ourselves "as far as we can" from objects that create "unease" (*SP II* 206). For Astell, unease, indeed even unhappiness, is the motor of human perfection and happiness; unease and desire are not, as in Locke's account, demons haunting human morality, nor are they symptoms of the fall.

---

19 Astell's argument in the second part is not wholly new, for she talks about the love of God in the first part also. It is rather a matter of emphasis: in the first she emphasizes reason and in the second the love of God.

20 Locke, *Essay*, 254, 230. In this, Locke is not far from Astell's earlier complaints about the lack of satisfaction in romantic relationships. But it is Locke who expands this point, to argue that humans find "imperfection, dissatisfaction, and want of complete happiness" in all earthly experience; for Locke, this is God's design, so that we seek full enjoyment in him "*at whose right hand are pleasures for evermore*" (130).

Astell also rhetorically invokes Locke's discussion of labor from the *Second Treatise of Government* (1689), transforming Locke's proprietary language of masculine labor into a feminine language of rational delight.[21] In Locke's text, he famously identifies labor as the foundation of both private property and personal identity. For Locke, the pursuit of property through labor is the foundation of society because it provides the motive for cooperation under government. Astell riffs on this idea rhetorically, by repeatedly referring to the kind of rationalization that she calls for as "labour" and "industry." In this way, she posits rational thought as a mode of establishing her own version of personal identity. She describes the process of achieving this, in the closing sentence of her *Proposal*, as "Labour of Love," and the goal of her proposal is to make this kind of labor—and love—available to women as well as to men (*SP II* 236). Where Locke proposes that labor is the key to property, Astell re-imagines such labor as both intellectual and amorous. She makes truth a kind of property that is achieved by the "Labor and Cost" that "inhances the value of everything" and whose teleology is human happiness (*SP II* 140). Astell's admonition—"If you *Wish*, why should you not *Endeavor*"—is not merely an argument for linking desire to the will, it is also a re-conceptualization of labor, or "endeavor," as properly belonging to the realms of happiness and of rationality rather than to a personal identity based upon property rights (*SP II* 132). If a marker of modernity is a vexed relationship between identity and happiness, exhibited in anxiety about labor versus desire, Astell, in these rhetorical invocations of Locke's vocabulary, offers an insight into another possible model of subjectivity.

In terms of the alienation that all modern theories of subjectivity posit, Hobbes famously splits conscience and action and Locke divides desire and will. Astell of course maintains the Cartesian mind and body split, but she does not imagine the mind and body to be at odds; in fact she insists that the body carry out the intellectual and moral imperatives shaped in the mind (including desire). Her rhetorical questions—"If you *approve*, Why do you not follow? And if you *Wish* why shou'd you not *Endeavor*?"—show in microcosm how Astell moves from an idea of morality that resides in reason and depends upon sanctioned (or customary) actions to one that is based in desire and is measured by acts of the will that may very well resist customary morals (*SP II* 120). "Approving," an act of the understanding, is linked via parallel grammatical structure to the "wishing" of her desirous subject. "Following" becomes, in Astell's deft translation of a moral imperative, "endeavoring." Although part of Astell's conservatism is her emphasis on the immaterial Christian world of the hereafter, *A Serious Proposal* shows how far from a passive acceptance of the material world Astell envisions for the moral subject. Her subject is neither a passive acceptor of social custom nor a spirit who transcends it by relying on grace. Astell's implication that "prudence," which she defines as being "all of a piece," provides the foundation for morality is not a naive belief that a coherent subject is an easy end or an inherent fact. Nor is it merely a reiteration of High Church notions of authenticity, but rather it emerges from her theorization of *how* the subject is divided and thus how it may be *reconciled* (*SP II* 170).

---

21   John Locke, *Two Treatises on Government*, ed. Peter Laslett (Cambridge, 1967).

For Astell, it is social custom, the "Opinions and Practices of the World," that "very fallacious," poses obstacles to successful development of human subjectivity and thus human morality and human happiness (*SP II* 170). The "frequent repetition" of "unreasonable Choices" makes immoral ideas "Customary" (*SP II* 206). But nothing, according to Astell, can make such customary ideas reasonable or allow them to lay claim to the authentic desire of reasonable human beings. In this, Astell anticipates, not the psychological subject in need of repression that Locke may be seen as predicting, but rather the subject hindered (but not crippled) by false consciousness, who is able to resist such colonization of the mind via education. Astell forwards an argument about the moral imperative of action against "custom," and, in so doing, imagines a subject with much more agency (in the personal if not political realm) than Locke's conflicted and repressive model. Locke may be the champion of liberal, inalienable rights, but Astell's philosophy of mind prioritizes individual development and the power of rational autonomy much more strongly than does that of Locke.

It is true, as William Kolbrener argues, that Astell's resistance to the model of rights that Locke (as well as proponents of latitudinarian orthodoxy) propounded can be viewed as nostalgia for authenticity as it was conceived by the Stuarts.[22] Astell's conservatism famously puts her theories out of the reach of contemporary politics: for a Jacobite/Tory, passive obedience to the legitimate Stuart king is positively contrasted with the self-serving and scheming machinations necessary for what we consider modern politics. Astell is certainly not advocating modern politics. But she does articulate a theory of morality that has social implications. Though she advocates passionate devotion to God, she cautions against its excess. She suggests that when one's rationality, passions, and "habits" are properly developed, one will naturally exercise one's will in "acts" towards our "Fellow Creatures" that imitate "God's beneficence" (*SP II* 224–25). Although pleasing God is primary, Astell doesn't imagine that such an endeavor can be accomplished outside of social action. Women who wish to follow her plan must be willing to be "Laugh'd at for Fools" when they resist the "evil Customs of the Age" (*SP II* 226). She does aver that she does not wish to challenge the "management" of the world, and she admits that she has no idea how to correct "Old and inveterate" minds. Her proposal nonetheless seeks to persuade women to think for themselves and to resist the diminution of their desires that tying them to secular objects entails (*SP II* 229). An "Active Life" for Astell consists of both "*Being in the World*" and "*doing much Good in it*," but it does not require the martyrdom of individual, especially female, happiness (*SP II* 232). In fact, it depends upon just the opposite.

In positing the subject who develops and who necessarily challenges social orthodoxy (in the realm of ideas and personal relations if not politics), Astell prefigures a version of the liberal subject that differs quite a bit from Locke's and that in fact predicts a key aspect of debates about liberalism that develop over the nineteenth and twentieth centuries. Her vision of rational autonomy and voluntary

---

[22] William Kolbrener, "Gendering the Modern: Mary Astell's Feminist Historiography," *The Eighteenth Century: Theory and Interpretation* 44 (2004): 1–24, 19.

agency anticipates the theory of positive liberalism that is hinted at by Jean-Jacques Rousseau, who argues that one is free when one acts according to one's true will.[23] Astell's insistence on individual development as the foundation of moral and social good, as opposed to Locke's emphasis on the correction of moral errors via the will's subjection of desire, puts her in the camp of perfectionism, a theory of morality that assumes that human development—not civil rights—is the highest goal of liberal society. Astell, of course, advocates individual development in the name of God's will and not social justice, but nonetheless she makes a persuasive case for the moral imperative of the rational *and* passionate development of an autonomous mind. The same Mary Astell who is so commonly, and rightly so in many regards, held to be the conservative, admonishes her audience to "live well," imagining that their "Natural Liberty" will lead them toward the good life via "perfect[ing]" themselves "as much as may be" (*SP II* 201). The good life is, for Astell, the traditional Tory Anglicanism in that it imagines that social, individual, and spiritual good are linked, but for the Astell of the second part of the *Proposal*, social good happens only at the level of individual desire, reason, and happiness. In positing the "good in general" as a theological and decidedly *not* political end, Astell puts forward a version of Anglicanism critiques latitudinarian orthodoxy as well as its vexed dependence on a repressive (Lockean) model of desire. The subject that emerges from Astell's mediation of Locke and Norris is not based on the claim that a "law of the heart" will regulate social life, and it does not situate the drama of ethical conflict within the subject. Instead, Astell locates conflict between subjects and the social spaces in which unreflective and unrestrained self-interest will inevitably exclude some from access to the social privileges that others enjoy. Those privileges, especially the social opportunity to implement a desire not subject to arbitrary repression as well as to obtain the education that can correct defects of understanding are, according to Astell, the things that allow for the development of authentic desire and happiness.

---

23  There are of course vast differences between these thinkers that I cannot develop here. For example, for Rousseau the true will of the individual is figured as the general will, while for Astell it accords with God's will and not with any secular version of "general will." Further, Rousseau rejects the notion that progress comes from reason, whereas Astell, even as she emphasizes the heart, does not. My argument, however, is that Astell, like Rousseau, argues against the external imposition of moral ideas, and for the importance of individual development as the keys to both happiness and virtue (Jean-Jacques Rousseau, *Emile*, trans. Barbara Foxly [London, 1986], especially pages 329–60). The famous discussion of the difference between negative and positive liberalism is in Isaiah Berlin's *Two Concepts of Liberty* (Oxford, 1958).

Chapter VII

# Religious Nonconformity and the Problem of Dissent in the Works of Aphra Behn and Mary Astell

Melinda Zook

Comparing Aphra Behn (1640?–89) and Mary Astell (1666–1731) may seem like an odd enterprise.[1] The genres that these two women practiced and the manner in which they led their lives were indeed disparate. Behn drank life deeply. She partook in and celebrated worldly living, including rakish men and cross-dressing women. She wrote about youth, beauty, and sexual adventure. Astell lived a far more reclusive, woman-centered existence. She placed the highest value not in seeking "only the wisdom of this World," but in striving toward the perfection of the next.[2] Behn used her pen to entertain and earn herself a living, mastering numerous literary styles along the way. Astell sought to enlighten and persuade through her pamphlets on education, religion, and marriage, and to pulverize the political opposition through her virulent polemics.

Yet despite all the vast differences between Aphra Behn and Mary Astell, numerous scholars have time and again linked their names, labeling them both early feminists and ardent Tories.[3] They have become the prototype "Tory feminists." Feminist writers have long been interested in Behn and Astell, especially as maverick women writers who sometimes, although not always, challenged the customs that subordinated women. Investigations into the sexual politics of these two women have been extraordinarily illuminating. Still, the literary output of both women indicates that they were more preoccupied with the bitter partisan politics and religious crises of their age than they were by the treatment of women.[4] As scholars,

---

1 There is no evidence to suggest that these two women ever met. Patricia Springborg believes that Behn "made fun" of Astell, presumably in one of her plays. But this is unlikely. Behn did satirize the stereotypical "learned lady," such as in the case of Lady Knowall in *Sir Patient Fancy* (1678), but there is certainly no reason to believe that Behn had Astell in mind. Behn died in 1689 and Astell did not start publishing until 1694. Springborg, ed., *Astell: Political Writings* (Cambridge, 1996), xv.

2 [Mary Astell,] *Moderation Truly Stated* (London, 1704), 27. Hereafter cited parenthetically as *MTS*.

3 For example, they are linked as feminists in Hilda L. Smith, *Reason's Disciples: Seventeenth-Century English Feminists* (Urbana, 1982), 3; and in Joan K. Kinnaird, "Mary Astell and the Conservative Contribution to English Feminism," *Journal of British Studies* 19.1 (1979): 59, 19n. They are linked as Tories in Bridget Hill, *The First English Feminist: Reflections upon Marriage and other Writings by Mary Astell* (New York, 1986), 53; and in Rachel Weil, *Political Passions: Gender, the Family and Political Argument in England, 1689–1714* (Manchester, 1999).

4 Mary Astell wrote eight works. If we count *Some Reflections on Marriage* as both feminist and

then, we need to read their feminist impulses within the political contexts that their writings consistently sought to defend. For both Behn and Astell, the preservation of the traditional order against its enemies was more pressing than attacking the treatment of women. Their Toryism required a defense of custom. Certainly, they understood that English custom was not always kind to women, but their larger concerns dedicated them to a defense of the political and social structures of English society before the Enlightenment.

This being the case, their Tory politics are central to any understanding of their work. Yet beyond the general label, "Tory women writers," we often find little analysis of the precise kind of Toryism Behn and Astell espoused and defended.[5] In part, this is a result of the understudied nature of Tory ideology. Scholars of political thought are well aware of the "varieties of Whiggism"[6] during the Restoration, but they are far less likely to parse the different strands of Toryism, particularly for the 1680s and 1690s.[7] Further, the political dimensions of women writers in the seventeenth and early eighteenth centuries have also received insufficient attention or have been lost in special collections devoted solely to women. Both Behn and Astell contributed to the political culture of the Restoration, but rarely do we find their work treated in the scholarship devoted to the Exclusion Crisis (1678–83), or to the approach of the Revolution of 1688/89 (for Behn), or to the crisis in the Church during the 1690s and early 1700s (for Astell).[8]

The political dimensions of the works of Aphra Behn and Mary Astell not only beg for further analysis, but in my view, they beg for comparison. Here we have the two most prominent women writers of the Restoration. Both lived and wrote during times of heated political and religious debate which they keenly observed and recorded, and to which they contributed. Both evoked memories of the Civil Wars, the martyrdom of Charles I, and the Interregnum, comparing those times of chaos and disorder (the 1640s and 1650s) to their contemporary world. And both believed that the cause of England's discontent was the enemy within. Those who fomented crisis and acrimony were not agents for Louis XIV or popish incendiaries, but what

---

as deeply concerned with current politics, then five of her tracts are keenly political in nature while only three are overtly feminist. Aphra Behn's plays, particularly in the prologues, certainly contain feminist sentiments. But her plays, poems, and prose works are far more filled with satirical references and portraits of Whigs and Dissenters and celebrations of royalism than they are critiques of the treatment of women.

5   Weil, *Political Passions*, 10.

6   J.G.A. Pocock, "The Varieties of Whiggism from Exclusion to the Revolution," in *Virtue, Commerce and History: Essays on Political Thought and History* (Cambridge, 1985).

7   For Tory political thought in the 1680s, see Tim Harris, "Tories and the Rule of Law in the Reign of Charles II," *The Seventeenth Century* 8.1 (1993): 9–27; for the post-Revolution era, the best analyses of Tory ideology are Mark Goldie, "Tory Political Thought, 1689–1714" (PhD diss., University of Cambridge, 1978) and Linda Colley, *In Defense of Oligarchy* (Cambridge, 1982).

8   For example, neither Tim Harris, *London Crowds in the Reign of Charles II* (Cambridge, 1987) nor Mark Knights, *Politics and Opinion in Crisis, 1678–81* (Cambridge, 1994) mention Behn in their excellent studies of the politics of the Exclusion era. There is no mention of Astell in Geoffrey Holmes, *British Politics in the Age of Anne* (London, 1967); W.A. Speck, *The Birth of Britain: A New Nation, 1700–1710* (Oxford, 1994); or even, G.V. Bennett, *The Tory Crisis in Church and State, 1688–1730* (Oxford, 1975), which is devoted to the life of Francis Atterbury, Bishop of Rochester, someone with whom Astell associated.

Astell called "self-ended politicians," who stirred up the ignorant mob with the canting discourse of Protestant nonconformity and Whiggery. In short, the problem was dissent, which neither Behn nor Astell saw as a matter of conscience, but rather as a veil for greed, lust, and self-interest.

Anglican loyalists in the late seventeenth and early eighteenth centuries commonly envisioned Dissent as a combination of Protestant nonconformity and Whig politics. Neither Behn nor Astell truly distinguished between them. After all, the so-called "Protestant Cause" was so very formidable in the eyes of Tories and High Anglicans precisely because of its combination of Whig practical politics, liberal political philosophies, and Protestant nonconformity. Whether they were called "the *Presbyterians* or *Whiggs*," according to Astell, "they are all of the same Original, they act upon the same Principles and Motives, and tend to the same End."[9] Sectarians were seen by loyalists as a particularly destabilizing force within English society. Their emphasis on liberty of conscience and individual inspiration, and the prominence of active women within their societies, frightened High Anglicans. Furthermore, nonconformist Protestants, ranging from those that had their origins in the heady days of the New Model Army such as the Baptists and Quakers, to the more moderate Presbyterians and Congregationalists, claimed numerous adherents among the mercantile, middling, and lower classes. The empowerment of merchants, tradesmen, and yeoman farmers meant nothing less than the world turned upside down, according to their detractors.

Behn's and Astell's vision of dissent had much in common with that of other Tories. They propagated the same Tory slogans, whether it was "playing the old game [of 41] over again" for Behn or "the Church in danger" for Astell. Astell's high flying polemics of 1704, as her biographer Ruth Perry points out, were often "indistinguishable from her [Tory] male contemporaries."[10] Behn's satiric depiction of Whigs and Dissenters in her plays and poetry were similar to those of John Dryden, Nathaniel Lee, and other Tory playwrights. Like other Tories, they both manipulated the history of the mid-century crisis, haranguing their audience with frightening images of fratricide and social anarchy (all, of course, depicted as the consequences of regicide). Where these two Tory advocates differed from their fellow (male) travelers is what makes a comparative analysis of their work instructive.

For both Behn and Astell, Protestant dissent represented a direct threat to the social and sexual order as well as to the church and state. They posited a gendered view of dissent, condemning what they saw as the sexual double standards, hypocrisy, and dissimulation of Protestant nonconformity. Dissenters were hypocrites who cried up liberty and conscience in the public sphere while acting as autocrats in the domestic arena. Above all, the sectarians' dissembling, both in public and in private, corrupted the nation and pushed the traditional order to the brink of collapse. Their religious cant was corrosive. It might seem harmless to some moderate conformists, low churchmen and latitudinarians, who allowed it to grow and infiltrate the polity. It might even seem liberating to women, artisans, and tradesmen. But, ultimately, it was

---

9  [Mary Astell,] *Impartial Enquiry into the Causes of the Civil War* (1704), in *Astell: Political Writings*, ed. Springborg, 185. Hereafter cited parenthetically as *IE*.

10  Ruth Perry, *The Celebrated Mary Astell: An Early English Feminist* (Chicago, 1986), 189.

simply a tool used by deceitful men, grasping for power, and bent on the destruction of the old order. Tory politics and culture, on the other hand, were transparent. The rules of political, social, and sexual behavior were not hidden in a coded language but plainly visible in the common currency of English traditions.

Aphra Behn and Mary Astell may have expressed themselves in wholly different literary genres, but their Tory politics similarly revolved around the image of the hypocritical, ambitious, dissembling, canting, and often lustful Dissenters. They were "that Race, whence *England's* Woes proceed" and "where all our Mischiefs breed," according to Behn.[11] "They Bribe, they Threaten, they Solicit, they Fawn, they Dissemble, they Lye, they break through all the Duties of Society, violate all the Laws of GOD and Man," according to Astell (*IE* 139). Both women were equally confident of this portrait of dissent, and they did not spare their words. "If the picture of a Hypocrite, a Schismack, a Factious Person, etc, offends some sort of People," wrote a vehement Astell, "let them not reproach the painter, but themselves, for the resemblance" (*MTS* 81).

In the early 1680s, Aphra Behn lived in a metropolis that seemed very much on the verge of revolution: the atmosphere was deeply politicized, contentious, rancorous, and thick with a sense of apprehension. The series of political and religious crises that began with the Popish Plot in 1678 and continued through the controversy over the royal succession, commonly known today as the Exclusion Crisis, produced a highly volatile political culture.[12] "The devil take this cursed plotting Age," as Behn quipped in 1679, "'T has ruin'd all our Plots upon the Stage."[13] Dutch fops and forced marriages were no longer to the taste of fashionable London in the first age of party. Audiences craved topical plays, filled with allusions to contemporary politics and personalities. London's playhouses, as much as the bookshops and coffee houses, became sites of partisan politics. Behn did not shy away from this new "Disease o'th' Age," as she called it.[14] She certainly knew a market when she saw it, and like John Dryden, Thomas Shadwell, and other dramatists of the Exclusion Crisis, Behn's plays became markedly partisan from 1678 to 1682. The most keenly political were *Sir Patient Fancy* (1678); *The Roundheads* (1681); and *The City Heiress* (1682), all Tory plays that mocked the opposition in the form of the old, canting, rabble-rousing Dissenter, and celebrated royalism in the form of the young, handsome, womanizing Cavalier.

After 1682, when the popularity of the stage began to decline, Behn turned to other literary genres to make her living, including translation, fiction, and poetry. Her novels and short stories continued to promote her royalism and to decry the opposition. Between 1685 and 1689, Behn became a strident champion of James II,

11  Aphra Behn, *On a CONVENTICLE* (1692), in Janet Todd, *The Works of Aphra Behn* (Columbus, 1992), 1:355.

12  On the Exclusion Crisis, see Mark Knights, *Politics and Opinion*; Gary De Krey, "The London Whigs and the Exclusion Crisis Reconsidered," in *The First Modern Society: Essays in English History in Honor of Lawerence Stone*, eds. A.L. Beier, D. Cannadine, and J.M. Rosenheim, (Cambridge, 1989), 457–82.

13  Aphra Behn, *The Feign'd Curtizans* (1679) in Todd, *Works*, 6:89.

14  Aphra Behn, *The Second Part of the Rover* (1681) in Todd, *Works*, 2.6:231.

even as the Catholic King's Romanizing policies made many of his Anglican and Tory supporters increasing queasy. Behn also established herself, through her many panegyrics to James and his Queen, Mary of Modena, as a leading poet on affairs of state, so much so that in the spring of 1689, following the ascension of William III and Mary II, Behn was asked by the leading Williamite propagandist, Reverend Gilbert Burnet (later Bishop of Salisbury), to provide the new king with celebratory verses. She kindly refused. My "Loyalty," she wrote in honest reply, "Commands with Pious Force."[15] Aphra Behn died a few weeks later, an unreformed Tory, a new-made Jacobite.

In the 1690s and early 1700s, Mary Astell lived in a political climate no less divided than that of Aphra Behn. The Glorious Revolution had done nothing to stifle the rage of party which continued to dominate London's political culture. The Williamite Whigs of the 1690s and moderate Tories of Queen Anne's administration of the early 1700s still maintained that the kingdom's foremost enemy was Catholic France. But zealous Tories and high-flying Anglicans, including Astell, were no more convinced than Behn had been by Whigs' cries of "popery and slavery" during the 1680s. For Tories like Astell, the real antagonists who had divided and disrupted English society since the time of the Civil Wars were Protestant Dissenters. "'Tho names of contempt have been often changed on either side," she wrote in 1704, "as Cavalier and Roundhead, Royalist and Rebels, Malignants and Phanaticks, Torys and Whigs, yet the Division has always been barely the Church and the Dissenter, and there it continues to this Day."[16]

While nonconforming Protestants—Presbyterians, Independents, Baptists, and Quakers—continued to constitute only a small minority of the English population, they had earned the "Liberty of Worshipping God to our Consciences," as Daniel Defoe put it, with the passage of the Act of Toleration (1689).[17] Although the Corporation and Test Acts continued to apply to Dissenters, many qualified for office by "occasionally" taking communion in the Established Church. For Dissenters, the practice of occasional conformity allowed them access to political office and influence. This was particularly important at the local level where they were often able to promote the election of Whig MPs.[18] But for the High Church party, occasional conformity was simply another means by which their influence at Westminster and Whitehall was eroded and Whigs and Dissenters gained further power and prominence. The Revolution of 1688/89 had also divided the church itself. To accept the revolution was to accept either the practice of popular resistance and nullify the principle of a divinely-ordained succession, or to accept "the pious fiction of an abdication by James II."[19] Some four hundred inferior clergy and seven

---

15  Aphra Behn, "A PINDARIC POEM TO THE Reverend Doctor Burnet ON THE Honour he did me of Enquiring after me and my MUSE" (1689), in Todd, *Works*, 1:309.

16  [Mary Astell,] *A Fair Way with Dissenters and Their Patrons* (1704), in *Astell: Political Writings*, ed. Springborg, 109. Hereafter cited parenthetically as *FW*.

17  Daniel Defoe, *More short-WAYS with the DISSENTERS* (1704), 14.

18  On the issue of occasional conformity, see John Flaningham, "The Occasional Conformity Controversy: Ideology and Party Politics, 1697–1711," *Journal of British Studies* 17.3 (1977): 38–62; George Every, *The High Church Party, 1688–1718* (London, 1956), 108–12.

19  Norman Sykes, *Church and State in England in the XVIIIth Century* (Hamden, 1962), 29.

bishops, including Mary Astell's first patron, Archbishop William Sancroft, simply could not do so. They refused to take the Oath of Allegiance to the new regime and thus were deprived of their benefices.[20] The mere presence of the nonjurors was a painful reminder to the church of the moral costs and compromises it had made in 1689 in order to secure a Protestant succession. Anglicans were further frightened by events in Scotland in the 1690s where Presbyterians had abolished episcopacy and Episcopal incumbents and professors were "outed and ill-us'd," in the words of Astell (*FW* 102).

These events together, and not the controversy over occasional conformity alone, resulted in what Geoffrey Holmes has aptly called the "tortured state of the Established Church after the Settlement."[21] During William III's regime, there was little hope among High Anglicans of turning the tide and buttressing the church's power.[22] But with the ascension of a true daughter of the Church of England, Queen Anne, in 1701, the aspirations of the High Church party were raised. It was within this context that Astell wrote her three most political tracts: *A Fair Way with Dissenters*; *Moderation Truly Stated*; and *An Impartial Enquiry into the Causes of the Civil Wars*—all published in 1704. Astell, by this point in her writing career, had already established herself as a serious philosopher of a Platonic bent, an advocate of women's education, and a critic of the customs governing courtship and marriage. Her work was admired by Dissenters like Daniel Defoe as well as by nonjurors such as George Hickes and Henry Dodwell.[23] For the most part, the tenets of her fervent Tory tracts of 1704 did not undermine those of her earlier feminist work. While *A Serious Proposal to the Ladies* (1694) challenged the customs that subordinated women and restricted their intellectual lives, it did not advocate the liberation of women in any worldly sense. Astell's later *Some Reflections upon Marriage* (1700) was similar. While a biting critique of the inequities and double standards women endured in marriage, *Reflections* strongly asserted that it was an indestructible, God-given union. She who marries "Elects a Monarch for Life."[24] Astell never suggested that the order of society should be altered or that women should do the business of men that is "without Doors."[25] Rather she argued that women like herself, women of the middling and gentle orders, should be better educated so that they may better attend to the "Grand Business that Women as well as Men have to do in this World"

---

[20]  Geoffrey Holmes, *The Making of a Great Power: 1660–1722* (London, 1993), 358.

[21]  Geoffrey Holmes, *Religion and Party in Late Stuart England* (London, 1975), 6.

[22]  William III favored a broad toleration, including Catholics. Jonathan I. Israel, "William III and Toleration," in *From Persecution to Toleration: The Glorious Revolution and Religion in England*, eds. Ole Peter Grell, Jonathan I. Israel, and Nicholas Tyacke (Oxford, 1991), 129–70.

[23]  In his *An Essay upon Projects* (1697) Defoe, like Astell, promoted the idea of women's colleges and in his preface speaks of his "very great Esteem" for the author of *A Serious Proposal*. Astell corresponded with both nonjuring Bishop and antiquary, George Hickes (1642–1715), and the scholar and theologian, Henry Dodwell (1641–1711), both of whom admired her tracts on occasional conformity. Perry, *Celebrated Mary Astell*, 100, 211–12.

[24]  *Some Reflections on Marriage* (1706), in Hill, *First English Feminist*, 38. Hereafter cited parenthetically as *SRM*.

[25]  [Mary Astell,] *The Christian Religion as Profess'd by a Daughter of the Church of England* (1705), excerpts in Hill, *First English Feminist*, 201.

which is "to prepare for the next."[26] Astell's high Anglicanism and divine-right Toryism may have limited her class-based feminism, but they did not contradict it.

Aphra Behn was an equally firm supporter of England's traditional order, and, like Astell, marked out Dissenters as the cause of the deterioration of the old bonds of society: loyalty to the monarchy and deference to birth. Although neither Behn nor Astell were truly members of an elite class, they placed a high value on the old social hierarchy. Behn "enjoyed the fringes of louche aristocratic society" and "internalized" their views and values, according to her biographer, Janet Todd.[27] Astell, the daughter of a provincial merchant, had "an over-developed sense of class." She defended hereditary privilege with a "fervor far more characteristic of a Tory gentleman living on his family's estate than a merchant's daughter in genteel poverty in London," according to Ruth Perry.[28] Both women were profoundly hostile to what they saw as a new world of opportunistic politicians, religious fanaticism, mercantile values, and the leveling politics of city merchants and tradesmen.

Both Behn and Astell were well aware of the discourses and tropes of dissenting politics and the hypnotic thrall they seemed to have over London's middling and lower classes. They were also highly critical of social disorder and inappropriate class behavior, so painfully reminiscent of the Civil Wars and Interregnum. London's merchants and tradesmen were guilty of over-reaching by asserting themselves into the domains of their betters in the 1680s and 1690s. But both Behn and Astell asserted that these "little Londoners" were egged on, manipulated by the "pretended saints," who employed the discourses of Whiggism and dissent to "corrupt the people and fire the Mob," as Astell put it (*FW* 111). These "demagogues who drove the people thus," industriously instilling "evil principles" into the heads of the rabble through their seditious cant, were to blame: for the chaos of the mid-century crisis; for the Exclusion Crisis of 1678–83; for the Revolution of 1688/89; and, for Astell, for the increasing threats to the Established Church in the 1690s and early 1700s (*MTS* xxxvii, xxxvii). The opening scene of Behn's comic satire on the last days of the Commonwealth, *The Roundheads*, poignantly depicts the power of Puritan-Dissenting/Whig discourse on London's lower ranks.[29] A group of soldiers confront two artisans, a joiner and a felt-maker, members of the "sanctify'd mobile." The artisans speak the language of the godly and reiterate the rhetoric of the Good Old Cause. After the joiner boldly declares himself a "free-born" subject, the soldiers tell him to get "ye home, and mind your Trade, and save the Hangman a Labour." To this the joiner responds, "I fear no Hang-man in Christendom; for Conscience and Publick Good, for Liberty and Property, I dare as far as any Man."[30] For Behn's audience the joiner's mishmash of Whig slogans was not only amusing, it firmly

26   [Mary Astell,] *A Serious Proposal to the Ladies, for the advancement of their True and Greatest Interest. In Two Parts* (London, 1697), *Part II*, 203.

27   Janet Todd, *The Secret Life of Aphra Behn* (London, 1996), 224.

28   Perry, *Celebrated Mary Astell*, 24, 32.

29   I discuss this scene in more detail in "Contextualizing Aphra Behn: Plays, Politics, and Party, 1679–1689," in *Women Writers and the Early Modern British Political Tradition*, ed. Hilda L. Smith (Cambridge, 1998), see 80–81.

30   Aphra Behn, *The Roundheads* (1681), in Todd, *Works*, 2:367. Hereafter cited parenthetically as *R*.

linked the Roundheads and Puritans of the 1650s with Whigs and Dissenters of the 1680s. The Whigs of the Exclusion Crisis were simply, "playing the old game over."[31] Behn's audience would have also known that the soldier's admonition to the joiner to "save the Hangman a Labour" was an allusion to the fate of Stephen College. The so-called "Protestant joiner" College had inappropriately meddled in the politics of the Exclusion era, authoring anti-court ditties and propagating Whig slogans until he was tried for seditious behavior at the Oxford assizes of August 1681 and hanged.[32]

Astell also made it clear that the "old game" was being played out again before her:

> They had their *Pryns*, *Burtons* and *Bastwicks*, as we have our *Tutchins*, *Stevens's* and *Defoe's*,[33] to corrupt the People and fire the Mob ... they had their Petitioners and Tumults as we have had our Petitioners and Legions[34] ... There being no Difference, that I can find between *those* times and *these*. (*FW* 111–12)

When politics becomes unhinged from reason and religion, and every man "even the Scum of them" is told they have a "Native Right to set up what they please," then even a little fellow like Stephen College "takes upon himself to be a leader, that is, seducer of the people" (*FW* 103; *MTS* iii). This seduction, according to Behn and Astell, was done by means of artifice and meaningless jargon. Both Behn and Astell took some delight in parodying and mimicking the tropes and idioms of their opponents. The rhetoric of the pretended saints and the Lockean discourse of the Whigs were easy targets.[35] Astell was particularly keen to dissect what she saw as the "double

---

31  Behn, *Rover*, 2:231.

32  Melinda Zook, *Radical Whigs and Conspiratorial Politics in Late Stuart England* (University Park, PA, 1999), 89–91.

33  William Prynne (1600–1699) was a lawyer and Puritan pamphleteer; Henry Burton (1578–1648) was an Independent minister and like John Bastwick (1595?–1654) a religious controversialist. All three were silenced by Archbishop William Laud in 1637; Laud had them tried, pilloried, ear-lopped, and imprisoned for life. The Long Parliament released them in 1640. John Tutchin (1661?–1707) was a Dissenter, a Monmouth rebel, and the principle author of the popular Whig martyrologies (published in 1689, 1693, 1705), among other Whig tracts; William Stephens (1650–1718) was an outspoken Whig divine and controversialist; Daniel Defoe (1660?–1731) was a Dissenter, a Williamite Whig, and author of *More short-WAYS with the DISSENTERS* (1704), to which Astell is responding in her *A Fair Way with Dissenters*.

34  By "legion" Astell is probably referring to Daniel Defoe's *Legion's Memorial* (London, 1701) which was written in defense of some citizens of Kent who petitioned Parliament to support King William's War. *Legion's Memorial* was published anonymously and concluded with the line, "*Our name is* LEGION, *and we are Many*." This line is found in Mark 5:30 wherein Jesus asks an unclean spirit, "What is your name?" The demon, trying to hide its name, answers, "My name is Legion and we are many." Defoe probably employed the line because he was trying to hide his authorship and assert a sense of collective strength. But as Defoe's authorship became known his detractors quickly associated him with the devil. Further, "Legion" was already commonly linked in Restoration literature with Satan, division, unrest, and strife. Tories like Behn connected Dissent with "Legion" as in her poem, "On a CONVENTICLE." Astell was thus able to use it to link Whig politics, Dissent, and demonology.

35  I am using the term "Lockean" as a short-hand for the political rhetoric, reiterated by Whigs, of early Enlightenment liberalism. Locke was hardly alone among Whig pamphleteers in his discussion of the origins of government, the rights of Englishmen, and the dissolution of government—all of which was common fare in the political debates prior to and following the Glorious Revolution. But Locke's *The Two*

meanings, equivocal expressions, Innuendo's and secret Hints and Insinuations" of Whig rhetoric (*IE* 139–40). In her *Impartial Enquiry into the Causes of the Civil War*, she juxtaposed the "plain and honest" speech of the High Church party with that of the Dissenters and their allies. The traumatic experience of the Civil Wars has

> taught us to decypher their Gibberish! We know too well, that in their Dialect *Popery* stands for the *Church of England*; the *Just* and *Legal Rights* of an English Monarch are call'd *Arbitrary Power*; by the *Privileges* of either *House*, they mean such exorbitant Power as may enable them to *Tyrannize* over their Fellow Subjects, nay over their very Sovereign; *Liberty of the People*, in their Language, signifies an unbounded Licentiousness .... (*IE* 195)

Astell expertly unpacks the political double-talk of the opposition, unmasking what she saw as the true, far more sinister meanings of Whiggism.

For both women, the truth was bare-faced, plain, without disguise. Behn's Cavaliers and Tories hate dissimulation, hypocrisy, and falseness. "Secrecy," declares the roving Cavalier, Willmore in *The Second Part of the Rover*, "is a damn'd ungrateful sin, Child, known only where Religion and Small Beer are current."[36] Behn's aristocratic heroes love mirth, wit, generosity, and maintain the old ethos of chivalry and unwavering loyalty to the monarchy. The Dissenters, on the other hand, practice "Dissimulation, Equivocation, and mental Reservation." They outdo even the Jesuits in their capacity to manipulate language (*R* 6:374; *IE* 187).[37]

Behn and Astell maintained that Dissenters practiced such deception to mask their true interests: self-empowerment. "Their Interest then, say I, is the main of their Religion," Astell states flatly in *A Fair Way with Dissenters*. What they call "tender Consciences and grievous Persecutions" is "in plain *English*, the keeping a Man out of a Place" (*FW* 93, 92). Dissenters only profess piety for appearance, "upon Occasion, and to Serve a turn; a seeming to act upon Religious Motives when they are only, or chiefly mov'd by Secular." They "never come to Church," (that is, practice occasional conformity), "but for a Place" (*MTS* 33, 34). Behn makes this point as well in her comedy, *The City Heiress* (1682), in which the old dissembling Whig, Sir Timothy Treat-all, states that he goes to an Anglican service on occasion to maintain his city offices: "I go to save my Bacon, as they say, once a Month, and that too, after the Porridge is serv'd up." Behn and Astell envisioned the established Church as homely and plain, preaching, as the Tory knight Sir Anthony Meriwill states, "wholesome Doctrine, that teaches Obedience to my King and Superiors." But at sectarian meeting houses they rail at "the Government ... quoting Scripture for Sedition, Mutiny and Rebellion."[38] In one of her most vivid and comic passages, in the preface to *Moderation Truly Stated*, Astell allegorizes dissent as "Liberty of Conscience" and the Church of England as "Religion":

---

*Treatises of Government* (1690) do cogently sum up basic radical Whig ideology. Further, Locke's work does seem to be one of Astell's main targets of attack, particularly in *Some Reflections on Marriage*.

36  Behn, *Rover*, 6:245. Small beer was less alcoholic and associated with Puritans who were concerned about drunkenness.

37  Astell also calls Dissenting cant "Jesuitical."

38  Aphra Behn, *The City Heiress*, in Todd, *Works*, 7:15.

Stand off now, and make Room for Religion and Liberty of Conscience, bring them hand in hand! Alas Sir! Religion is left at the Door; she can't crowd in, for Liberty of Conscience has got the Start of her. Liberty of Conscience is the Goodlier Person, uses a little Art, goes Finer, has better Address and more plausible Eloquence. Religion is a Plain, Honest Matron, and this as Times go is no great Recommendation. (*MTS* xli)

This passage is revealing not only in that it speaks to Astell's representation of the Church of England as "plain" and "honest," while Dissenters uses "art" and "eloquence," but also because it depicts religion and liberty of conscience as women. The one is an "honest matron," although that is "no great recommendation." The other, using a little art, seductively slips through the crowd.

The seductive nature of dissent, especially for women, was something both Behn and Astell found disturbing. Protestant nonconformity with its promotion of individual conscience and Whig slogans about rights and privileges certainly had broad appeal, not just to city merchants and tradesmen, but also to women. Many sectarian groups placed a heavy emphasis on the spiritual equality of men and women and were receptive to women preachers, missionaries, and prophets.[39] During the mid-century crisis and early Restoration, many dissenting women garnered considerable publicity through their prophesying, their spectacle stunts, such as going into trances, appearing in sackcloth and ashes or, for Quakers, "going naked as a sign," and for the cruel punishments they endured for their faith.[40] The late Stuart era did witness a quieting down of some of the excesses of sectarian inspiration and enthusiasm. Yet women were still active in patronizing dissenting preachers, providing meeting houses for the brethren, and evangelizing the faith. During the Exclusion Crisis, many nonconforming women also became active in the so-called "Protestant Cause," printing and disseminating Whig propaganda, hiding Whig outlaws, and supporting the pretensions of the would-be Protestant successor, James Scott, Duke of Monmouth.[41] In 1685 Behn may well have witnessed the notorious burning at Tyburn of the Baptist woman, Elizabeth Gaunt, for her Whig activism, which including harboring a Monmouth rebel.[42] In the 1690s, dissenting women were still active in missionary circles and in voicing their religious and political

---

[39] The historiography on this subject is plentiful. But see in particular, Diane Willen, "Godly Women in Early Modern England: Puritanism and Gender," *Journal of Ecclesiastical History* 43.4 (1992): 561–80; Phyllis Mack, *Visionary Women: Ecstatic Prophecy in Seventeenth-Century England* (Berkeley, 1992); Hilary Hinds, *God's Englishwomen: Seventeenth-Century Radical Sectarian Writings and Feminist Criticism* (New York, 1996).

[40] Kenneth Carroll, "Early Quakers and 'Going Naked as a Sign,'" *Quaker History* 67.2 (1978): 69–87; Diane Purkiss, "Producing the Voice, Consuming the Body: Women Prophets of the Seventeenth Century," in *Women, Writing, History 1640–1740*, eds. Isobel Grundy and Susan Wiseman (Athens, GA, 1992), 140–58; Phyllis Mack, "Women as Prophets During the Civil War," *Feminist Studies* 8.1 (1982): 19–45.

[41] Melinda Zook, "Nursing Sedition: Women, Dissent, & the Whig Struggle," in *Fear, Exclusion and Revolution: Roger Morrice & His World, 1675–1700* (Ashgate, forthcoming).

[42] Elizabeth Gaunt (d. 1685) and her husband were active in the most extreme Whig conspiracies of the early 1680s. She was finally captured and tried in October 1685. Convicted of high treason, she was burned to death at Tyburn. Her execution was witnessed by many including William Penn who described it to Gilbert Burnet. See Burnet, *History of His Own Time*, 6 vols. (Oxford, 1933), 3:61.

opinions in print. Astell would have no doubt noticed the many tracts written by nonconformist women as she browsed the bookstalls of London.[43]

Both Aphra Behn and Mary Astell were also aware, as were many contemporaries, of the domestic implications of Whig contractarian ideas. After all, if the people can absolve their oaths to their liege lord, what prevented men and women from dissolving their marriage vows? If the people can rebel against arbitrary kings, surely then women, children, and servants may do so as well against their husbands, fathers, and masters. Behn and Astell understood that such ideas could liberate in the extreme, to the point of license. Thus Olivia in Behn's *The Younger Brother* (1696) declares "when Parents grow Arbitrary, 'tis time we look into our Rights and Privileges."[44] But, of course, this was the world turned upside down, and for Tories it evoked bitter memories of the chaos of the Civil Wars and Interregnum. Astell knew that the Republicans and Whigs who spouted such Lockean rhetoric had no desire to extend such rights to the private sphere. They were, once again, hypocrites, for "how much soever Arbitrary Power may be dislik'd on a Throne, not Milton himself wou'd cry up liberty to poor *Female Slaves*, or plead for the Lawfulness of Resisting a Private Tyranny" (*SRM* 46–47).

Behn ridiculed both dissenting men and women by representing them as base-born, lewd, and hypocritical. In *The Roundheads*, the Puritans act as though "harmless Wit and Mirth's a Sin, laughing scandalous, and a merry Glass, Abomination," but actually, "they drink as deep, and entertain themselves as well with this silent way of lewd Debauchery" (*R* 6:385). The Presbyterian elder, Ananias Gogle, takes the beautiful Lady Desbro aside, and can hardly speak as he fondles her breasts: "who in the sight of so much such Beau - -ty-- can think of any Bus'ness but the Bus'ness!– Ah! hide those tempting Breasts – Alack, how smooth and warm they are--" (*R* 6:394–95). In *Sir Patient Fancy*, Lady Fancy complains to the Tory Wittmore about her husband's dissenting friends, "... a Herd of sniveling, grinning Hypocrites, that call themselves the teaching Saints; who under pretence of securing me to the number of their Flock, do so sneer upon me, pat my Breasts, and cry fy, fy upon this fashion of tempting Nakedness."[45]

If dissenting men were old and impotent, nonconformist women were alluring and sexually insatiable. In *The Roundheads*, the Cavalier Loveless sneers at his friend, Freeman, who has a nonconformist mistress: "They are all sanctify'd *Jilts*," he declares, "Make Love to 'em, they answer you back in Scripture." But Freeman responds, "Ay, and lye with you in Scripture too. Of all Whores, give me your zealous Whore; I never heard a Woman talk [so] much of Heaven, but she was much for the Creature too" (*R* 6:369).[46]

---

43  Astell would have certainly seen the religious writings of Quaker sufferer, Mary Mollineux (d. 1695), whose collection of pious verse *Fruits of Retirement* (1702) passed into six editions; Anne Docwra (d. 1710), a prolific Quaker writer of the 1680s and 1690s; and Joan Vokins (d. 1690), whose works were collected and published in 1691, among other female-authored works in the print shops.

44  Aphra Behn, *The Younger Brother*, in Todd, *Works*, 7:368. Thus, Olivia tells her brother, he should "Assist my Disobedience."

45  Aphra Behn, *Sir Patient Fancy*, in Todd, *Works*, 6:19.

46  "Creature" was an alcoholic drink, usually whiskey.

In *The City Heiress*, Behn portrays two dissenting women, both of whom are sexually promiscuous. Mrs Clackett is a "most devout Bawd ... A Saint in the Spirit, and a Whore in the Flesh / A Doer of the Devil's Work in God's Name."[47] Sir Timothy Treat-all's nonconformist housekeeper, Mrs Sensure, also confuses sex and religion. When caught running from Sir Timothy's bed, a book of the Presbyterian writer Richard Baxter's sermons drops from her coat.

For Behn, dissenting meetings were sites of lewdness and promiscuity. In her poem, "On a CONVENTICLE," they are places that villains find refuge and women vent their "lust."[48] In *The Roundheads*, Lady Lambert asserts that the first lesson women learn in the conventicles is the importance of "jilting": "Kings are despos'd, and Commonwealths are rul'd; / By Jilting all the Universe is fool'd" (*R* 6:409). And thus they cuckold their impotent husbands. Lady Lambert finds the sexual prowess of dashing Cavalier Loveless irresistible. They are about to make love when Loveless spies Charles I's crown and scepter. He is duly reverent, bowing and kneeling before the "sacred Relicks of my King," and he tells Lady Lambert that they should "Either withdraw, or hide that Glorious Object." But Lady Lambert is sexually aroused: "Thou art a Fool, the very sight of this – Raises my Pleasure higher" (*R* 6:405). The Dissenters, women and men alike, know nothing of reverence, honor, and respect. They mingle the sacred, be it devotion to God or the monarchy, with the profane.

Behn's depiction of dissenting women was meant to titillate as much as condemn. She wrote first and foremost to entertain and earn her living. Any feminist sentiments Behn may have espoused were only meant for elite Cavalier women, who by right of birth, wealth, and fashion were allowed to entertain gallant lovers, cross dress, and even defy parents and husbands. But for dissenting women, Behn relied on traditionally negative representations of women as fickle, seductive, and sexually insatiable. Maximizing the audience's pleasure and further disparaging the enemy were important to Behn, certainly more so than any bonds of sisterhood.

Astell, on the other hand, with her more developed feminist conscience, and with little or no concern for marketability, did not entirely dismiss nonconformist women. Whereas Behn's main preoccupation was her art and what it could earn for her, Astell was indeed a true "lover of her SEX." "Fain would I rescue my Sex, or at least as many of them as come within my little sphere, from that meanness of Spirit into which the Generality of em are sunk."[49] She certainly had no desire to simply reduce women, even Dissenters, to the old proverbial stereotypes about female inferiority. But the activism of some nonconformist women did pose a real quandary for Astell. When addressing the matter, she betrays a divided conscience. Astell found the boldness of these women both attractive and deeply disturbing.

In the preface to *Moderation Truly Stated*, Astell indulges in a bizarre digression on the topic of women. It starts modestly enough during the dialogue of John a Nokes (a Tory) and William a Styles (a Whig). Styles provokes the discussion of

---

47  Behn, *City Heiress*, 7:47.

48  Todd, *Works*, 1:355.

49  Mary Astell, *A Serious Proposal to the Ladies for the Advancement of their True and Greatest Interest* (1696), title page; *Letters concerning the Love of God, between the Author of The Proposal to the Ladies and Mr. John Norris* (1695), excerpted in Hill, *First English Feminist*, 195.

women when he remarks that the Dissenters "have not a few of the Female Sex" and even more adherents among "Sea-faring Men, likewise very many Tradesmen, or Retailers, Artificers, Manufacturers and Day-Labourers." "Now you must consider," he continues as a sort of warning, "that these tradesmen are mostly employ'd by the female sex, and if the ladies should put themselves in the Head of these Multitudes, what a formidable Insurrection would it make! What a shock it would give to the throne! And how fatal might the consequences prove!" These women, along with dissenting barristers and doctors, would harangue the mob and use "Gally-pots, Law-books, Recipes, Chancery Bills, Attorney's and Apothecaries Items, and such like Instruments of Destruction, more fatal than Bullets and Gun-powder." Worse still, some "Amazon" might seize the fleet for all the seamen of Dissenters too (*MTS* xlix).

Astell's mocking sense of humor is on display here, but she also uses Styles to recount a long history of heroic women who have led armies, fought in wars, or appeased mutinies. It is an impressive list. Ruth Perry believes that at this point in the dialogue, Astell's feminism "bubbles up."[50] Perhaps so, but it is quickly moderated by Astell's contempt for dissent. The Tory Nokes fulfills this task by declaring that it is particularly repulsive for "noisy" dissenting women to "Cabal against the Government especially in a Ladies [Queen Anne] Reign." Astell was so confident that self-interest alone compelled Dissenters that she could not fathom why these women crossed the boundaries of traditional female decorum and voiced their opinions. "What can be their design in it," asks an indigent Nokes. "To get Preferments? To be admitted to the Board? And to Command our Armies and Fleets?" Astell was obviously troubled by the very public behavior of some dissenting women. What did it mean? In print, she could not admit that these women may have been just as driven by their faith to express themselves as was she. Yet this passage betrays that she was aware that her argument that Dissenters were only interested in power fell apart when it came to women. She quickly neutralizes this troubling specter by having Nokes end the discussion on an altogether different note, asserting that "the Young and the Handsome, the Witty and the Gay, the Intriguing and Politick Ladies are all on the Factious side; and only the Old and the Ugly, the Praying and the Women of Thought are on the other" (*MTS* li).[51]

Still, the image of the factious, intriguing woman did not leave Astell. The following year, she vented her concerns about such women in *The Christian Religion as Profess'd by a Daughter of the Church of England* (1705), linking them once again to the "Good-old-Cause." Astell was puzzled and unnerved by these women. Why did they meddle in the affairs of state in which they clearly had no business? "And since we are not allow'd a share in the Honourable Office in the Commonwealth, we ought to be asham'd and scorn to drudge, in the mean trade of Faction and Sedition."

---

50    Perry, *Celebrated Mary Astell*, 202.

51    Astell is referring to herself as one of the praying women of thought. She and her church are ancient, plain, and undesirable while dissent and dissenting women are young, seductive, and fashionable. It is unclear to whom she is referring as witty and factious. Although no Dissenter, Sarah Churchill, duchess of Marlborough, was certainly a prominent and very beautiful intriguer in Whig politics at this time.

Those that do must surely be mere "Tools of Crafty and Designing Demagogues," Whigs and Dissenters. Such women were, in short, "Ridiculous."[52]

Astell was more critical, however, of the sexual politics and double standards of male Whigs and Dissenters. She made this particularly plain in her *Some Reflections on Marriage*, a keenly political tract which, as Patricia Springborg points out, seeks to respond to and undermine the fundamentals of Lockean political philosophy.[53] From the outset, Astell mocks the kind of Whig language used to justify the Glorious Revolution, aptly applying it to the domestic sphere. It is not her wish to prompt women to "Resist, or to Abdicate the Perjur'd Spouse," states Astell in a sly reference to the Declaration of Rights, which maintained that James II, having broken his contract with the people, had "abdicated" his throne (*SRM* 9). She continues by taking the family–state analogy to task, wondering why Whigs find kingly absolutism so abhorrent: "if Absolute Sovereignty be not necessary in a State, how comes it to be so in a Family?" Why do these men practice "Arbitrary Dominion in their Families, which they abhor and exclaim against in the State?" (*SRM* 17).[54]

Astell was not advocating the application of Lockean political philosophy to the private sphere. Quite the contrary, she was a lifelong adherent of divine right kingship and found the political and social tenets of the Enlightenment detestable. Rather, she made the hypocrisy of the men who spouted such contractarian formulas transparent. Did they really want their wives to resist their authority should it be deemed arbitrary? "If he abuses [his marital rights], according to modern Deduction, he forfeits it." Astell knew that these men never intended for wives to question the authority of their husbands. Her point was that the notion of a justifiable rebellion was as ludicrous for subjects as it was for wives. And neither did she wish for women to rebel: "a peacable Woman indeed will not carry it so far, she will neither question her Husband's Right nor his Fitness to Govern" (*SRM* 79).

In Astell's truly Platonic configuration of life—peace of mind, domestic security, and political and social harmony came from one source, order. In one of the more revealing passages of *Moderation Truly Stated*, Astell states:

> As for Order, as it needs no external Arguments to enforce, no rhetorical persuasions to recommend it, so it stands in as little need of Art and logic to define it. Like Beauty, Harmony, and Mathematical Proportions, which are nothing else but that Order that Mind observes in those several objects about which it is employ'd, 'tis discerned by its own Native Light, and shines by its own Brightness.

Astell's paean to "order" here is truly poignant. On the one hand, it places her squarely within that Augustan frame of mind that so emphasized reason, symmetry, and clarity. But it also seems to represent a plea on Astell's part. It is clear that "Order" *does*

---

52  Astell, *Christian Religion*, 199, 202.

53  Patricia Springborg, "Mary Astell (1666–1731), Critic of Locke," *The American Political Science Review* 89.3 (1995): 621–33.

54  In *The Two Treatises*, Locke demonstrates the inapplicability of the patriarchal family–state analogy. Familial relations, he argues, do not provide a model for political associations and thus he effectively de-politicizes the domestic sphere. Astell responds that this is duplicitous; an effort to liberate all men while maintaining all women in chains.

require recommendation in the early eighteenth century, and that it is exactly the thing that Astell believed was missing in the world around her, endangered as it was by the social leveling, political maneuvering, and religious hypocrisy of the Whigs and Dissenters. Order, which for Astell meant the traditional order of the church and state—loyalty, hierarchy, and social deference—is transparent, not dressed up in some new-fangled rhetoric. It is "common sense," she asserts, "informing everyone that Order is nothing else but that which is most proper, most becoming, and every way best in its kind." "Obedience, Order, and Uniformity, the Peace and safety of the Church" was exactly what the Dissenter sought to undermine in his quest for power and privilege. What "the Dissenter desires of the church is the slacking the Reins of Discipline, the Violation of Order and Breach of Laws" (*MTS* 4, 13). Writing twenty years earlier, Aphra Behn was less fixated on the health and status of the church and more concerned with the stability of the monarchy and aristocracy, on the fringes of which artists like herself made their living. But she was no less confident about the source of the threat to all that she cherished. In short, it was "Puritanical, Schismatical, Fanastical, Small-beer Face[d]" Whigs and Dissenters. And she, too, longed for a return to traditional order where tradesmen knew their place and women did not mask their sexuality in the sacred, did not hide sermons in their sheets. "Let all things in their own due Order move," sings the Tory gentleman, Sir Charles Meriwill in *The City Heiress*, and "Let Ceasar be the Kingdom's Care and Love."[55]

Clearly, Aphra Behn and Mary Astell were disturbed by what they saw as the slow demise of traditional England, with the monarchy as its sacred center, and the increasing acceptance of religious pluralism, social mobility, and parliamentary government. In this, they were not alone. Many High Church men and Tory politicians felt a similar repulsion to the ethos of the Enlightenment. But for Behn and Astell there was also the disturbing specter of nonconformist women zealously peddling their religion in the streets and abroad, meddling in the male domain of politics. For Behn they posed an obvious opportunity for humor and so she ridiculed them, dismissing them as purely sexual creatures. But for Astell the issue of dissenting women was more complex: she seemed to be thinking out loud in the few passages in which she addressed them. Were they the mere tools of Whigs and demagogues? What could they possibly want? Her Anglican feminism could not bring her to the point of acknowledging the sincerity of their devotion. Dissent, after all, was a fraud. Astell was hesitant to simply dismiss these women, but ultimately they had no place in her Tory worldview.

---

55  Behn, *City Heiress*, 7:75.

# Chapter VIII

# "Great in Humilitie": A Consideration of Mary Astell's Poetry

## Claire Pickard

In 1689 Mary Astell addressed a small volume of poems to William Sancroft, Archbishop of Canterbury, apparently as a thanks offering for the financial assistance and introductions he had provided her with shortly after her arrival in London. Archbishop Sancroft was an appropriate figure for Astell to approach. Ruth Perry describes how he was noted for his charitable works and also how, as one of the leading nonjuring clergy, he was a figure whom Astell admired and respected. The volume itself is modest in appearance; hand stitched, it measures 15 cm by 20.5 cm and contains twelve poems, a dedication, and concluding address, over the course of forty-eight folios. This volume remained unpublished as a whole until reproduced as an appendix to Perry's biography in 1986.[1]

Unsurprisingly, given the dedicatee, the poems in the volume all address religious concerns. Astell focuses on themes such as the spiritual value of suffering, the judgment of the damned, the salvation of the blessed, and the importance of submission to God's will. Yet the single idea that Astell returns to most consistently throughout this volume is the worthlessness of earthly rewards and the allied belief that those who suffer in this life will achieve recompense in Heaven. In this essay I will argue that it is Astell's belief in a compensatory afterlife as explored in the poems that ultimately enables her to invert the worldly hierarchies that exclude women; she thus confronts the problem of gender inequality by shifting her reader's attention from an earthly existence in which women are disadvantaged to a spiritual one in which such disadvantages are eradicated. I wish to suggest that Astell's religious verse, which remains largely unexplored by critics, demonstrates the author's first sustained attempt to develop a technique of transference—a technique that she likewise employs in two of her early prose works, *A Serious Proposal to the Ladies* and *Some Reflections upon Marriage*.

In the opening pages of *A Serious Proposal Part I* Astell echoes the model of displacement expressed in her poetry with her call to "fix" her readers' "Beauty" by "transferring it from a corruptible Body to an immortal Mind."[2] In this treatise,

---

1 All quotations from the poetry are from the original manuscript (Bodleian Library, MS Rawlinson Poet 154, fols. 50r–97v). The text of this manuscript is reproduced in Ruth Perry, *The Celebrated Mary Astell: An Early English Feminist* (Chicago and London, 1986), Appendix D. See Perry, 66–69 for further information about the manuscript volume.

2 Mary Astell, *A Serious Proposal to the Ladies Parts I & II*, ed. Patricia Springborg (London,

Astell calls on her readers to shift their focus from the body, which is subject to social conventions and gender roles, to the mind, which through the exercise of reason can free itself from gender constraints. Her poems likewise shift the reader's attention from the false valuation of this transient material world to an arena in which spiritual worthiness, *not* gender distinctions, are paramount, that is, to the afterlife, to Heaven. In both texts then, Astell establishes a dichotomy between a corporal reality in which women are undermined and an ideal world in which they can fulfill their potential unhindered by "custom." The *Proposal*, perhaps unique in Astell's canon, focuses upon suggestions for reform in this world, promoting a pragmatic solution to the problems that women of her era confronted. Her verse, however, written without the prudential and this-worldly aims of the *Proposal*, provides its author with the opportunity to explore the concept of justification in the next world. That is, while *A Serious Proposal* turns towards the possibility of social reform through Astell's proposed educational retreat for women, the collection of poems has not social withdrawal, but rather personal martyrdom and suffering as its model. In this sense, while the *Proposal* addresses concretely the problems that women confronted at the time at which Astell lived, the poetry emerges out of a different sensibility, one probably closer to the one which Laura Knoppers identifies with the sensibility of the martyr Charles I: removed from the realms of "time and contingency" and abstracted into a realm of idealized suffering.[3] Perry has written that Astell's poetry is informed by an idealization of the "wronged Stuarts," and in particular the "royal martyr." In Astell's poetry, written at the time of the revolutionary settlement, her political and gender commitments overlap. The aura of suffered isolation it imparts, however, serves not only as a political model as a means to identify with Charles, who left "Empires for a Cell," but also presents a non-material solution to the problems of gender inequality.[4]

Of course, even when Astell's ostensible focus is upon the transformation of women's material circumstances (as in *A Serious Proposal*), her concern with their spiritual welfare remains paramount. Astell's interest is, after all, not simply in the misguided orientation of women's minds but in their *immortal* minds. At the close of *Part I* of the *Proposal* Astell makes clear that whilst she has attempted to advance the cause of women's education, this is fundamentally in order to further their spiritual interests:

> Whereas, a wise and good Woman is useful and valuable in all Ages and Conditions; she who chiefly attends the *one thing needful*, the *good part which shall not be taken from her*, lives a cheerful and pleasant life, innocent and sedate, calm and tranquile, and makes a glorious Exit; being translated from the most happy life on Earth, to unspeakable happiness in Heaven; a fresh and fragrant Name embalming her Dust, and extending its Perfume to succeeding Ages. (*SP I* 46)

---

1997), 5. Hereafter cited parenthetically as *SP I* and *SP II*.

   3 Laura Lunger Knoppers, "Reviving the Martyr King: Charles I as Jacobite icon" in *The Royal Image: Representations of Charles I*, ed. Thomas Corns (Cambridge, 1999), 263–87.

   4 Perry, *Celebrated Mary Astell*, 42.

A similar dynamic operates in Astell's *Some Reflections*. Whilst Astell decries the disadvantages of marriage for women and suggests some ways of ameliorating these, her belief in marriage as a sacrament and as part of a divinely ordained social order prevent her from suggesting a radical reinvention of the institution. Instead, she can only truly perceive marriage as beneficial in relation to a woman's spiritual life. That is, while *A Serious Proposal* entails a social program for the purposes of female spiritual advancement, *Some Reflections* views the existence of the institution of marriage as only an impediment best to be avoided. Yet a rational woman still can conceive of such an arrangement, for while "it is no advantage to her in this World, if rightly manag'd it may prove one as to the next." As a result:

> ... she who Marries purely to do Good, to Educate Souls for Heaven, who can be so truly mortify'd as to lay aside her own Will and Desires, to pay such as intire Submission for Life, to one whom she cannot be sure will always deserve it, does certainly perform a more Heroic Action than all the famous Masculine Heroes can boast of, she suffers a continual Martyrdom to bring Glory to GOD and Benefit to Mankind, which consideration indeed may carry her through all Difficulties, I know not what else can ...[5]

Thus, in this sense, the later *Reflections* is more in keeping with the sensibility articulated in the poems where material disadvantage becomes the means to claim eminence in relation to the claims of Heaven. For the Astell of both *Some Reflections* and the poems, it is through martyrdom (inevitably associated in Astell's own royalist languages with the martyrdom of Charles) through which her own spiritual superiority can be asserted. Yet, Astell's own "continual Martyrdom"—manifested through mortification and submission—emerges as "a more Heroic Action" than those of "all the famous Masculine Heroes." This essay will demonstrate that Astell's poetry in her 1689 volume, by focusing solely upon spiritual rather than earthly solutions to questions of gender inequality, elaborates her own feminine conception of other-worldly martyrdom and heroism.

Astell's compensatory approach to earthly unhappiness is introduced in the very first poem in the collection, "The Invitation" (fol. 52r–v). In this poem the speaker finds comfort through the knowledge that Heaven will provide a refuge in which worldly troubles are turned to joy:

> Hark how he calls, come unto me
> All that are laden and opprest,
> My service is true Libertie,
> My bosom an Eternal Rest,
> With open arms he begs of thee to come,
> Make hast my Soul, leave all & thither run.

---

[5] *The First English Feminist: Reflections upon Marriage and other Writings by Mary Astell*, ed. Bridget Hill (Aldershot, 1986), 130–31.

> Wipe thy blind eyes dark'ned with tears,
> From all but Penitentiall ones,
> Harbour only Religious Fears,
> And for thy Sins keep all thy Groans;
> Then he who never lets us sigh in vain,
> Will turn to brightest Joy thy Greif & pain. (fol. 52r)

More significantly, if paradoxically in this context, in the first stanza of this poem Astell also validates her own ambitions by merging her literary with her religious aspirations:

> Come Muse, and leave those wings that soar
> No further than an Earthly flight,
> Let us the GOD of Heav'n implore,
> And tune our Notes AEtherial height;
> Heav'n thy Parnassus be, thence learn thy Song,
> Thy Saviour's side shall be thy Helicon. (fol. 52r)

Heaven is thus not only a place of spiritual fulfillment, it is also the poet's "Parnassus." By here linking literary fame—which she dismisses as irrelevant in other poems such as "In emulation of M^r. Cowleys Poem call'd the Motto page I" and "Ambition"—to Christ's passion, and a Heavenly muse, Astell makes her poem an expression of the conventional view that true glory comes through the praise and service of God, as well as suggesting that through such service she will, finally, win her "bays":

> Teach ev'ry word to chant his Praise,
> And ev'ry verse to sing his Love,
> His Crown of thorns shall be thy bays,
> His Cross shall be thy shady Grove,
> Which will at last be to a Kingdom blown,
> And thy sharp bays will sprout into a Crown. (fol. 52r–v)

Astell thus commences her volume with a presentation of the afterlife that combines a conventional view of an "Eternal Rest" with a far more active fulfillment of her own earthly ambitions. The opening lines set the tone for this distinctly aspirational view of Heaven; a Muse that inspires a merely "Earthly flight" is of no interest to Astell, her sights are set on an "AEtherial height."

Astell further complicates and validates the worldly theme of ambition in *A Serious Proposal Part I* by redirecting it towards spiritual ends, thus removing the pejorative connotations normally associated with the term. "You may be as ambitious as you please," she writes,

> so you aspire to the best *things*; and contend with your Neighbours as much as you can, that they may not out-do you in any commendable Quality. Let it never be said, that they to whom pre-eminence is so very agreeable, can be tamely content that others shou'd surpass them in *this*, and precede them in a *better* World! (*SP I* 6–7)

It is in the light of these comments that the ambition of "The Invitation" can be most fully understood. In this poem, and indeed throughout the volume dedicated to Archbishop Sancroft, Astell presents a poetic persona who is assertive and profoundly aspirational. Yet this self-belief is consistently related to spiritual concerns—it is not the false "self-love" Astell abhors. Rather, it is the genuine self-respect that comes from a commitment to pursuing only "the best *things*." Even the desire for literary fame, for "bays," is freed from the taint of worldliness through its association with the attainment of a Heavenly "Crown." For Astell, articulating something like a metaphysical paradox, it is only by means of "service" that "true Liberty" emerges—and hence distinguishes her aspirations from the mere "earthly flight" associated with classical literary aspiration. Indeed, Astell's classical and pastoral landscape gives way to the "sharp bays" associated with the penitential "Groans" of "Greif & pain." For Astell, her own Christian ambitions, distilled in the image of "sharp bays"—at once signifying both suffering and Christian ambition—are realized through the service of chanting "his Praise."

Astell further develops the theme of a consolatory afterlife in her second poem, "In emulation of M$^r$. Cowleys Poem call'd the Motto page I" where such consolation is now intimated as a necessary recompense for the gender constrictions suffered in this life. The poem is worth quoting in full:

> What shall I do? not to be Rich or Great,
> Not to be courted and admir'd,
> With Beauty blest, or Wit inspir'd,
> Alas! these merit not my care and sweat,
> These cannot my Ambition please,
> My high born Soul shall never stoop to these;
> But something I would be thats truly great
> In 'ts self, and not by vulgar estimate.
>
> If this low World were always to remain,
> If th'old Philosophers were in the right,
> Who wou'd not then, with all their might
> Study and strive to get themselves a name?
> Who wou'd in soft repose lie down,
> Or value ease like being ever known?
> But since Fames Trumpet has so short a breath,
> Shall we be fond of that w$^{ch}$. must submit to Death?
>
> Nature permits not me the common way,
> By serving Court, or State, to gain
> That so much valu'd trifle, Fame;
> Nor do I covet in Wits Realm to sway:
> But O ye bright illustrious few,
> What shall I do to be like some of you?
> Whom this misjudging World dos underprize,
> Yet are most dear in Heav'ns all-righteous eyes!

How shall I be a Peter or a Paul?
That to the Turk and Infidel,
I might the joyfull tydings tell,
And spare no labour to convert them all:
But ah my Sex denies me this,
And Marys Priviledge I cannot wish,
Yet hark I hear my dearest Saviour say,
They are more blessed who his Word obey.

Up then my sluggard Soul, Labour and Pray,
For if with Love enflam'd thou be,
Thy JESUS will be born in thee,
And by thy ardent Prayers, thou can'st make way,
For their Conversion whom thou may'st not teach,
Yet by a good Example always Preach:
And tho I want a Persecuting Fire,
I'le be at lest a Martyr in desire. (fols. 52v–53r)

In the opening stanza of the poem Astell dismisses those qualities that bring earthly renown—wealth, greatness, beauty, wit, fame—yet she does so in a way that inverts conventional hierarchies, obscuring her own sense of exclusion. Instead of arguing simply that she will be recompensed for such exclusion in Heaven, Astell reverts to the previously introduced idea of personal ambition, and rejects as beneath her the very assets of which she feels deprived: "These cannot my Ambition please, / My high born Soul shall never stoop to these." Astell thus refuses "the common way" of aspiring to "Fames Trumpet" from which she is barred on earth by her "Nature" and her sex. She justifies her ambition by making it the product of her "high born Soul" and not her worldly personality. In doing so, however, she is unable to emulate the very Christian figures she invokes and admires. The fourth stanza of the poem draws the reader's attention to the central dilemma of women such as Astell, who sought an active role yet could see no viable means of achieving such a position within the contexts of Anglican Christianity (not, that is, until the perspective advanced in *A Serious Proposal*). The only female role model she is able to identify is Mary, whose "Priviledge," Astell writes, as bearer of the Christian Messiah, she simply "cannot wish."

Astell does not disavow the notion of women assuming prominent religious functions; in fact, in the second part of *A Serious Proposal* Astell does express her longing for the opportunity to fulfill an apostolic role:

Tis a Godlike thing to relieve even the Temporal wants of our Fellow Creatures, to keep a *Body* from perishing, but it, is much more Divine, to *Save a Soul from Death*! A Soul which in his estimate who best knows the value of it is worth more than all the World. They who are thus *wise shall shine as the brightness of the Firmament, and they who turn many to Righteousness as the Stars for ever*; which is a Glory we may honestly Contend for, a Beauty we may lawfully Covet; O that we had but Ambition enough to aspire after it! (*SP II* 151)

Astell's message is here exoteric—addressing all women. Indeed, the conception of women performing apostolic functions derives from the first part of the tract where the "Piety and solid Knowledge" acquired in Astell's proposed retreat will prepare women "to propagate Religion" upon their "return to the World" (*SP I* 37). In the earlier poetry, however, Astell demonstrates that while she herself possesses the ambition to aspire to such a position she finds no means for its fulfillment. Although the option of educator is closed off to the Astell of the poetry (who cannot "be a Peter or a Paul"), the final stanza of the poem does provide an alternative to the pedagogical option modeled by the apostles. Though Astell had earlier rejected the emulation of Mary's role, in the final stanza, she in fact embraces it; she fulfills Mary's mission through both labor and prayer. Calling out to her soul, she affirms: "if enflam'd thou be, / Thy JESUS will be born in thee." The apostles may bear witness to Jesus, yet Astell's more physical bearing of Jesus through "ardent Prayers" constructs a place for herself (as well as other women)—both comparable to that of the male apostles as well as to that of Mary. By becoming "a Martyr in desire," Astell, though she "may'st not teach," can by her "good Example always Preach." Here the feminine martyrdom of desire—founded on obedience ("They are more blessed who his Word obey")—gives Astell a stature equal to, or perhaps surpassing, those of the apostles. Astell intimates a perspective which will become more explicit in the later poems of the volume: feminine suffering is not only a preparation for a consolatory afterlife, but itself functions as a primary means to become "most dear in Heav'ns all-righteous eyes."

The sheer force of the speaker's self-representation in this poem is further underlined if one compares Astell's version of this poem with Cowley's original; the most immediately apparent difference between Cowley's poem and Astell's is the latter's substitution of spiritual for literary immortality. Cowley's poetic speaker reflects in closing that whereas others are born to fame and wealth, if he is to achieve a similar renown "Out of *my self* it must be *strook*." Significantly, Cowley articulates an aspiration for worldly honor where Astell has devoted her efforts to Heavenly reward.[6] He then dedicates himself to the pursuit of literary glory and dismisses all distractions, committing himself solely to his books, where Astell aspires to both solitary devotion and to public service. Cowley's poem concludes with the speaker devoting himself to the study of Aristotle, Cicero, and Virgil, whom he figures as looking down upon him from the great height of a mountain, presumably Parnassus, while Astell's anticipates rather the scrutiny of "Heav'ns" more exalted and "all-righteous eyes."

More interesting, however, is Astell's alteration of the entire tone of Cowley's poem. Although both poems end with a sense of the gulf between the speakers' aspirations and their current status, in Astell's poem there is an emphasis upon the ultimately worthy character of that speaker. Whereas Cowley accentuates his own inferiority and his need to be taught by his literary masters, Astell stresses her own "high born Soul"—which will enable her to teach others through living example. The contrast between the two poems draws attention to the greater self-assertion

---

6  Abraham Cowley, *The English Writings of Abraham Cowley*, ed. A.R. Waller (Cambridge, 1905), 15.

and resolve that Astell conveys by virtue of a spiritual ambition which validates her personal sense of worth by placing it within the context of a religious meditation.

The complexity of Astell's reworking of Cowley's text is further emphasized if one contrasts it to the poem "Ambition," which follows shortly after it in Astell's volume (fols. 54v–55r). In this text Astell returns to the notion that she is superior to those who seek earthly success yet reverses the dynamic of the poem written in emulation of Cowley. Following upon the assertion of Astell's martyrdom in the preceding poem, "Ambition" is distinctly triumphant in its expression of the potential of women's religious experience:

> What's this that with such vigour fills my brest?
> Like the first mover finds no rest,
> And with it's force dos all things draw,
> Makes all submit to its imperial Law!
> Sure 'tis a spark 'bove what Prometheus stole,
> Kindled by a heav'nly coal,
> Their sophistry I can controul,
> Who falsely say that women have no Soul. (fol. 54v)

The second stanza of the poem sustains this tone of assured self-assertion:

> Vile Greatness! I disdain to bow to thee,
> Thou are below ev'n lowly me,
> I wou'd no Fame, no Titles have,
> And no more Land than what will make a grave.
> I scorn to weep for Worlds, may I but reign
> And Empire o're my self obtain,
> In Caesars throne I'de not sit down,
> Nor wou'd I stoop for Alexanders Crown. (fol. 54v)

Perfecting the maneuver that enables her to reject the very earthly rewards she is unable to possess, this stanza expertly positions the speaker as one whom, whilst excluded from "Fame," "Titles," "Land," and "Empire," is simultaneously greater than that "Greatness" she dismisses as "Vile." The reference to "lowly me" should be read in the context of her remark in *A Serious Proposal Part II* that:

> The only difference therefore between the Humble and the Proud is this, that whereas the former does not prize her self on some Imaginary Excellency, or for any thing that is not truly Valuable; does not ascribe to her self what is her Makers due, nor Esteem her self on any other account but because she is GOD's Workmanship, endow'd by him with many excellent Qualities, and made capable of Knowing and Enjoying the Sovereign and Only Good; so that her Self-Esteem does not terminate in her *Self* but in GOD, and she values her self only for GOD's sake. The Proud on the contrary is mistaken both in her Estimate of Good, and in thinking it is her Own; She values her self on things that have no real Excellency, or which at least add none to her, and forgets from whose Liberality she receives them .... (*SP II* 179)

In "Ambition" Astell encapsulates this distinction between the conviction that she is "lowly" in herself while of great value as the product of "God's Workmanship."

The third stanza of "Ambition" extends that value judgment to Astell's literary work, essentially rendering her impervious to the whims of "Town" critics as it establishes Astell herself as the primary judge of her own work:

> Let me obscured be, & never known
> Or pointed at about the Town,
> Short winded Fame shall not transmit
> My name, that the next Age may censure it:
> If I write sense no matter what they say,
> Whither they call it dull, or pay
> A rev'rence such as Virgil claims,
> Their breath's infectious, I have higher aims. (fol. 55r)

To "write sense" becomes the speaker's objective, a "higher aim" to which she can aspire regardless of her position in the world or its judgment of her. Although not directly linking her religious and literary aspirations here as she did in "The Invitation," Astell's pre-emptive rejection of the opinions of others and alignment of her writing with "higher aims" simultaneously dignifies her writing whilst also avoiding the charge of worldly ambition. Having likened the "vigour" that "fills [her] brest" to that of the "first mover," and situating her inspiration a "spark 'bove what Prometheus stole," the spiritual source of her poetical muse is clear; as is its resultant imperviousness to any secular judgment.

Having already established in her poem in emulation of Cowley that it is spiritual rather than earthly achievement that is of true value, Astell continues to assert this conviction in the final stanza of "Ambition":

> Mean spirited men! that bait at Honour, Praise,
> A wreath of Laurel or of Baies,
> How short's their Immortality!
> But Oh a Crown of Glory ne're will die!
> This I'me Ambitious of, no pains will spare
> To have a higher Mansion there,
> Where all are Kings, here let me be,
> Great O my GOD, Great in Humilitie. (fol. 55r)

The contrast between those "Mean spirited men" who seek worthless fame and her firm assertion in the final line of the first stanza that women are possessed of the feature that is essential for true glory—a soul—enables Astell to finally dispose of the idea, voiced in the first poem, that her sex restricts her. Indeed her gender, which implicitly bars her from the possession of many forms of earthly power, itself becomes an aid in her quest for "a Crown of Glory." This image is the very one Astell uses in the closing pages of *Some Reflections upon Marriage* to sum up the spiritual benefits she believes women can gain from an improved education. This education, she argues, can lead women:

to such a pitch of Perfection, as the Human Soul is capable of attaining in this Life by the Grace of GOD, such true Wisdom, such real Greatness, as tho' it does not qualifie them to make a Noise in this World, to found or overturn Empires, yet it qualifies them for what is infinitely better, a Kingdom that cannot be mov'd, an incorruptible Crown of Glory.[7]

Here, as in the final stanza of "Ambition," Astell envisions her eternal "Crown of Glory"; this is not a merely compensatory view of the afterlife, but one in which women's exclusion from worldly power actually *increases* their chances of Heavenly splendor. Thus, in the poem, the speaker's very lowliness in earthly terms would seem to aid her desire to be "Great in Humilitie." As her earlier reference to "lowly me" in fact asserts the poet's spiritual worth, Astell's aspiration to be "Great in Humilitie" appears, at first reading, to be paradoxical. For Astell, however, as she explains in *A Serious Proposal Part II*, true greatness can be achieved only *through* humility. Charles's greatness would time and again, in the Jacobite languages of the period, be asserted through praising the Royal Martyr's rejecting of the heroic actions of earthly fame in favor of the passivity of martyrdom.[8] Astell appropriates such a notion, and genders it. It is only when one frees oneself from a "Self-Esteem" based upon "Self" and instead achieves a "Self-Esteem" based, not upon heroic actions, but upon God, that one can attain spiritual glory. For Astell, women's very exclusion from earthly power, its temptations and aggrandizements, is in fact a spiritual advantage; their martyrdom, as Charles's, is but a sign of their true greatness.

The lengthy poem "Heaven" builds upon these ideas and extends them further (fols. 75r–79v). The poem opens with a reference to the poet's humble status and her temerity in addressing religious topics: "In a poor simple Girl 'tis a bold flight, / To aim at such a glorious height" (fol. 75r). However, as the poem develops, Astell reverses this viewpoint. Subverting the idea common in the work of many early modern female poets that writing by women can be justified *only* if it originates from God, Astell claims instead that religious topics are the only ones worthy of *her* attention and ambition.[9] Dismissing the suggestion that women should write about worldly "trifles" she states:

But none of these my Genius please,
Alas we were not born for these,
They're not our business they're but our disease.
No, to its native place my Soul aspires,
And something more than Earth desires,
Heav'n only can it's vast Ambition fill,
And Heav'n alone must exercise my mind and quill. (fol. 75v)

---

7 Astell, *Reflections*, 129.

8 See William Kolbrener, "'Forc'd into an Interest': High Church Politics and Feminine Agency in the Works of Mary Astell," *1650–1850: Ideas, Aesthetics, and Inquiries in the Early Modern Era* 10 (2004): 3–31.

9 See Elaine Hobby, *Virtue of Necessity: English Women's Writing 1649–88* (London, 1988), Chapter Two. Hobby demonstrates how the poets "Eliza," An (*sic*) Collins and Elizabeth Major justify their writing by arguing that it proceeds from God and speaks His truths.

Astell's recurrent theme of the worthlessness of earthly rewards here reaches its apotheosis. She returns to the desire she expressed in the opening lines of "The Invitation" that her Muse should help her reach an "AEtherial height," as here her "mind and quill" will only be satisfied when focused on "Heav'n alone." Far from being "a poor simple Girl," she has now achieved the spiritual confidence to view Heaven not as the "Eternal Rest" of the earlier poem, but as the only state that can fulfill her own "vast Ambition." The realization that her "Self-Esteem" is now based not upon her own worth but upon God's love for her enables Astell to view Heaven, with its attendant glory, and not an earthly sphere that excludes women, as her "native place."

In the final poem in the volume, "The Thanksgiving," Astell synthesizes her belief that worldly gifts are a distraction from the love of God with an exploration of the idea that earthly "suffering" is in fact a blessing as it focuses the mind on spiritual redemption (fols. 90v–93r). This celebration of suffering as enabling spiritual growth recurs throughout Astell's works, notably in *Some Reflections upon Marriage* where husbands' power to "render Life miserable" is turned to spiritual benefit as it allows wives to "Exercise … their Vertue."[10] In "Thanksgiving" Astell continues to present a distinction between the "vile" worldly aspect of her personality, which she associates with unhappiness and exclusion, and God's care and love for her eternal soul. In relation to God's bounty, Astell emphasizes her own unworthiness:

> What am I Lord, ah what am I?
> That of me thou shou'dst take such care,
> And for my sake thy one dear Son not spare!
> Dost thou behold me with a Friendly eye,
> Vile me, on whom the world dos look awry? (fol. 91r)

Yet in relation to the wider world, the speaker underlines her separateness and her confidence of God's love for her. This stanza continues:

> Then I'le no more the world regard,
> Value it's loss, nor care for it's reward,
> Thou kindly has withdrawn from me
> All other things, that I might only Love & think on thee. (fol. 91r)

The features that more worldly individuals might perceive as lacking from her life are thus transmuted into signs of God's favor. Even her "Friendless" (92r) state is a blessing:

> Thrice blessed be thy Jealousie,
> Which would not part
> With one smal corner of my heart,
> But has engross'd it all to Thee! (fol. 92v)

---

10  Astell, *Reflections*, 76, 75.

The speaker is ultimately shown as vindicated in relation to those who pity her:

> From my secure and humble seat,
> I view the ruins of the Great.
> And dare look back on my expired days,
> To my low state there needs no shameful ways. (fol. 91v)

Her inversion of worldly hierarchies complete, Astell concludes the volume with this poem in which her speaker marks herself out as an individual beloved of God and "secure" in her dismissal of those who possess the earthly gifts she lacks. Five years later, Astell was to extend this sense of security to women in general in *A Serious Proposal*:

> You are therefore Ladies, invited into a place, where you shall suffer no other confinement, but to be kept out of the road Of Sin: You shall not be depriv'd of your Grandeur, but only exchange the vain Pomps and Pageantry of the world, empty Titles and Forms of State, for the true and solid Greatness of being able to despise *them. (SP I* 19)

This contrast between Astell's focus on her individual soul in her religious verse, and her attention to the needs of a wider community of female readers in her prose work tells us much about the different functions of Astell's writing in these two distinct genres. Astell's poetry remained in manuscript and was addressed to the nonjuring Sancroft at the time of the revolutionary settlement when Astell's personal and political prospects were at their nadir.[11] It is essentially a record of a personal spiritual journey and its focus is thus entirely upon persona of the poet. The prose work, published after her correspondence with John Norris had established her more public persona, was a more assured intervention in a public debate about the role of women in society. Yet despite the difference of emphasis in the separate genres, the central preoccupations remain the same. *A Serious Proposal* may have articulated a more concrete role for women in society (albeit one also presupposed on withdrawal), but it does nonetheless foreground women's otherwordly aspirations and ends. In both the poetry and the prose Astell thus combines a critique of those aspects of society which disadvantage women with a concentration upon the possibility of a Christian afterlife in which such disadvantages are removed. Her verse collection enables Astell to work through for the first time the connection between her spiritual beliefs and her concern with the status of women in ways that both prefigure and illuminate the arguments of her later prose.

---

11  Perry, *Celebrated Mary Astell*, 42.

Chapter IX

# "Tis better that I endure": Mary Astell's Exclusion of Equity

Ann Jessie Van Sant

In my mental bookcase, Astell's feminist essays stand next to Monique Wittig's *The Straight Mind* because both writers were committed to denaturalizing *woman* as a category constituted by custom: Wittig insisted that both *woman* and *man* were relational terms; Astell, by contrast, regarded neither woman nor man as relational to the other in any fundamental sense. Astell's "progressive" thinking about gender has long been understood to arise in part from her grafting of a philosophical modernity onto her High Church Tory and Platonized Anglicanism. Cartesianism (as interpreted by Nicholas Malebranche, via the Cambridge Platonists) was useful to her not only because the *cogito* accommodated an ungendered thinking being, but also because Descartes's erasure of the authority of the past converted history to a record of mistakes that ought to be corrected by the right method of reasoning.[1] Astell could thus reject, in its most significant elements, what we would call a gendered definition of women and a non-gendered definition of men. She was, as we know, by no means alone. Something like a feminist *literature of dissent* emerged in the course of the seventeenth century, much of it centering on women's education, that is, on an effort to *change women's minds*.[2] Astell used not only her education proposal but also,

I would like to thank the members of the Berkeley Eighteenth-Century Studies group, especially Len von Morze; my colleagues, Victoria Silver and Jayne Lewis; and graduate students in my course "Women, Prescriptive Authority, and Equity," Amelia Parkin and Emily Liu. I also want to acknowledge the careful and generous comments of the editors of this volume, Michal Michelson and William Kolbrener.

1  Joan Kinnaird considers *Part II* of *A Serious Proposal to the Ladies* "little more than an elaborate exposition of Descartes's *Discourse on Method*" ("Mary Astell and the Conservative Contribution to English Feminism," *The Journal of British Studies* 19.1 [1979]: 62). See as well Ruth Perry's "Radical Doubt and the Liberation of Women," *Eighteenth Century Studies* 18.4 (1985): 472–93, and Cynthia B. Bryson, "Mary Astell: defender of the 'disembodied mind,'" *Hypatia* 13.4 (1998): 40.

2  Many studies contribute to our knowledge of arguments for women's education. See, for example, Hilda Smith, *Reason's Disciples: Seventeenth-Century English Feminists* (Urbana, 1982); Patricia Crawford, "Women's Published Writings 1600–1700," in *Women in English Society 1500–1800*, ed. Mary Prior (London, 1985), 211–82; and Ralph A. Houlbrooke, *The English Family: 1450–1700* (London, 1984). For the "woman question," see Diane Purkiss, "Material Girls: The Seventeenth-Century Woman Debate," in *Women, Texts & Histories 1575–1760*, eds. Clare Brant and Diane Purkiss (London, 1992), 69–101. For an argument that Astell's apparently contradictory intellectual genealogies point to "complementary languages of critique," see William Kolbrener's "Gendering the Modern: Mary Astell's Feminist Historiography," *The Eighteenth Century: Theory and Interpretation* 44.1 (2004): 1–24.

scattered throughout her work, her aggressive wit, to ridicule the gender asymmetry in which women were customarily trained:

> The Service [a woman] at any Time becomes oblig'd to pay to a Man, is only a Business by the Bye, just as it may be any Man's Business and Duty to Keep Hogs; he was not Made for this, but if he Hires himself out to such an Employment, he ought conscientiously to perform it.[3]

For Astell, being a wife is rather like being a hog keeper, but neither has anything to do with the end for which a human being was created. Not only should a woman not be taught that "marriage [is] her only preferment," she should see her service to a man as "only a Business, by the Bye" (*SRM* 60).

Ever since Joan Kinnaird argued that Astell's feminism was enabled by her conservative religious principles, part of the critical conversation about Astell's immense contribution to the project of establishing women's intellectual, spiritual, and subjective equality has centered around the sense that she presents a paradox—that the radical and conservative, or progressive and traditional elements of her thinking require a good deal of interpretive work to establish both an historical grounding and a theoretical explanation adequate to her thinking. Opposing a fully articulated and generally approved gender asymmetry, thoroughly normalized in law, custom, and religion, was almost an epistemological task in the late seventeenth century. It required a sturdy capacity to reject the authority of the past and to insist that reason, detached from the weight of history, should override the authority of accumulated tradition.[4] In some respects, Astell might be said to fit the profile for early modern women writers outlined by Catherine Gallagher—which employs Max Weber's contrast between traditional and legal-rational authority.[5] But even making use of that analysis of authority, we still must take into account how Astell's rejection of the authority (she labels it the "tyranny") of custom is deeply embedded in her philosophical framework. In her Platonist epistemology, living according to custom is equivalent to being entrapped in the sensory world, to being cut off from the

---

3 *Some Reflections upon Marriage, to which is added a Preface in Answer to Some Objections*, 3rd edition, in *Astell, Political Writings*, ed. Patricia Springborg (Cambridge, 1996), 11. Hereafter cited parenthetically as *SRM*.

4 As Sarah Ellenzweig has recently observed, many students of Astell's work have "attempted to elucidate [the] complex mix of traditional and progressive tendencies" in her thinking ("The Love of God and the Radical Enlightenment: Mary Astell's Brush with Spinoza," *Journal of the History of Ideas* 64.3 [2003]: 379–97). Ellenzweig points in particular to the term "Tory feminist" and to Hilda Smith's *Reason's Disciples*, Kinnaird's "Mary Astell and the Conservative Contribution to English Feminism," Ruth Perry's "Mary Astell and the Feminist Critique of Possessive Individualism," *Eighteenth Century Studies* 23.4 (1990): 444–57, and Catherine Gallagher's "Embracing the Absolute: The Politics of the Female Subject in Seventeenth-Century England," *Genders* 1.1 (1993): 24–39. Ellenzweig's own argument is that "Astell's closest proximity to radical thinking, however unintentional, is to be found not in her feminism but rather in her theology and her philosophy" (396). Rachel Weil has further explored the extremes in Astell's thinking in "Mary Astell: The Marriage of Toryism and Feminism," in her *Political Passions: Gender, the Family, and Political Argument in England, 1680–1714* (Manchester, 1999), 142–60.

5 See Catherine Gallager, "A History of the Precedent: Rhetorics of Legitimation in Women's Writing," *Critical Inquiry* 26.2 (2000): 309–27.

intelligible world. It is therefore a matter of particular interest that Astell validates—for the sake of social order—the authority that rests on ancient usage. I want here to suggest that Astell's complex political and theological position centering on obedience can be understood in terms of the contemporary opposition between law and equity, with law associated with customary, time-out-of-mind or prescriptive authority and equity with an appeal to conscience in each individual case. Although Astell was profoundly committed to women's equality, she was as profoundly distrustful of equity in a legal sense. Her extreme commitment to obedience, which includes but is not limited to the Christian doctrine of surrender of the will to God, aligns her on the side of law in the law versus equity debates.[6] Despite her rejection of the authority of the past *qua* past—"Nor can Error, be it as Antient as it may, ever plead Prescription against Truth," a view consistent with Equity—she finds it necessary to do precisely what she enjoins against: to bend to prescriptive authority even when that authority is opposed by a reasoned truth (*SRM* 10).[7] And, finally, as we will see, she rejects the individual exceptionality to law on which equity depends.

In order to argue that an essential framework for Astell's thinking is to be found in the opposition between law and equity, I will begin by bringing into view the liberty she takes as an interpreter of Biblical material, a liberty characteristic of equity rather than law. By contrast, the intransigency of her polemic against dissenters and their practice of occasional conformity, I will show, works against any appeal to individual circumstance, the very ground of equity. Astell's apparently paradoxical positioning rests on her Platonized Christian commitment to an intelligible rather than a sensible world, but it is defined as well by the repugnance she feels for dissent, which she cannot see in any terms but rebellion, even treason. Indeed, the rejection of equity manifested in Astell's works emerges, in some sense, from her commitment to a vision of the Church of England (and the obedience which it entailed) which, though articulated provisionally in *Some Reflections upon Marriage*, would reach its fullest articulation in her *Christian Religion*, first published in 1705. A complete accommodation of equity in the sphere of the domestic would have also meant an accommodation of an exceptionality which would manifest itself historically in the phenomenon of Dissent. The unambivalent rejection of principles of equity in Astell's later works (in both *Christian Religion* and her *A Fair Way with the Dissenters*, written at the height of the crisis of occasional conformity in 1704) elaborates a rejection of the exceptionality of dissent—which itself entailed the most powerful challenge to her own political and theological ideals.[8]

---

6  See Perry's *The Celebrated Mary Astell: An Early English Feminist* (Chicago, 1986) for discussions of Astell's perspective on obedience, especially ch. 6, 165–66, 168–69 and 171–72. See also Weil, *Political Passions*, 142–60.

7  The relevant definition of *prescriptive*, from the *OED*, is "Uninterrupted use or possession from time immemorial, or for a period fixed by law as giving a title or right; hence, title or right acquired by virtue of such use or possession: sometimes called *positive prescription*" and "(a) Ancient or continued custom, esp. when viewed as authoritative, (b) Claim founded upon long use." For an analysis of the importance of prescription and "time immemorial" to common law, see J.G.A. Pocock, *The Ancient Constitution and the Feudal Law* (Cambridge, 1987).

8  For an analysis of Astell's treatment of the language of commercial culture, like her treatment of the language of dissent, through appropriation, see William Kolbrener's "Forc'd into an Interest: High Church

**I**

Countering both traditional and contemporary arguments, Astell claims in *Some Reflections upon Marriage* that there is no Biblical authority for the subjection of women. She famously interprets even Paul as her ally, insisting that he says nothing contrary to her claim that women were made for the service of God, not man.

> Nor can anything be concluded to the contrary from St. *Paul*'s Argument, *I Cor. 11*. For he argues only for Decency and Order, according to the present Custom and State of things. Taking his Words strictly and literally, they prove too much, in that *Praying and Prophecying in the Church* are allow'd the Women, provided they do it with their Head Cover'd, as well as the Men; and no inequality can be inferr'd from hence, neither from the Gradation the Apostle there uses, that *the Head of every Man is Christ, and that the Head of the Woman is the Man, and the Head of Christ is GOD*; It being evident from the Form of Baptism, that there is no natural Inferiority among the Divine Persons, but that they are in all things Coequal. The Apostle indeed adds, that *the Man is the Glory of God, and the Woman the Glory of the Man*, Etc. But what does he infer from hence? he says not a word of Inequality, or natural Inferiority, but concludes, that a Woman ought to Cover her head, and a Man ought not to cover his, and that *even Nature itself teaches* us, that *if a Man have long hair it is a shame unto him*. Whatever the Apostle's Argument proves in this place nothing can be plainer, than that there is much more said against the present Fashion of Men's wearing long Hair, than for that Supremacy they lay claim to. For by all that appears in the Text, it is not so much a Law of Nature, that Women shou'd Obey Men, as that Men shou'd not wear long Hair. Now how can a Christian Nation allow Fashions contrary to the Law of Nature, forbidden by an Apostle and declared by him to be a shame to Man? Or if Custom may make an alteration in one Case it may in another, but what then becomes of the Nature and Reason of things? (*SRM* 11–12)

Astell's boldness as an interpreter allows her to characterize apostolic statement as a mere delineation of custom. Paul argues, she says, "only for Decency and Order, according to the present Custom and State of things"; the assertion that "Women shou'd Obey Men" appears parallel to the assertion that "Men shou'd not wear long Hair." Both are customs and subject to alteration over time. With ease, she accepts the idea that various elements of scriptural statement are embedded in a particular time and place and cannot, without absurdity, be elevated to universal applicability. In insisting on her own reading of Paul's words, Astell permits herself not only to be an interpretive dissenter (she knows that she argues against long-standing tradition) but to introduce historical contingency into Biblical material. Astell takes a similar liberty, also in *Some Reflections*, with God's words to Eve. It's true, Astell writes,

> that GOD told *Eve* after the Fall that *her Husband shou'd Rule over her*: And so it is that he told *Esau* by the mouth of *Isaac* his Father, that he shou'd serve his *younger Brother*, and shou'd in time, and when he was strong enough to do it, *break the Yoke from off his Neck*. Now why one Text shou'd be a Command any more than the other, and not both of them be

Predictions only; or why the former shou'd prove *Adam's* natural Right to Rule, and much less every Man's, any more than the latter is a Proof of *Jacob's* Right to Rule, and of *Esau's* to Rebel, one is yet to learn? The Text in both Cases foretelling what wou'd be; but, neither of them determining what ought to be. (*SRM* 19–20)

Astell's ingenious hair-splitting here—between what would be and what ought to be—is not without precedent (Locke similarly interprets this Biblical material in *Two Treatises*), but it does show her willingness to treat a sacred text as if it were subject to her own reason—rather than necessitating absolute acceptance of precedent interpretive authorities.[9]

Interpretive liberty might also be said to characterize Astell's strategy in *A Fair Way with the Dissenters*, where she argues not only against occasional conformity but against all religious dissent.[10] Although she allows interpretive liberty to herself, her aim in this polemical piece is to erase denominational difference in order to recreate the possibility of a universal religious practice based in the Church of England.[11] Absorbing the language of Daniel Defoe's *More Short-Ways with the Dissenters* (his words indicated by italics and sometimes by page numbers) within her own rhetoric, she unapologetically proclaims that "the *Total Destruction of Dissenters as a Party* ... is indeed our Design." She tries to normalize the idea that destruction—"to strike at *the Root of the Dissenting Interest* (4), *to extirpate and destroy* Dissention (3), and hinder its *Succession in the Nation*"—is no undue injury to Dissenters, since their polemics are not a reflection of true conviction, but rather merely "Fancies and Prejudices."[12] Treating beliefs of Dissenters as if they belonged entirely to the world of appearances, Astell assimilates them to the "Cut and Fashion" of contemporary style. Although her destructive aim might be said to be modified by qualified phrasing (she rejects, for example, only "Dissenting *Interest*"), Astell does, in fact, suggest a method for ridding the country of all Dissenters: forbidding them the right to educate their children in independent dissenting schools, in fact, destroying all dissenting academies. "Were it not," Astell inquires,

> better both for their own Posterity, and for the Nation in general (to which certainly these great Pretenders to Publick Spiritedness ought to have some regard) to lay the Seeds of Dissention as much out of their Children's way as possible, and not beat into their Heads such Fancies and Prejudices as would ne'er come there, were they not drove in by an aukward Education, or afterwards taken up upon Worldly and Unchristian Views, and for Temporal Advantage?

---

9  I refer to Locke's interpretation of Genesis. Like Astell, Locke uses the Jacob/Esau story to justify his reading of a different passage of scripture. In the case of Jacob and Esau, God merely "foretold what should *de facto* come to pass." Similarly, God's saying that women should be in subjection to their husbands did not give Adam any authority over Eve but "only foretels what should be the Womans Lot" (John Locke, *Two Treatises of Government*, ed. Peter Laslett [Cambridge, 1999], I.v.48, 47, 174). Although they have different rhetorical purposes, both Locke and Astell use the Jacob/Esau story to dissent from traditional interpretive claims about God's subjection of Eve to Adam, and by extension woman to man.

10  *A Fair Way with the Dissenters and their Patrons*, in Astell, *Political Writings*, 87–127.

11  See Kolbrener, "'Forc'd into an Interest,'" especially 14 ff.

12  *Fair Way*, 90.

If, as Astell continues, "a Method be found out to prevent Posterity from falling into the Separation, it would be one of the greatest Benefits could be done this Kingdom, and no manner of Prejudice to the Toleration Suppressing of their Schools would be a very good and necessary Work, were it like to destroy a Faction."[13] Astell, like other extreme Tory polemicists, cannot conceive of the religious and political nation except in what we might call "totalizing" terms. Despite her opportunistic use of rhetoric, whereby she shows herself willing to operate from momentarily advantageous points of view in order to undermine her opponent, she is so completely committed to a universalized and absolute truth that she regards exceptionality, even when it appeals to conscience, as dangerous. She is contemptuous of occasional conformity not only because its claim to exceptionality to the law is a strategy aimed at worldly advantage, but also because its necessary "doubleness" offends her concept of truth as absolute. Further, she is wholly unsympathetic to the fragmenting appeal to individual case and conscience on which it rests. Thus, in a major strand of her thinking, Astell must, as we will see, exclude the possibility of equity.

## II. Equity

In a general sense, equity is a corrective supplement to the law (*Aequitas erroribus medetu*). Following the spirit rather than the letter, it "softens the rigor" or "mitigates the harshness" of the law and corrects the law's generality, which necessarily causes the law's incapacity to deal justly with all particular cases. Equity does what the law would do if it could anticipate all the circumstances of particular cases and take into account the intention of agents.[14]

In England, equity emerged as a jurisdiction separate from the common law.[15] The special power to step outside legal constraints in order to accomplish a just end gradually devolved onto the Chancellor but originally lay in the King's inherent power as the "Fountain of justice." Before emerging as equity, the power was simply termed the King's "grace." The tradition of identifying equity with the Christian "new dispensation" in contrast to the "old dispensation" of the law was absorbed

---

13  *Fair Way*, 93–94.

14  Although writers on English equity beginning with William Blackstone frequently separated its historical development from this theoretical distinction, earlier eminent writers on equity laid claim to these distinctions in explaining and justifying their work. For studies of law and equity, see William Holdsworth, *History of English Law*, 4th edition (London, 1927); C.K. Allen, *Law in the Making* (Oxford, 1961); R.C. Van Caenegem, *The Birth of the Common Law* (Cambridge, 1997); Theodore F.T. Plucknett, *A Concise History of the Common Law* (Boston, 1956); Joseph Story, *Commentaries on Equity Jurisprudence* (Washington DC, 2000); William Maitland, *Lectures on Equity* (Cambridge, 1929); H.D. Hazeltine, "The Early History of Equity" in *Essays in Legal History*, ed. Paul Vinogradoff (Oxford, 1913), 261–85; Frederick Pollock, "The Transformation of Equity" in Vinogradoff, *Essays*, 286–96; D.M. Kerly, *An Historical Sketch of the Equitable Jurisdiction of the Court of Chancery* (Littleton, CO, 1986); William F. Walsh, *A Treatise on Equity* (Chicago, 1930). For an extensive discussion of the intellectual history of equity, see Kathy Eden, *Poetic and Legal Fiction in the Aristotelian Tradition* (Princeton, 1986), 136ff, and *Hermeneutics and the Rhetorical Tradition* (New Haven, 1997).

15  The separate jurisdictions, once developed, lasted until the Judicature Acts in the nineteenth century.

into the idealization of the king's special powers. How thoroughly this analogue continued to be embedded in legal thinking, long after it ceased to function in the idealization of monarchy, can be seen in Maitland's explanatory vocabulary when he strenuously insists that equity was never opposed to the law: "Equity had come not to destroy the law but to fulfil it."[16]

Routinely called an "extraordinary" form of justice, equity was, generally speaking, a jurisdiction concerned with matters of good faith and conscience, and in its purview were such matters as trusts (and uses, an earlier form of the trust), fraud, and accidents. While common law was said to deal with the *thing* (*in rem*), equity was said to deal with the *person* (*in personam*), whose conscience could be probed in an effort to obtain a form of evidence not available to law. Equity's procedure was inquisitorial rather than dependent on fact-finding (the procedure central to juries in common law courts). Repayment of loans provides a standard example for explaining equity's greater flexibility, its concern with matters of conscience, and its attention to the details of a particular case (as opposed to the relevant legal principle). If B, for example, failed to repay A a loan by a pre-determined date, A could initiate an action against B in common law.[17] The common law courts, however, only examined the facts concerning the thing itself (*in rem*). But B, resorting to courts of equity, was empowered to file a complaint in the form of a bill or a petition. Accordingly, the chancellor could issue an injunction against a judgment received by A at law and compel the parties to appear and answer questions. The chancellor might then discover extenuating or exceptional circumstances that would emerge from viewing the case from a perspective of equity: that, for example, B was *en route* to pay when prevented by a flood which made all roads impassable; or that B had paid 75 percent of the loan and was only defaulting on the last quarter. The chancellor could rule according to the particulars of the case—according to the perspectives of equity— accounting for the intent of the parties, the partial rather than full payment, and so on. Similarly, if B had in fact repaid the loan in its entirety but had failed to get (or could not produce) the proper releasing document, B *would have no case at law* (and would be responsible for paying the debt twice), but *would have a case at equity* where the acknowledged fact of repayment would be considered even without the document required by the law's procedures. The equity court could thus deal with contingencies—having to do with exceptions not immediately present in the facts themselves—that the law could not accommodate.[18]

Many matters found no remedy at law because they did not fall into recognized actionable categories. The common lawyers knew that some cases of injustice would occur, but in order to avoid eroding an established legal principle, they refused to make allowances for particular circumstances and exceptional cases. As the historian

---

16   Maitland (*Lectures*, 17) here echoes Matthew 5:17–18: "Think not that I am come to destroy the law … I am not come to destroy, but to fulfil." See also J.H. Baker's echo of Maitland, *An Introduction to English Legal History* (London, 1990), 118.

17   The Common Law's treatment of debt repayment is a common example among legal historians. See, for example, Baker, *An Introduction*, 118.

18   The law had its own delaying procedures, called "essoins," but could not vary its procedures to accommodate information outside them.

D. M. Kerly notes, "[I]n most cases even of admitted hardship, a medieval statesman would undoubtedly have declared, as the Judges and the Chancellor himself on many occasions did, that it were better a single individual should suffer than that the law and constitution of the land should be changed."[19] As the common law developed (it is frequently said to have "hardened"), its tendency to exclude the extraordinary and exceptional grew more pronounced, which gave rise to the maxim, "Better a mischief than an inconvenience." As explained by legal historian Theodore Plucknett, the lawyers thought it was better to "tolerate a 'mischief' (a failure of substantial justice in a particular case) rather than an 'inconvenience' (a breach of legal principle)."[20] With the common law increasingly excluding the exception, one of the principal tasks for the equitable jurisdiction was to determine how to deal with cases that lay outside of the strict application of the law.

One of the forms of exceptional justice developed at equity, central to the present discussion of Astell, was the doctrine of married women's separate property. As William Holdsworth explains,

> The common law had no place for [the "newer ideas which limit the husband's control in the interest of the wife"], and therefore the alterations in the status of the married woman which a changed order of ideas demanded were unable to take place within its sphere. They were made in the rival system of equity, which gave effect to the demand for an improvement in the status of the married woman by creating for her a peculiar proprietary capacity.[21]

The development of married women's limited legal right to own separate property illustrates the relationship between law and equity. On the one hand, equity's jurisdiction was a supportive supplement to the common law (allowing the law not to clutter or compromise its principles—"Equity follows the Law"; *Aequitas sequitur legem*), but on the other hand equity was in competition with the common law (as Holdsworth's use of the term "rival" conveys). This double relationship was explicitly recognized. As Maitland explains, as early as the fourteenth century "complaints about this extraordinary justice grew loud," even while it was acknowledged that the courts of equity (under jurisdiction of the chancellor) were doing useful work "that could not be done ... by the courts of common law" (like "enforcing uses or trusts").[22] Thus equity, in taking on the role of "helper," solving problems that the law could not (or did not want) to recognize, allowed the law itself to maintain internal consistency. By developing such areas of "legal" concern, however, equity increased its jurisdiction, and therefore its power, and became a genuine rival to the common law. It was a power outside the law and potentially, in the view of the common lawyers, "lawless."

Because equity was in many instances "situational," it was, or was at least conceived to be, less bound by precedent.[23] Although by the Restoration and the

---

19   Kerly, *Historical Sketch*, 4.

20   Plucknett, *Concise History*, 680. See also Baker, *An Introduction*, 94–95.

21   Holdsworth, *English Law*, 3:532–33.

22   Maitland, *Lectures*, 6.

23   The most famous (and most frequently quoted) criticism of equity comes from John Seldon (1584–1654): "Equity is a roguish thing. For Law we have a measure, know what to trust to. Equity is according

eighteenth century equity had developed a concern for precedent, its use of precedents differed from that of common law. Holdsworth, in discussing the nature of equity, quotes Jessell: "It must not be forgotten," he said,

> that the rules of equity are not like the rules of the common law, supposed to have been established from time immemorial. It is perfectly well known that they have been established from time to time—altered, improved, and refined from time to time ... the older precedents in equity are of very little value. The doctrines are progressive, refined, and improved; and if we want to know what the rules of equity are, we must look, of course, rather to the more modern than the more ancient cases.[24]

"Time immemorial," so central to the concept of common law, is conceptually opposed by the "time-to-time" character of equity. With the printing of equity reports and with equity textbooks, the rules of the equitable jurisdiction became more settled, and in fact, equity's judgments often included a remarkable plethora of references to previous judgments.[25] But, in comparison with law, equity seldom called on prescriptive or time-out-of-mind authority.[26] Law was ancient custom; equity, operating on a reasoned principle of fairness and good conscience in the particular case, could set aside custom. For equity, the antiquity of a custom could not be its salient feature. Equity, as Jessel remarked, looked "rather to the more modern than the more ancient cases."

Because the equity courts were historically associated with the King's prerogative (with his power to go beyond the boundaries of the law to ensure justice or allow mercy), one might have expected equity to be an attractive model for Astell. Its exceptionality might have seemed a realization or reification of her profoundly royalist political commitments and her High Church religious loyalties. But, as we will see, the political valence of equity was multi-layered, and even the King's claim of prerogative, as it actually operated, ran counter to Astell's principles. Arthur Annesley defended James's dispensing powers in specifically equitable terms in his pamphlet, *The King's Right of Indulgence in spiritual Matters, with the Equity thereof, Asserted*. The King has a right to indulge and permit "Persons to serve God as they think most for the good of their own Souls, especially when they agree in

---

to the conscience of him that is Chancellor, and as that is larger or narrower, so is Equity. 'Tis all one as if they should make the standard for the measure we call a 'foot' a Chancellor's foot; what an uncertain measure that would be! One Chancellor has a long foot, another a short foot, a third an indifferent foot. 'Tis the same thing in the Chancellor's conscience" (Richard Milward, "Equity," in *Table Talk of John Selden*, ed. Frederick Pollock [London, 1927], 43).

24  Holdsworth, *English Law*, 1:465–66.

25  For examples, see *Reports of Cases Argued and Determined in the High Court of Chancery ... Collected by William Peere Williams*, 2 vols. (London, 1740).

26  The appeal to antiquity was sometimes made for Equity: Louis A. Knafla, discussing the rivalry of Sir Edward Coke and Lord Ellesmere (and the corresponding conflict between law and equity), nevertheless discusses the earlier period of amicability between the Common Law and other courts. "Readers at the inns of court lectured on the antiquity of the Chancery. Among the lectures of famous Readers, Edward Coke called the law of the Court 'time out of mind'" (*Law and Politics in Jacobean England: The Tracts of Lord Chancellor Ellesmere* [Holmes Beach, FL, 1986], 158). But this claim was a minor rather than a major element in the historical characterization of equity.

Fundamentals with the rest of their Brethren." Invoking principles deriving from equity, Annesley argues that "these may not be punished in their *Estates* or *Liberties*, much less in their *Lives*, for Nonconformity."[27] James's "equitable" use of his prerogative operated in favor of both Roman Catholics and dissenters, which might be seen as compromising the Crown's unwavering commitment to the integrity of the Anglican Church. Yet, Astell's own works evidence an almost exclusive affiliation with authority and obedience, and not the equitable tendencies which Annesley associates even with James's royal prerogative.

Despite her aversion to equity, however, Astell does invoke the more conventional connotations of equity on several occasions. In introducing herself to John Norris in what would become the first letter of *Letters Concerning the Love of God*, Astell attributes her own expectation that Norris will be receptive to her query rather than "remit [her] to the Distaff or the Kitchin," to his being more "Equitable" than other men.[28] Here she uses a recognizable framework: established cultural attitude and practice (custom) would cause a learned man to "remit" Astell and all other women to the feminine spheres of "the Distaff or the Kitchen." She acknowledges Norris's own exceptionality because he can set aside custom and respond to her particular case. In *A Serious Proposal, Part II*, insisting on the necessity for women to attain knowledge through education, Astell similarly calls on the principle of equity:

> For if the Grand business that Women as well as Men have to do in this World be to prepare for the next, ought not all their Care and Industry to Centre here? and since the matter is of Infinite Consequence *is it equitable to deny 'em the use of any help?* If therefore Knowledge were but any ways Instrumental, tho at the remotest distance, to the Salvation of our Souls, it were fit to apply our selves to it.[29]

In a sense, Astell's proposal itself, which parallels and displaces a proposal of marriage, can be seen as setting up an equitable alternative not available to women in the custom-regulated world. Her proposal would create a world of intellectual *femmes soles*. The two parts of *A Serious Proposal* can be understood as Astell's attempt to provide equitable remedies for women, removed from an unjust world governed by custom and the prescriptions of men.

Yet in Astell's more substantial and explicit writings on equity issues in *Some Reflections*, she first delineates, and then resigns herself to the inequities that stem from property arrangements. A woman, she affirms, must place "her Fortune and Person entirely in [the Husband-Monarch's] Powers":

> She and all the Grants he makes are in his Power, and there have been but too many instances of Husbands that by wheedling or threatening their Wives, by seeming Kindness

---

27   Arthur Annesley, *The King's Right of Indulgence in Spiritual Matters, with the Equity Thereof, Asserted by a Person of Honour* (London, 1688 [published posthumously]).

28   *Letters Concerning the Love of God*, Letter I, 1–2. Later, in answering Letter V, Astell writes: "Your Hypothesis, as you now explain and rectifie it, runs clear and unperplext, and has nothing in it but what equitably understood challenges my full Consent ..." (103).

29   Mary Astell, *A Serious Proposal to the Ladies*, ed. Patricia Springborg (Peterborough, ON, 2002), 147, emphasis added.

or cruel Usage, have perswaded or forc'd them out of what has been settled on them ... A Man enters into Articles very readily before Marriage, and so he may, for he performs no more of them afterwards than he thinks fit ... [H]e is sure to perswade her out of her Agreement, and bring her, it must be suppos'd, *Willingly*, to give up what she did vainly hope to obtain, and what she thought had been made sure to her ... For Covenants betwixt Husband and Wife, like Laws in an Arbitrary Government, are of little Force, the Will of the Sovereign is all in all."

The husband, she concludes, does not act "like an equitable or honest Man" (*SRM*, 51–52).

In her complaint, Astell outlines equity's solution—separate property settled on the wife. She insists, however that such a solution cannot work—notwithstanding any agreements made before marriage—because husbands dominate the scene at home: "the Will of the Sovereign is all in all." One would not guess from Astell's objections that the courts, too, had husbands in their view, to prevent the very problems she identifies.[30] One could say that she simply recognizes, perhaps in a somewhat exaggerated form, the problems experienced by women on a daily basis.[31] We should note, however, that equity's arrangements for separate property were not mere private agreements—"Covenants betwixt Husband and Wife"; they involved in most cases real limitations on the power of the husband to act.[32] Equity restricted the husband's power to reject a legally binding arrangement more significantly than Astell's account implies. Furthermore, the courts (albeit in their paternalist and protectionist mode) were aware of strategies of men who sought, in Astell's term, to "wheedle" their wives out of money settled on them. Without suggesting that equity created a panacea for propertied women, it is important to note that Astell shows no interest in the real, if partial, remedies that equity did provide for married women.

The standard example of repayment of a loan may seem very distant from Astell's concerns. But in fact, the situations Astell outlines for women often have a comparable structure. She repeatedly identifies an egregiously unfair and asymmetrical domestic situation and then simply accedes to the injustice, schooling her audience not in any potentially remedial practice, but rather resignation. The discussion of women's legal standing in marriage is throughout a substantive case

---

30  "'[S]ince Queen Elizabeth's time it hath been the constant course of this court to set aside and frustrate all incumbrances and acts of the husband upon the trust in the wife's term, and that he shall neither charge or grant it away; and 'tis the common way of proceeding for the jointures of women, to convey a term in trust for them upon marriage, that it may be out of the power and reach of the husband'" (Doyley v. Perful [1673]; quoted in Holdsworth, *English Law*, 6:644).

31  The courts were not always consistent. "[T]he court sometimes seems to have regarded devices used by the wife to withdraw her property from her husband's control as frauds upon the husband's legal rights, unless the husband had received consideration for the abandonment of his rights" (Holdsworth, *English Law*, 5:312). For a discussion of limitations in the developing doctrine of women's separate property, see Susan Staves, "No Dower of a Trust" in *Married Women's Separate Property in England, 1660–1832* (Cambridge, 1990), 27–55.

32  As Staves suggests, separate property arrangements can be seen as agreements by which fathers limited the power of husbands over the property of wife and future children. Women were not usually principals in the arrangements. Nevertheless, such arrangements did restrict the power of husbands. Staves, "No Dower of a Trust," 53, 84.

for equity and a procedural case for law. Astell has no desire to "soften the rigor" or "mitigate the harshness" of the law. The extremity of the law's remedy-less structure for married women fits Astell's purposes. While equitable practice may lead, over time, to fundamental changes in the law, as it did in the case of married women's separate property, equity, for Astell, is necessarily an ameliorative and not a "radical" structure.[33] Though *A Serious Proposal* is in the "genre" of improvement projects, and Astell's own practical charitable work sought to provide "equitable" solutions to women's social and legal predicaments, equitable remedies do not provide solutions for the wrongs she identifies in the context of marriage. For her polemical purposes, a better functioning system of equitable relief would only enable women to live more happily in the world. For Astell, women had a simple (and stark) choice: marriage, at best an opportunity for martyrdom, or an unmarried life, devoted to selfless divine service. Astell saw these extreme choices—a function of her rejection of equity in marriage—as providing the conditions necessary to move women's aspirations toward spiritual and intellectual goals.

Astell thus shows herself to be more comfortable with the severity of law than with the mere mitigation of its harshness. The opposition between law and equity underlies her presentation of women's situation in marriage, and she employs it to suggest that God is the only true source of equity. His form of equity, however, is to give women the strength to bear their trials, not to improve their situations. As Astell writes in *Some Reflections*, reflecting on the relation between divine justice and equity: "How it agrees with the Justice of Men we inquire not, but certainly Heaven is abundantly more Equitable than to injoin Women the hardest Task, and give them the least Strength to perform it."[34] Divine equity, for Astell, lies precisely in rendering women able to suffer the injustices (unameliorated by a principle of human equity) imposed by men.

In what she considered her most important work—*The Christian Religion as Profess'd by a Daughter of the Church of England*—Astell delineates a perspective which evidences an even greater distance from principles of equity (elucidating as well the commitments present in the earlier work on marriage) "[I]n reference to Superiors, 'tis better that I endure the Unreasonableness, Injustice, or Oppression of a Parent, a Master, etc. than that the Establish'd Rules of Order and good Government shou'd be superseded on my account."[35] It would be better, in other words, for her to suffer an injustice than for justice achieved on the basis of an exception (that is, on her own account) to weaken long-established principle. What Astell says here, from which I take my title, paraphrases the legal maxim "Better a mischief than an inconvenience." This maxim, like Astell's paraphrase of it, disallows that exception, even when the exception opposes "Unreasonableness, Injustice, or Oppression." "Better a mischief than an inconvenience" is central to Astell's thinking, and her

---

33  For discussions of equity as a source of law, see Walsh, *A Treatise on Equity*, 31–34, and Allen, *Law in the Making*, 396–404.

34  Mary Astell, *Some Reflections upon Marriage* (New York, 1970), 62. (This is a republication of the London, 1730 edition).

35  *The Christian Religion, as Profess'd by a Daughter of the Church of England* (London, 1717), 138. Hereafter cited parenthetically as *CR*.

commitment to this principle requires her to counter-thematize equity. In Astell's view, exceptionality, on which equity depends, is dangerous and is only countered by an almost relentless commitment to law.[36]

## III. Exceptionality is lawless

In part, Astell rejects exceptionality for good feminist reasons: the exceptional woman, unless a queen, tends to become a satiric figure—the learned lady, the *rara avis*, or, in Astell's case, Madonella in the *Tatler*.[37] But Astell rejects the exceptionality inherent in equity because the acceptance of exceptionality is too close to toleration of religious dissent. If the degree of religious toleration delineated in the Declaration of Breda had been maintained, dissent would have found a place within the law. With the Clarendon Code, however, dissent was once again outside the law, and any argument made for toleration had to be based on some special allowance, some charitable interpretation of the law. Despite equity's association with the royal prerogative as a widely acknowledged cultural ideal, it could be associated as well with non-conformity and religious toleration, in particular concerning the Quakers. In a pamphlet entitled "The Conscientious Cause of the Sufferers, called Quakers," the use of the term *conscientious* reveals the equitable basis of its appeal.[38] Astell's mentor and philosophical correspondent, John Norris, was directly involved in this quarrel. In his *Reflections Upon the Conduct of Human Life*, he disparaged the Quakers and was answered by "A Just Reprehension to John Norris … for his Unjust *Reflections* on the Quakers."[39] An earlier pamphlet takes up the defense, in specifically

---

36  Many of Astell's contemporaries who opposed Equity's exceptionality also thought it was dangerous, but on different grounds. Because Equity could create an exception to a judgment at law, it was dangerous in the same way that the King's prerogative was dangerous—on constitutional grounds. For a theoretical discussion of the exception, see George Schwab, *The Challenge of the Exception: An Introduction to the Political Ideas of Carl Schmitt between 1921 and 1936* (New York, 1970).

37  Astell is figured as "a profess'd Platonne" and "the most unaccountable Creature of her Sex" (*The Tatler*, ed. Donald F. Bond [Oxford, 1987], 1:240 [#32]).

38  George Whitehead, *The conscientious cause of the sufferers, called Quakers pleaded and expostulated with their oppressors in this nation of England, and particularly in and about the city of London: and those in power that go about to transport, banish, or suppress them for their meetings, innocently informed, and impartially cautioned, from the innocent and oppressed seed of God, which herein calls for justice and equity, and utterly exclaims against severity and persecution for matters of conscience or religion: wherein first and principally is shewed, the use and end of the publick assemblies of the said sufferers, in answer to several objections against them, 1. with respect to their conscientiousness, as it being their duty to meet, 2. with respect to their innocency and peaceable deportment both to the nation and government therein* (London, 1664). Another similar title of the same year: *For the King and both Houses of Parliament being a declaration of the present suffering and imprisonment of above 600 of the people of God, in scorn called Quakers, who now suffer in England for conscience sake … together with a particular relation of some of the late inhumane cruelties inflicted on some of the aforesaid people …* (London, 1664).

39  John Norris, *Reflections Upon the Conduct of Human Life with reference to the study of learning and knowledge: in a letter to the excellent lady, the Lady Masham; to which is annex'd a visitation sermon, by the same author* (London, 1690); Richard Vickris, *A just reprehension to John Norris of Newton St. Loe, for his unjust reflection on the Quakers in his book, entituled, Reflections Upon the Conduct of*

legal terms, of non-conformists more generally: "The Conformist's Plea for the Non-Conformist" (1681) deals with the "Reasonableness and Equity of their Desires and Proposals."[40] Non-conformists could be seen as deserving charity in religious terms and equity in legal terms; neither Norris nor Astell embraced principles of equity for they threatened the very integrity of the Church of England.

Occasional conformity might, in fact, be seen as an equitable solution; without compromising a legal principle, it allowed for exceptional practice. This was a quarrel in which Astell was vehemently engaged—one in which she reveals her absolute intolerance for a principle of exceptionality. Dissenters are for her fundamentally lawless. That they took law and authority into their own hands makes them both a conceptual and actual danger to the Church of England. Her ironic treatment of Daniel Defoe and others in *A Fair Way with the Dissenters* makes clear that mercy and forgiveness had no application in the context of dissent. Her recommendation is to return to the full force of the law; charity remains beyond consideration.

> If usurping all Royal Authority and maintaining a Bloody Civil War against their Sovereign, and at last, with an unheard of Impudence, arraigning him at their Bar, and beheading him at his own Palace-Gate; if these be Lawful Means we are sure they have made use of them. But then I pray what Means can be unlawful? These are the Dissenters gradual Steps in suppressing what they called Tyranny, and when we *catch them upon the first Round of the Ladder*, we may, *without Breach of Charity, conclude, that they mean, as soon as they are able, to mount to the top of it.*[41]

It is true that the pamphlet-war genre can often be characterized as *strident*, but Astell's extremity—"when we catch them on the first Round of the Ladder"—precludes any possibility of an equitable solution. Astell reels from the disorder of the Civil War; her consequent commitment to order overrides everything else. The intensity of her argument arises from the sense that the order of her society is under siege. The Civil Wars—and Civil War accommodation, indeed celebration of exceptionality—mark the transgression of a fundamental, quasi-sacred boundary.

The Dissenters' failure of obedience places them in a lawless category, forcing Astell to reiterate the foundational necessity of obedience to law. Parallel to the political tract on dissent, Astell also centralizes the question of obedience in her *Christian Religion*. In doing so, she compromises the principle upon which she has put forward her earlier proposal to the ladies: the preeminent place of reason. This may seem only an apparent contradiction. Astell, after all, carefully articulates a caveat, distinguishing ecclesiastical authority from all others: "But when I speak of the little deference that is to be given to Names, Authorities, and receiv'd Opinions,

---

*Human Life, &c together with his false representation of their principle of the light* ... (London, 1691).

40 Edward Pearse, *The conformists plea for the nonconformists, or, A just and compassionate representation of the present state and condition of the non-conformists as to I. The greatness of their sufferings, II. Hardness of their case, III. Reasonableness and equity of their desires and proposals, IV. Qualifications, and worth of their persons, V. Peaceableness of their behaviour, VI. The churches prejudice by their exclusion, &c. humbly submitted to authority / by a beneficed minister, and a regular son of the Church of England* (London, 1681).

41 *Fair Way*, 99–100, emphasis added.

I extend it no farther than to matters purely Philosophical to mere Humane Truths, and do not design any Prejudice to the Authority of the Church which is of different consideration."[42] As a daughter of the Church of England, she must rely on its authorities. But she extends the principle even further, affirming that she will with confidence submit "to him or them who shall have Lawful Authority over" her. And even if those in authority should be wrong, her submission remains, she affirms, necessary and unapologetic:

> For tho' they should happen to lead me into error, yet in this case they, and not I must answer for it; as for me *I am safer in my Obedience, than I cou'd have been even with Truth in a disorderly way.* (*CR* 34, emphasis added)

It is better for her to be *obedient and wrong* than to discover truth in the wrong way. Such an assertion would at least seem to be in conflict with her discussion in *A Serious Proposal, Part I*: "She is, it may be, taught the Principles and Duties of Religion, but not Acquainted with the Reasons and Grounds of them; being told 'tis enough for her to believe, to examine why, and wherefore, belongs not to her."[43] Even Truth acquired in a disorderly way must be subordinated to order, a view that runs counter to her description of "blind Obedience" in *Reflections*:

> A blind Obedience is what a Rational Creature shou'd never Pay, nor wou'd such an one receive it, did he rightly understand its Nature. For Human Actions are no otherwise valuable, than as they are conformable to Reason, but a blind Obedience is an Obeying *without Reason*, for ought we know, *against it*. God himself does not require our Obedience at this rate; he lays before us the goodness and reasonableness of his Laws, and were there any thing in them whose Equity we could not readily comprehend, yet we have this clear and sufficient Reason on which to found our Obedience, that nothing but what's Just and Fit, can be enjoin'd by a Just, a Wise, and Gracious GOD; but this is a Reason will never hold in respect of Mens Commands, unless they can prove themselves infallible, and consequently Impeccable too. (*SRM* 75)

God can be counted on for Equity—even if its operation is not comprehensible— but this is not the case with men. Although she says in *Christian Religion* that her "Teachers and Spiritual Pastors ... don't require blind Obedience," the formulation that she uses to explain why it is safer for her to obey without question allows little distinction between that and blind obedience (*CR* 3).

But there are further problems here. Astell's defense—"God never requires us to submit our Judgments to our Fellow-Creatures, except in cases wherein He makes them, and not us, answerable for the Error and all its evil Consequences"—replicates the legal reasoning behind the husband's culpability for a wife's wrong if done in his presence and justifies the husband's position (*CR* 4). Astell's explanation for her confidence in authority even when the authority is wrong parallels the protection/ dependence formula fundamental to feudal relations and to early modern political and marital arrangements. Further, Astell's formula for obedience rests on the

---

42  *Serious Proposal*, 92.
43  *Serious Proposal*, 16.

necessity to obey prescriptive authority—when there is no better. Obedience is the cornerstone of her set of principles: It is "[i]mpossible," she writes, "to be Happy unless Obedient."

> That all Authority being deriv'd from God's Absolute Dominion ... consequently the reason and ground of Superiority is the suppos'd Excellency of the Superior. *But because Order and Government must be maintain'd,* which cou'd not be, considering the Corruption and Partiality of Mankind, were every one left to be Judge in this matter, therefore we must Submit to him, who *by the laws and Usages of the Place,* or by *Prescription when there is not a better title,* has a claim to Superiority, even tho' he be not really better than his Neighbours. (*CR* 61, 138–39, emphasis added)

Obedience is a necessary response to God—entailing not merely an ethical imperative, but an epistemological one as well, providing the only grounds for the apprehension of God. Astell almost apotheosizes obedience, making submission to those merely validated by "the laws and Usages of the Place" analogous to that larger Christian requirement to surrender the will to God. In such a system, there is no room for exception. "Because order and government must be maintained," Astell almost turns the new dispensation back into the old. The "Corruption ... of Mankind" seems to allow law to trump grace.

There is hardly any better way to describe a husband than he "who by the laws and Usages of the Place, or by Prescription when there is not a better title, has a claim to Superiority." It is interesting to interline this text with Astell's ironic treatment of men's prescriptive authority in *Reflections*: Men "govern the World, they have Prescription on their side," which women are "too weak to dispute"; "Who shall contend with them? Immemorial Prescription is on their Side in these Parts of the World, antient Tradition and modern Usage!" (*SRM* 79, 29).[44] Her irony here is clearly aimed at long-standing custom and prescriptive right. While in *Some Reflections* the rejection of equity is nonetheless paired (somewhat paradoxically) with the ironic attack on custom, in *Christian Religion*, the advocacy of obedience against equity is unambiguous. In this tract, she calls on her readers for compliance with outward marks of status: "There is also a more Peculiar *Outward* Respect and Honour due to *some*, according to the Laws and customs of the Place we live in; and an *Inward* Esteem to *others*, in proportion to their Real Worth" (*CR* 113).

In *Christian Religion*, then, Astell defends prescriptive authority and reinstates custom. She thus makes a direct counter move to her earlier statement: "Nor can Error, be it as antient as it may, ever plead Prescription against Truth" (*SRM* 10). Although even in *Some Reflections*, Astell had rejected the remedies of equity, in the theological tract, written after the occasional conformity crisis (when exceptionality had raised its head in the form of Dissent) Astell's condemnation of equity is far more unqualified. That is, in *Christian Religion*, Astell aligns her thinking unequivocally

---

44  She continues, "Our Fathers, have all along, both taught and practiced Superiority over the weaker Sex, and consequently Women are by Nature inferior to Men, as was to be demonstrated. An Argument which must be acknowledged unanswerable; for, as well as I love my Sex, I will not pretend a Reply to *such* Demonstration!" (Springborg, ed., *Some Reflections* [1730], 123).

with the prescriptive power of law as ancient custom and against the exceptionality of equity.

As Perry points out in her biography, Astell quotes with approval the Earl of Halifax's *The Lady's New-year's Gift; or, Advice to a Daughter* in the 1730 edition of *Some Reflections upon Marriage*:[45] "For, as a noble Lord, who knew the World perfectly well, instructs his Daughter, she may as well play with Fire, as dally with Gallantry":

> The *Extravagancies* of the Age have made *Caution* more necessary ... the unjustifiable Freedom of some of your Sex, have involved the rest in the Penalty of being reduced. And though this cannot so alter the Nature of Things, as to make that *Criminal*, which in it self is *Indifferent*; yet if it maketh it *dangerous*, that alone is sufficient to justify the *Restraint*. (*SRM* [1730] 13)

Any deviation from the rule is dangerous, even if not "criminal." It is not surprising to find Astell allying herself, in *Christian Religion*, with Halifax. Under the guidelines he articulates, exceptionality is not possible, as we can further see from the explicit case he makes against equity for women: "You must first lay it down for a foundation in generall," he writes, "that there is inequality in the Sexes."[46]

> It may be alleadged by the Counsel reteined by your Sex, that as there is in all other Lawes, an appeal from the letter to the equity ..., it is as reasonable, that some court of a larger jurisdiction might be erected, where some wives might resort and plead specially. And ... they might have releif and obtein a mittigation in their own particular, of a sentence which was given generally against woman kind.[47]

But after entertaining the possibility of equity for some married women, he makes clear its impossibility: "*it is safer some injustice should be connived at ... than to breake into an establishment upon which the order of humane Society doth so much depend*" (emphasis added).[48] As Astell will later do, Halifax, too, denies equity by relying upon his own version of the maxim, "Better a mischief than an inconvenience," paraphrased as "it is safer some injustice should be connived at ... than to breake into an establishment upon which the order of humane Society doth so much depend." Astell of the 1730 edition of *Some Reflections* concurs with a Halifax who sees in marriage, as Astell saw in dissent, any accommodation to exceptionality as disruptive if not dangerous. Astell's and Halifax's reasons may have been different, but they seem to see similarly potent risks in implementing the principle of equity. For Astell of 1730, exceptionality, the disturbance of principle by an individual case—whether in the context of politics, theology, or marriage—would lead to a world of intolerable contingency.

---

45  Perry, *Celebrated Mary Astell*, 160. (Perry points out Astell's use of Halifax but does not quote the section relevant to my argument). George Saville, Marquis of Halifax, *The Works of George Saville, Marquis of Halifax*, ed. Mar, N. Brown, vol. 2 (Oxford, 1989), 363–406.

46  Halifax, *Works*, 369–70

47  Halifax, *Works*, 370–71.

48  Halifax, *Works*, 371.

Chapter X

# Mary Astell on the Causation of Sensation

Eileen O'Neill

While scholarship on Mary Astell has shed light on her significant contributions to seventeenth-century social and political philosophy, it has, until quite recently, largely neglected her work in natural philosophy, metaphysics, and theology.[1] In this chapter, I examine her views on a topic that cuts across all three neglected areas of her thought: the causation of sensation.

In the scant literature on this topic, there has been considerable disagreement about the content of Astell's initial response to John Norris's quasi-occasionalist theory of sensation in *Letters Concerning the Love of God* (1695), which she co-authored with Norris. There is also no consensus about whether Astell altered her views on this topic in her subsequent works: *A Serious Proposal to the Ladies, Part II* (1697), and *The Christian Religion as Profess'd by a Daughter of the Church of England* (1705). The bulk of the scholarship to date has treated Astell's views primarily in terms of its relation to British philosophy—especially the positions of Norris, John Locke, Henry More, and Damaris Masham. In this chapter I show that by also exploring the relation of Astell's views to Descartes's in more detail than has heretofore been done, a new reading of Astell on sensation emerges. I also examine the philosophical force of her arguments by setting them against the historical backdrop of longstanding philosophical debates between Aristotelian naturalist philosophers and theologians advocating occasionalism.

For helpful comments on this paper and encouragement with my work on Astell I would like to thank Desmond Clarke, Karen Detlefsen, Daniel Garber, Sarah Hutton, Sukjae Lee, Paul Lodge, Stephen Menn, Gary Ostertag, Tad Schmaltz, Ralph Schumacher, and the members of my 2006 graduate seminar. The paper is dedicated to Stephen Menn.

1   This point is made in E. Derek Taylor, "Mary Astell's Ironic Assault on John Locke's Theory of Thinking Matter," *Journal of the History of Ideas* 62.3 (2001): 505–22. Others, in addition to Taylor, who have discussed Astell's views in natural philosophy, metaphysics, or theology include Richard Acworth, *The Philosophy of John Norris of Bemerton (1657–1712)* (Hildesheim, 1979); Ruth Perry, *The Celebrated Mary Astell: An Early English Feminist* (Chicago, 1986); Kathleen M. Squadrito, "Mary Astell's Critique of Locke's View of Thinking Matter," *Journal of the History of Philosophy* 25.3 (1987): 433–39, and "Mary Astell," in *A History of Women Philosophers*, vol. 3, ed. Mary Ellen Waithe (Dordrecht, 1991), 87–99; Patricia Springborg, "Astell, Masham, and Locke: Religion and Politics" in *Women Writers and the Early Modern British Political Tradition*, ed. Hilda L. Smith (Cambridge, 1998), 105–25; Eileen O'Neill, "Mary Astell," in *Routledge Encyclopedia of Philosophy* (London, 1998), 1:527–30; Jacqueline Broad, *Women Philosophers of the Seventeenth Century* (Cambridge, 2002) and "Adversaries or Allies? Occasional Thoughts on the Masham–Astell Exchange," *Eighteenth-Century Thought* 1 (2003): 123–49.

In the first section, I argue that in *Letters* Astell provides a philosophically substantial reason for resisting Norris's Malebranche-inspired view that God is the *sole* efficient cause of our sensations. I show, *contra* those who hold that Astell accepted Norris's account of sensation, that her arguments entail that bodies play a causal role in the production of sensation.[2] While commentators have rightly noted an overlap in these arguments and John Locke's posthumously published ones against seventeenth-century occasionalism, I show that Astell's two main criticisms of occasionalism are prefigured in St Thomas's arguments against medieval Islamic occasionalism.[3] In order to evaluate the force of Astell's strongest argument against Norris, I compare Norris's brand of occasionalism with the medieval versions, and that of Malebranche.

In the second section, I examine Astell's own account of the causation of sensation. She suggests that there may be a "sensible congruity" between features of external bodies and the powers of the soul employed in sensation. That is, although there are no sensations in bodies, specific bodies are fitly disposed to "draw forth" specific sensations in fitly disposed souls.

Some scholars have interpreted this theory of "sensible congruity" as a departure from the Cartesian view that matter is inert, and thus as a departure from the orthodox form of Cartesian dualism.[4] I argue, however, that Astell's brief remarks in *Letters* are largely compatible with Descartes's account of sensation, which Norris had outlined and criticized in "A Discourse Concerning the Measure of Divine Love" (1693)—the very text that had motivated Astell's letters to Norris.

In the final section, I turn to disagreements in the recent literature about Astell's views on sensation in her publications subsequent to *Letters*. Some scholars contend that while in *Letters* she agreed with Norris's rejection of bodies as causes of sensations and embraced his Malebranchean view of "seeing all things in God," she abandoned this position in *A Serious Proposal, Part II*, only to reaffirm it in *The Christian Religion*.[5] Others maintain that she resisted occasionalism in *Letters*, but embraced it in *The Christian Religion*.[6] Still others argue that by the time she wrote *A Serious Proposal, Part II*, she had decided to suspend judgment about the issue of mind-body interaction.[7] I agree with the majority of the commentators that she unquestionably held an orthodox Cartesian account of sensation in *A Serious Proposal, Part II*. I also argue that there is insufficient evidence to support the claim of Astell's late conversion to occasionalism in *The Christian Religion*.

---

2   For the view that in *Letters* Astell held that God is the only efficient cause of our sensations, see Springborg, "Astell, Masham and Locke," 112; cf. Squadrito, "Mary Astell," 97.

3   On the overlap between Astell's anti-occasionalist arguments in *Letters* and Locke's arguments in "Remarks Upon Some of Mr. Norris's Books, Wherein he asserts P. Malebranche's Opinion of our seeing all Things in God," in *The Works of John Locke*, 10 vols. (London, 1812), 10:249, see Perry, *Celebrated Mary Astell*, 79; Taylor, "Ironic Assault," 510; Broad, *Women Philosophers*, 104, 125.

4   Broad, *Women Philosophers*, 108; Taylor, "Ironic Assault," 509–10.

5   See Springborg's introduction and notes to her edition of Astell's *A Serious Proposal, Parts I & II*, (London, 1997) esp. 189, n. 3. Hereafter cited parenthetically as *SP I* and *SP II*.

6   See Acworth, *Philosophy of John Norris*, 174, 178; Taylor, "Ironic Assault," 511–12.

7   See Broad, *Women Philosophers*, 109.

## I. Anti-occasionalism in *Letters*: Astell's arguments and their historical precedents

In *Letters* Norris reiterates his view, for which he had earlier argued in "A Discourse Concerning the Measure of Divine Love," that (1) God deserves to be the sole object of our love, and that (2) God is the only efficient cause of all our sensations, and thus of all our pleasures. And he again argues that (2) provides grounds for (1). While Astell admits that Norris has convinced her of the truth of (1), well into the correspondence she indicates that she has not been convinced that (2) is needed as grounding for (1).[8] And in her final, appended letter, Astell makes clear that although she had initially accepted (2), she now has two objections to it: "First, That this Theory renders a great Part of GOD's Workmanship vain and useless. Secondly, That it does not well comport with his Majesty" (*L* 278; see *L* 4). As will become clear in what follows, these arguments are challenges to an occasionalist account of sensation. Thus, I reject the position of Patricia Springborg and Kathleen Squadrito that in *Letters* Astell holds (2); I instead concur with the majority of scholars who view Astell in *Letters* as resisting Norris's account of the production of sensation.[9] Indeed Astell's two arguments have precedents in the centuries-old philosophical debates concerning occasionalism.

Western theistic philosophers have typically agreed that God is the *primary* cause of all phenomena. Some, however, have argued for the further claim that God is the *sole* efficient cause of phenomena (other than the volitions of free agents whom God has endowed with intellect and free will). These latter philosophers, who have denied that there are genuine secondary (or creaturely) causes in nature, I will call "occasionalists."[10] Medieval Muslim thinkers, such as al-Ghazali of the eleventh century, and medieval Christian philosophers, such as Gabriel Biel of the fifteenth century, discussed some form of the position long before Malebranche in the seventeenth century.

Scholastic Aristotelians held that the world is filled with individual corporeal substances, which are instantiations of the different species of things. For example, this particular body might be an instance of the species, fire. Individual substances have natures that determine their causal powers and dispositions—powers and dispositions that are definitive of the various species of things. For instance, the nature of this fire determines that it has the active causal power to burn appropriately disposed substances, such as this cotton. In its turn, the cotton has the passive causal power to be burned by appropriately disposed substances, such as this fire. The Aristotelians, in opposition to the occasionalists, held that corporeal

---

8  See [Mary Astell and] John Norris, *Letters Concerning the Love of God* (London, 1695), 208–9. Hereafter cited parenthetically as *L*.

9  Springborg, "Astell, Masham and Locke," 112; Broad, *Women Philosophers*, 104–8; Perry, *Celebrated Mary Astell*, 78–79; Acworth, *Philosophy of John Norris*, 174; Taylor, "Ironic Assault," 509–10. Cf. Squadrito, "Mary Astell's Critique," 439.

10  My characterization of occasionalism and its relation to Scholastic Aristotelianism is indebted to the following outstanding article: Alfred J. Freddoso, "Medieval Aristotelianism and the Case against Secondary Causation in Nature," in *Divine and Human Action: Essays in the Metaphysics of Theism*, ed. Thomas V. Morris (Ithaca, 1988), 74–118.

substances both *have* and *exercise* their own causal powers; God's activity in nature does not make substances' causal powers superfluous. Rather, God in his non-miraculous activity in nature is a universal cause who "concurs with" secondary causes.

Further, Aristotelians claimed that substances have many of their active and passive powers *essentially*. In other words, fire has the active causal power to burn a suitably disposed piece of cotton by a necessity of nature. This substance cannot be fire, if it does not burn this piece of cotton that is ready to burn, all other things being equal (e.g., you have not coated the cotton with a fireproof substance). Critics of Aristotelian essentialism, such as al-Ghazali, argued that any such account of corporeal substances is blasphemous: it puts constraints on the kind of power which the sacred texts describe God as regularly exercising. For God is described as having the power to make it the case that human beings that have been thrown into roaring fires are not burned. But according to Aristotelian essentialism it is metaphysically necessary that this flesh be burned when brought into contact with this fire, all other things being equal. A theistic essentialist might argue that God changes the flesh of the holy person into metal during his time in the fire, or that God covers the body with a protective substance. But occasionalists reject this view of God's causal power, since God would have to work around the necessary connections in the natural world that he created; he would have to continually preempt the causal activities of corporeal substances.[11]

One position in logical space that an Aristotelian impressed with these occasionalist worries might hold—a position that will be useful in examining the seventeenth-century debates—is what Alfred Freddoso has called "the no-essence theory" of occasionalism.[12] This theory consists of: (1) the doctrine of occasionalism (viz., the doctrine that, barring the causal contributions of agents endowed with intellect and free will, God is the sole efficient cause of states of affairs in nature), (2) the anti-essentialist thesis that no corporeal substance has any active causal power *essentially*, and (3) the claim that every corporeal substance has active causal power. Notice that this form of occasionalism is not that held by Malebranche. Instead, he holds what Freddoso has called the "modified no-nature theory": (1) the doctrine of occasionalism, (2) the anti-essentialist thesis that no corporeal substance has any active causal power *essentially*, and (3*) the claim that no corporeal substance has any active causal power. It is a modified form of the full no-nature theory of Berkeley,

---

11  See al-Ghazali, *The Incoherence of the Philosophers*, trans. Michael E. Marmura (Provo, UT, 1997), 170–82.

12  Freddoso does not attribute the "no-essence theory" to al-Ghazali. Rather, he notes that in the *Incoherence of the Philosophers* al-Ghazali offers two distinct theories: the first consists of the doctrine of occasionalism and the anti-essentialist thesis; the second consists of the anti-essentialist thesis and the view that corporeal substances not only *have* active and passive causal powers, but they also *exercise* these powers. Only the first of these theories is an occasionalist one; thus the debate about whether to count al-Ghazali as an occasionalist. The no-essence theory is a hybrid of al-Ghazali's two theories. See Freddoso, "Medieval Aristotelianism," 96. Michael E. Marmura argues that in the *Incoherence of the Philosophers* al-Ghazali presents both theories as possible, but that in *Moderation in Belief* he clearly endorses the occasionalist theory. See Marmura's introduction to his translation of al-Ghazali, *The Incoherence*, xxiv–xxv.

who replaces (3*) with (3**): the claim that no corporeal substance has any *active or passive* causal power.

A common Aristotelian objection to occasionalism is that drawn from God's power and perfection. In *Summa contra Gentiles* St Thomas argued against the position of occasionalism in this way:

> The perfection of the effect demonstrates the perfection of the cause, for a greater power brings about a more perfect effect. But God is the most perfect agent. Therefore, things created by Him obtain perfection from Him. So, to detract from the perfection of creatures is to detract from the perfection of divine power. But, if no creature has any active role in the production of any effect, much is detracted from the perfection of the creature. Indeed, it is part of the fullness of perfection to be able to communicate to another being the perfection which one possesses. Therefore, this position [occasionalism] detracts from the divine power.[13]

I want to suggest that it is this broad argumentational strategy, with a lineage going back to the Middle Ages, that Astell offers when she writes: "It seems more agreeable to the Majesty of God, and that Order he has established in the World, to say that he produces our Sensations *mediately* by his Servant Nature, than to affirm that he does it *immediately* by his own Almighty Power" (*L* 281–82).[14] Of course, as commentators have been ready to point out, this objection is not conclusive. Occasionalists will attempt to show that those who hold that God concurs with real secondary causes in effect hold that God's causal contribution to natural change is not sufficient to determine the specific nature of effects. Occasionalists, then, can claim that their position comports with God's majesty or sovereign power better than the concurrentists' position.

Consider, however, St Thomas's more powerful Aristotelian criticism of occasionalism, an objection which, in *Summa contra Gentiles*, he states thus:

> Again, it is contrary to the rational character of wisdom for there to be anything useless in the activities of the possessor of wisdom. But, if created things could in no way operate to produce their effects, and if God alone worked all operations immediately, these other things would be employed in a useless way by Him, for the production of these effects. Therefore, the preceding position [occasionalism] is incompatible with divine wisdom.[15]

This objection poses a formidable problem for the no-essence brand of occasionalism. For according to this theory, God has given to material substances hidden causal powers and dispositions none of which they will ever exercise. Such superfluous powers would appear to serve no role in the divine scheme of things; they appear to have been created to no purpose. I believe that Astell uses this broad argumentational strategy in response to Norris's account of sensation. I will set out a formal statement

---

13 Saint Thomas Aquinas, *Summa contra Gentiles, Book Three: Providence Part I*, trans. Vernon J. Bourke (South Bend, IN, 1975), ch. 19, para. 15.

14 In his "Remarks upon Some of Mr. Norris's Books," Locke gives us his version of this criticism of ocassionalism. See Locke, *The Works of John Locke*, 10:255.

15 Aquinas, *Summa Contra Gentiles*, III, I, 69.13.

of Astell's argument shortly. But in order to determine its force in response to Norris's theory, we first need to see precisely which type of occasionalist theory Norris embraces.

Norris holds a hybrid theory of causation. With respect to body–soul causation, for example, in the production of sensation, he endorses Malebranche's modified no-nature theory: (1) the doctrine of occasionalism, (2) the anti-essentialist thesis that no corporeal substance has any active causal power *essentially*, and (3*) the claim that no corporeal substance has any active causal power.[16] But with respect to body–body causation, Norris rejects Malebranche's occasionalist account; he holds that each body *has* and *exercises* active causal power. What we can attribute to body is "to be able to act upon other Bodies, either by moving all their parts at once out of their place, or by changing the Order and Situation of the Parts among themselves."[17] And in the case of sensation, the "proper Power, Force and Activity" of an external body consists of its motion, by which power it produces an impression on the human body. This impression, in turn, is the occasion by which God causes a sensation in the soul, in accordance with his general law that establishes that certain sensations will follow certain impressions.[18] Recall that St Thomas's argument caused difficulties especially for a causal theory that blended a roughly Aristotelian metaphysics of corporeal natures instantiated by individual substances, with a denial of essentialism, and an endorsement of the doctrine of occasionalism.[19] So the question before us is whether Astell's use of St Thomas's argumentational strategy will have any force against Norris's hybrid account of causation.

Here is Astell's statement of her argument:

> Allowing that Sensation is only in the Soul, that there is nothing in Body but Magnitude, Figure and Motion, and that being without Thought it self it is not able to produce it in us, and therefore those Sensations, whether of Pleasure or Pain, which we feel at the Presence of Bodies, must be produced by some higher Cause than they; yet if the Objects of our Senses have no natural Efficiency towards the producing of those Sensations which we feel at their Presence, if they serve no further than as positive and arbitrary Conditions to determine the Action of the true and proper Cause, if they have nothing in their own Nature to qualifie them to be instrumental to the Production of such and such Sensations, but that if GOD should so please (the Nature of the things notwithstanding) we might as well feel Cold at the presence of fire as of water, and heat at the Application of Water or

---

16   That Norris holds the modified no-nature theory with respect to body–soul causation is supported by the following textual evidence from *Practical Discourses upon several Divine Subjects* (London, 1693), vol. 3: Occasionalism: "'Tis *God* and God only that acts in us, and is the true and proper Cause of all our Sensations" (54). Anti-essentialism: "May not that very Motion which is *de facto* follow'd with Pleasure, be as well the Occasion of Pain for any Proportion, Affinity, or Natural Connexion that is in the things themselves? 'Tis most certain that it may" (28). No material substance has active causal power: "Bodies neither have any thing in them resembling our Sensations, nor any Power to produce them in us" (55).

17   Norris, *Practical Discourses*, 3:34–35.

18   Norris, *Practical Discourses*, 3:47–48.

19   St Thomas explicitly says that if occasionalism were true, then the "forms and causal powers" with which corporeal substances are endowed would have no purpose. Thus, he appears to be arguing against a no-essence occasionalist theory. See *De potentia Dei*, Question 3, Article 7, resp.

any other Creature, and since God may as well excite Sensations in our Souls without these positive Conditions as with them, to what end do they serve? And then what becomes of that acknowledged Truth that GOD does nothing in vain, when such Variety of Objects as our Senses are exercised about are wholly unnecessary? (*L* 279–80)

One might think that Astell here treats Norris as holding the no-essence theory. For, she says that "if GOD should so please (the Nature of the things notwithstanding) we might as well feel Cold at the presence of fire as of water." In other words, she attributes to Norris the view that fire has a nature from which flow its causal powers, for example, the power to heat human beings. But notwithstanding fire's nature, there is no necessity that this human being feels heat when she approaches the fire, for the power to heat is not had by the fire essentially. It is understandable that she might treat Norris as a no-essence theorist. Astell would simply take the claim that bodies have active causal powers (from Norris's account of body–body causation) and add it to his anti-essentialist and occasionalist theory of the causation of sensation. Norris, however, could reply that in his view God has *not* created bodies with the causal power to produce sensations in us, where this causal power is never exercised. For in Norris's theory, bodies have no such causal power. And while God *has* created bodies with causal powers in relation to other bodies, these bodies also *exercise* those powers. So, Norris might argue, Astell's argument poses no threat to his theory. (In fact, as we will see shortly, Astell's own argument appears to attribute to Norris a no-nature form of occasionalism with respect to sensation.)

But I think that Astell's argument questions not only the creation of causal power that is never exercised, but also what reason God could have in creating bodies at all if he is the sole cause of our sensations. For according to occasionalism, God does not use bodies as instruments when he produces our sensations. And surely, Astell adds, he does not require occasions. So, bodies appear to have been created to no purpose. In Norris's reply to Astell in *Letters*, he argues that it is false that bodies "serve for nothing," since they do something, namely, they "make an Impression upon our Bodies." While metaphysically speaking God could arbitrarily cause in us any sensation he chose, given his concern for the welfare of embodied human souls, external bodies provide God with a reason why he should, for example, make us feel pain when we get too close to fire rather than pleasure (*L* 303–5). For this is most conducive to the preservation of the body. This response by Norris assumes the existence of human bodies. But why does God create any bodies at all? Astell's argument hints at the view that if one goes the route of occasionalism, the Berkleyean elimination of material substances will be theologically more appealing.

I think that in this argument Astell is giving Norris a run for his money. Nonetheless, there are responses ready to hand for Norris and Malebranche. They could argue that a theory of sensation in which there are no bodies, human or otherwise, with God directly causing our sensations, makes no sense. For, the sole purpose of sensation is that it is the most efficient way to ensure the preservation of the human body. If humans were not embodied, we would simply have our intellectual ideas through the vision in God, and we would have no need for sensations. God would create sensations in vain, if he were to cause them in disembodied humans. To be sure,

Berkeley would deny this claim. But I am not going to pursue this dialectic further. Instead, I want to look more closely at Astell's argument, in order to be in a better position to understand the positive account of the causation of sensation that she goes on to offer in *Letters*.

The argument, although not precisely a *reductio ad absurdum*, nonetheless tries to show that Norris's claims about sensation jointly appear to lead to a theologically untenable implication, given in (14); below. Thus, most of the argument provides us with Norris's views; Astell herself will accept only some of these propositions. Here is a formal statement of Astell's argument quoted above:

1  There is nothing that exists [formally] in body except magnitude, figure, and motion.

2  Therefore, thought does not exist [formally] in body. (By 1)

3  Sensation is a species of thought. (Unstated assumption)

4  Therefore, sensation does not exist [formally] in body. (By 2 and 3)

5  Sensation exists [formally] only in the soul.

6  Whatever is in an effect must exist formally or eminently in its total efficient cause.[20] (Unstated assumption)

7  Sensation does not exist eminently in body. (Unstated assumption)

8  Therefore, body is not *the* [total efficient] cause of sensation in the soul. (By 4, 6, and 7)

9  Bodies have nothing in their nature [i.e., no properties, powers, or dispositions] (a) to qualify them to be partial efficient causes of sensations, for example, instruments that the true and proper cause may use, or (b) to in any other way causally contribute to the production of sensations.

10  Therefore, sensation is caused by something higher [up in the chain of reality] than body [viz., finite or infinite Spirit]. (By the background assumptions of dualism and a Platonic/Cartesian ordering of reality, together with 6, 8, and 9)

11  Bodies are mere positive conditions that determine the action of the true and proper cause of sensation [viz., God].

12  God could, if he so chose, produce in our souls the sensation of cold at the presence of fire (notwithstanding the magnitude, figure, and motion in fire); he could also produce the sensation of heat at its presence. (Anti-essentialist premise)[21]

---

20  Squadrito attributes a different causal principle to Astell, which she calls a "causal likeness principle" ("Mary Astell's Critique," 437). According to this principle, bodies can produce modifications in bodies, but not in minds; minds can produce modifications in minds, but not in bodies. I find no evidence of Astell's endorsement of this principle in the texts. Further, it is inconsistent with Astell's hypothesis of sensible congruity.

21  As commentators have noted, Astell's argument bears a resemblance to one that Locke offers in "Remarks Upon Some of Mr. Norris's Books" (see n. 3 above). But the arguments are not identical. As premise (12) makes clear, the focus of Astell's argument is bodies external to our own, such as fire, and the issue of whether they play any causal role in sensation. But Locke's argument focuses on internal bodies—the corporeal organs of sense—and the question of their causal role in sensation. See Locke, *The Works of John Locke*, 10:249. Locke's argument, however, is stronger than Astell's. For even if external bodies play no causal role in sensation, they might be useful for some other divine purpose. But it is harder

13   God could produce sensations in our souls without these positive conditions [viz., bodies].

14   Therefore, [to the extent that bodies are neither the total causes, partial causes, instruments, or conditions necessary for the production of sensations, to that extent] God's creation of the variety of bodies is to no purpose. (By 8, 9, and 13)

15   But God does not create anything to no purpose.

In the absence of an occasionalist account of the purpose of bodies, Astell suggests that we may wish to consider an alternative theory of the causal role of bodies in the production of sensation to that given by occasionalism, namely, the theory of sensible congruity.

Let us examine which of the above propositions Astell endorses. She accepts (1), the Cartesian, mechanical understanding of body. She also accepts (2)–(5), which are elements of Descartes's dualism and philosophy of mind. It is worth pointing out that in this argument Astell is following Norris in understanding sensation in what Descartes terms the "material" sense, namely, as a modification (mode) or operation of the mind, rather than in the "objective" sense, namely, as the object represented by that operation.[22] Thus, (5) is the orthodox Cartesian view that, taken as a mode or operation, a sensation exists "formally" only in a soul. And a mode exists formally in a substance just in case the substance actually has that precise mode. For example, a particular magnitude, figure, or motion may be contained formally in a particular bodily substance. But a particular act of will cannot be formally contained in a body, since bodies do not have volitions.

(6) is one version of Descartes's causal principle, which Norris explicitly endorses in *An Essay Towards the Theory of the Ideal or Intelligible World, Part II*, and intimates in "A Discourse of Divine Love," and of which Astell explicitly endorses the general form in *A Serious Proposal, Part II*.[23] While there has been considerable disagreement in the recent literature about what Descartes means by the "eminent containment" of modes, we do have Norris's own gloss:[24]

And though some of the Modern *Reformers* of Philosophy have thought fit to reject the *former* part of the Supposition, *viz.* That Bodies have in themselves something answerable to the Sensations which we feel in the use of them; yet they generally retain the *Later,*

---

to see what role sense organs might play, if they have none in the production of sensation.

22   Descartes, *The Philosophical Writings of Descartes*, 3 vols, trans. John Cottingham et al. (Cambridge, 1991), 2:7. Hereafter cited parenthetically as *PW*.

23   John Norris, *An Essay Towards the Theory of the Ideal or Intelligible World, Part II* (London, 1704), 291–92 and *Practical Discourses*, 3:33. Astell uses the general form of the causal principle, "none can give what he has not" in *A Serious Proposal II* 131.

24   See, for example, Geoffrey Gorham, "Descartes's Dilemma of Eminent Containment," *Dialogue* XLII (2003): 3–25; Thomas Vinci, *Cartesian Truth* (Oxford, 1998); Eileen O'Neill, "Mind–Body Interaction and Metaphysical Consistency: A Defense of Descartes," *Journal of the History of Philosophy* 25.2 (1987): 227–45; Louis E. Loeb, *From Descartes to Hume: Continental Metaphysics and the Development of Modern Philosophy* (Ithaca, 1981); Kenneth Clatterbaugh, "Descartes's Causal Likeness Principle," *Philosophical Review* 89 (1980): 379–402.

*viz.* That they produce and cause those Sensations in us, and do so accordingly allow, that Fire (for instance) is *Eminently* and *Potentially*, though not *Formally* hot, that is, That though it has not any thing resembling the Sensation of Heat in it self, yet it has a Power to produce such a Sensation in those that shall approach it. This they not only *allow*, but *contend* for. For whereas according to the Old Distinction, some things were said to be both Formally and Eminently hot too (as Fire) and some only eminently, (as the Sun) the Moderns have ventured to cut off the former part of the Distinction, and reduce all to the later, by supposing all Bodies that we call Hot, to be so only *Eminently* and *Potentially*, as they are productive of Heat in us. And by this they explain the *Phenomenon* of Heat in Bodies, supposing it to be nothing else in the Bodies themselves, but only a Power of producing such a Sensation. But then by this they manifestly hold that they do produce it; and I know but of One amongst them that thinks any *Otherwise*, or any *Farther* (* Mr. Malebranche).[25]

For Norris, the condition that needs to be met for a substance to contain a mode eminently, according to the modern view is this: (i) the substance has the power to bring about the existence of the property in another substance. In fact, however, there are two other conditions that the moderns require for eminent containment to obtain: (ii) the substance does not contain the property formally, and (iii) the substance must be more perfect than the substances that formally contain the property—it must be higher up than them in the chain of reality, which starts with the most perfect and independent being, God, and descends to the most imperfect and dependent modification of corporeal substance.[26]

Now (4) together with (6) and (7) implies (8), namely, that body is not the total efficient cause of sensation in the soul. Astell grants (7) for the sake of her argument, and she genuinely accepts (8). We will have to see, when we examine her own account of sensation, whether she truly endorses (7). She will reject most of the remaining claims in the. For example, she will reject (9), that bodies have nothing in their natures to qualify them to be partial efficient causes of sensations, and thus she will argue that what follows from the Cartesian background assumptions and (6) and (8) is *not* (10). Rather, what follows is: Therefore, sensation is *at least partially* caused by something higher up in the chain of reality than body.

Norris himself thought that the claim embedded in (11), namely that the true cause of sensations is the infinite spirit (God), followed from (10) together with the claim that finite spirits (such as human souls, angels, or demons) cannot be the cause of our sensations. In "A Discourse of the Love of God," Norris mounts numerous arguments

---

25  Norris, *Practical Discourses*, 3:21–22. Norris does not mention Descartes by name when he gives this sketch; instead he refers to the "Modern *Reformers* of Philosophy." But it is reasonable to assume that he has in mind those who were replacing traditional Aristotelian natural philosophy with the new mechanical philosophy, for example, figures such as Descartes and Locke. Descartes's contemporaries (accurately to my mind) saw him as both denying the view that "Bodies have in themselves something answerable to the sensations that we feel," while retaining the view that these bodies "produce and cause those Sensations in us." And the language of the formal and eminent containment of properties is a scholastic leftover retained in Descartes's causal principle. I think it is safe to assume that Descartes is one of Norris's "Reformers."

26  On conditions (ii) and (iii), see Francisco Suárez, "Metaphysical Disputations" in *Descartes' Meditations: Background Source Materials*, ed. Roger Ariew et al. (Cambridge, 1998), 34.

in support of this latter claim. As we will see, on Astell's own account, bodies are more than mere conditions; they, along with human souls, causally contribute to the production of sensation. In this argument, however, she simply assumes (11), along with the anti-essentialist premise (12), in order to raise her challenge to Norris's theory of sensation: Since God can produce sensations in us without the need of bodily occasions (13), and since we are assuming with Norris that bodies are also neither total nor partial efficient causes in the production of sensation, then to that extent God created bodies to no purpose (14). But this conclusion is untenable.

At the heart of the disagreement between Norris and Astell at the end of *Letters*, then, are their divergent views with respect to (9). Astell rejects Norris's strong occasionalist position (which berges on the modified no-nature theory) that bodies have no powers or dispositions that could qualify them to be even partial causes of sensations. I now want to examine Astell's positive account of sensation. I hope to show that, contrary to what some recent commentators have suggested, she does not embrace a neoplatonist alternative to Norris's views. I will argue that her position is closer to Descartes's—at least as I read Descartes on sensation.

## II. Astell's account of sensation in *Letters*: a Cartesian reading of "sensible congruity"

Having raised two objections to Norris's account of sensation, Astell suggests an alternative:

> Why therefore may there not be a *sensible Congruity* between those Powers of the Soul that are employed in Sensation, and those Objects which occasion it? Analogous to that vital Congruity which your Friend Dr. *More* (*Immor. Of the Soul, B*. II. *Chap.* 14. *S.* 8.) will have to be between some certain Modifications of Matter, and the plastick Part of the Soul. ... For as the Soul forsakes her Body when this vital Congruity fails, so when this sensible Congruity is wanting, as in the Case of Blindness, Deafness, or the Palsie, &c. the Soul has no Sensation of Colours, Sounds, Heat and the like, so that although Bodies make the same Impression that they used to do on her Body, yet whilst it is under this Indisposition, she has not that Sentiment of Pleasure or Pain which used to accompany that Impression, and therefore though there be no such thing as Sensation in Bodies, yet why may there not be a *Congruity* in them by their Presence to draw forth such Sensations in the Soul? (*L* 280–81)

Here Astell makes reference to Henry More's understanding of soul–matter union. More held that it is this union which explains why (1) our souls stay "tied" to a single body during our mortal life, and (2) matter can cause sensations in the soul, among other phenomena. He argued that no mechanical explanation of two things uniting (in virtue of their textures, and in virtue of their surfaces coming into contact) can account for life and sensation. Rather, while neither life nor sensation exists in matter *per se*, there is a vital union, agreement or congruity, which "is chiefly in the *Soul* it self, it being the noblest Principle of Life; but is also in the *Matter*, and is there nothing but such modification thereof as fits the *Plastick* part of the Soul, and tempts out that Faculty into act."[27] In other words, the soul stays with a particular body, or has a sensation, because of a harmony or agreement between fitly disposed matter and the plastic and perceptive faculties of a particular soul. But this harmony is not merely concomitance; when matter is organized in a certain way it affects the soul so that the soul has a particular sensation. Thus, matter fitly disposed to produce the sensation of whiteness in a particular soul is a *cause* of the soul's experience of whiteness, despite the fact that whiteness is not in the matter.[28]

Astell's view, which so far agrees with More's, seems to be precisely the view of the "Reformers" that Norris rejected. That is, Astell and More hold that while neither color nor pain are formally contained in bodies, they are eminently contained in bodies insofar as bodies have the causal power to elicit sensations in souls.[29] But More's account of sensation has a further element. More notes:

> I affirm with *Des-Cartes*, that nothing affects our Senses but such Variations of *Matter* as are made by difference of Motion, Figure, Situation of parts, &c. but I dissent from him in this, in that I hold it is not mere and pure Mechanical motion that causes all these sensible Modifications in Matter, but that many times the immediate Director thereof is this *Spirit of Nature* (I speak of) one and the same every where, and acting always alike upon like occasions ....[30]

More's spirit of nature is a departure from Descartes's position of two created substances.[31] For it is a single "Substance incorporeal," distinct from human souls, lacking sense and reason, which pervades matter and causally acts upon it "according to the sundry predispositions and occasions in the parts it works upon, raising such *Phaenomena* in the World, by directing the parts of the Matter and their Motion, as

---

27  Henry More, *The Immortality of the Soul*, reprinted in, *A Collection of Several Philosophical Writings, 1662*, vol. 2 (New York, 1978), 120–21.

28  For More on bodies containing nothing but matter and motion, see *Immortality*, 2:120; on bodies being incapable of having sensations, 67; on extended substances causing sensations in the soul, 11, 120.

29  Given the gloss on eminent containment given in the body of this chapter, the question naturally arises how bodies can eminently contain sensations (taken materially as modes), since bodies are less perfect than souls, that is, since they are lower in the chain of reality than souls. This is a complicated issue, which has received considerable treatment in the recent literature. For my reasons for attributing this account to Descartes, see my "Mind and Mechanism: An Examination of Some Mind–Body Problems in Descartes' Philosophy," (PhD diss., Princeton University, 1983). For a similar treatment, see Margaret Wilson, "Descartes on the Origin of Sensation," *Philosophical Topics* 19 (1991): 293–323. For an alternative view, see Janet Broughton, "Adequate Causes and Natural Kinds," in *Human Nature and Natural Knowledge: Essays Presented to Marjorie Grene on the Occasion of her Seventy-Fifth Birthday*, ed. Alan Donagan et al. (Dordrecht, 1986), 107–27.

30  More, *Immortality*, 2:199.

31  On More's spirit of nature see: John Henry, "Henry More Versus Robert Boyle: The Spirit of Nature and the Nature of Providence," in *Henry More (1614–1687), Tercentenary Studies*, ed. Sarah Hutton (Dordrecht, 1990), 55–76; and his "A Cambridge Platonist's Materialism: Henry More and the Concept of Soul," *Journal of the Warburg and Courtauld Institutes* 49 (1986): 172–95; Alan Gabbey, "Henry More and the Limits of Mechanism," in *Henry More (1614–1687), Tercentenary Studies*, 19–35; J.E. Saveson, "Differing Reactions to Descartes Among the Cambridge Platonists," *Journal of the History of Ideas* 21.4 (1990): 560–67.

cannot be resolved into mere Mechanical powers."[32] If Astell is advocating More's complete account of sensation, spirit of nature and all, then Jacqueline Broad would be correct in claiming that Astell's "theory not only empowers and enlivens matter (when it would otherwise be dead and inert), but also avoids an extreme dualism. The doctrine of plastic nature to which she appeals introduces a 'middle way,' an intermediary sphere that bridges the gulf between spiritual and material substances."[33] But does Astell endorse More's immaterial spirit of nature?

She clearly holds that "when this sensible Congruity is wanting, as in the Case of Blindness, Deafness, or the Palsie, &c. the Soul has no Sensation of Colours, Sounds, Heat and the like" (*L* 281). Does this imply that when the incorporeal spirit, which pervades the sense organs, does not act upon the soul, the soul has no sensations? Or does she agree with More just to the extent that when the corporeal sense organs are damaged, such that they fail to be able to affect the soul, the soul has no sensations? I find no evidence in *Letters* that Astell, in opposition to Descartes and Norris, had eschewed a mechanical understanding of even body–body interactions such that mechanism had to be supplemented with a vitalistic, immaterial principle of nature. Given Astell's acceptance throughout *Letters* of a Cartesian metaphysics, where her one problem is with the occasionalist account of sensation, it seems reasonable to read her as agreeing with More only to the extent that, while bodies do *not* formally contain sensations, they *do* have the power to affect the soul so as to be causally efficacious in their production. And this is how Norris reads Astell. Arguing from the supposition that Astell shares his Cartesian dualistic metaphysics, he states:

> If by sensible Congruity you mean (as you seem to do) that ... by virtue of this Analogy such an Impression has any natural Efficacy to produce, or (in your Language) to *draw forth* such a sentiment, in this sense I deny that there is any such thing as a sensible Congruity, that is, I deny that sensible Objects have any such Congruity with our sensations as to be able to contribute any thing by way of a Physical Efficacy towards the Production of them. Not so much as by the way of *Instruments*. (*L* 306)

Norris understands an impression to be a purely material image, and it is to *this* that he believes Astell attributes the power to educe sensation in the soul—not an immaterial spirit acting through the material image.

Further, two years after the publication of *Letters*, Astell states in *A Serious Proposal, Part II* that body is "an Extended Substance" and that mind is "a Spiritual or Thinking Substance" (*SP II* 132). To be sure, she does not say that these two are the *only* created substances. But neither does she say that body is permeated with an incorporeal soul of the world, spirit of nature, or hylarchic principle. And in *The Christian Religion* she writes: "Now all Beings whatsoever are either Material or Immaterial."[34] And she glosses "Body and Mind" as "Material and Immaterial being directly opposite, and in their own Natures inconsistent; to say that the Mode of

---

32  More, *Immortality*, 2:193.

33  Broad, *Women Philosophers*, 108. Cf. Taylor, "Ironic Assault," 509–10.

34  Mary Astell, *The Christian Religion as Profess'd by a Daughter of the Church of England* (London, 1705), 251.

the one may be the Mode of the other, amounts to as much as to say, That a Thing may Be and may not Be, at the same time." Thus, Astell holds that God, who is an immaterial thinking thing "cannot be Extended."[35] Astell's metaphysics, then, does not seem to leave any room for an immaterial yet extended, created being, which lacks sense and reason, and which produces bodily modifications. In short, it does not leave room for More's spirit of nature.

I read Astell in *Letters* as endorsing Descartes's view that there are only two created substances, mind and body—a view that she will continue to hold throughout her writings. She aligns herself with More, over against Norris, on the issue of whether bodies may be partial efficient causes of sensation, despite the fact that bodies do not formally have sensations. But whereas Astell thinks bodies are purely material, extended substances, More holds that it is in virtue of the immaterial spirit of nature pervading matter that bodies are able to cause sensations.[36] In the end, Astell's view is closer to the view that Norris attributes to the "Reformers," such as Descartes, than it is to More's.[37]

Descartes, like Astell, maintains a "middle way" between taking bodies to be "proper" or primary causes of sensations, or taking them to be mere occasions by which the primary cause acts in the specific way it does. For both, that middle way is the view that bodies are *partial* efficient causes, or at least they causally contribute to the production of sensations.[38] Particular bodies have dispositions to produce specific sensations in suitably disposed minds; they have the causal power to excite sensations in the mind. In the *Principles of Philosophy*, Part Four, Descartes states:

> We know that the nature of our soul is such that different local motions are quite sufficient to produce all the sensations in the soul. What is more, we actually experience the various sensations as they are produced in the soul, and we do not find that anything reaches the brain from the external sense organs except for motions of this kind. In view of all this we have every reason to conclude that the properties in external objects to which we apply the terms light, colour, smell, taste, sound, heat and cold … are, so far as we can see, simply various dispositions in those objects which make them able to set up various kinds of motions in our nerves which are required to produce all the various sensations in the soul. (*PW* 1:285)

---

35  Astell, *Christian Religion*, 252.

36  Astell does make the following remark in *The Christian Religion*: "But tho' some may dispute, (how reasonably I am not now to enquire) whether Extension be the Essence of Body, none will pretend that Thought is its Essence" (251). I suppose one could argue that here Astell has left open whether body is simply extended substance, or whether it is extended substance pervaded by an immaterial spirit of nature. But this seems unlikely to me, given that on the preceding page she has given her version of Descartes's "real distinction argument," including the claim that our idea of an extended being provides us with a "complete idea" of body.

37  The view here is a departure from my earlier hypothesis in O'Neill, "Mary Astell," 1:528.

38  Scholars are divided on the issue of whether bodies have any causal power, for Descartes. See Daniel Garber, "Descartes and Occasionalism," in *Causation in Early Modern Philosophy*, ed. Steven Nadler (University Park, PA, 1993), 9–26; Desmond Clarke, "Causal Powers and Occasionalism from Descartes to Malebranche," in *Descartes' Natural Philosophy*, ed. Stephen Gaukroger et al. (London, 2000), 131–48; and Steven Nadler, "Descartes and Occasional Causation," *British Journal for the History of Philosophy* 2.1 (1994): 35–54.

For Descartes, mind, in addition to body, is also an efficient cause of our sensations. He writes: "It can also be proved that the nature of our mind is such that the mere occurrence of certain motions in the body can stimulate it to have all manner of thoughts which have no likeness to the movements in question. This is especially true of the confused thoughts we call sensations or feelings" (*PW* 1:284). And in *Comments on a Certain Broadsheet*, Descartes provides an analogy, which suggests the causal roles that he ascribes to minds and bodies in the production of sensation. Here the relations between an external body, the mind, and sensations (taken objectively) are compared to the relations between a boss, the work crew, and the work accomplished:

> Something can be said to derive its being from something else for two different reasons: either the other thing is its proximate and primary cause, without which it cannot exist, or it is a remote and merely accidental cause ... Thus workers are the primary and proximate causes of their work, whereas those who give them orders to do the work, or promise to pay for it, are accidental and remote causes, for the workers might not do the work without instructions. (*PW* 1:305)

By analogy, then, the external body is the remote, *per accidens* cause, which stimulates or triggers the mind, which is the primary and proximate cause, to produce a sensation of a certain kind, and to produce it now rather than at another time. The remote cause is not merely an occasion for the mind to produce the sensation—as Norris understands occasions—because, as we have seen, occasions are mere conditions; they have no causal power. But remote efficient causes, as Descartes understands them, causally contribute to the production of sensation, albeit indirectly via causing changes in the primary cause. This is why something can partially "derive its being" from a remote cause.

Although Astell does not discuss in the detail that Descartes does the division of causal labor in the production of sensation, it seems that she too counts not only bodies, but also minds, as efficient causes of sensation. For in her characterization of sensible congruity she speaks not only of the causal contribution of body, but also of "those Powers of the Soul that are employed in Sensation" (*L* 280).

In this section, I have argued that Astell's own account of the causation of sensation in *Letters* is closer to Descartes's than to More's. The question remains, however, whether Astell eventually embraced Norris's occasionalist account of sensation in her later works.

### III. The account of sensation in Astell's later works: occasionalist, or concurrentist and interactionist?

With respect to her views in *A Serious Proposal Part II*, able scholars such as Springborg and Taylor have agreed that here Astell rejects an occasionalist account of sensation.[39] I throw in my lot with these commentators. That Astell adopted the

---

[39] Taylor, "Ironic Assault," 513; Springborg, "Introduction," to *A Serious Proposal II*, xvii; 189,

interactionist view is indicated by the following passage: "Contemplation requires a Governable body, a sedate and steady Mind, and the Body and the Mind do so reciprocally influence each other, that we can scarce keep the one in tune if the other be out of it" (*SP II* 112). In fact, Astell also appears to have been committed to the pneumatic details of Descartes's account of sensation and voluntary motion in his *Passions of the Soul* (*SP II* 161). In that text Descartes notoriously held that both of these forms of mind–body interaction take place in the pineal gland in the brain by means of a refined corporeal wind, which he called animal spirits (*PW* 1:341).

Broad, however, has argued that in *A Serious Proposal Part II* Astell decided to "suspend her judgment" about whether to endorse or reject Norris's occasionalist account of sensation. The textual evidence that she offers is this: "We know and feel the Union between our Soul and Body, but who amongst us sees so clearly, as to find out with Certitude and Exactness, the secret ties which unite two such different Substances, or how they are able to act upon each other" (*SP II* 101).[40] As I read this passage, Astell is in fact endorsing Descartes's own position on our lack of clear and distinct ideas concerning mind–body causal interaction. Compare her remarks with Descartes's: "What belongs to the union of the soul and body is known only obscurely by the intellect alone or even by the intellect aided by the imagination, but it is known very clearly by the senses" (*PW* 3:227). Further, in response to Frans Burman's question, "How can the soul be affected by the body and vice versa, when their natures are completely different?," Descartes replies, "This is very difficult to explain; but here our experience is sufficient, since it is so clear on this point that it just cannot be gainsaid" (*PW* 3:346). According to Descartes, then, we feel through sensation that soul and body interact. But there is no theory, graspable by the intellect, and comparable to the mechanical theory of body–body interaction, which can explain soul–body interaction. When Astell claims that she knows and feels the union of soul and body, while lacking certitude and exactness about how such different substances can act upon each other, she seems to be voicing views quite close to those expressed by Descartes to his interlocutors.

Another set of commentators, notably Taylor, have argued that in *The Christian Religion* Astell provides a "defense of 'occasionalism' as expounded by Norris."[41] I cannot on this occasion explore all of the reasons to be suspicious of Taylor's view. But consider the two passages in Astell's later work, which Taylor thinks it will be difficult to read in any other way than as defenses of Norris's occasionalist account of sensation.[42] The first is:

---

n. 93. To be more precise, what Springborg claims is that Astell retracts the doctrine that "we see all things in God" in *A Serious Proposal, Part II*. But Springborg appears to take this latter doctrine about intelligible ideas to be Norris's occasionalist theory of sensation, since she remarks elsewhere that "'seeing all things in God' renders perceptual apparatus of sensation irrelevant'; see Springborg, "Astell, Masham, and Locke," 118.

   40  Broad, *Women Philosphers*, 109.

   41  Taylor, "Ironic Assault," 511. Acworth, *Philosophy of John Norris*, 178 puts forward this view, but provides no textual evidence. Springborg, "Introduction," to *A Serious Proposal II*, xvii, 189, n. 93 argues that Astell here re-endorses the principle of "seeing all things in God"; see n. 39 above.

   42  Cited in Taylor, "Ironic Assault," 512–13.

Without controversie, it is for very good Reasons that He [God] has *so* united a Corruptible Body to an Immortal Mind, that the impressions which are made on the former, shall be perceiv'd and attended with certain Sensations in the other, and this by ways altogether mysterious and incomprehensible, and only to be resolv'd into the Efficacy of the Divine Will.[43]

Taylor is surely correct that one way we could read this passage is as an endorsement of Norris's brand of occasionalism. But it is not hard to imagine an orthodox Cartesian interactionist saying what Astell does in Taylor's first passage. After all, Descartes maintains as well that God so unites the soul to the body that by "the mere occurrence of certain motions in the body" the soul is stimulated to "have all manner of thoughts which have no likeness to the movements in question" (*PW* 1:284). And as I have noted above, Descartes appears to think that soul–body interactions are not comprehensible at the level of theory. Rather, Descartes has recourse to final causes—God's decree to annex certain sensations to certain modifications of matter for the purposes of the preservation of the soul–body union. Thus, Descartes would agree that soul–body interactions are "only to be resolv'd into the Efficacy of the Divine Will." Does this mean that Descartes thinks that God is the sole, immediate cause of sensations in the soul on the occasion of motions in the body? Not as I read him: "It is the movements ... which, acting directly upon our soul in so far as it is united to our body, are ordained by nature to make it have such sensations" (*PW* 1:167). The *motions* act directly upon our soul, not God. Since in this chapter I have been attributing to Astell a roughly Cartesian account of the production of sensation, and since Taylor's first text is compatible with such an account, I do not yet find reason to attribute to Astell a change in her views in the direction of occasionalism.

Here is Taylor's final piece of textual evidence for his view:

Having therefore upon your Mind that truly Rational and Sublime Pleasure, of approving your self to GOD and enjoying Him, you are not at leisure to attend the little poignancy of Meat and Drink, tho' the health and soundness of your Constitution makes these as relishing to you as to any body. If meditation and a just disquisition of Truth has carry'd you beyond the prejudices of sense, you are convinc'd that GOD is the True Efficient Cause of all our Good, of all our pleasing Sensations, and that without any reflection on the Purity of His Nature. You look thro' the Creature to the Creator as the Author of all your Delight, and thus every morsel gives a double Pleasure, considering the hand that feeds you, or to speak more correctly, the Power of GOD giving you divers modifications.[44]

There appear to be three main points here: (1) meditation can lead us beyond the prejudices of the senses, (2) God is the true efficient cause of all our pleasing sensations, and (3) bodies "give" us a double pleasure, if we recall that God "gives" our souls our various modifications. (1) is a view that Norris would hold. But of course so would Descartes; it is one of the main themes of his *Meditations*. Similarly, (2) is held by occasionalists and concurrentists alike. Descartes, for example, states

---

43  Astell, *Christian Religion*, 337.
44  Astell, *Christian Religion*, 140–41.

not only that God is the true efficient cause of all our sensation, but also that "God is the universal cause of everything in such a way as to be also the total cause of everything" (*PW* 3:272). How can Descartes claim that God is the total cause, if he also holds that bodies are also efficient causes of sensations? As a concurrentist, he maintains that a secondary cause, as well as God the primary cause, can both be total causes of an effect, since these causes are of different orders, and secondary causes are essentially subordinated to the primary cause, that is, they exist and act through a dependence on God. So far, then, nothing in this Astell passage requires that we attribute a turn toward occasionalism to her.

Taylor, however, puts the greatest stress on (3). He states that in this second passage we find Astell "offering Norris's occasionalist version of 'efficient causality' (God's unimpeachable, differential power to produce 'modifications' on the soul) as the technically 'correct' way to 'speak' of the 'pleasing Sensations' of taste."[45] And Taylor makes much of the fact that in *Letters* Norris had said that God "has the sole Power to act upon our Spirits, and to give them new Modification. I say *Modifications*, for that well expresses the general Nature of Sensation" (*L* 288–89).[46] But, of course, the interactionist Descartes also takes sensations (in the material sense) to be modifications of the soul. The pressing question with respect to (3) is whether in this second passage Astell is saying that God alone is the efficient cause of the modifications of our soul (in which case she is embracing Norris's account of sensation) or whether she is offering a concurrentist account. I do not claim that this passage provides substantial evidence that Astell is giving a soul–body interactionist and concurrentist account, but I think such a reading is unforced. As I understand the passage, Astell claims that bodies "give" or causally contribute to our receiving two pleasures: The first is the pleasurable sensation that it causes in us. Here the morsel/body is acting as a secondary cause of the modification of my soul. But if meditation has carried me beyond the senses to the realm of the intellect, I can consider the intelligence who uses the morsel/body to produce pleasure in me; this is the second, intellectual pleasure. That is, I can grasp that secondary causes receive their existence and power from God, who concurs with them in modifying our souls. Thus, bodies are both efficient causes of my sensation, and instrumental causes that I can use to put myself in mind of the infinite first cause. On this reading of the second passage, Astell remains a Cartesian soul–body interactionist; again, there is no reason to saddle her with a late conversion to Norris's brand of occasionalism.

Even if the texts are not decisive, Taylor intimates that Astell would have had powerful motivation ultimately to reject her doctrine of sensible congruity. From Norris's "Cartesian perspective" sensible congruity requires a formal likeness between the modes in body and the sensation in the soul. Given this assumption, sensible congruity threatens the real distinction between soul and body: that they are essentially distinct substances that share no properties in common. Astell would have come to see that without the real distinction, the door is open for the possibility of thinking matter. And this latter possibility jeopardizes arguments for the immortality

---

45  Taylor, "Ironic Assault," 512.
46  Taylor, "Ironic Assault," 512–13.

of the soul—which is untenable. Thus, Astell chose to jettison her doctrine of sensible congruity and sign on to Norris's occasionalist theory of sensation.

But I have argued in this chapter that Astell's sensible congruity does not require that bodies formally contain sensations such as redness or heat.[47] So Astell would not have had to give up sensible congruity in order to maintain the real distinction of soul and body, which she thought had important theological implications. And her hostility towards Locke's hypothesis of thinking matter is as well explained by attributing to her steadfast orthodox Cartesian views, as it is by attributing to her a retreat, in *The Christian Religion*, to Norris's views.

It would seem that there is no unequivocal textual evidence to support the claim that Astell embraced occasionalism in her later work. Absent such evidence, and given the general commitment to orthodox Cartesian views in Astell's corpus, it seems reasonable that throughout her career Astell held the Cartesian, anti-occasionalist, concurrentist position about bodies as partial efficient causes of sensations.

---

[47] Norris did see the attribution of causal power to bodies as a slippery slope that led to thinking matter. For he argued that if bodies can produce sensation in a soul, why can they not produce it in themselves? But the interactionist response is this: Bodies are partial efficient causes of sensations in the sense of being disposing causes. I am a disposing cause of the leafiness of my plant: I do not possess leafiness, but I have the power to stimulate or trigger the plant to produce leafiness by means of my actions on the plant (e.g. watering and fertilizing it). So too, on the interactionist account, bodies act on souls and produce sensations in them, although bodies do not formally possess sensations.

Chapter XI

# Astell, Cartesian Ethics, and the Critique of Custom

Jacqueline Broad

In her final work, *Bart'lemy Fair: Or, An Enquiry After Wit* (1709), Mary Astell declares that

> A Man who lives by Principle, is steady and consistent with himself, Master of his Passions, and therefore free from the Torment of opposite Inclinations and Desires impossible to be Gratify'd; always at ease in his own Mind, whatever happens without him; enjoying Self-satisfaction, which, in the Opinion of a great Philosopher, is the sweetest of all the Passions.[1]

Although there is no explicit acknowledgment, René Descartes is undoubtedly the "great Philosopher" to whom Astell refers, and the opinion in question comes from his final treatise, *Les Passions de l'Ame* (1649). In the 1650 English translation of this work, *The Passions of the Soule*, Descartes defines self-satisfaction as "an inward satisfaction, which is the sweetest of all the Passions."[2] The satisfaction gained from the performance of a good action is so sweet, he says, because it depends upon ourselves alone. For Astell scholars, the author's obscure reference to the "great Philosopher" should come as no surprise: many have interpreted Astell as a "Cartesian philosopher" or as someone who grounds her feminist views on Cartesian epistemological principles.[3] From her first letter to the occasionalist John

This essay was completed during my tenure as an Australian Research Council postdoctoral fellow in the School of Philosophy and Bioethics at Monash University, Melbourne. I am extremely grateful to the ARC for their financial assistance, and to Karen Green, for her helpful comments and suggestions.

1 [Mary Astell,] *Bart'lemy Fair: Or, An Enquiry after Wit; In which due Respect is had to a Letter Concerning Enthusiasm, To my LORD \*\*\** (London, 1709), 140. Hereafter cited parenthetically as *BF*.

2 René Descartes, *The Passions of the Soule In three Books. The first, Treating of the Passions in Generall, and occasionally of the whole nature of man. The second, Of the Number, and order of the Passions, and the explication of the six Primitive ones. The third, of Particular Passions. By R. des Cartes. And Translated out of French into English* (London, 1650), Article 63, 52. It is possible that Astell refers to this translation. For a modern translation, see René Descartes, *Passions of the Soul*, in *The Philosophical Writings of Descartes*, trans. John Cottingham, Robert Stoothoff, and Dugald Murdoch, 3 vols. (Cambridge, 1985), vol. 1, section 63:351–52. Unless otherwise indicated, all subsequent citations refer to this edition and are cited parenthetically as *Passions*.

3 Margaret Atherton, "Cartesian Reason and Gendered Reason," in *A Mind of One's Own: Feminist Essays on Reason and Objectivity*, eds. Louise M. Antony and Charlotte Witt (Boulder, 1993), 19–34; Catherine Gallagher, "Embracing the Absolute: The Politics of the Female Subject in Seventeenth-Century England," *Genders* 1.1 (1988): 24–39; Joan K. Kinnaird, "Mary Astell and the Conservative Contribution

Norris in 1693, to her last work in response to the third Earl of Shaftesbury in 1709, Astell reveals herself to be a strong supporter of Cartesian ideas.[4] But perhaps it is surprising that here Astell refers to Descartes's ethical theory of the passions—not to the familiar Descartes of the *Meditations* (1641), but to Descartes in his guise as a philosopher in search of happiness and the good life. Today we do not tend to interpret Descartes as a moral philosopher. Modern historians of philosophy examine Descartes's legacy according to a rather narrow set of philosophical concerns—his skeptical challenge, his rationalist epistemology, and his dualist theory of mind and body, in particular. But recent scholarship suggests that we ought to revise our conception of Descartes as a thinker who is solely preoccupied with questions about knowledge and metaphysics.[5] In his 1996 essay on "Cartesian ethics," John Cottingham points to evidence that Descartes conceives of the ultimate aim of his philosophical project to be human happiness. In the Preface to the French edition of his *Principles of Philosophy* (1647), Descartes says that

> By "morals" I understand the highest and most perfect moral system, which presupposes a complete knowledge of the other sciences and is the ultimate level of wisdom. Now just as it is not the roots or the trunk of a tree from which one gathers the fruit, but only the ends of the branches, so the principal benefit of philosophy depends on those parts of it which can only be learned last of all.[6]

On this subject, far from challenging his ancient and scholastic forebears, Descartes accords with their traditional conception of a philosopher as someone who provides guidance on "how best to live."

In the standard accounts of Astell's debt to Cartesianism, the impact of Cartesian ethics has not been examined in full. Yet Descartes's conception of the ethical character of the passions is a recurring theme in many of Astell's works. In the final chapter of *A Serious Proposal to the Ladies, Part II* (1697), Astell makes explicit reference to Descartes's account of the passions, and this discussion forms a crucial part of Astell's feminist project to teach women how to lead useful lives of virtue and wisdom.[7] In this paper, I examine Astell's philosophy in light of her ethical theory of the passions in the second part of the *Proposal*. A proper understanding of Astell's ethics, I maintain, might assist us in recognizing the various interconnections and

---

to English Feminism," *The Journal of British Studies* 19.1 (1979): 53–75; Ruth Perry, "Radical Doubt and the Liberation of Women," *Eighteenth Century Studies* 18.4 (1985): 472–93; Ruth Perry, *The Celebrated Mary Astell: An Early English Feminist* (Chicago, 1986), 57–97; and Hilda L. Smith, *Reason's Disciples: Seventeenth Century English Feminists* (Urbana, IL, 1982), 115–39.

4  Mary Astell to John Norris, September 21, 1693; in [Mary Astell and] John Norris, *Letters Concerning the Love of God* (London, 1695).

5  See John Cottingham, "Cartesian Ethics: Reason and the Passions," *Revue Internationale de Philosophie* 50.195 (1996): 193–216; Cottingham, *Philosophy and the Good Life: Reason and the Passions in Greek, Cartesian and Psychoanalytic Ethics* (Cambridge, 1998), esp. chapter 3; Susan James, "Reason, the Passions, and the Good Life," in *The Cambridge History of Seventeenth-Century Philosophy*, eds. Daniel Garber and Michael Ayers, 2 vols. (Cambridge, 1998), 2:1358–96.

6  Descartes, *Principles of Philosophy*, in *Philosophical Writings*, 1:186.

7  Mary Astell, *A Serious Proposal to the Ladies, Parts I and II*, ed. Patricia Springborg (London, 1997), 165. Hereafter cited parenthetically as *SP I* and *SP II*.

continuities between Astell's works. In the past, scholars have highlighted Astell's debt to Descartes's egalitarian conception of reason, his mistrust of custom and unexamined prejudices, and his method of attaining clear and certain knowledge. But on these common interpretations, a tension inevitably arises between Astell's philosophical stance and her conservative political outlook.

In his recent study of the rise of modernity, Jonathan Israel maintains that Descartes's philosophy played a significant role in the political upheavals of the early Enlightenment.[8] Several key aspects of Cartesianism are associated with the rationalization and secularization of opinions across early modern Europe—including its challenge to ancient tradition and authority, the doubting of past prejudices and assumptions, its reverence for natural reason, and its emphasis upon the individual mind. Descartes's challenge to custom—his call for a revolutionary change in our customary ways of thinking—forms the basis of what Israel calls "the crisis of the European mind," a crisis that prepared the way for a "Radical Enlightenment."[9] The radical aspects of Cartesianism are directly opposed to Astell's core political values: her support for divine authority and absolute monarchy, her defense of traditional social hierarchies, her opposition to atheism, and her emphasis upon the importance of communal values, rather than individualism. If Astell were a faithful adherent to the "New Philosophy," as many scholars represent her to be, then there would appear to be a striking tension between her political allegiances and her philosophical thought. I argue that such tensions disappear, however, if we interpret Astell as a Cartesian according to an ethical rather than an epistemological paradigm.

# I

In 1697, following the publication of *A Serious Proposal to the Ladies, for the Advancement of their True and Greatest Interest* (1694), Astell published a second part outlining a method for "the Improvement of their Minds." Although Astell's original work was well received, her central proposal—the founding of an academy or a "religious retirement" for single gentlewomen—failed to find active support. Astell wrote this second work in order to persuade women to improve their minds through their own efforts, till a seminary could be established. She specifically targets those women who are so inured to a life of ignorance and idleness that they are loath to begin a reformation: "they know not how to look into their Souls, or if they do, they find so many disorders to be rectified, so many wants to be supplied, that frighted with the difficulty of the work they lay aside the thoughts of undertaking it" (*SP II* 76). The second *Proposal* offers a method that will enable such women to overcome a purely sensuous and animal life, and to "procure such a temper of mind" as will make them "happy in all Conditions" (*SP II* 73). The explicit aim of this work is not just to assist women in the attainment of truth, but to teach them how to attain happiness by leading lives of virtue.

---

8  Jonathan I. Israel, *Radical Enlightenment: Philosophy and the Making of Modernity 1650–1750* (Oxford, 2001).

9  Israel, *Radical Enlightenment*, 14.

For Astell, one of the greatest obstacles to obtaining true virtue is the influence of *custom* on one's moral judgments. In the first *Proposal*, Astell says that "Ignorance and a narrow education lay the Foundation of Vice, and imitation and Custom rear it up. Custom, that merciless Torrent that carries all before it" (*SP I* 14). The Cambridge Platonist Henry More defines custom as "a corporeal Impression, by which the Soul is extremely bent to judge of things, as true, good, or amiable; for no other Motive, but because it has been accustomed so to judge, and so to act."[10] Though Astell occasionally equivocates, her use of the term "custom" generally accords with that of More. For Astell, custom inclines us to judge an action as right or wrong for no other reason than that such an action has been deemed right or wrong by long use and by the sanction of our forebears.[11] Custom thus constitutes a powerful but potentially irrational influence on our judgments about how we should or should not act. In the second *Proposal*, Astell observes that most women are "so little improved" because of "Ill-nurture, Custom, loss of time, the want of retirement, or of not knowing how to use it, so that by the disuse of our Faculties we seem to have lost them if we ever had any[,] are sunk into an Animal life wholly taken up with sensible objects" (*SP II* 78).

One cause of this moral decay is that custom reverses the proper relation between the *understanding* and the *will*. The understanding or the intellect is that faculty of "Receiving and Comparing Ideas," and the will is "the Power of Preferring any Thought or Motion, of Directing them to This or That thing rather than to another" (*SP II* 153). Although the understanding ought to govern the will, under the influence of custom the will becomes a "head-strong and Rebellious Subject" (*SP II* 84). Moral judgments are made when the will either accepts or rejects the intellect's notion of "what is fit." Such judgments can go wrong when the intellect is fettered by obscure and confused ideas, and the will is compelled to accept them anyway (*SP II* 93). Astell observes that in our early life, before our reason has matured, the passions incite the will to make certain choices (*SP II* 90–91). The will fixes our thoughts on a "present uneasiness which it says must be remov'd," and we fail to consider our future happiness. In later life, we become habituated to this way of thinking, and thus "we generally take that course in our search after Happiness, which Education, Example, and Custom puts us in" (*SP II* 156, 83). The key problem for Astell is to explain how ignorant, uneducated women are to overcome those early influences that set their inclinations on the wrong path.

First, Astell emphasizes that the will is free. Custom, she says, erects "a Tyranny over our free born Souls" and makes it seem as though we are not at liberty to resist our inclinations. Yet this is simply an illusion: human beings, unlike animals, have the free capacity to regulate their will according to their understanding (*SP II* 89). "Because," as Astell writes,

---

10   Henry More, *An Account of Virtue: Or, Dr. Henry More's Abridgment of Morals, Put into English*, trans. Edward Southwell (Bristol, 1997), 87. Hereafter cited parenthetically as *Virtue*.

11   On Astell's use of "custom," see Rebecca M. Mills, "'That Tyrant Custom': The Politics of Custom in the Poetry and Prose of Augustan Women Writers," *Women's Writing* 7.3 (2000): 391–409.

as Irrational Creatures act only by the Will of him who made them, and according to the Power of that Mechanisme by which they are form'd, so every one who pretends to Reason, who is a Voluntary Agent, and therefore Worthy of Praise or Blame, Reward or Punishment, must *Chuse* his Actions and determine his Will to that Choice by some Reasonings or Principles either true or false, and in proportion to this Principles and the Consequences he deduces from them he is to be accounted, if they are Right and Conclusive a Wise Man, if Evil, Rash and Injudicious a Fool. If then it be the property of Rational Creatures, and Essential to their very Natures to Chuse their Actions, and to determine their Wills to that Choice by such Principles and Reasonings as their Understandings are furnish'd with, they who are desirous to be rank'd in that Order of Beings must conduct their Lives by these Measures, begin with their Intellectuals, inform themselves what are the plain and first Principles of Action and Act accordingly. (*SP II* 82)

Like many moral philosophers before her, Astell recognizes a vital connection between a creature's essence and its ultimate good. Following Aristotle, Astell maintains that a life of well being is a life lived in accordance with our intellectual nature. For rational creatures, it is essential to their nature to choose their actions through the exercise of reason. To emphasize this point, Astell highlights the crucial differences between women and mere mechanisms or animals. Whoever denies their liberty, she says, "denies that he is capable of Reward and Punishments," and simply turns himself into "a more curious piece of Mechanism" (*SP II* 101). She says that "till we are capable of Chusing our own Actions and directing them by some Principle, tho we move and speak and so many such like things, we live not the life of a Rational Creature but only of an Animal" (*SP II* 82). Astell thus urges women to embrace their essential humanity and to recognize that "Natural Liberty within" them (*SP II* 148).

While Astell's use of the language of "custom," "tyranny," and "liberty" echoes the party political debates of her time, her sentiments are firmly Cartesian.[12] Astell subscribes to Descartes's view that we can esteem ourselves only on "the exercise of our free will and the control we have over our volitions. For we can reasonably be praised or blamed only for actions that depend upon this free will" (*Passions* 384). For Descartes too, the will consists in our ability to affirm or deny, or to pursue or avoid something, and the understanding is that faculty by which we are able to apprehend or perceive ideas. In his view, erroneous judgments are made because "the scope of the will is wider than that of the intellect; but instead of restricting it within the same limits, I extend its use to matters which I don't understand."[13] I can avoid error, however, if I am careful and self-disciplined, and let my understanding determine the will: "If ... I simply refrain from making a judgement in cases where I do not perceive the truth with sufficient clarity and distinctness, then it is clear that I am behaving correctly and avoiding error."[14] In the *Passions of the Soul*, Descartes declares that the key to acquiring virtue consists in "a firm resolution to make good use" of the will (*Passions* 388).

Similarly, for Astell, erroneous judgments can be avoided if we carefully follow a reliable method for thinking. Astell borrows her "rules for thinking" from Descartes's

---

12   See Mills, "The Politics of Custom," 395.
13   Descartes, *Meditations*, in *Philosophical Writings*, 2:40.
14   Descartes, *Meditations*, in *Philosophical Writings*, 2:41.

followers, Antoine Arnauld and Pierre Nicole, the authors of *Logic, or the Art of Thinking* (first published in 1662). This work is a practical guide to rational thought, based on the manuscript of Descartes's *Rules for the Direction of the Mind* (first written in 1628), and his *Discourse on the Method of Rightly Conducting One's Reason* (1637). The English translators of the *Art of Thinking* (also known as the *Port Royal Logic*) assert that their work is "no less Useful for the Conduct of Human Life, than to instruct and guide us wandring in the Labyrinths of Unsettled Reason."[15] Although the *Art of Thinking* is not a book of ethics, the authors intend to provide a way of overcoming irregularities in all aspects of human life. They assert that "no one is exempted from forming judgments about good and evil, since these judgments are necessary for conducting our lives, directing our actions, and making ourselves eternally happy or miserable" (*Logic* 54). Arnauld and Nicole aim to correct the errors and defects of judgment, so that our judgments might be of value in everyday, practical life—and for the spiritual life to come.

Astell's theory of judgment begins with the recommendation that we acquire a clear understanding of any terms or concepts to be used in our judgments. Like Arnauld and Nicole, she says that we should reason only about those things "of which we have clear and distinct ideas" (*SP II* 126; *Logic* 235). Implicitly, this requires that we "Disengage our selves from all our former Prejudices, from our Opinion of Names, Authorities, Customs and the like, not give Credit to any thing any longer because we have once believed it, but because it carries clear and uncontested Evidence along with it" (*SP II* 89). Our train of thought should proceed in a natural and logical order, beginning with the simplest ideas and moving by degrees to the more complex (*SP II* 126–27; *Logic* 238). We must assure ourselves that we have not left any part of our subject unexamined, and divide our subject into as many parts as we can in order to understand it (*SP II* 127; *Logic* 238). We must also keep the subject matter close in mind, avoiding a hasty and partial examination (*SP II* 115). Then finally we must "judge no further than we Perceive, and not … take any thing for Truth, which we do not evidently Know to be so" (*SP II* 128; *Logic* 238). Sometimes this will mean that we cannot readily make a judgment about a particular subject. In this case, reason dictates that we must "suspend our Assent" and avoid judging things we do not understand (*SP II* 115, 128). We ought to "suspend our Inclinations as we both May and Ought, and restrain them from determining our Will, till we have fairly and fully examin'd and ballanc'd, according to the best of our Knowledge" (*SP II* 155).

Many scholars interpret this key section of the *Proposal* in terms of Astell's epistemological commitments. Joan Kinnaird asserts that it is "little more than an elaborate exposition of Descartes's *Discourse on Method*."[16] Hilda L. Smith

---

15  Antoine Arnauld and Pierre Nicole, *Logic: Or, the Art of Thinking. In which, Besides the Common, are contain'd many Excellent New Rules, very profitable for directing of reason, and acquiring of Judgement, in things as well relating to the Instruction of a Man's self, as of others* (London, 1696), "The Translators to the Reader," sig. A3v. For a modern edition, see Antoine Arnauld and Pierre Nicole, *Logic or the Art of Thinking*, trans. and ed. Jill Vance Buroker (Cambridge, 1996). Subsequent citations are from this edition and hereafter cited parenthetically as *Logic*.

16  Kinnaird, "Mary Astell," 62.

describes the second *Proposal* as "primarily an elaboration of Astell's Cartesian epistemology."[17] Smith explains:

> Her writings reveal that Astell was a dedicated Cartesian, but one of a particularly religious bent. She began with a philosophical doubt about all knowledge, and, working from the assumption that we know there is a God because we can imagine perfection in our minds, she, like Descartes, reasoned toward the truth of our own existence and on to a surety that God created us and we are obliged to follow his plan. Her works combined Christian faith with a sophisticated rationalist construction in a system that paralleled Descartes's "Discourse on Method."[18]

In "Radical Doubt and the Liberation of Women," Ruth Perry similarly asserts that "Cartesian rationalism was the very cornerstone of [Astell's] feminism."[19] These writers suggest that Astell bases her feminism on the Cartesian insight that all human beings—including women—are essentially thinking things. On this basis, they argue, Astell asserts that women are capable of attaining clear and certain knowledge provided that they follow the appropriate rules.

It is true that Astell's method closely resembles that of Descartes, even though she never explicitly refers to his *Discourse*. But when Astell's remarks are placed in their proper context—in the context of her design to effect a moral reformation in women—the standard descriptions are somewhat misleading. First, in the second *Proposal*, Astell does not articulate "a philosophical doubt about all knowledge," or, for that matter, raise skeptical hypotheses in order to challenge beliefs acquired through the senses. Nowhere does she advocate the "willful doubting of all previous knowledge" as a forerunner to an explication of Descartes's *cogito* or *res cogitans*.[20] In the second *Proposal*, the inspiration behind Astell's program is not "radical doubt," but a theory of judgment—one that has an ethical objective, like that of Arnauld and Nicole. While the Port Royal Logic might provide a means for acquiring knowledge, for Astell, these "rules for thinking" are a way of attaining moral truths. This is evidenced by the fact that Astell's two sample judgments are "that the Existence of an All-Perfect Being is Absolutely necessary" and that "Riches and Happiness are two distinct things"—two insights that are crucial to our happiness (*SP II* 131, 132). To say that Astell is influenced by Cartesian epistemology *alone* fails to capture this ethical dimension of her feminist project. Astell endorses Descartes's mistrust of custom and unexamined prejudices, as well as his method of attaining clear and certain knowledge, but she does so for a moral purpose.

Second, if we interpret Astell as offering an epistemological program alone, then this would not leave her with a practical theory of reform. The Cartesian method of attaining knowledge would not provide Astell with a remedy for those idle women who are sunk in an animal life, with almost no possibility of rectifying their behavior. Oftentimes these women might be capable of judging what is good, but they do not

---

17  Smith, *Reason's Disciples*, 129.
18  Smith, *Reason's Disciples*, 119.
19  Perry, "Radical Doubt," 491.
20  Perry, "Radical Doubt," 479.

have the inclination to pursue it. One must not, therefore, ignore Astell's theory of the passions in the closing chapter of the second *Proposal*: here Astell proposes a remedy for *these* women. While the method of the early chapters provides women with a means of recognizing the good, in the final chapter Astell proposes a way of overcoming the influence of custom on the passions, so that one might *do* what is good. "It is to little purpose to guard our selves against the Sophisms of the Head," Astell says, "if we lie open to those of the Heart. One irregular Passion will put a greater Obstacle between us and Truth, then the bright[est] Understanding and clearest Reasoning can easily remove" (*SP II* 133). Astell therefore advocates the "Art of Prudence," the practical art of governing and mastering the passions *(SP II* 120, 162). The pinnacle of Astell's method of improvement for women is about rectifying "their false Ideas, [forming] in their Minds adequate conceptions of the End and Dignity of their Natures," such that women "not only feel Passions, but be able to direct and regulate their Motions" (*SP II* 78).

## II

In the seventeenth century, several thinkers were engaged in an ongoing dispute about the proper place of the passions in a virtuous life. On the one hand, as Susan James observes, there was the Stoic position, in which the passions are intrinsically undesirable and something to be avoided altogether in the good life.[21] On the other, there was the Aristotelian tradition, in which the passions are desirable features of a moral life—so long as they are directed toward their proper objects. In this debate, Descartes occupies something like the Aristotelian position: he says of the passions that "they are all by nature good, and that we have nothing to avoid but their misuse or their excess" (*Passions* 403). Like Descartes, Astell does not regard the passions as intrinsically bad in themselves. She says that "it appears that it is not a fault to have Passions, since they are natural and unavoidable, and useful too" (*SP II* 162).[22] We cannot receive any injury from the passions if we regulate them accordingly. After all, God has made the passions part of human nature, and "God being Infinitely Wise all his Judgments must be Infallible, and being Infinitely Good he can will nothing but what is best, nor prescribe anything that is not for our advantage" (*SP II* 153). A wise and benevolent God would not have given us passions, if he did not intend for them to contribute toward our good.

In his *Passions of the Soul*, Descartes says that "Even those who have the weakest souls could acquire absolute mastery over all their passions if we employed sufficient ingenuity in training and guiding them" (*Passions* 348). First, we must recognize that the passions are simultaneously both physical and mental events—they are a

---

21   James adds that very few writers adopt the Stoic position without some qualification; a life entirely devoid of passion is generally held to be unattainable (James, "Reason, the Passions, and the Good Life," 1373–74).

22   Here Astell echoes her position in the *Letters*, where she says "I am not for a *Stoical Apathy* ... The Fault is not in our Passions considered in themselves, but in our voluntary Misapplication and unsuitable Management of them" (Astell and Norris, *Letters*, 130).

product of the soul–body union. Although the soul and body are distinct substances, according to Descartes, my soul is "not merely present in my body as a sailor is present in a ship."[23] Instead, I am closely joined and connected to this body such that I feel pain when it is injured, hunger when it is famished, and so on. In the *Principles*, Descartes affirms that I experience certain "things which must not be referred either to the mind alone or to the body alone. These arise … from the close and intimate union of our mind with the body." His list includes "the emotions or passions of the mind which do not consist of thought alone, such as the emotions of anger, joy, sadness and love."[24] For Descartes, any remedy for the irregularity of the passions must take into account this close connection between the soul and body. While I am part of the soul–body hybrid, I will never be able to eliminate the passions—but I might be able to modify or reprogram them.[25]

Like Descartes, Astell affirms that "Humane Nature consists in the Union of a Rational Soul with a Mortal Body" (*SP II* 158). "Suffice it briefly to observe," she begins,

[t]hat by the Oeconomy of Nature such and such Motions in the Body are annext in such a manner to certain Thoughts in the Soul, that unless some outward force restrain, she can produce them when she pleases barely by willing them, and reciprocally several Impressions on the Body are communicated to, and affect the Soul, all this being perform'd by the means of the Animal Spirits. The Active Powers of the Soul, her Will and Inclinations are at her own dispose, her Passive are not, she can't avoid feeling Pain or other sensible Impressions so long as she's united to a Body, and that Body is dispos'd to convey these Impressions. And when outward Objects occasion such Commotions in the Bloud and Animal Spirits, as are attended with those Perceptions in the Soul which we call the Passions, she can't be insensible of or avoid 'em, being no more able to prevent these first Impressions than she is to stop the Circulation of the Bloud, or to hinder Digestion. All she can do is to Continue the Passion as it was begun, or to Divert it to another Object; to Heighthen or to let Sink by degrees, or some way or other to Modifie and Direct it. The due performance of which is what we call *Vertue*, which consists in governing Animal Impressions, in directing our Passions to such Objects, and keeping 'em in such a pitch, as right Reasons requires. (*SP II* 161)

While Astell's definition of virtue seems to come from Henry More, her "remedy" for the passions is essentially that of Descartes.[26] Like Descartes, Astell addresses the question of how we are to attain virtue as embodied creatures, and not just as immaterial minds. Any adequate theory of virtue must take into account the fact that we cannot avoid feeling passions or sensible impressions as long as we are part of the soul–body composite. In proposing a remedy for idleness and impertinence, we cannot just suppose that women can use their reason to direct their inclinations as

---

23  Descartes, *Meditations*, in *Philosophical Writings*, 2:56.

24  Descartes, *Principles of Philosophy*, in *Philosophical Writings*, 1:209.

25  On this topic, see Cottingham, "Cartesian Ethics."

26  Henry More writes that "Virtue *is an intellectual Power of the Soul, by which it over-rules the animal Impressions or bodily Passions; so as in every Action it easily pursues what is absolutely and simply the best*" (More, *Virtue*, 11).

a disinterested pilot might direct a ship. Such women are intimately associated and intermingled with their bodies—as all human beings must be. But while we cannot prevent the passions from having an impact on the mind, we can direct or divert them to objects of greater worth by a process of transference or channeling. Astell says that "tho we may find it difficult absolutely to quash a Passion that is once begun, yet it is no hard matter to transfer it" (*SP II* 169). In her moral theory, she does not attempt to suppress or deny the passions, but gives them a vital role in the attainment of virtue. Virtue consists in governing the animal impressions and re-directing the passions, not in obliterating them.

By making selective use of Descartes's ideas, Astell follows the lead of her fellow Englishmen, the Cambridge Platonists Henry More and Ralph Cudworth. The Cambridge men are suspicious of the atheistic overtones of Cartesian mechanism and Descartes's separation between spirit and extension. But they embrace the positive moral and theological aspects of Descartes's philosophy, such as his arguments in favor of spiritual substance and the existence of God. In his *Treatise of Freewill* (probably written c. 1670–78), Cudworth appeals to Descartes's theory of the will and understanding in his account of practical moral judgment.[27] In his Latin text, *Enchiridion Ethicum* (1667), More gives an account of the role that the passions might play in the virtuous life, an account that is heavily indebted to Descartes's *Passions of the Soul*. Astell resembles these early English readers of Descartes in her recognition of the moral and spiritual aspirations of the Cartesian project. Not surprisingly, in her account of the proper objects of the passions, Astell draws on the 1690 English translation of More's *Enchiridion Ethicum*, titled *An Account of Virtue* (*SP II* 165).

Astell's approach is similar to More's in that they both emphasize the importance of regulating the passions in the service of a religious or "divine life." Following More's approach, Astell partakes in a long tradition of philosophical attempts to classify the passions in terms of a few key or primitive passions.[28] In the *Passions of the Soul*, Descartes claims that there are *six* principal passions: admiration, love, hatred, desire, joy, and sadness. Initially, Astell approves of More's contraction of these passions to three: admiration, love, and hatred. She confirms More's view that "Admiration gives Rise to all the Passions; for unless we were affected by the Newness of an Object, or some other remarkable Circumstance, so as to be attentively engag'd in the Contemplation of it, we shou'd not be any wise mov'd, but it wou'd pass by unregarded" (*SP II* 165; *Virtue* 44).[29] Astell's notion of love also strongly echoes that of More: while More defines love as a "Passion of the Soul, by which it is excited willingly to join it self unto Objects which seem grateful thereunto," Astell describes it as "*a motion of the Soul to joyn itself to that which appears to be grateful to it*" (*Virtue* 84; *SP II* 166).

---

27  Ralph Cudworth, *A Treatise of Freewill*, in *A Treatise Concerning Eternal and Immutable Morality, with A Treatise of Freewill*, ed. Sarah Hutton (Cambridge, 1996), 180.

28  On this tradition, see Susan James, *Passion and Action: The Emotions in Seventeenth-Century Philosophy* (Oxford, 1997), 4.

29  More paraphrases the 1650 English translation of Descartes's *Passions of the Soule*, in which "Admiration" (*l'admiration*) is "the first of all the Passions" (Descartes, *Passions*, 47).

But Astell departs from More in reducing all the passions to different modifications of *love*. Love, she says, is "at the bottom of all the Passions, one wou'd think they're nothing else but different Modifications of it, occasion'd by some Circumstance in the Subject or Object of this Passion" (*SP II* 166). In her analysis of love as the chief passion, Astell follows the Augustinian–Neoplatonic moral tradition.[30] In *The City of God* (c. 412–26), Augustine explains all the basic types of passion in terms of love, saying that love "desiring to enjoy what it loves is desire: and enjoying it, is joy: flying what it hates, it is fear; feeling it, it is sorrow."[31] Astell likewise reduces the passions to species of love: for her, desire is simply a love of future good, joy is the pleasure received from love, sorrow is occasioned by the absence of what we love, and "even Hatred tho it appear directly opposite to Love, may be referr'd to it, the very same motion that carrys the Soul towards Good, carrying her also from those things that wou'd deprive her of it" (*SP II* 166). The upshot of Astell's emphasis on love is to claim that "if therefore our Love be Right, the rest of our Passions will of course be so" (*SP II* 166). For Astell, as for Augustine, love is the key to leading a virtuous life. The passions are good when they are those that right reason disposes us to, or when they are inclined towards their proper objects. The passion of love is well regulated when we have saved it for things of the greatest worth; and what could be worthier, she asks, than the love of God? We should, therefore, have "no Passion but for God's service" (*SP II* 171). The passions of esteem, veneration, love, desire, and so on, need not disturb us if they are directed toward our one true end: the glory of our maker.

> To wind up all; The Sum of our Duty and of all Morality, is to have a Temper of Mind so absolutely Conform'd to the Divine Will, or which is the same in other words, such an Habitual and Intire Love to GOD, as will on all occasions excite us to the Exercise of such Acts, as are the necessary consequent of such a Habit. (*SP II* 171)

It is curious that, at this point, Astell does not explicitly refer to the work of her correspondent John Norris. First, Astell echoes Norris's position in the *Theory and Regulation of Love* (1688), where he suggests a way of approaching ethics according to "the reduction of all Vertue and Vice to the various Modifications of Love."[32] Second, Astell reiterates a central thesis in Norris's "Discourse concerning the Measure of Divine Love," the first essay in the third volume of Norris's *Practical Discourses* (1693). In that essay, drawing from Nicolas Malebranche's occasionalist philosophy, Norris argues that we love only that which brings us pleasure, and because God is the only true cause of our pleasure, God alone is truly deserving of our love. In her final letter to Norris (August 14, 1694), Astell says that even if material things were the true causes of our pleasure, God would still be the only deserved object

---

30  On this tradition, see James, *Passion and Action*, 6.

31  St Augustine, *The City of God*, trans. J. Healey (London, 1962), 33.

32  John Norris, *The Theory and Regulation of Love. A Moral Essay. In Two Parts. To which are added Letters Philosophical and Moral between the Author and Dr Henry More* (Oxford, 1688), "To the Reader."

of our love—because all our good is brought about solely by his will.[33] Likewise, in the second *Proposal*, Astell argues that God "is the only proper and adequate Object of our Love." And "if we love GOD with *All* our Soul," then our passions will be naturally regular (*SP II* 166). Third, Astell repeats Norris's sentiments when she affirms that "Conformity to his Will" is "the Duty and Perfection of all Rational Beings" (*SP II* 173). In the "Postscript to the First Discourse," Norris adds that "if we would sincerely consult the Perfection of our Rational Nature, we should at least as much endeavour to conform our Wills to the Will of God, as to conform our Understanding to the Understanding of God."[34]

It is possible that Astell is reluctant to name Norris out of fear of being branded a heretic. In a recent paper, Sarah Ellenzweig suggests that in the 1690s Astell may have distanced herself from Malebranche and Norris because their philosophy had been unfavorably associated with Spinozism and irreligion.[35] But whatever Astell thinks of occasionalism, she never abandons Norris's central moral–theological claim that God ought to be the sole object of our love.

## III

It is apparent, then, that Astell's feminist project is based not on Cartesian epistemology alone, but also on Cartesian ethical principles. Descartes' theory of the regulation of the passions plays an integral role in Astell's philosophy. In the second *Proposal*, Astell intends for her project for reform to be a practicable one, something that ordinary women can put into practice. She recommends a program that will enable women to overcome bad habits and fortify their "minds against foolish Customs" (*SP II* 96). For this purpose, it is not enough for Astell simply to assert that reason can triumph over custom; she also needs to explain *how* it can do so, despite the influence of the passions on the will. Toward this end, Astell develops a remedy for redirecting passions to their proper objects. Although Astell departs from Descartes in treating love as the predominant passion, she accords with his notion that the passions are not intrinsically undesirable in themselves. Like Descartes, Astell regards a life of well-being as a life in which the passions play a vital role.

An understanding of Astell's ethical theory of the passions, and of love as the predominant passion, can assist in our conception of Astell's philosophical project as a continuous whole. First, and most obvious, Astell's second *Proposal* is a natural continuation of the central thesis of *Letters Concerning the Love of God*—the notion that in order to attain true happiness, we must love and desire God alone. In this earlier work, Astell declares that "if Love which is the leading and Master Passion were but once wisely regulated, our Passions would be so far from rebelling against and disquieting us, that ... they would mightily facilitate the great Work we have to

---

33  Astell and Norris, *Letters*, 284–85.

34  John Norris, *Practical Discourses Upon several Divine Subjects* (London, 1693), III:340.

35  Sarah Ellenzweig, "The Love of God and the Radical Enlightenment: Mary Astell's Brush with Spinoza," *Journal of the History of Ideas* 64.3 (2003): 387.

do."[36] In the *Proposal*, Astell expresses some ambivalence about "seeing all things in God," but she still upholds Norris's Malebranchean view that a virtuous life is one devoted solely to the love of God (*SP II* 117). A true Christian must have "a true Notion of the Nothingness of Material things and of the reality and substantialness of the immaterial, and consequently contemn the present World as it deserves, fixing all their Hopes upon and exerting all their Endeavours to obtain the Glory of the next" (*SP II* 78). A few years later, in *Some Reflections upon Marriage* (1700), Astell once again provides women with a salient lesson about letting the misguided passions dictate their life choices. When a woman accepts a suitor's marriage proposal, Astell warns that she must not base her decision on "brutish Passion."[37] A woman must marry for spiritual motives: if "the Soul be principally consider'd and regard had in the first Place to a good Understanding, a Vertuous Mind," then this will contribute a long way toward her happiness.[38] But if a woman's decision is blinded by improper lust, greed, or mistaken self-love, then it would be better if she did not marry at all.

In *The Christian Religion, as Profess'd by a Daughter of the Church of England* (1705), Astell continues to urge women to lead virtuous lives by regulating their passions according to their "noblest Objects":

> In a word, we judge and chuse amiss, because our Judgments are hasty and partial; 'tis our Passions for the most part that make our Judgments thus precipitate and defective, we suffer Passion to lead when it ought to follow; and sensible things, the Love of this World and present Pleasure, is that which moves our Passions. Wise Men of all Ages have exclaim'd against Prejudices and Prepossessions, and advis'd us to get rid of them, but they have not inform'd us how, nor enabled us to do it, Christianity only does this. And it does it by stripping sensible things of their deceitful appearances, and finding us nobler Objects of our Passions than any this World affords.[39]

The good Christian woman must recognize that her happiness does not consist in the mutable things of this world. She must re-direct her passions from the love of sensible things to the love of an eternal and immutable God. "And how," Astell says,

> can a Life thus led but abound with *Self-satisfaction*? which as a Great Man who had throughly consider'd this Subject tells us, is *the sweetest of all the Passions*. None indeed but the Good Christian can have it, or enjoy that *Tranquility of Mind* which is his Portion, both in the Nature of things, and by his Great Masters Promise. Which Tranquility he enjoys in the midst of all outward Troubles. (*CR* 286–87)

Here again we see the significance of Descartes's ethical theory for Astell's wider philosophy. In the *Passions of the Soul*, Descartes says that "The satisfaction of those who steadfastly pursue virtue is a habit of their soul which is called 'tranquillity' and

---

36 Astell and Norris, *Letters*, 130.

37 Mary Astell, *Reflections upon Marriage*, in *Political Writings*, ed. Patricia Springborg (Cambridge, 1996), 37.

38 Astell, *Reflections*, 53.

39 [Mary Astell,] *The Christian Religion, As Profess'd by a Daughter Of The Church of England* (London, 1705), 283.

'peace of mind'" (*Passions* 396). For Descartes, the path to happiness lies within our very own souls because it depends solely upon the exercising of our free will. Provided that a man always does what he judges to be best, "the most violent assaults of the passions will never have sufficient power to disturb the tranquillity of his soul" (*Passions* 382). Similarly for Astell, the steadfast pursuit of virtue can lead to a calm and detached acceptance of outward circumstances.

This emphasis on "satisfaction" or "Tranquility of Mind" provides the key to understanding how Astell could embrace the Cartesian challenge to custom while at the same time occupying a conservative political position. In *Bart'lemy Fair*, her final sustained attack on Whiggism, Astell once again extols the benefits of "self-satisfaction."[40] In this tract, Astell responds to the *Letter Concerning Enthusiasm* (1708), an anonymous work written by Anthony Ashley Cooper, the third Earl of Shaftesbury. In the *Letter*, Shaftesbury puts forward a novel suggestion for evaluating the worth of extreme theological positions. Rather than test such religious beliefs by the light of reason or truth, he proposes that we subject them to a test of public ridicule. If a certain belief is genuine and sincere, then it will stand the test of ridicule and laughter; if it is spurious, then it will be detected and exposed. Shaftesbury's wry suggestion stems from his conviction that there can be no true "freedom of censure" (or, in modern terms, freedom of speech) if certain customs or opinions are exempt from criticism.

Astell sees this method as tantamount to exposing all religion to the contempt of the people (*BF* 23). "To Laugh ourselves out of the little Knowledge we have," she says, "will be so far from being *Wit* and *good Humor*, that it will be the height of Folly and Madness" (*BF* 123). Shaftesbury's freedom of censure, in her view, is the freedom to challenge and undermine the religious and political order. The logical extension of Shaftesbury's "libertine" viewpoint is that "we shall never be a perfectly free Nation, till the Guards are remov'd, the Court Gates thrown open, and every body at Liberty to be as merry as they please with their Sovereign" (*BF* 50). Shaftesbury's failure to treat sacred institutions with due reverence can lead to nothing but moral and political chaos. "To make Libertines," Astell says, "is to make so many Beasts of Prey, Foxes and other vermin; and do all one can to reduce Mankind to a state of open Violence, or dissembled Malice, which some, taking the *Measure* from themselves, have falsly call'd a State of Nature" (*BF* 90).

Astell has a different conception of liberty: not a radical political one, but a strictly philosophical conception of liberty as freedom of the will. For Astell, the will is free either to choose to love the transitory things of this world, or to place our hopes on attaining "an eternal and immutable Crown of Glory" in the next (*SP II* 114). To choose the latter course is the only sure means to peace and harmony. An understanding of religion helps to subdue "those Passions which imbitter Life; sets us above those little Designs, which make us angry with them who stand in our way; fills our Souls with the Noblest Hopes, and the most Regular Desires" (*BF* 124). By contrast, the libertine—a person who values material goods and shows nothing but

---

40   For details, see Van C. Hartmann, "Tory Feminism in Mary Astell's *Bart'lemy Fair*," *The Journal of Narrative Technique* 28.3 (1998): 243–65.

contempt for religion and God—can never achieve tranquillity. Astell points out that "Libertine Pleasures depend on limited and precarious Objects, which are often out of our Power, and which must be engross'd and many times destroy'd, are continual occasions of Solicitude, Disquiet, and Grief; so that the Pain they give is generally greater than the Delight" (*BF* 90). The Libertine is "a Slave to his Appetites, and for this Reason to every Thing without him; uneasy to himself, as well as to every one who happens to stand in his way" (*BF* 140).

While the radical enlightenment might have found fuel in the Cartesian challenge to custom, Astell's writings show that radicalism is not a necessary outcome of Descartes's philosophy. Instead of promoting radical change, a pursuit of Cartesian ethical ideals might result in a calm acceptance of the status quo. While we cannot master our external circumstances—such as the cruel tyranny of an abusive husband or the despotism of an unjust prince—we can master our own inner aspirations. The culmination of our re-direction of the passions toward the love of God is an inner tranquility and peace of mind, regardless of "what happens without us." Astell's challenge to custom, therefore, is not one that logically leads to the undermining of political authority. It is a challenge, rather, to our customary judgments of right and wrong, judgments that go astray because we allow our passions to be directed toward unworthy ends rather than the love of God.

## Chapter XII

# Are You Experienced?: Astell, Locke, and Education

### E. Derek Taylor

Assuming her writings offer some indication of her mind's wanderings, Mary Astell must have pondered regularly during the thirty-five years of her publishing career some version of the following question: Why are human beings so dumb? As a staunch Anglican Christian and inveterate reader of Scripture, of course, Astell always, on one level, knew the answer to this question before asking it; if Sin, as Milton had suggested, was the mother of Death, so too did it beget Stupidity; all three were, with the fall of Adam and Eve, original aspects of the human condition, as Astell noted in *Some Reflections upon Marriage* (1700): "If Mankind had never sinn'd, Reason would always have been obey'd."[1] Astell also firmly believed, however, that as with Sin, and as with Death, human beings could overcome intellectual inanity, and in precisely the same manner: by learning to turn away from the material creation and toward the immaterial creator.

We do not only need saving, in other words. We also need schooling—a point Astell stressed in her first and most ambitious pedagogical work, *A Serious Proposal to the Ladies, Part I* (1694). Women—flighty, fashion-conscious, romance-reading, husband-hunting women—were, of course, her particular concern. Men blamed them for their vacuity, she complained, while hypocritically withholding any systemic opportunity to prove themselves otherwise; the "narrow Education" fathers generally provided their daughters "lay the Foundation" for the ignorance and superficiality toward which women were thought by nature to tend.[2] If women were allowed a substantive education, Astell contended, the vicious cycle energized by that "Tyrant Custom" finally would be broken (*SP I* 15).

Of course, Astell's vision of a useful education might itself strike modern readers as decidedly "narrow." Like the institution she seriously proposes constructing, it is essentially, *explicitly*, religious—which sounds more limiting to our ears than it probably should. Astell, to be sure, saw no clear distinction between a solid education and a religious one. Indeed, she took it as a strictly logical proposition that a woman must "get religion" to "get" anything. It was a woman's immaterial soul, "that particle of Divinity" within "which is really [her] self" that rendered her

---

1 Mary Astell, *Some Reflections upon Marriage*, in *Mary Astell: Political Writings*, ed. Patricia Springborg (Cambridge, 1996), 15. Hereafter cited parenthetically as *SRM*.

2 Mary Astell, *A Serious Proposal to the Ladies, Parts I & II*, ed. Patricia Springborg (London, 1997), 14. Hereafter cited parenthetically as *SP I* and *SP II*.

inherently teachable, and, Astell maintained, inherently equal to the other sex in the only important respect (*SP I* 6).

Astell would never abandon her early contention that a full understanding of religion provided a necessary catalyst in the development of a capacious intellect. "She then who desires a clear Head," she wrote in *A Serious Proposal, Part II* (1697), "must have a pure Heart" (*SP II* 82). Having acquired both, she slyly observed in *Some Reflections upon Marriage*, women might so "Improve themselves" in the acquisition of "true Wisdom" as to make men "Blush" at the lusty and materialistic employments of their own "immortal mind[s]" (*SRM* 76). "If GOD had not intended that Women shou'd use their Reason, He wou'd not have given them any," Astell insisted in *Christian Religion* (1705; 2nd edition 1717), unrepentant in her dedication to defending the inherent intellectual potential of women. "If they are to use their Reason, certainly it ought to be employ'd about the noblest Objects, and in business of the greatest Consequence, therefore in Religion," she contended in the same work, equally unwavering in her conflation of piety and understanding.[3]

Given the fact that Astell's most sustained educational works rest firmly on sacred ground, it is not surprising that in arguably her most religious work, Astell is still interested in education. Indeed, if we are to believe Astell, *Letters Concerning the Love of God* (1695; 2nd edition 1705), a collection of the correspondence between the well-known Christian Platonist John Norris and herself, only exists in printed form *because* Astell so desperately wished to teach. She agrees to publish, she tells Norris in a prefacing letter, only in hopes that she might, in the first place, "perswade" members of her sex "to leave their insignificant Pursuits for Employments worthy of them" and, furthermore, dispel the "Wonder" of the other sex at meeting "with an ingenious Woman."[4] But education, Astell knew, was Janus-faced; if it could enlighten, it could also benight. An education that teaches the wrong lessons sullies the intellect just as surely as no education at all.

Consider, Astell explains to Norris, the fundamentally flawed lessons human beings learn about their relationship to God and His creation by dint of living as a body among bodies:

> 'Tis our Misfortune that we live an animal before we live a rational Life; the Good we enjoy is mostly transmitted to us through Bodily Mediums, and contracts such a Tincture of the Conveyance through which it passes, that forgetting the true Cause and Sourse of all our Good, we take up with those occasional Goods that are more visible, and present to our animal Nature. Besides, the Mistakes of our Education do too much confirm us in this Error. We suck in false Principles and Tendencies betimes, and are taught, not to thirst after *GOD* as our only Good, but to close with those visible Objects that surround us, to rest and stay in them. (*L* 117)

We *learn* to accept the existence and importance of secondary causes, in other words, as children; we are *taught* to believe in the efficacy of the fire that warms our hands,

---

3  [Mary Astell], *The Christian Religion, as Profess'd by a Daughter of the Church of England*, 2nd edition, (London, 1717), 5. Hereafter cited parenthetically as *CR*.

4  Mary Astell and John Norris, *Letters Concerning the Love of God*, ed. E. Derek Taylor and Melvyn New (Aldershot, 2005), 66. Hereafter cited parenthetically as *L*.

the rose that delights our noses, the cake that melts on our tongues. To "imagine," however, "that Nature not Custom is the Author" of this fundamental misreading of human experience, Astell continues, "certainly is a very gross Mistake."

One can only assume, then, that Astell would have applied this phrase—"a very gross Mistake"—to that monumental work of philosophy that had been published some three years prior to the composition of her letter to Norris, John Locke's *Essay Concerning Human Understanding* (1690). Locke, of course, begins the *Essay* by elaborating the very "lesson" Astell admonishes her readers to unlearn, namely, that the sensory perception of the physical world is central to the acquisition of all human knowledge. Far from rejecting secondary causality, Locke argues that human understanding of God's creation is, in fact, limited to secondary qualities; he refers without hesitation to the "Power" of physical objects "to produce various Sensations in us."[5]

If, in the passage from *Letters*, Astell seems with one hand to distance herself from Locke, however, she seems with the other hand, Patricia Springborg has suggested, to draw him near. After all, the body does, in Astell's account, teach lessons, albeit the wrong ones. According to Springborg, Astell thus makes a "surprising concession to the principles of Lockean sensationalist psychology."[6] Is not Astell, in other words, proposing the human being as a *tabula rasa*, a blank slate on which the body writes its experiences? Was she, with regards to education at least, implicitly a true empiricist, and of Locke's party without knowing it? (My apologies to Blake.)

There are, it seems to me, three ways to account for Astell's apparent contradiction, all of them perhaps true in part, the third, I believe, more true than the others.

In the first place, it may simply be that Astell was inconsistent on this point. *Letters* is, after all, one of Astell's earliest published works, probably *the* earliest composed.[7] Surely a nascent philosopher can be forgiven if, like a host of more seasoned thinkers, she was still grappling in 1693 with the epistemological upheaval Locke had introduced three years earlier with his "new way of ideas."[8] But even if we conclude that Astell is a contradictory philosopher, we would do well to consider what good company she keeps. It was Norris's own inconsistency regarding the nature of sensation, after all, that had inspired Astell to send her opening letter. In his "Discourse Concerning The Measure of Divine Love," the first of a series of essays in the third volume of *Practical Discourses* (1693), Norris adduces Nicolas Malebranche's theory of occasionalism, according to which God, and not His creation, is directly responsible for all human sensation and perception, as philosophical justification for the theological admonition to love Him only. "For if God be the only

---

5  John Locke, *An Essay Concerning Human Understanding*, ed. Peter H. Nidditch (Oxford, 1988), II.8.137. Hereafter cited parenthetically as *Essay* and by book, chapter, and page.

6  Patricia Springborg, "Astell, Masham, and Locke: Religion and Politics," in *Women Writers and the Early Modern British Political Tradition*, ed. Hilda L. Smith (Cambridge, 1998), 121.

7  *Serious Proposal, Part I* was published one year prior to *Letters*. However, when one couples Astell's gracious recommendation of Norris's works to her audience (21–22) with her frequently rapturous religious language, it becomes difficult not to suspect that Astell composed *Serious Proposal, Part I* either during or just after her correspondence with Norris.

8  For a useful summary of various hostile, puzzled, and admiring contemporary reactions to Locke's *Essay*, see Allan P.F. Sell, *John Locke and the Eighteenth-Century Divines* (Cardiff, 1997), 16–61.

true Cause that acts upon our Spirits, and produces our Pleasure, then he only does us good," Norris there argues; thus "he only is lovely"; thus "'tis plain that we ought to love none but him, and him intirely."[9] If, Astell acutely notes in her letter, Norris is correct in linking God's role as the occasional cause of all our pleasant sensations to our need to love Him entirely, then are we not also required to loathe Him utterly for his equally necessary role as the cause of all our pain? Norris quickly accepted Astell's remedy to his theoretical difficulty, which was to posit God more broadly as the source of our *good*, whether inflicting pleasure or pain.[10] Other contemporary philosophers, too, might have told Astell something about changing intellectual course—Henry More, for instance, or Locke himself.[11]

Or perhaps, in the second place, Astell's "concession" is not as "surprising" as Springborg suggests—or is not a "concession" at all. Neither Norris nor Astell, it is important to note, bears Locke particular hostility in *Letters*. (Actually, Locke is never even mentioned.) Indeed, as has often been noted, Astell's final letter to Norris, published as an "Appendix" to *Letters*, attempts to strike a balance between, on the one hand, a Lockean acceptance of the efficacy of the senses and, on the other hand, the Malebranchean version of human experience she and Norris had developed throughout their correspondence.[12] She writes, "it seems more agreeable to the Majesty of *GOD*, and that Order he has established in the World, to say that he produces our Sensations *mediately* by his Servant Nature, than to affirm that he does it *immediately* by his own Almighty Power" (*L* 132). It may not have occurred to Astell in 1693 that she could not, or should not, mingle her own theocentric philosophical tendencies with "the principles of Lockean sensationalist psychology." At this point in time, Edward Stillingfleet, Bishop of Worcester, had yet to launch his debate with Locke over the alleged moral, philosophical, and theological dangers of Locke's positions; Damaris Masham had yet to compose her biting assault (which Astell took

---

9  John Norris, "Discourse Concerning the Measure of Divine Love, with the Natural and Moral Grounds upon which it stands," in *Practical Discourses Upon Several Divine Subjects*, vol. 3 (London, 1693), 57.

10  See the opening four letters of Astell and Norris's *Letters*. Norris's initial response in letter two is defensive and fumbling, but by letter four, he has wisely recognized the significance of Astell's suggestion.

11  As with other of the Cambridge Platonists, More initially praised Descartes; in a letter of 1648 to the French philosopher, More rejects "all other philosophers as mere pygmies next to Descartes" (C.A. Patrides, *The Cambridge Platonists* [Cambridge, 1970], 29). By 1671, however, he had severed all ties with Descartes and his atheistical (as More saw it) devotion to mechanism. For his part, Locke famously devotes the first book of his *Essay*, of course, to debunking the doctrine of innate ideas; writing three years later in *Some Thoughts Concerning Education*, however, he underscores the limitations of even the best instruction by noting, "God has stamped certain characters upon men's minds, which ... may perhaps be a little mended; but can hardly be totally altered ..." (John Locke, *The Works of John Locke*, 10 vols. [London, 1812] 9:47). Locke too, in other words, struggled to maintain a fully consistent relationship to "the principles of Lockean sensationalist psychology."

12  Astell appeals to Norris's "Friend Dr. *More*" (Cambridge Platonist Henry More, whose correspondence with Norris had been published as an appendix to Norris's *Theory and Regulation of Love* [1688]) in hypothesizing a middle path between soul and body that would preclude the necessity of Malebranche's strict occasionalism (*Letters* 132). It is important to note that even though, as Ruth Perry and others (myself included) have suggested, the tendency of Astell's argument is "Lockean," Astell does not mention Locke. See Perry, *The Celebrated Mary Astell: An Early English Feminist* (Chicago, 1986), 79.

to be Locke's) on Norris, Malebranche, and Astell.[13] Indeed, even as late as 1697, Astell had not arrived at any definite conclusions regarding Locke or his principles; her one direct reference to him is both perfunctory and admiring (*SP II* 139).[14]

With the publication of *Christian Religion* in 1705, however, Astell renounced all ties to Locke. Here, she excoriates him as "a Socinian, an Epicurean, a party man, and a defender of liberty, property, choice, and Dissent," to borrow Springborg's succinct summary.[15] She now openly attacks Locke's "sensualiz'd" philosophy, which takes "nothing to be Real but what ... is some way or other the Object of [the] Senses," and she just as openly defends Malebranchean occasionalism, explaining human sensation as the "Powers of GOD giving [the human soul] divers modifications" (*CR* 209, 320). And yet, even in this, her final dissenting statement on Locke, Astell continues to admit that we learn from our sensory interaction with the material world:

> If it be enquir'd whence [our] difficulties arise, we shall find that it is *the Corruptible Body that presseth down the Soul* ... [S]ensible Pleasures being present, intrude upon us and will be attended: Whereas Spiritual Pleasures tho' unspeakably greater, are more remote .... Therefore the main business of those who aspire to Perfection ... is to throw off the prejudices of Sense, which have nothing to plead but the prepossessions of Childhood. (*CR* 72–73)

Why, given her total rejection of Locke, would Astell continue in *Christian Religion* to hold a Lockean understanding of the role of experience, particularly *early* experience, in shaping the human being? Was Locke's "sensationalist psychology" ineluctable, a "truth" she simply could not deny, despite its source?

Not necessarily. In fact, I would suggest a third option, namely, that not only in *Letters* and in *Christian Religion*, but in all of her major works, Astell builds steadily on a point she had found in Norris and in Malebranche, in admitting, and lamenting, how certainly, and badly, living a corporeal existence educates us. She was neither more nor less Locke's follower in educational matters, in short, than were Locke's more famous (at the time) philosophical adversaries.

Long before Locke published his *Essay*, in should be noted, Malebranche had already argued along the lines of Astell's ostensibly "surprising concession" to Locke's *tabula rasa*; in order to contend that Astell is Lockean after the fact, we will have to agree that Malebranche was so beforehand. Those who believe the body has a "power" over the soul and vice versa, he contends in "Elucidation Fifteen" of

---

13  Stillingfleet and Locke carried on their open debate between 1696 and 1699. Masham's *Discourse Concerning the Love of God* appeared in 1696. For Astell's reaction to Masham, see my "Mary Astell's Ironic Assault on John Locke's Theory of Thinking Matter" in *Journal of the History of Ideas* 62.3 (2001): 505–22.

14  Even as late as 1715, as Astell revised her text for (I believe) an abortive second edition, she found several places in the text either that reminded her, for better or worse, of Locke's arguments, or that were inspired by them, leading her to add his name in pen to the margins. My essay on this particular copy of Astell's book (currently housed in the Northampton Records Office as part of the remainders from the William Law Library) is forthcoming from *Studies in Bibliography*.

15  Patricia Springborg, "Mary Astell (1666–1731), Critic of Locke," *American Political Science Review* 89.3 (1995): 629.

his *Search After Truth* (1674–75), "arrived at this view through prejudice; they have believed it to be so since infancy and as long as they have been capable of sensing."[16] Physiology accounts in large part for our susceptibility to the misinformation presented by our senses; "In childhood, the brain fibers are soft, flexible, and delicate," Malebranche explains, "and, consequently, all external objects make very deep imprints on it" (*Search* II.1.6.110; II.1.8.125). Properly understood, then, education ought to focus on combating the "disruption of [the] brain caused by the impression of external objects" from the moment of "coming into the world"; unfortunately, educational practice too often reinforces in children the centrality of "sensible impressions" in the search after truth, thereby "stifl[ing] their reason and corrupt[ing] their better inclinations" (*Search* 126; 128–29). It may be "easier for a child of seven years to be delivered from the errors to which his senses have brought him than for a person of sixty who has followed the prejudices of his childhood throughout his life"—but "easier" does not equate to "easy." It is both predictable and unfortunate, Malebranche muses, that, even in adulthood, the soul, "fancying its own modifications as modifications of bodies," should "[lose] its bearings and altogether [misunderstand] itself" (*Search* 127; I.13.63). Notwithstanding his staunch philosophical support for Cartesian dualism, in short, Malebranche nevertheless maintains in his Preface that human "errors are almost all consequences of the mind's union with the body" (*Search* xxxix). "Since Original Sin," he explains, "man is, as it were, but flesh and blood. The least impression from his sense or passions interrupts his mind's closest attention, and the flow of spirits and blood sweeps the mind along with it and continually drives it toward sensible objects" (*Search* III.2.9.249).

Norris ("The English Malebranche," as John Sergeant pejoratively but justly labeled him[17]) proves equally "Lockean" in adducing a causal link between human experience and human error; for him too, our predilection for folly is an effect both of physiology, which we cannot help, and of pedagogy, which we can. On the one hand, the soul is hindered in any search after truth from the outset because of the physical baggage it necessarily carries; the body and the soul may be separate essences, but, as for Malebranche, those essences are thoroughly, even bewilderingly, intertwined. "[O]ur thick Houses of Clay" respond only to that which is somehow "*Sensible*," rather than "*Intelligible*," "visible to our *Eyes*," rather than "to our *Minds*," Norris explains in *Reason and Religion* (1689); thus, we are "always strongly inclined to sensible good."[18] "I suppose in the first place," Norris writes in his most thoroughly didactic work, *Reflections Upon the Conduct of Human Life: With Reference to the Study and Learning of Knowledge* (1690), "that the Soul sees through a *Medium*: Secondly, That this Medium is our *Terrestrial Vehicle*: Thirdly, That the *Grosness* of

---

16  Nicolas Malebranche, *The Search After Truth*, trans. and ed. Thomas M. Lennon and Paul J. Olscamp; with *Elucidations of the Search After Truth*, trans. and ed. Thomas M. Lennon (Columbus, 1980), 670. *Elucidations* first appeared as part of the third edition of *Search* in 1677. Hereafter, all references will treat these as a single text, and will be cited parenthetically as *Search*. Where applicable, I have provided book, part, chapter, and page—though, it should be noted, some books contain no parts, only chapters.

17  See Charles J. McCracken, *Malebranche and British Philosophy* (Oxford, 1983), 179.

18  John Norris, *Reason and Religion, or the Grounds and Measures of Devotion*, in *Treatises Upon Several Subjects* (New York, 1978), 32, 151. Hereafter cited parenthetically as *Reason*.

the Medium *hinders* the *Vision* of the Soul."[19] Norris elaborates a strictly logical—and, as with Malebranche, notably material—cause and effect explanation for how the body accomplishes this epistemologically unhappy feat: "[T]he Motion of the Passions Ferments the Spirits, and the Fermentation of the Spirits agitates the Blood, and by agitation raises all the feculent and drossie parts of it; and makes it like a troubled Fountain thick and muddy" (*Reflections* 211). The body quite literally obfuscates Truth, in Norris's analysis, all the while inculcating the mind with its own fallacious lessons. Indeed, in *Reason and Religion*, Norris points to the alleged "remoteness" of Malebranche's theocentric explanation of human experience as proof enough of "the prejudices of our Education" (*Reason* 110). "Education is the great Bias of Human Life" he again maintains (*Reflections* preface). Even he has been "long imposed upon," Norris there admits, by the near invincibility of "the Impressions of an early Prejudice," though attentive meditation and his reading of the "deservedly admired Monsieur *Malebranche*" have partially corrected his own error (*Reflections* 178–79). It is to Malebranche's *Search*, not surprisingly, that Norris directs his own children in the course of his open letter to them, *Spiritual Counsel: Or, The Father's Advice to his Children* (1694); there they will learn, he promises, the "Fundamental Theories" that "will rid you of all your Prejudices and Sensible Prepossessions."[20]

Astell was writing neither to nor about children in *Serious Proposal, Part I*, of course, but she was quite consciously stepping into an educational void that had, in her view, effectively infantilized much of her female audience. In recommending Norris's as an "ingenious pen" whose *Reflections Upon the Conduct of Human Life* would teach women to "busy themselves in a serious enquiry after *necessary* and *perfective* truths," and in suggesting "*Des Cartes*" and "*Malbranch*" as appropriate reading material in place of "idle *Novels* and *Romance*," Astell was not only graciously acknowledging her recent (or current) correspondent and his philosophical mentor—though, undoubtedly, she was in part doing just that (*SP I* 21, 21, 24).[21] More important, she was providing an apt reference to authors who had adumbrated perfectly her fundamental argument that, as she put it, "The Incapacity [of women], if there be any, is acquired not natural" (*SP I* 10). In her note to this passage, Springborg points to the confusion Astell has generated through her adherence to a cultural explanation for female "incapacity"—and we are back to the original problem, according to which any commitment to an experiential explanation for human intelligence would appear to amount to a "concession" to Locke, despite the fact that, as Springborg notes, Astell herself "does not subscribe to Lockean sensationalist psychology."[22] I hope it is becoming clear that she did not need to.

19  John Norris, *Reflections Upon the Conduct of Human Life: With reference to the Study of Learning and Knowledge*, in *Treatises Upon Several Divine Subjects* (New York, 1978), 211. Hereafter cited parenthetically as *Reflections*.

20  John Norris, *Spiritual Counsel: Or, the Father's Advice to his Children*, in *Treatises Upon Several Divine Subjects* (New York, 1978), 501.

21  Norris refers to Descartes—not Malebranche, somewhat surprisingly—as his "most admired Philosopher" in *Letters* (96). His unexpected distinction would appear to be based on the simple fact that without Descartes, there would be no Malebranche.

22  Springborg, *A Serious Proposal*, 50, n. 25.

Indeed, I believe that in shining so insistently Lockean light on Astell's treatment of the respective roles of the body and the mind in the acquisition of knowledge, we have failed to identify not only the more appropriate intellectual context for her educational thought, but the remarkable degree of *consistency* she maintains on this point throughout her major works. From her first work to her last, Astell reveals an unwavering devotion to the essentially rationalist account of learning developed by the likes of Norris and Malebranche, one that allowed her simultaneously to account for and to dismiss the operations of the body without having to consider, or rebut, Locke's arguments in any particularly careful fashion. It is unwittingly misleading, in other words, to read, as Springborg does, the following passage in the context of Locke:

> [T]he Mind being prepossess'd and gratefully entertain'd with those pleasing Perceptions which external Objects occasion, takes up with them as its only Good, is not at leisure to taste those delights which arise from a Reflection on it self, nor to receive the *Ideas* which such a Reflection conveys, and consequently forms all its Notions by such *Ideas* only as it derives from sensation, being unacquainted with those more excellent ones which arise from its own operations and a serious reflection on them, and which are necessary to correct the mistakes, and supply the other. (*SP I* 29–30)

Springborg suggests that Astell here "uses the language of Locke on ideas and sensation, but with none of the theoretical rigour she displays in *A Serious Proposal, II*" (60, n. 163). Astell's reading of and correspondence with Norris, in fact, provides a far better precedent for Astell's "language" in this case; Astell uses "Reflection" here not in the Lockean sense of the mind's consideration of ideas formed through sensory impressions, but rather in the Cartesian sense favored by Norris and Malebranche, that is, "reflection" as a rationalist form of meditation wherein the mind purposefully divorces itself from sensory input in order to concentrate on its own inner workings, and thus on "*necessary* and *perfective* truths," as Astell, quoting Norris, puts it (*SP I* 22).

Furthermore, what theoretical rigor Astell does display with respect to this matter in *Serious Proposal, Part II* likely derived more from her continued relationship with Norris and her reading of Malebranche, whose *Search* finally had been translated in 1694, than from any remarkable attention to Locke.[23] As is well known, Astell pointedly refuses in *Serious Proposal, Part II* to include "the Senses" in her "enumeration of the several ways of Knowing." "[W]e're more properly said to be *Conscious* of than to *Know* such things as we perceive by Sensation," Astell explains, and "that Light which we suppose to be let into our Ideas by our Senses is indeed very dim and fallacious, and not be relied on till it has past the Test of Reason" (*SP II* 103). Springborg suggests in her note that this passage offers "an important objection to Locke's notion of ideas as a mental reflex produced by sensations"; I have argued elsewhere that it represents an attempt on Astell's part to bridge the gap between Malebranche's and Locke's respective theories of sensation.[24] But it must now be

---

[23]  In fact, *Search After Truth* was twice translated in 1694, once by Richard Sault, again by Thomas Taylor.

[24]  Springborg, *A Serious Proposal*, 187, n. 58. See my "Ironic Assault," n. 13.

admitted that Astell did not, in fact, need Locke as her rhetorical foil to produce such an argument; she very well may not have been thinking of Locke as she wrote it. She is reproducing, with one small if significant change, a point she had found in Norris's *Reflections Upon the Conduct of Human Life*, composed, it should be remembered, before Locke had thrown down the empirical gauntlet in his *Essay*.[25]

This point needs to be stressed because *Serious Proposal, Part II* has been characterized so variously—as a "training manual for Norris's brand of Christian Platonism," a full-fledged Cartesian critique of Locke on the model of Antoine Arnauld, a retreat from the conflict between Locke and Norris, a middle path between Locke and Norris, and a confused amalgam of all of these positions and more.[26] As is so often the case, there is probably some truth in all of these descriptions. For our present purposes, it will suffice to show that, with respect to the relationship between material existence and the development of the intellect, Astell's story remains the same. It is true that Astell backs away in this text from endorsing explicitly Malebranche's related theocentric theories of occasionalism and of vision in God, both of which she and Norris had elaborated and praised over the course of the bulk of *Letters*. Her hesitancy on this score, however, did not prevent Astell from embracing Malebranche's more general, and fundamental, description of human understanding as a battle between a mind that could learn well, if rightly applied, and a body that will teach badly, if allowed. The human condition is such, Astell maintains, that "we feel the force of our Passions e're we discern the strength of our Reason" and thus "take up with such Principles and Reasonings ... as Education or Accident not Reason disposes us to" (*SP II* 90–91). In order effectively "to Conquer the Prejudices of Education, Authority and Custom," then, "it will be necessary to apply to the body as well as to the Mind" (*SP II* 94). Like Malebranche and Norris, Astell insists that if the mind is to meditate efficiently, "The Animal Spirits must be lessen'd, or rendered more Calm and Manageable," for "the Body and Mind do so reciprocally influence each other, that we can scarce keep the one in tune if the other be out of it." We must "withdraw our Minds from the World," Astell concludes, "from adhering to the Sense, from the Love of Material Beings, of Pomps and Gaieties; for 'tis these that usually Steal away the Heart, that seduce the Mind to such unaccountable

---

25  Norris describes the created world as follows: "[I]t is all throughout Darkness and Obscurity; and tho God has placed a Sensible Light in it, or rather something that may be an occasional Cause of such a Sensation, yet as to any purpose of Intellectual Illumination, it is still a blind confused Chaos, and Darkness does still sit upon the Face of the Deep" (*Reflections* 216). Astell shifts Norris's strong occasionalist caveat—"or rather something that may be an occasional Cause of such a Sensation"—into a more general caveat—"that Light which we *suppose* to be let into our Ideas by our Senses" (emphasis mine). I continue to believe that such moments are representative of Astell's general inclination in *Serious Proposal, Part II* away from Malebranche and Norris's more radical positions; but I wonder if much that I and others have assumed is "Lockean" in Astell's writing, both here and elsewhere, might not simply be what Norris and Malebranche's theories look like once stripped of their explicit allegiance to Occasionalism and Vision in God.

26  See, respectively, Perry, *Celebrated Mary Astell*, 83; Springborg's introduction and notes to her edition of *Serious Proposal, Part II*; Bridget Hill, *The First English Feminist: Reflections Upon Marriage and other writings by Mary Astell* (New York, 1986), 49; Taylor, "Ironic Assault," 513; and Sarah Ellenzweig, "The Love of God and the Radical Enlightenment: Mary Astell's Brush with Spinoza," *Journal of the History of Ideas* 64.3 (2003): 389.

Wandrings, and so fill up its Capacity that they leave no room for Truth, so distract its Attention that it cannot enquire after her" (*SP II* 112–13). Neither Norris nor Malebranche could have put it better.

Indeed, throughout her text Astell tips her hat to Malebranche's influence, in particular, by treating the title of his famous work as a synonym for thinking well— and always, it should be said, in the midst of thoroughly Malebranchean arguments. "Prejudices" are the "grand hindrance in our search after Truth" (*SP II* 89). We must "disengage our selves from the deceptions of sense" if we mean "honestly to search after Truth" (*SP II* 91). Only through dedicated and rigorous meditation will the unpracticed prove successful "in their search after Truth" (*SP II* 112). Such references are more than mere coincidence, as evidenced by Astell's direct echo of Malebranche in her recommendation that we "withdraw our selves as much as may be from Corporeal things, that pure Reason may be heard the better" and "make that use of our senses for which they are design'd and fitted, the preservation of the Body, but not to depend on their Testimony in our Enquiries after Truth" (*SP II* 115–16).[27] Sarah Ellenzweig is surely correct, then, in detecting a continuing alliance between Astell and Malebranche in *Serious Proposal, Part II*, however otherwise unconvincing her explanation of Astell's relationship to his theories.[28] Even Astell's somewhat dismissive characterization of Malebranche's "Notion That we see all things in GOD" amounts, upon close inspection, to a ringing endorsement of his educational influence:

> Whatever the Notion That we see all things in GOD, may be as to the Truth of it, 'tis certainly very commendable for its Piety, in that it most effectually humbles the most dangerous sort of Pride, the being Proud of our Knowledge, and yet does not slacken our Endeavours after Knowledge but rather Excites them. (*SP II* 117)

Accepting or rejecting Malebranche's strict account for *how* the body relates to the soul, it seems clear, was a matter Astell could, and did, put aside as she wrote her educational treatise. What mattered far more to her was Malebranche's recognition that the body *does* relate to the soul, and that in so doing, it limits, not furthers, the

---

[27] We have an "obligation to struggle continually against our senses" in the search after truth, Malebranche maintains, but this is not because the senses are themselves "altogether corrupted and disordered"; rather, we have failed to understand that "they are given us for the preservation of the body," to which end "they fulfill their purpose perfectly well" (*Search* 23). Cf. the section entitled "*That our senses are given us only for the preservation of our body*" (*Search* I.20.1.85). Norris had covered this aspect of Malebranche's thought in his and Astell's *Letters*, though not in precisely the language used by Astell and Malebranche; in his final letter, Norris defends the role of the senses in the "Preservation of the Machine, and the good of the bodily Life" (*Letters* 136).

[28] Ellenzweig, "The Love of God," 379–97. Ellenzweig suggests that Astell feared being labeled a Spinozist, but she supplies no convincing evidence in support of her claim. That Malebranche was looked on by some as faintly Spinozist is roughly as meaningful as the fact that Locke received the same treatment; as with charges like "enthusiast," or "Hobbesian," "Spinozist" served as an all-purpose, equal-opportunity canard during the closing decade of the seventeenth century and beyond. It is telling of the question-begging approach Ellenzweig takes in her essay that, in the midst of warning the reader of the political complexity involved in the Locke-Malebranche debate, she writes, "Locke served primarily as a spokesman for theological orthodoxy in the period" (391).

human being's "search after Truth." Whatever the "Truth" of this particular aspect of his theory (that is, however the soul and body interact), its overall tendency is not only theologically commendable, but pedagogically efficacious.

Thus it is that even when Astell returns explicitly to Norris and Malebranche's twin theocentric positions in *Christian Religion*, her theory of education has changed not at all. Here too, in Astell's account, the human being's propensity for intellectual error may be traced to the usual suspects—"Prepossessions and Prejudices so inveterate! the byass that Education and Custom, Example and Authority have put on our Minds so strong! the deep impressions that sensible objects have made upon our Imaginations so hard to be wrought off!" (*CR* 181–82). Here as well, the only path to knowledge lies in pursuing "Pure Speculations," especially those that are "Metaphysical, Moral, and Divine," as outlined by "an excellent Pen [Norris]" who has proved that "True Knowledge ... is a *Divine thing*" (*CR* 208).[29] Even when Astell takes unmistakable shots at Locke's materialism—and she does so, and more, frequently—her arguments are perfectly in keeping with those she had long been making about the role of the senses in the acquisition of knowledge:

> Most Men are so Sensualize'd, that they take nothing to be Real but what they can Hear and See, or which is some way or other the Object of their Senses. Others who wou'd seem the most refin'd, make Sensation the fund of their Ideas, carrying their Contemplations no farther than these, and the Reflections they make upon the operations of their Minds when thus employ'd .... But the Contemplation of Immaterial Beings and Abstracted Truths, which are the Noblest Objects of the Mind, is look'd on as Chimerical and a sort of Madness; and the studying to live up the pure Morals of the Gospel, is in their account Visionary. (*CR* 209)

That Astell now has Locke directly in her sights, that she again admits with Norris and Malebranche that the sensory union of "a Corruptible Body to an Immortal Mind" can "only ... be resolv'd into the Efficacy of the Divine Will"—these facts are, properly weighted, irrelevant to her theory of education (*CR* 244).

Like Norris and Malebranche, Astell rejected the notion that a sound education should be based upon "the principles of Lockean sensationalist psychology." Yet, also like them, she did not hesitate to accept the ugly truth that in the acquisition of knowledge, bodies matter. Astell learned early on that "advocating a theory of causation that reaffirms the body's interaction with the soul" neither distinguished her from Norris and his philosophical mentor, as Jacqueline Broad contends, nor put her necessarily in the company of Locke.[30] None of these philosophical opponents

---

29 Astell does not mention Norris by name, but it is clear from the terms she uses that his is the "excellent pen" in question: "[W]e are chiefly, and in the first place, to consider such Truths as are not only *Necessary* in their own Nature, as *Necessary* is oppos'd to *Contingent*, but such as are also most *Necessary for us* to know, because of greatest Importance, as helping us to regulate our Actions according to the Will of our Creator" (*Christian Religion* 208). Norris complains that "Learning is generally placed in the Knowledge of *Contingent*, not of *Necessary* Truth" in *Reflections Upon the Conduct of Human Life* (183); this is the text, it is worth remembering, that Astell had recommended in *Serious Proposal, Part I*, where Norris is described as "an ingenious pen" (21–22).

30 I am quoting Jacqueline Broad, "Adversaries or Allies? Occasional Thoughts on the Masham–Astell

to Locke denied the existence or—rightly understood—the utility of eyes, ears, skin, muscles, nervous systems, blood, guts, brains, and the host of physical objects they variously encountered (though, it should be remembered, George Berkeley and Arthur Collier were just around the historical bend[31]). What they disputed was the validity of the lessons taught by bodies, and taught by those, like Locke, who, as they saw it, had fallen under their seductive spell. To characterize these thinkers' material concerns as untenable, contradictory, inconsistent—"Lockean"—is to repeat the mistake made by Daniel Whitby, a contemporary critic of Norris and Astell's *Letters*. Whitby attacked Norris for, among other ostensible hypocrisies, having a wife.[32] One may as well blame Malebranche for his scientific study of magnets and muscles, or Astell for founding a charity school.[33]

"Experience," Milton's Eve crows upon finishing her meal; "not following thee, I had remained / In ignorance."[34] True enough, Astell and Locke agreed. And most unfortunate, Astell might have added—with a nod toward Norris and Malebranche.

---

Exchange," *Eighteenth-Century Thought* 1.1 (2003): 140. Broad vastly overemphasizes the importance of Astell's final contribution to *Letters*—and completely ignores Norris's rather crucial response—as a means of aligning her away from Norris and alongside Damaris Masham. It is important to recognize that, with the exception of this one speculative letter, Astell consistently demonstrates both her belief in the "utter separation of spirit and matter" *and* her acceptance of the "interaction between souls and bodies" (Broad 145, 134)—as did Norris, as did Malebranche.

31  Berkeley and Collier arrived almost simultaneously at similarly immaterialist conclusions; see Berkeley's *A Treatise Concerning the Principles of Human Knowledge* (1710); and Collier's *Clavis Universalis: Or, a New Inquiry after Truth, Being a Demonstration of the Non-existence, or Impossibility, of an External World* (1713). Collier, it should be noted, credits Norris's influence throughout his work.

32  See Daniel Whitby, *A Discourse of the Love of God* (London, 1697), 127. Richard Acworth provides a fine summary of Whitby's attack and Norris's response in *The Philosophy of John Norris of Bemerton (1657–1712)* (Hildesheim, 1979), 175–76; see also my and Melvyn New's introduction to *Letters*, 34 and n. 76.

33  See Malebranche, *Search*, V.2.8.498; cf. John W. Yolton's discussion of this chapter in *Thinking Matter: Materialism in Eighteenth-Century Britain* (Oxford, 1984), 128–31. Perry describes in detail Astell's indefatigable—and successful—work toward the establishment of the Chelsea school for girls, founded in 1709; see especially chapter eight of her biography of Astell, "The Company She Keeps," (232–81).

34  John Milton, *Paradise Lost* (New York, 1992), 9: 807, 809–10.

# Chapter XIII

# "Cry up Liberty": The Political Context for Mary Astell's Feminism

Hilda L. Smith

The scholarship concerning Mary Astell has consistently viewed her royalist politics and Anglican loyalties either as a significant drag on her feminism, or as barriers which she successfully overcame. Differing perspectives on this issue tend to be tied to the assessment of the seriousness of her feminism; those who see her as a limited "protofeminist" are more apt to view her as essentially conservative, but venturing into a critique of women's standing in the seventeenth century. Those who view her as a more profound and committed feminist are more apt to stress her overcoming conservative principles to develop a systemic feminist understanding.[1]

---

1 Ruth Perry has argued most extensively for the political significance of Astell's works in advance of Patricia Springborg's edition of Astell's political writings (*Astell: Political Writings*, ed. Patricia Springborg [Cambridge, 1996]), but she has accepted the view that in developing her feminist thought Astell was forced to overcome her royalist and Anglican loyalties, not that they propelled her into a feminist analysis. In her analysis of Astell's response to Enlightenment principles, she concludes that "all the contradictions" of the Enlightenment emerged in Astell who "argued for the rights of women yet she upheld absolute monarchy in the state. She believed in Reason but distrusted the materialism of the new way of ideas" and she was "an extremely devout Anglican." This series of descriptors encapsulate the perspective of most scholars on Astell, with the exception of those who believe her conservatism prevented her from developing a set of ideas that could truly be termed "feminist." (Ruth Perry, "Mary Astell's Response to the Enlightenment," in *Women and the Enlightenment*, eds. Margaret Hunt, Margaret Jacob, Phyllis Mack, and Ruth Perry [ NY, 1984], 13–40, 13); Perry's most important political analysis of Astell appears in "Mary Astell and the Feminist Critique of Possessive Individualism," *Eighteenth Century Studies* 23.4 (1990): 444–57, where she argued that "in bypassing the political contract made by men, Astell at once invoked the earlier doctrine of the divine right of monarchs over all subjects alike and at the same time denied the power of all men over all women" (452). In her introduction to the edition of Astell's political writings, Springborg also stresses the limitations inherent in her conservative values, but she is more apt to contextualize Astell's dualistic use of terms relating to individual liberty and to monarchical legitimacy within her explicit response to Locke's *Second Treatise*: "Most of Astell's references to 'liberty,' 'property,' and 'natural rights' like those for 'self-preservation,' seem to be veiled references to Locke as a member of Shaftesbury's party, or to Defoe as a member of Locke's, characterized by her as sycophantic schemers, peddling theories for political advantage" (xxiv). Those scholars who see Astell as a limited protofeminist whose commitment to women is restricted by her conservative ideology build on the early essay, Joan Kinnaird, "Mary Astell and the Conservative Contribution to English Feminism," *The Journal of British Studies* 19.1 (1979): 53–75, and the theorizing of royalism's significance for early modern treatments of the female self in Catherine Gallagher's "Embracing the Absolute: The Politics of the Female Subject in Seventeenth-Century England," *Genders* 1.1 (1988): 24–89. Each approach downplays the centrality of Astell's feminism and portrays royalist ideology as a restrictive force as regards questioning women's status in early modern England.

This essay, in contrast to either perspective, views her conservative values as essential to developing her feminist arguments during the late 1600s. Here, I contend that Astell is drawn to a critique of women's intellectual and familial status precisely because her royalist and Anglican loyalties put her in direct conflict with the values and actions of mid-century revolutionaries. It was the dialectical conflict between the egalitarianism of sectarians and her own royalist agenda that allowed her to raise questions—seemingly distinct, but related in Astell's thought—about the motives of the enemies of Charles I and his successors, and their implications for women's standing in society and the family. While women on the political left, and among the religious sectarian movement, held values more conducive to questioning women's subordinate status in society, their position within those movements denied them the independence and incentive to question the basic principles of their factions (not to mention their leaders). In addition, to link those values directly to women's status would have separated them from their male compatriots and their efforts to undermine the authority of the established church and the monarchy. These women were subordinate to a broader agenda; for them to have focused exclusively upon the status of women would have raised questions about their loyalty and their full commitment to political and religious change.

From the earliest period of contemporary feminist scholarship, the insight gained by women from their perspective as among those standing outside the dominant structures of power has been reiterated in basic women's studies texts.[2] Astell's own thought was served by her distance from her Whig and dissenting contemporaries, as well as their Civil War antecedents. But further, Astell developed her idiosyncratic feminism out of the conflict of sometimes seemingly opposing tendencies in her own worldview. Indeed, Georg Wilhelm Hegel's epistemology which stresses the centrality of the dialectic, especially among thinkers who seek to refine their thought processes in the face of contradiction, may have an unexpected bearing on the works of Astell. Obviously, Astell lived well before Hegel; the philosopher who most influenced her own work was René Descartes. The operation of the dialectic has nonetheless entered into our epistemological lexicon and forms one of the fundamental ways in which we understand how individuals raise and resolve questions. That is, the dialectical principle articulated by Hegel has ramifications beyond his own circle, even beyond the sphere of those who claim him as an antecedent influence. In the analysis offered here, such a dialectical process of thought emerges clearly in the works of Mary Astell.[3]

---

2  Two often-used textbooks that stress women's outsider status among other themes are Jo Freeman, *Women: A Feminist* Perspective, 3rd edition (Palo Alto, CA, 1984) and Virginia Sapiro, *Women in American Society: An Introduction to Women's Studies* (Mountain View, CA, 1990); for a history of women's studies as a specialty in the United States, see Marilyn J. Boxer, *When Women Ask the Questions: Creating Women's Studies in America* (Baltimore, 1998).

3  Among the massive literature on Hegel's contribution to modern philosophy, see Karl-Otto Apel, "Kant, Hegel, and the Contemporary Question Concerning the Normative Foundations of Morality and Right," in *Hegel on Ethics and Politics*, eds. Robert B. Pippin and Otfried Höffe, trans. Nicholas Walker (Cambridge, 2004), 49–77; for a broad discussion of the nature of the dialectic and its relationship to religion see Stephen Crites, *Dialectic and Gospel in the Development of Hegel's Thinking* (University Park, PA, 1998).

While Astell dealt with a thesis and its antithesis in relationship to seventeenth-century politics, counter-posing a greater focus on liberty and an expanded political populace on the one hand, to values of order, stability, and absolutism on the other, the outcome that emerged from this intellectual process was not a resolution of these two opposing positions, but rather a synthesis that evolved into her understanding of women's role in society, and which formed the basis for her distinctive feminist ideology. Astell's earliest and most substantial works centered on women, and it was a loyalty to her sex that most defined her identity, writ large in the signature to the first part of a *Serious Proposal*, by "a Lover of her Sex." As the correspondence found in the George Ballard papers at Oxford reveal, it was the status and treatment of women that likewise occupied her later years, especially the negligence of women's learning that she witnessed everywhere by 1720.[4]

Astell considered the principles as outlined by those seeking greater religious and political flexibility and involvement in contrast with traditional royalist and Anglican values, and found (some would say paradoxically) the former wanting. The development of Astell's feminism out of the dialectical conflicts implicit in her thought did not result in the shifting of political loyalties; rather her own Tory feminism is tied to a critique which employs progressive arguments to undermine parliamentarian and sectarian understandings of family and gender relationships. That is, Astell did not fully dismiss egalitarian and democratic principles, even given her royalist and Tory politics, but she did not apply them to the political realm. Rather, she applied them to the issues that mattered most to her: the assessment and treatment of women. Further, her attack against the opponents of Charles I, and later the Whigs, was based less on the errors within their core principles (some of which she herself adopted) than on an understanding which linked their motives and their false assessment of what constituted tyranny within England, in particular as it related to their libelous judgments concerning the Royal Martyr, Charles I. In Astell's eyes, the Whig failure to express loyalty to the true authority of Charles was sign of a moral failure and hypocrisy, which registered further—and most significantly for her—in the disparity between their stated doctrines of equality and their attitudes towards women.

The impetus for, and outcome of, Astell's feminism emerge from her commitment to three primary principles: (1) an understanding of God's creation as guarantor of

---

4  In a letter addressed to Lady Ann Coventry in 1720, she critiques society's assessment of Mary Wortley Montagu as follows: "And we hear no more of Lady Mary Wortley's Wit, but of her Bargains," (reproduced in Ruth Perry, *The Celebrated Mary Astell: An Early English Feminist* [Chicago, 1986], 392); the importance of women's learning, and the influence of the *Serious Proposal* is made clear in George Ballard's *Memoirs of Several Ladies of Great Britain* (Oxford, 1752). There were approximately 585 subscribers to the work (which included disproportionately large numbers of Anglican officials and Oxford dons); Astell, Ballard wrote, had "a piercing wit, a solid judgment, and tenacious memory, [which] made her ... a complete mistress of every thing she attempted to learn" (445); Ballard himself assessed the *Proposal* as "an ingenious treatise" which garnered public attention and financial support (446). Subscribers to the volume, in addition, included large numbers of women who chose to have their names listed individually and not subsumed under the name of a male family member, although he was often included as well. Women listed as individuals, for example, come from the Cavendish-Bentinck family, the Bridgwaters, the Bridgmans, and the Gurnseys; the list also includes influential figures such as William Blackstone and Sir George Grenville.

an equality between the sexes; (2) a loyalty to the Church of England based on its permitting the fullest development of women's minds and souls; and, (3) a distrust of the motives, and a rejection of factual claims, implicit in the revolutionaries' (and later Dissenters') critique of monarchy and the Anglican faith. These principles emerge from an application of Cartesian strictures to serious learning, methods of discovery, and logical thinking as expressed in *A Serious Proposal to the Ladies, Parts I* and *II*. They emerged as well from her understanding of the basic religious tenets of Christianity and their application to politics and society as outlined in *The Christian Religion as Profess'd by a Daughter of the Church of England*. They further culminated in her application of these separate, but analogous, arguments to the institution of marriage as it operated in the late 1600s in *Some Reflections upon Marriage*. While *Christian Religion* was published after *Some Reflections*, the principles presented in the later work nonetheless had their origins in her earlier tracts; they were simply expressed in their fullest and most systematic fashion in this last religious work published in 1705. Out of Astell's varied, but interlocking philosophical, theological, and even political arguments, her feminist perspective emerges.

While Astell took part in contemporary political disputes through publishing Tory tracts, she was first and foremost a feminist intellectual. She strongly believed in the importance and reliability of Cartesian epistemology, and applied Descartes's critical methodology to English institutions broadly. However, it was consistently to institutions and values that restricted women's lives that her attention was drawn. To pursue this process in Astell's thinking and writing, one must begin with *A Serious Proposal*, her first—and most influential—work. As Ruth Perry affirms in her conclusion to *The Celebrated Mary Astell*, for Astell, the Miltonic principle, "'He for God only, she for God in him' was not a clear and distinct idea."[5]

That Astell chose to write about women's learning (and its relationship to their faith) reflected first the denial of a systematic advanced training to herself and, second, her attachment to reason and philosophy as the central and abiding interests of her life. Scholars over the last twenty-five years have certainly analyzed the *Proposal*, but more attention has been paid to its institutional aspects—to its existence as the earliest substantial plan for a separate women's college. Judgments have related to the social classes admitted or excluded from her proposed residential setting for women's serious education. Others have questioned the dominant role of religion in both the curriculum and the personal ends for the students. Still others have focused on its practicability or likelihood of the establishment of such an institution during the reign of Queen Anne.

Astell's proposal for a women's college, a "convent" or "female retreat," to use terms more appropriate to the period, gained her much recognition and led the likes of Defoe and Steele to both mimic her idiom and appropriate many of her ideas. She became a public figure discussed in London society, but often, merely as a stereotypical addled-headed old maid. However, here I want to stress the significance and centrality of *Part II* of *A Serious Proposal*, for it is in this work that Astell articulates the arguments most central to the intellectual bases for her feminism. This

---

5  Ruth Perry, *Celebrated Mary Astell*, 328–29.

tract, arguably, stands in many ways as her most lasting contribution to women's advanced training, since the actual proposed institution of *A Serious Proposal Part I* was never put into practice. Patricia Springborg also sees the latter installment of *A Serious Proposal* as most significant, but more within the context of Astell's differences with Locke and her debate with Damaris Masham over the nature of rational Christianity. Springborg considers *Part II* as constituting "the lineaments of [Astell's] mature arguments" and sees a shift away from a more religious and faith-based regimen to one that stressed rationalism. The publication of 1697 differs from its antecedent, because, Springborg claims, "Astell takes seriously Masham's claim that to deny the relative autonomy of individual cognition is gratuitous Platonic quietism."[6]

Accepting Springborg's categorization of *Part II* as the mature statement of Astell's epistemological method, I would not, however, emphasize the differences with Masham, or Masham's influence on Astell's thought, as what characterizes the primary contribution of the tract. Springborg claims that only in response to Masham did Astell deny that "her house of retirement for women was ever intended as other than a primarily academic establishment," but I would argue that she always saw her proposed retreat for woman as founded primarily upon philosophical principles. In *Part I* of her proposal Astell justifies the need for such a female academy, seeking pupils and financial support from parents and others potential donors, while, more generally, convincing the public of the good such an institution could accomplish. In *Part II* she clarifies the types of materials to be studied, "those that require serious dedication," outlines Cartesian epistemology, and makes the search for "clear and distinct" ideas the central goal of her curriculum. But in both parts, her aim remains constant: to produce a faithful Christian who will further Christ's cause. Such a cause is best furthered by a believer who accepts the principles of religion not through memorization of the catechism or adhering blindly to the words of husbands or ministers, but through personal study and rigorous thought grounded in philosophical and ethical principles, as well as serious scrutiny of the scriptures and theology.

Astell thus introduces *A Serious Proposal to the Ladies* of 1694 with an integrated synthesis of reason, religion, and an analysis of women's lowly status in the late 1600s. Such a synthesis dominates both the *Serious Proposal* (*Parts I* and *II*) and *Some Reflections upon Marriage*; unlike later scholarly commentators on her work, Astell herself saw these texts as promoting complementary aspects of her feminist ideology. They dictated an alteration in the way women were to be viewed—not as objects in the market of courtship, but as rational souls. Such a shift mandated, as a consequence, a necessary change in conception of the manner in which women should pursue their lives, culminating in the learned, religious, and self-respecting women she hoped her proposals would produce. Both works are expressly directed towards women—providing them the evidence needed first to understand and then resist the harmful advice they were following against their own true interests. Astell's work thus encourages women to "heighten" their own "Value," removing them from that

---

6 Patricia Springborg, ed., *A Serious Proposal to the Ladies Parts I and II* (London, 1997), 19. Hereafter cited parenthetically as *SP I* and *SP II*.

realm of courtship in which they are merely "cheap and contemptible." Following her program would allow women to attain a true "Beauty," associated not with the "coruptible Body," but rather the "immortal Mind." Interestingly, while Astell's contemporaries might have used the more conventional term, immortal soul, Astell employs, in her ideal conception of woman, the phrase "immortal Mind," providing a synthesis that encompassed reason, religion, and female identity (*SP I* 51).

While Astell establishes her basic philosophical arguments for the need for women's serious learning in *Part I*, she devotes the greatest attention to convincing women of what they will gain from abandoning a life of superficiality, centering on the self-promotion demanded of them in the male marketplace of courtship. She urges her female compatriots to be "Wise" and to avoid the "Toys and Vanities" of the world, a realm devoid of internal worth, existing only for external show (*SP I* 92). In these urgings she employs uncompromisingly harsh tones against her sex, intoning sarcastically, "How can you be content to be in the World like Tulips in a Garden, to make a fine *shew* and be good for nothing?" In this section of the tract, she again combines intellectual reach and religious belief as the qualities that will promote both self-awareness and accomplishment not possible through conformity to fashion and society. "What a pity it is," she writes,

> that whilst your Beauty casts a lustre round about, your Souls which are infinitely more bright and radiant (of which if you had but a clear Idea, as lovely as it is …) shou'd be suffer'd to overrun with Weeds, lye fallow and neglected. (*SP I* 54)

Significantly, Astell does not delay until *Part II* for an appeal to Descartes's "clear and distinct ideas," but links them, in the earlier tract, to her conception of the soul and the method women should follow to discover their real worth and to pursue a sober life of study and devotion.

Astell's arguments in apparently different spheres are always parallel and interlocking: her commitment to Cartesian philosophical principles, the advocacy of royalist politics, and the critique of gender relations emerge in her work as inter-related. Astell's analysis of the politics of courtship in *A Serious Proposal, Part I*, dovetails with her philosophical principles. For the restrictions on women's self-fulfillment are a consequence of the roles constructed for them within a gender system that denies women the ability to make rational choices—barring them from intellectual achievement, and as a consequence, rendering them unable to make the discriminations necessary for the selection of a worthy mate. As women are continually pushed to attract men through their mastery of the economy of fashion, and to think of their future marriage as *the* end of their existence, the process of courtship irreparably harms their ability to pursue more serious philosophical goals. Again, in Astell's direct and graphic language, following a pejorative reference to the always gazing "eyes of men," she warns:

> We value *them* too much, and our *selves* too little, if we place any part of our worth in their Opinion; and do not think our selves capable of nobler Things than the pitiful Conquest of some worthless heart. (*SP I* 55–56)

This gendered power analysis of the practices of courtship does not exist in isolation from her philosophical program. Indeed, it is crucial to see Astell's feminist works as expressing an integrated vision that incorporates her political values and intellectual interests, as well as a gendered analysis of social and cultural politics. While each of her works may highlight one aspect of this tripartite vision to a greater extent, still all incorporate her basic synthesis.

In *Part II* of the *Serious Proposal*, Astell focuses especially on the liberating nature of serious intellectual and philosophical engagement. This work begins with her posing questions relating to the extent to which knowledge or goodness must dominate women's lives, and set the standards for their learning and future behavior. Affirming first the priority of goodness—"She then who desires a clear Head must have a pure Heart"—Astell then shows her hesitation with her own formulation, and re-phrases her question: "what degrees of Purity are requisite in order to Knowledge, and how much must we Know to the end we may heartily endeavour to Purify?" (*SP II* 127). To answer this query, she begins a lengthy disquisition on the nature of reason and reasonable minds. This discussion forms the basis for her judgments as to the extent and methods best suited to women's learning. In seeking a first principle as regards the origins of knowledge and their relation to its ultimate pursuit, she concludes that "there are some degrees of Knowledge necessary before there can be *any* Human Acts." In delineating such principles, she again establishes the basic goal of the work as a whole, to encourage women to pursue their natural abilities to the fullest.

> Not to dispute the Number of 'em here, no body I suppose will deny us one, which is, *That we ought as much as we can to endeavour the Perfection of our Beings, and that we be as happy as possibly we may.* (*SP II* 129)

While she uses such a principle to elaborate the goals women should pursue, she also reminds them that not any pursuit of happiness will do. Fulfillment, for Astell, must always be grounded on the intersection of philosophical engagement and religious pursuit. It is thus the reciprocal interaction between the "Understanding" and the "Moral Conduct of the Will" that should drive women's learning and their actions, not the one isolated from the other, and certainly not the promise of personal gain or interest promised in the realm of courtship and marriage (*SP II* 129).

In her subsequent discussion of Cartesian epistemology, Astell continues to incorporate faith into her educational program, seeing faith, science, and opinion as the three separate faculties, with only the latter lacking a justifiable basis. She equates the truth and wisdom gained from the competing realms of science and faith and claims: "Science is the following the Process our Selves upon Clear and Evident Principles" while faith is relying on others. Yet, she affirms, the "Objects of Faith are as Certain and as truly Intelligible in themselves as those of Science" (*SP II* 151). One should use Descartes's model as the means for best pursuing knowledge, but just as with the French philosopher, she ultimately bases the ability to accept reality and know truth on God's guarantee of what we perceive (*SP II* 165–78).[7]

---

7   In this discussion of Cartesian methodology, she both reiterates her belief in the centrality of God's

The homologies in Astell's work are not only between her arguments about philosophy, theology, and gender, but also between gender and politics. Springborg's editorial inclusion of *Some Reflections* in her edition of the *Political Writings*, reveals the extent to which, for Astell, arguments about politics and gender were inter-related, showing points of similarity between the earlier tract about marriage, and the more polemical political tracts of 1704, *A Fair Way with the Dissenters* and *An Impartial Enquiry into the Causes of Rebellion*. Though *Some Reflections* was written first, it was nonetheless the most substantial of the three. Still, in attempting to document the use of her conservative and royalist politics as impetus for her feminism, one needs to focus on the last two works, for it is in these texts that she presents the most comprehensive arguments on behalf of a monarchical state and an established church. True, both works, published in 1704, emerged out of the local political concerns that surrounded the controversy surrounding occasional conformity. Yet, as one enters into the arguments of the tracts, one is drawn to more fundamental issues than early-eighteenth-century disputes over occasional conformity and party politics. As previously noted, Astell was an intellectual most concerned with rationally-based arguments. Like any author, she was apt to see her own arguments, and those attached to her political values, as more reasonable and less self-interested than those of her opponents. This is certainly the case with her assessment of the earlier opponents of Charles I and the contemporary Whigs whom she attacked. Yet, out of the *ad hominen* arguments, partisan rejectionism, and attribution of disreputable motives to her opponents, emerge the intellectual bases central to her position—in which arguments about politics and gender overlap.

As an uncompromising supporter of Charles I, Astell rejected those who would not defend the king in all of his actions. Whether they were his outright opponents or only lukewarm supporters, she saw them as disloyal. In her eyes this disloyalty defined their nature more than the rhetoric of equality and liberty that many of them used (and which she herself would appropriate). She thus lacked any sympathy for Whigs and Dissenters, even though she often employed their language when postulating women's place within the family and English society more broadly. Their lack of respect for legitimate authority meant that they were of questionable character, and that character was not overcome by their espousing principles that might benefit women as well as men. Thus Astell's works, especially *Some Reflections upon Marriage*, continually returned to her political opponents' hypocritical nature— their clamoring for a standing equal to their king for themselves while demanding submission from women in the home and within society generally. It was such an evaluation of both their motives and character that drove her critique of them more

---

role in providing the bedrock of truth and scaffolding for human knowledge, and links the process of Cartesian rationalism to the limitations on women's access to opportunities for serious learning: "so is Truth, we are surrounded with it, and GOD has given us Faculties to receive it" (Springborg, ed., *A Serious Proposal II*, 174). But, Astell continually reminds her readers that learning and knowledge are more than society conceives them to be, and that institutions alone do not contain them, nor can they restrain those (most importantly women) who they exclude from obtaining them: "All have not leisure to Learn Languages and pore on Books, nor Opportunity to Converse with the Learned; but all may *Think*, may use their own Faculties rightly, and consult the Master who is within them" (Springborg, ed., *A Serious Proposal II*, 168).

than a thorough difference with their political pronouncements. If the opponents of Charles hold such moderate, compromising positions, she asks, why do they insist on expressing themselves in the most radical fashion, while maintaining institutions that provide little leeway for women to function with autonomy? Further, whether addressing the Whigs and occasional conformity or those who fomented rebellion against Charles I, she asks why they do not apply their most progressive values to the women in their midst.

While clearly there was even less questioning about the status of women in society among the supporters of Charles I and Anglican officials than among their political and religious opponents, the aforementioned were at any rate not attempting to alter the status quo by incorporating the voices and power of a broader segment of the population. While one can look at what has been termed the "Laudian Revolution" of the early seventeenth century as an attempt to alter fundamentally the Elizabethan Settlement of the Anglican Church, Laud is dead by 1645. The changes wrought by the Laudian Revolution had been made some years before Margaret Cavendish (in the 1650s and 1660s) and Astell and others (in the 1690s) called attention to the omission of the question of women's equality from both Puritan and Dissenting visions. Astell saw the discrepancy between the principles of those who—from mid-century—sought to undermine the Anglican establishment and expand political standing to include all independent Englishmen and their practices as manifested in the realms of family, courtship, and marriage. Not surprisingly, it was those outside these dissenting frameworks, like Cavendish and Astell, who were able to see more clearly the limitations of their ostensibly progressive contemporaries, and thus to speak openly against them, foregrounding their negative impact on women in the family and society more broadly. Of all the authors fitting this category (those whom Gallagher would call Tory feminists), Mary Astell offered the clearest and most systematic, critical analysis of the Whig and dissenting movements.

Not unexpectedly then, the connections between Astell's conservative politics and her feminist principles emerge most clearly in her explicitly political—and royalist—writings. Indeed, Astell's attachment to the "cult of the royal Martyr" placed her among a late-seventeenth-century generation mired in earlier Stuart tragedies which distanced her own strong Tory loyalties from current internecine politics. While she clearly sided with the Tories in support of nonjurors and was skeptical about policies showing greater leniency to Dissenters, the issues that truly roused her emotions and loyalty were those bred in her uncompromising support of Charles I. Furthermore, since as a woman she lacked the impetus of office seeking and party maneuvering as bases for her beliefs and publications, it was the political principles themselves that were always central to both the expression of her thought and the ultimate goals she identified for herself and other women. The centrality of the Royal Martyr thus emerges as crucial to her feminism. For her core beliefs were consistently tied to the politics of a half century earlier and the perfidy of those who offered falsely democratic and inclusive language while both destroying the monarchy and relegating women to familial dependence, domestic ignorance, and cultural insignificance. It was her allegiance to the cause which the Royal Martyr represented which allowed her to expose the inconsistency of her more "progressive" contemporaries. Further, it was her isolation from any political controls—the strictures, for example, imposed upon female members by sectarian movements or later latitudinarian orthodoxy—that allowed her to attack the realities of women's subordination within the family and their culturally imposed general ignorance without offending politically powerful male allies.

Such freedom was, paradoxically enough, not afforded to the women of sectarian movements who had aggressively promulgated the causes of liberty and equality. For sectarian and Leveller women to point to women's continued subordination in the home (or their omission, for example, from the 1647 *Agreement of the People*) would have placed them in disagreement with movements and leaders to whom they were devoted. Rather, in their petitions to Parliament and their efforts within Quaker women's groups and other sectarian congregations, they argued only for spiritual equality, and devoted most of their attention to fighting for male Leveller and Quaker prisoners, as well as overseeing the spiritual and conjugal purity of the families of co-religionists. Patricia Crawford, at once noting the democratic potential of sectarian congregations, nonetheless emphasizes that "there was no demand for any extension of the franchise to women, even though women were voting in some separatist churches. Nor were there any demands for increased female participation in local government."[8] Ann Hughes has argued that the Levellers postulated an ephemeral individualism that centered on the patriarchal family, and that Leveller women were not speaking for their own interests. "The wives were supporting their husbands and defending their families, and it was made clear that theirs was not an independent voice."[9] Basically, sectarian and Leveller women argued for their public voice either as Quaker preachers or as pamphleteers addressing Parliament as citizens of England. They did not, however, utilize that standing to critique the power relations of a patriarchal society, and Margaret Fell Fox in fact explicitly denied the right to speak to women who sought to "usurp authority over the man." While sectarian

---

[8] Patricia Crawford, "The Challenges to Patriarchalism: How Did the Revolution Affect Women?" in *Revolution and Restoration: England in the 1650s*, ed. John Morrill (London, 1994), 127; Crawford's most recent analysis of women's political standing in early modern England takes a more positive perspective on the assumed inclusion of women in democratic language, but still does not document women being included in any of the major Leveller or sectarian works defining English citizenship. See "'The Poorest She': Women and Citizenship in Early Modern England," in *The Putney Debates of 1647*, ed. Michael Mendle (Cambridge, 2001), 219–40. Crawford discusses a range of efforts by women to exercise some form of political action during the 1600s including signing petitions, taking parliamentary loyalty oaths, and protesting incarceration of their compatriots. She points to a number of authors ranging from Filmer to Lilburne who claimed women had originally been created as men's equals, yet denied women's full political rights because "women lost their liberty when they consented to marriage and placed themselves in subordination to their husbands" (201). Still, she offers no evidence that single or widowed women voted alongside their brothers. And, most important for the arguments of this essay, while these women used religious justifications as "we are assured of our creation in the image of God" to claim that they held "a proportionable share in the freedoms of this Commonwealth," they did so not to press their own case but to petition for Leveller prisoners. Nor did they use these arguments to confront the inequality of the patriarchal family, as did Astell, and Cavendish before her (210).

[9] Ann Hughes, "Gender and Politics in Leveller Literature," in *Political Culture and Cultural Politics in Early Modern England: Essays Presented to David Underdown*, eds. Susan D. Amussen and Mark Kishlansky (Manchester, 1995), 170.

women spoke up in their congregations and Quaker women resisted the opposition of some male members of the Society of Friends to either restrict or shut down the women's meetings, they failed to question these same men's authority within the family. And, as vessels of Christ's word, rather than as overt spokeswomen for their sex, their voices were disembodied and removed from both their personal identity and the identity of women generally. Separatist women thus represented strong examples of women's public and private religious roles, but they did not use their pulpit or congregational representation to press for greater power for women within the family or society at large.

It is thus the dialectical relationship that Astell experienced with the mid-century religious and political left that underlay her feminist origins: she turned their progressive principles against them, showing how radical movements had relegated women's earthly status to little more than an irrelevance while synthesizing her own distinctive feminism from the contradictions she saw in their position. True, Astell's strong Anglican loyalties underlay her support of the institution of marriage, yet her distrust of male dominance in the home was continually linked to a discourse built upon the perception of men's threat to order in the state. Not merely in her famous charge against "even Milton" for "not crying up liberty to poor female slaves," but more broadly in her analysis of the structures of family relations, does Astell persistently contrast revolutionary principles with their hypocritical perspectives and practices in relation to the family:

> Again, if Absolute Sovereignty be not necessary in a State, how comes It to be in a Family? Or if in a Family why not in a State; since no Reason can Be alleg'd for the one that will not hold more strongly for the other?

She continues, for anyone who doubts that her understanding of the family is basically a political one, "If the Authority of the Husband, so far as it extends, is sacred and inalienable, why not of the Prince?[10]

While many authors of the period see women as occupying a unique place in discourses concerning power and authority, one that focused on their place in the family, Astell argues analogously to other groups or nations that might have struck most of her contemporaries as simply inappropriate. In arguing against the basic inferiority of women because they have been traditionally under the authority of men, she contends that the Holy Scriptures do speak of women "in a state of subjection," yet,

> and so do they of the Jews and Christians when under the Dominion of the *Chaldeans* and *Romans*, requiring of the one as well as of the other a quiet submission to them under whose Powere they liv'd. But will any one say that these had a *Natural Superiority* and a Right to Dominion?[11]

---

10  Mary Astell, *Some Reflections upon Marriage*, in *Astell: Political Writings*, ed. Patricia Springborg, 46–47, 17.

11  Astell, *Some Reflections*, 14.

Astell's analogy between the clearly temporally specific subjection of the "Jews and Christians" to the "Dominion" of the rule of the "Chaldeans and Romans," and the likewise merely situational ascendancy of men over women in her society, places her assertions of women's natural equality in the political and theological contexts so important to her thought. Out of her critique of mid-century political and dissenting hypocrisy, Astell thus synthesizes a feminist perspective which was, in some sense, more far-reaching than that of her contemporaries.

Such a synthesis emerges from the same perspective—outside the contexts of power—which would allow a Royalist such as Cavendish to assert that women owed no loyalty to the commonwealth, or Astell herself to wonder rhetorically, "If all Men are born free how is it that all Women are born Slaves?"[12] Indeed, nowhere can one find such fundamental critiques of women's standing in seventeenth-century England among their religious and political opponents. This can be attributed not only to the dialectical aspects of Astell's thought, born of her outsider status, but also, in the case of Astell, to her strong attachment to Cartesian doubt (Cavendish, by contrast, found energies for her argument from other sources).[13] Out of the dialectical tension between her own conservative cultural politics and the most radically democratic and individualistic politics of mid-century, Astell would develop her own critical evaluation of contemporary Whigs and Dissenters, based primarily on their exclusion of women. Since both Cavendish and Astell were associated with the socially and politically conservative royalist cause, neither was part of a movement pressing for political and social change in ways that excluded individuals—that is, women—such as themselves. While subjection to a monarch's rule limited one's standing and individuality, it limited men's and women's in equal measure, whereas men—from Levellers to Dissenters—who were pressing for a new form of citizenship during the second half of the seventeenth century constructed an ideology that elevated them, while leaving their sisters behind. Although Margaret Cavendish had offered a more fragmentary understanding of this insight earlier in the century, no one saw this more clearly than Mary Astell: from this insight, her idiosyncratic—and radical—feminism emerges.

---

12  Astell, *Some Reflections*, 18.

13  For an analysis of Margaret Cavendish's unique political perspective see my "'A General War Amongst the Men [but] None Amongst the Women': Political Differences between Margaret and William Cavendish," in *Politics and the Political Imagination in Later Stuart Britain*, ed. Howard Nenner, (Rochester, NY, 1997): 143–60. Cavendish, of course, raised some of the most far-reaching questions concerning women's standing in seventeenth-century England, including asking why women should desire children: "yet a Woman hath no such Reason to desire Children for her Own Sake, for first her Name is Lost ... [and] neither Name nor Estate goes to her Family." And if they be daughters, they "are but Branches which by Marriage are Broken off from the Root ... so that Daughters are to be accounted but as Moveable Goods or Furnitures that wear out" (from *Sociable Letters* [#93] quoted in *Women's Political and Social Thought: An Anthology*, eds. Hilda L. Smith and Berenice A. Carroll (Bloomington, 2000). And on women's relationship to the state, she articulated in letter sixteen, "we are not tied, nor bound to State or Crown; we are free, not sworn to Allegiance, nor do we take the Oath of Supremacy; we are not made Citizens of the Commonwealth ... and if we be not Citizens in the Commonwealth, I know no reason we should be Subjects" (81).

# Select Bibliographies

**Primary Bibliography**

Al-Ghazali (1997), *The Incoherence of the Philosophers*, a parallel English–Arabic text, trans. Michael E. Marmurra, Provo, UT: Brigham Young University.

[Allestree, Richard] (1673), *The Ladies Calling. In Two Parts*, Oxford: Printed at the Theater.

—— (1673), *The Gentleman's Calling*, London: R. Norton for Robert Pawlet at the Sign of the Bible in Chancery-Lane near Fleetstreet.

Arnauld, A., and P. Nicole (1696), *Logic: Or, the Art of Thinking. In which, Besides the Common, are contain'd many Excellent New Rules, very profitable for directing of reason, and acquiring of Judgement, in things as well relating to the Instruction of a Man's self, as of others*, 3rd edition, London: T.B.

Astell, Mary, Bodleian Library, MS Rawlinson Poet 154, fols. 50–97.

—— (1694), *A Serious Proposal to the Ladies, For the Advancement of their true and greatest Interest. By a Lover of Her Sex*, London: Richard Wilkin at the King's Head in St Paul's Church-Yard.

—— (1695), *A Serious Proposal to the Ladies, For the Advancement of their true and greatest Interest, Part I. By a Lover of Her Sex*, The Second Edition Corrected. London: Printed by T.W. for Richard Wilkin at the King's Head in St Paul's Church-Yard.

—— (1696), *A Serious Proposal to the Ladies, For the Advancement of their true and greatest Interest, Part I. By a Lover of Her Sex*, The Third Edition Corrected. London: Printed by T.W. for Richard Wilkin at the King's Head in St Paul's Church-Yard.

—— (1697), *A Serious Proposal to the Ladies, Part II. Wherein a Method is offer'd for the Improvement of their Minds*, London: Richard Wilkin at the King's Head in St Paul's Church-Yard.

—— (1700), *Some Reflections Upon Marriage, Occasion'd by the Duke & Dutchess of Mazarine's Case; which is also consider'd*, London: John Nutt near Stationers-Hall.

—— (1703), *Some Reflections Upon Marriage. The Second Edition*, London: R. Wilkin, at the King's Head in St Paul's Church-Yard.

—— (1704), *A Fair Way With The Dissenters And Their Patrons. Not Writ by Mr. L---y, or any other Furious Jacobite whether Clergyman or Layman; but by a very Moderate Person and Dutiful Subject to the Queen*, London: E.P. for R. Wilkin, at the King's Head in St Paul's Church-Yard.

—— (1704), *An Impartial Enquiry Into The Causes of Rebellion and Civil War In This Kingdom: In an Examination of Dr. Kennett's Sermon, Jan. 31. 1703/4. And Vindication of the Royal Martyr*, London: E.PL. for R. Wilkin at the King's Head in St Paul's Church-Yard.

—— (1704), *Moderation Truly Stated: Or, A Review Of A Late Pamphlet Entitul'd, Moderation a Vertue. With a Prefatory Discourse to Dr. D'Aveanant Concerning His late Essays on Peace and War*, London.

—— (1705), *The Christian Religion, As Profess'd by a Daughter Of The Church of England. In a Letter to the Right Honourable, T.L. C.I.*, London: R. Wilkin.

—— (1706), *Reflections Upon Marriage. The Third Edition. To which is Added A Preface, in Answer to some Objections*, London: R. Wilkin, at the King's Head in St Paul's Church-Yard.

—— (1717), *The Christian Religion, As Profess'd by a Daughter Of The Church of England*, London: Printed by W.B. for R. Wilkin.

—— (1722), *An Enquiry After Wit: Wherein the Trifling Arguing and Impious Raillery of the Late Earl of Shaftesbury in his Letter Concerning Enthusiasm and other Profane Writers are Fully Answer'd and Justly Exposed*, London.

—— (2002), *A Serious Proposal to the Ladies*, ed. Patricia Springborg, Toronto: Broadview Press.

—— (1996), *Astell: Political Writings*, ed. Patricia Springborg, Cambridge: Cambridge University Press.

[Astell, Mary] (1709), *Bart'lemy Fair: Or, An Enquiry after Wit; In which due Respect is had to a Letter Concerning Enthusiasm, To my LORD \*\*\**, London: R. Wilkin.

[Astell, Mary and] John Norris (1695), *Letters Concerning the Love of God, Between the Author of the Proposal to the Ladies and Mr. John Norris: Wherein his late Discourse, shewing That it ought to be Intire and Exclusive of All Other Loves, is Further Cleared and Justified*, London: J. Norris.

—— (1705), *Letters Concerning the Love of God, between the Author of the Proposal to the Ladies I.E., Mary Astell and Mr. John Norris: Wherein His Late Discourse, Shewing, That It Ought to Be Intire and Exclusive of All Other Loves, Is Further Cleared and Justified. The Second Edition, Corrected by the Authors, with some few Things added*, London: Printed for Samuel Manship ... and Richard Wilkin.

—— (2005), *Letters Concerning the Love of God*, eds. Derek E. Taylor and Melvyn New, Aldershot: Ashgate.

Atterbury, Francis (1698), *A Discourse Occasion'd by the Death of the Right Honourable the Lady Cutts*, London: Tho. Bennet at the Half-Moon in St Paul's Church-Yard.

Ballard, George (1752), *Memoirs of Several Ladies of Great Britain, who have been celebrated for their writings or skill in the learned languages arts and sciences*, Oxford: Printed by W. Jackson for the Author.

Bond, Donald (ed.) (1987), *The Tatler*, 3 vols, Oxford: Clarendon Press.

Burnet, Gilbert (1753), *The History of My Own Times*, 6 vols, Edinburgh: Hamilton, Balfour, and Neill.

[Chamberlayne, Edward] (1671), *An Academy or Colledge: Wherein Young Ladies and Gentlewomen May at a Very Moderate Expense be Duly Instructed in the True Protestant Religion ... According to the Pattern of Some Protestant Colledges in Germany*, The Savoy: Tho. Newcomb.

Cowley, Abraham (1905), *The English Writings of Abraham Cowley*, ed. A.R. Waller, Cambridge: Cambridge University Press.

Cudworth, R. (1996), *A Treatise Concerning Eternal and Immutable Morality, with A Treatise of Freewill*, ed. S. Hutton, Cambridge: Cambridge University Press.

Defoe, Daniel (1701), *Legion's Memorial*, London.

—— (1702), *The Original Power of the Collective Body of the* People, London.

—— (1704), *The Shortest Way with the Dissenters*, London.

—— (1704), *More Short-Ways with the Dissenters*, London.

Descartes, R. (1650), *The Passions of the Soule In three Books. The first, Treating of the Passions in Generall, and occasionally of the whole nature of man. The second, Of the Number, and order of the Passions, and the explication of the six Primitive ones. The third, of Particular Passions. By R. des Cartes. And Translated out of French into English*, London: A.C.

—— (1985–91), *The Philosophical Writings of Descartes*, 3 vols, trans. John Cottingham, R. Stoothoff, and D. Murdoch, Cambridge: Cambridge University Press.

[Drake, Judith] (1696), *Essay in Defence of the Female Sex*, London.

Filmer, Sir Robert (1991), "The Anarchy of a Limited or Mixed Monarchy (1648)," in Sommerville, Johann (ed.), *Patriarcha and Other Writings*, Cambridge: Cambridge University Press.

Halifax, George Savile, Marquis of (1688), *The Lady's New-years Gift, or, Advice to a Daughter: Under These Following Heads: viz. Religion, Husband, House and Family, Servants, Behaviour and Conversation, Friendship, Censure, Vanity and Affectation, Pride, Diversion, Dancing*, London: Printed for Matt. Gillyflower, and James Partridge.

—— (1989), *The Works of George Savile, Marquis of Halifax*, 3 vols, ed. Mark N. Brown, Oxford: Clarendon Press.

Hickes, George (1682), *A Discourse of the Sovereign Power*, London.

—— (1713), "A Sermon Preached at the Church of St. Bridget on Easter-Tuesday Being the 1st of April 1684," in *A Collection of Sermons Formerly Preached by the Reverend George Hickes D.D.*, 2 vols, London: John Churchill, pp. 357–401.

Hill, Bridget (ed.) (1986), *The First English Feminist: Reflections Upon Marriage and Other Writings by Mary Astell*, New York: St Martin's Press.

Hyde, Edward, Earl of Clarendon (1676), *A Brief View and Survey of ... Leviathan*, London.

Leslie, Charles (1704), *Cassandra. (But I Hope not) Telling what will come of it. In Answer to the Occasional Letter*, London.

—— (1702), *New Association of those Called Moderate Church-men with the Modern-Whigs and Fanaticks*, London.

Locke, John (1689), *Two Treatises of Government: in the former, the false principles, and foundation of Sir Robert Filmer, and his followers, are detected and overthrown. The latter is an essay concerning the true original, extent, and end of civil government,* London: Awnsham Churchill.

—— (1812), *The Works of John Locke,* 10 vols, London: W. Otridge.

—— (1967), *Two Treatises on Government,* ed. Peter Laslett, 2nd edition, Cambridge: Cambridge University Press.

—— (1987), *A Paraphrase and Notes on the Epistles of St Paul,* ed. Arthur Wainright, 2 vols, Oxford: Clarendon Press.

—— (1988), *An Essay Concerning Human Understanding,* ed. Peter H. Nidditch, Oxford: Clarendon Press.

—— (1997), *Some Thoughts Concerning Education,* in *The Works of John Locke,* vol. 8, London: Routledge.

—— (1999), *The Reasonableness of Christianity,* ed. John Higgins-Biddle, Oxford: Clarendon Press.

Malebranche, Nicolas (1980), *The Search After Truth,* trans. and ed. by Thomas M. Lennon and Paul J. Olscamp; with *Elucidations of the Search After Truth,* trans. and ed. by Thomas M. Lennon, Columbus: Ohio State University Press.

[Masham, Damaris] (1696), *Discourse Concerning the Love of God,* London: Printed for Awnsham and John Churchil, at the Black-Swan.

More, Henry (1978), *The Immortality of the Soul,* reprinted in *A Collection of Several Philosophical Writings, 1662,* vol. 2, New York: Garland Publishing.

—— (1997), *An Account of Virtue: Or, Dr. Henry More's Abridgment of Morals, Put into English,* trans. Edward Southwell, Bristol: Thoemmes Press.

Norris, John (1690), *Reflections Upon the Conduct of Human Life with Reference to the Study of Learning and Knowledge : In a Letter to the Excellent Lady, the Lady Masham / by John Norris ... ; to Which Is Annex'd a Visitation Sermon, by the Same Author,* London: S. Manship.

—— (1693), *Practical Discourses Upon several Divine Subjects,* London: S. Manship, vol. 3.

—— (1694), *The Theory and Regulation of Love: A Moral Essay,* London, S. Manship.

—— (1978), *An Essay Towards the Theory of the Ideal or Intelligible World 1701–1704,* vol. 2, New York: Garland Publishing.

—— (1978), *Reason and Religion, or the Grounds and Measures of Devotion,* in *Treatises Upon Several Subjects,* New York: Garland Publishing.

—— (1978), *Reflections Upon the Conduct of Human Life: With reference to the Study of Learning and Knowledge,* in *Treatises Upon Several Divine Subjects,* New York: Garland.

—— (1978), *Spiritual Counsel: Or, the Father's Advice to his Children,* in *Treatises Upon Several Divine Subjects,* New York: Garland Publishing.

[Shaftesbury, Anthony Ashley Cooper, Third Earl of] (1708), *A Letter Concerning Enthusiasm, to My Lord \*\*\*,* London: J. Morphew.

Sherlock, William (1684), *The Case of Resistance,* London.

Todd, Janet (ed.) (1992), *The Works of Aphra Behn,* Columbus: Ohio State University Press.

Whitby, Daniel (1697), *A Discourse of the Love of God,* London: Awnsham and John Churchill.

**Secondary Bibliography**

Acworth, Richard (1979), *The Philosophy of John Norris of Bemerton (1657–1712)*, Hildesheim: Gorg Olms Verlag.

Ashcraft, Richard (1969), "Faith and Knowledge in Locke's philosophy," in Yolton, John W. (ed.), *John Locke: Problems and Perspectives*, Cambridge: Cambridge University Press, pp. 194–223.

Atherton, Margaret (1993), "Cartesian Reason and Gendered Reason," in Antony, Louise M., and Charlotte Witt (eds.), *A Mind of One's Own: Feminist Essays on Reason and Objectivity*, Boulder: Westview Press, pp. 19–34.

Bahlman, D.W.R. (1957), *The Moral Revolution of 1688*, New Haven: Yale University Press.

Barash, Carol (1996), *English Women's Poetry*, Oxford: Oxford University Press.

Bennett, G.V. (1975), *The Tory Crisis in Church and State, 1688–1730*, Oxford: Clarendon Press.

Boxer, Marilyn J. (1998), *When Women Ask the Questions: Creating Women's Studies in America*, Baltimore: Johns Hopkins University Press.

Broad, Jacqueline (2001), *Women Philosophers of the Seventeenth Century*, Cambridge: Cambridge University Press.

—— (2003), "Adversaries or allies? Occasional thoughts on the Masham–Astell exchange," *Eighteenth-Century Thought*, 1 (1), 123–49.

Butler, Melissa A. (1991), "Early Liberal Roots of Feminism: John Locke and the Attack on Patriarchy," in Shandley, Mary Lyndon and Carole Pateman (eds.), *Feminist Interpretations and Political Theory*, University Park: Penn State University Press, pp. 74–94.

Champion, Justin A.I. (1992), *Pillars of Priestcraft Shaken: The Church of England and its Enemies, 1660–1730*, Cambridge: Cambridge University Press.

Clark, Alice (1919), *Working Life of Women in the Seventeenth Century*, London: G. Routledge & Sons.

Clark, J.C.D. (1985), *English Society, 1688–1832*, Cambridge: Cambridge University Press.

Claydon, Tony (1996), *William III and the Godly Revolution*, Cambridge: Cambridge University Press.

Colas, Dominique (1997), *Civil Society and Fanaticism*, trans. Amy Jacobs, Stanford: Stanford University Press

Cranston, Maurice (1957), *John Locke: A Biography*, Oxford: Oxford University Press.

Crawford, Patricia (1985), "Women's Published Writings 1600–1700," in Prior, Mary (ed.), *Women in English Society, 1500–1800*, London: Methuen, pp. 211–82.

—— (1994), "The Challenges to Patriarchalism: How Did the Revolution Affect Women?," in Morrill, John (ed.), *Revolution and Restoration: England in the 1650s*, London: Collins & Brown, pp. 112–28.

De Krey, Gary (1989), "The London Whigs and the Exclusion Crisis Reconsidered," in Beier, A.L., D. Cannadine, and J.M. Josenheim (eds.), *The First Modern Society: Essays in English History in Honor of Lawrence Stone*, Cambridge: Cambridge University Press, pp. 457–82.

Dunn, John (1969), "The Politics of Locke in England and America in the Eighteenth Century," in Yolton, John (ed.), *John Locke: Problems and Perspectives*, Cambridge: Cambridge University Press, pp. 29–52.

Ellenzweig, Sarah (2003), "The love of God and the radical enlightenment: Mary Astell's brush with Spinoza," *Journal of the History of Ideas*, 64 (3), 379–97.

Erickson, Robert (1997), *The Language of the Heart, 1650–1750*, Philadelphia: University of Pennsylvania Press.

Ezell, Margaret J.M. (1993), *Writing Women's Literary History*, Baltimore: Johns Hopkins University Press.

Ferguson, Moira (ed.) (1985), *First Feminists: British Women Writers 1578–1799*, Bloomington: Indiana University Press.

Flaningam, John (1977), "The occasional conformity controversy: ideology and party politics, 1697–1711," *Journal of British Studies*, 17 (3), 36–82.

Gallagher, Catherine (1988), "Embracing the absolute: the politics of the female subject in seventeenth-century England," *Genders*, 1 (1), 24–39.

—— (2002), "A history of the precedent: rhetorics of legitimation in women's writing," *Critical Inquiry*, 26 (2), 309–27.

Gilbert, Sandra M. and Susan Gilbar (eds.) (1985), *The Norton Anthology of Literature by Women*, New York: Norton.

Goldie, Mark (1978) "Tory political thought, 1689–1714," unpublished PhD diss., University of Cambridge.

—— (ed.) (1999), *Two Treatises: The Reception of Locke's Politics*, 6 vols, London: Pickering & Chatto.

——, Paul Seaward and Tim Harris (eds.) (1990), *The Politics of Religion in Restoration England*, Oxford: Blackwell.

Greer, Germaine, Jeslyn Medoff, Melinda Sansone and Susan Hastings (eds.) (1988), *Kissing the Rod: An Anthology of Seventeenth-Century Women's Verse*, London: Virago Press.

Grundy, Isobel and Susan Wiseman (eds.) (1992), *Women, Writing, History: 1640–1740*, Athens: University of Georgia Press.

Harris, Ian (1994), *The Mind of John Locke*, Cambridge: Cambridge University Press.

Harrison, John and Peter Laslett (1971), *The Library of John Locke*, 2nd edition, Oxford: Clarendon Press.

Harth, Erica (1992), *Cartesian Women: Versions and Subversions of Rational Discourse in the Old Regime*, Ithaca: Cornell University Press.

Hartmann, Van C. (1998), "Tory feminism in Mary Astell's *Bart'lemy Fair*," *The Journal of Narrative Technique*, 28 (3), 243–65.

Henry, John (1986), "A Cambridge Platonist's materialism: Henry More and the concept of soul," *Journal of the Warburg and Courtauld Institutes*, 49, 172–95.

—— (1990), "Henry More versus Robert Boyle: The Spirit of Nature and the Nature of Providence," in Hutton, Sarah (ed.), *Henry More (1614–1687), Tercentenary Studies*, Dordrecht: Kluwer Academic Publishers, pp. 55–76.

Hill, Bridget (1987), "A refuge from men: the idea of a Protestant nunnery," *Past and Present*, 117, 107–30.

Hinds, Hilary (1996), *God's Englishwomen: Seventeenth-Century Radical Sectarian Writings and Feminist Criticism*, New York: Manchester University Press.

Hobby, Elaine (1988), *Virtue of Necessity: English Women's Writing 1649–88*, London: Virago Press.

Holmes, Geoffrey (1967), *British Politics in the Age of Anne*, London: Macmillan Press.

—— (1975), *Religion and Party in Late Stuart England*, London: English Historical Association.

—— (1993), *The Making of a Great Power: 1660–1722*, London: Longman.

Hughes, Ann (1995), "Gender and Politics in Leveller Literature," in Amussen, Susan D. and Mark Kishlansky (eds.), *Political Culture and Cultural Politics in Early Modern England: Essays Presented to David Underdown*, Manchester: Manchester University Press, pp. 162–88.

Isaacs, Tina (1982), "The Anglican hierarchy and the Reformation of Manners, 1688–1738," *Journal of Ecclesiastical History*, 33, 391–411.

Israel, Jonathan I. (1991), "William III and Toleration," in Grell, Ole Peter, Jonathan I. Israel and Nicholas Tyacke (eds.), *From Persecution to Toleration: The Glorious Revolution and Religion in England*, Oxford: Clarendon Press, pp. 129–70.

—— (2001), *Radical Enlightenment: Philosophy and the Making of Modernity 1650–1750*, Oxford: Oxford University Press.

Kelly, Joan (1982), "Early feminist theory and the 'Querelle des Femmes,' 1400–1789," *Signs*, 8 (1), 4–28.

Kenyon, John (1977), *Revolution Principles*, Cambridge: Cambridge University Press.

Kinnaird, Joan K. (1979), "Mary Astell and the Conservative contribution to English feminism," *The Journal of British Studies*, 19 (1), 53–75.

Kolbrener, William (2004), "Gendering the modern: Mary Astell's feminist historiography," *The Eighteenth Century: Theory and Interpretation*, 44 (1), 1–24.

—— (2004), "'Forc'd into an interest': High Church politics and feminine agency in the works of Mary Astell," *1650–1850: Ideas, Aesthetics, and Inquiries in the Early Modern Era*, 10, 3–31.

Kramnick, Jonathan Brody (1999), "Locke's Desire," *Yale Journal of Criticism*, 12 (2), 189–208.

Mack, Phyllis (1982), "Women as prophets during the Civil War," *Feminist Studies*, 8 (1), 19–45.

—— (1984), "Women as Prophets during the English Civil War," in Jacob, Margaret and James Jacob (eds.), *The Origins of Anglo-American Radicalism*, London: Allen and Unwin, pp. 214–30.

—— (1992), *Visionary Women: Ecstatic Prophecy in Seventeenth-Century England*, Berkeley: University of California Press.

McCracken, Charles J. (1983), *Malebranche and British Philosophy*, Oxford: Clarendon Press.

McCrystal, John (1993), "Revolting women: the use of revolutionary discourse in Mary Astell and Mary Wollstonecraft compared," *History of Political Thought*, 14 (2), 189–203.

McDowell, Paula (1998), *The Women of Grub Street*, Oxford: Oxford University Press.

Mendelson, Sara Heller (1979), "The weightiest business: marriage in an upper-gentry family in seventeenth-century England," *Past and Present*, 85, 126–35.

—— and Patricia Crawford (1998), *Women in Early Modern England, 1550–1720*, Oxford: Clarendon Press.

Mills, Rebecca M. (2000), "'That tyrant custom': the politics of custom in the poetry and prose of Augustan women writers," *Women's Writing*, 7 (3), 391–409.

O'Neill, Eileen (1983), "Mind and mechanism: an examination of some mind–body problems in Descartes' philosophy," unpublished PhD thesis, Princeton University.

—— (1987), "Mind–body interaction and metaphysical consistency: a defense of Descartes," *Journal of the History of Philosophy*, 25 (2), 227–45.

—— (1998), "Mary Astell," in *Routledge Encyclopedia of Philosophy*, vol. 1, London: Routledge, pp. 527–30.

Outhwaite, R.B. (1986), "Marriage as Business: Opinions on the Rise in Aristocratic Bridal Portions in Early Modern England," in McKendrick, Neil and R.B. Outhwaite (eds.), *Public Life and Public Policy: Essays in Honour of D.C. Coleman*, Cambridge: Cambridge University Press, pp. 21–37.

Pateman, Carole (1988), *The Sexual Contract*, Stanford: Stanford University Press.

Perry, Ruth (1984), "Mary Astell's Response to the Enlightenment," in Hunt, Margaret R. (ed.), *Women and the Enlightenment*, New York: The Haworth Press, pp. 13–40.

—— (1985), "Radical doubt and the liberation of women," *Eighteenth Century Studies*, 18 (4), 472–93.

—— (1986), *The Celebrated Mary Astell: An Early English Feminist*, Chicago: University of Chicago Press.

—— (1990), "Mary Astell and the feminist critique of possessive individualism," *Eighteenth Century Studies*, 23 (4), 444–57.

Pocock, J.G.A. (1980), "The Myth of John Locke and the Obsession with Liberalism," in Pocock, J.G.A. and Richard Ashcraft (eds.), *John Locke*, Los Angeles: William Andrews Clark Memorial Library, University of California, pp. 1–24.

—— (1980), "Post-Puritan England and the Problem of the Enlightenment," in Zagorin, P. (ed.), *Culture and Politics*, Los Angeles: Clark Library, pp. 91–109.

—— (1985), *Virtue, Commerce and History: Essays on Political Thought and History, Chiefly in the Eighteenth Century*, Cambridge: Cambridge University Press.

—— (1987), *The Ancient Constitution and the Feudal Law: A Study of English Historical Thought in the Seventeenth Century: A Reissue with a Retrospect*, 2nd edition, Cambridge: Cambridge University Press.

—— (1995), "Within the Margins: The Definitions of Orthodoxy," in Lund, Roger D. (ed.), *The Margins of Orthodoxy*, Cambridge: Cambridge University Press, pp. 33–53.

—— (2004), "Quentin Skinner: the history of politics and the politics of history," *Common Knowledge*, 10 (3), 532–50.

Purkiss, Diane (1992), "Producing the Voice, Consuming the Body: Women Prophets of the Seventeenth Century," in Grundy, Isobel and Susan Wiseman (eds.), *Women, Writing, History 1640–1740*, Athens: University of Georgia Press, pp. 139–58.

—— (1992), "Material Girls: The Seventeenth-Century Woman Debate," in Brant, Clare and Diane Purkiss (eds.), *Women, Texts, and Histories, 1575–1760*, London: Routledge, pp. 69–101.

Ready, Kathryn J. (2002), "Damaris Cudworth Masham, Catharine Trotter Cockburn, and the feminist legacy of Locke's theory of personal identity," *Eighteenth-Century Studies*, 35 (4), 563–76.

Rivers, Isabel (1981), *Reason, Grace and Sentiment*, Cambridge: Cambridge University Press.

Rose, Craig (1991), "'Seminarys of faction and rebellion': Jacobites, Whigs, and the London Charity Schools, 1716–1724," *The Historical Journal*, 34 (4), 831–55.

—— (1993), "The Origins and Ideals of the SPCK 1699–1716," in Walsh, John, Colin Haydon and Stephen Taylor (eds.), *The Church of England c.1689–c.1833: From Toleration to Tractarianism*, Cambridge: Cambridge University Press, pp. 172–90.

—— (1999), *England in the 1690s: Revolution, Religion and War*, Oxford: Blackwell.

Runge, Laura (2001), "Beauty and gallantry: a model of polite conversation," *Eighteenth-Century Life*, 25 (1), 43–63.

Skinner, Quentin (2002), *Visions of Politics*, 3 vols., Cambridge: Cambridge University Press.

Smith, Florence Mary (1916), *Mary Astell*, New York: Columbia University Press.

Smith, Hannah (2001), "English 'feminist' writings and Judith Drake's *An Essay in Defence of the Female Sex* (1696)," *The Historical Journal*, 44 (3), 727–47.

Smith, Hilda L. (1982), *Reason's Disciples: Seventeenth Century English Feminists*, Urbana: University of Illinois Press.

—— (1997), "'General War amongst the Men but None amongst the Women': Political Differences between Margaret and William Cavendish" in Nenner, Howard (ed.), *Politics and the Political Imagination in Later Stuart Britain*, Rochester, NY: University of Rochester Press, pp. 143–60.

—— (ed.) (1998), *Women Writers and the Early Modern British Political Tradition*, Cambridge: Cambridge University Press.

—— and Berenice A. Carroll (eds.) (2000), *Women's Political and Social Thought: An Anthology*, Bloomington: Indiana University Press.

Sommerville, Margaret R. (1995), *Sex and Subjection: Attitudes to Women in Early-Modern Society*, London: Arnold.

Speck, W.A. (1994), *The Birth of Britain: A New Nation, 1700–1710*, Oxford: Blackwell.

Springborg, Patricia (1995), "Mary Astell (1666–1731), critic of Locke," *American Political Science Review*, 89 (3), 621–33.

—— (1998), "Astell, Masham, and Locke: Religion and Politics," in Smith, Hilda (ed.), *Women Writers and the Early Modern British Political Tradition*, Cambridge: Cambridge University Press, pp. 105–25.

—— (1998), "Mary Astell and John Locke" in Zwicker, Stephen (ed.), *Cambridge Companion to English Literature, 1650–1740*, Cambridge: Cambridge University Press, pp. 276–306.

—— (2001), "Republicanism, freedom from domination, and the Cambridge contextual historians," *Political Studies*, 49 (5), 851–76.

Spurr, John (1991), *The Restoration Church of England, 1646–1689*, New Haven: Yale University Press.

Squadrito, Kathleen (1987), "Mary Astell's critique of Locke's view of thinking matter," *Journal of the History of Philosophy*, 25 (3), 433–39.

—— (1991), "Mary Astell," in Waithe, Mary Ellen (ed.), *A History of Women Philosophers, 1600–1900*, vol. 3, Dordrecht: Kluwer Academic Publishers, pp. 87–99.

Staves, Susan (1990), *Married Women's Separate Property in England, 1660–1833*, Cambridge, MA: Harvard University Press.

Taylor, E. Derek (2001), "Mary Astell's ironic assault on John Locke's theory of thinking matter," *Journal of the History of Ideas*, 62 (3), 505–22.

Thomas, Keith (1958), "Women and the Civil War sects," *Past and Present*, 13, April, 42–62.

Thompson, Martyn (1976), "The reception of Locke's *Two Treatises of Government*, 1690–1705," *Political Studies*, 24 (2), 184–91.

Todd, Janet (1996), *The Secret Life of Aphra Behn*, London: Andre Deutsch.

Tully, James (ed.) (1988), *Meaning and Context: Quentin Skinner and his Critics*, Princeton: Princeton University Press.

Van Sant, Ann Jessie (2002), "Satire and Law: The 'Case' against Women," in Thomas, Brook (ed.), *Real, Yearbook of Research in English and American Studies*, Tubingen: Gunter Narr Verlag, pp. 39–64.

Weil, Rachel (1999), *Political Passions: Gender, the Family, and Political Argument in England, 1680–1714*, Manchester: Manchester University Press.

Weiss, Penny (2004), "Mary Astell: including women's voices in political theory," *Hypatia*, 19 (3), 63–94.

Yolton, Jean S. and John W. Yolton (1985), *John Locke: A Reference Guide*, Boston: G.K. Hall.

Yolton, John W. (1968), *John Locke and the Way of Ideas*, Oxford: Oxford University Press.

—— (1983), *Thinking Matter: Materialism in Eighteenth-Century Britain*, Oxford: Basil Blackwell.

Zook, Melinda (1989), "Contextualizing Aphra Behn: Plays, Politics, & Party, 1679–1689," in Smith, Hilda L. (ed.), *Women Writers and the Early Modern British Political Tradition*, Cambridge: Cambridge University Press.

—— (1999), *Radical Whigs and Conspiratorial Politics in Late Stuart England*, University Park: Penn State Press.

—— (2006), "Nursing Sedition: Women, Dissent, & the Whig Struggle," in McElligott, Jason (ed.), *Fear, Exclusion and Revolution: Roger Morrice & His World, 1675–1700*, London: Ashgate.

# Index